MW00561017

WOMEN PRIESTS
AND OTHER FANTASIES

NIHIL OBSTAT:
  Rev. William B. Smith, S.T.D.
  Censor Librorum

IMPRIMATUR:
  Most Rev. Joseph T. O'Keefe
  Vicar-General, Archdiocese of New York

December 28, 1984, New York, N.Y.

WOMEN PRIESTS AND OTHER FANTASIES

Reverend Vincent P. Miceli, S.J.

Roman Catholic Books

Post Office Box 2286, Fort Collins, CO 80522

Library of Congress Catalog Card Number 84-071718
ISBN 0-912141-94-8

Father Vincent P. Miceli, S.J.

Father Vincent Miceli was a highly regarded Jesuit professor of philosophy and a Catholic commentator whose writing career spanned four decades. Probably best known for his book *The Antichrist* (Roman Catholic Books, Box 2286, Fort Collins, CO 80522, $22.00, postage paid), he was also the author of *The Gods of Atheism* ($24.95). The latter was called by Archbishop Fulton Sheen "as complete a study of atheism as exists in any language."

Father Miceli earned his doctoral degree in contemporary philosophy under the renowned Dietrich von Hildebrand at Fordham University and later taught at Loyola University in New Orleans, Springhill College, the Gregorianum and Angelicum pontifical universities in Rome, and St John's University in New York. He wrote numerous essays and articles for journals and periodicals like *National Review, The New Scholasticism, Homiletic and Pastoral Review, Triumph, Christian Order, Social Digest, L'Osservatore Romano,* and *The New York Times,* to name some.

With Pope John Paul II

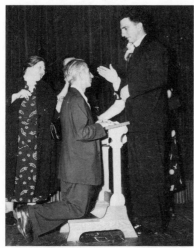

Vincent P. Miceli, S.J., on Ordination day, 1949

He co-founded Catholic Media Apostolate and appeared on hundreds of its radio and television programs, as well as on many secular television and radio programs debating various personalities of the left in the 1960s, 1970s, and 1980s. Born in 1915, in Manhattan, Father Miceli died on the Feast of Corpus Christi 1991, and the day after his death, a young priest by the name of Vincent Miceli — no relation — offered his first Mass in the Diocese of Brooklyn, New York, a sign, surely, of God's pleasure.

Preface

"And if disease...makes a man to be more out of his mind than
the rest of the world are..." *(Plato, Laws, 929)*

Plato wrote these words at the very end of his life. They sound
pessimistic indeed, for they clearly imply that a state of madness is fairly
common among human beings — these noble creatures endowed with
reason, and yet so reluctant to use it well, or even to use it at all.

Alas, the situation is not much changed today, and it is still true to
say that madness is a widespread disease. Basically, it is the incapacity of
distinguishing between true and false, good and evil, important and non-
important, enduring and fleeting, eternal valid and fashion bound. The
great Chesterton echoes a similar thought when he tells us that what
contemporary man needs most is a "steely sanity."

In the wake of Vatican II, the Roman Catholic Church — the rock
of Peter on which Christ built His Church — seemed suddenly to be
tottering under the avalanche which was hurled upon Her. All of a sudden,
it seemed as if everything that the Church had taught for centuries was
being questioned, re-examined, changed. Overnight, an impressive number
of "experts" (theologians, philosophers, sociologists, psychologists, etc.)
cast new ideas and new theories upon the Catholic population. In a few
years, the world was swamped with new publications which made the head-
lines of the New York Times, inundated the Catholic world, and the result
was that the average Catholic, baffled, confused and dizzy, lost his footing
and followed the way this tempestuous wind was blowing.

The power of the news media is such that one truly needs a very deep
grounding in one's faith, and a considerable amount of sanity, to remain
calm and follow the advice of St. Paul: "Test all things; keep what is good."

There is no doubt that, prior to Vatican II, innumerable Catholics
were dogmatically sound only because the climate of the time was relatively
favorable; but they lacked deep roots, and as soon as the hurricane of change
came over them, they were incapable of resisting its thrust and abandoned
the sound doctrines which the Church had taught, unchanged for two
thousand years. A bad captain can bring his ship to harbor when the weather
is fair; but his real talent as a navigator shows itself when the going is rough.
Alas, some Church leaders did not prove capable of leading their flock
through the tempestuous years which followed the Council, and they soon
discovered that priests were getting married, that nuns were breaking their
religious vows, that thousands of people were leaving the Church, no longer
believing in the Real Presence of Christ in the Holy Eucharist, and in the

dogmatic and moral teaching of the Church. She seemed to be shaking to her very foundations.

But thank God, not everyone lost his head; some people kept their sanity. And the series of articles Father Miceli now offers to the public testify that throughout the devastation which was taking place in the vineyard of the Lord, he kept his calm. The book addresses itself to a wide variety of topics, but all of them have a common thread. First of all, they all are timely; each one of them was written as an answer to some urgent problem which had arisen and called for an immediate remedy. Moreover, all of them are based on the unchanging teaching of the Church in matters of dogmas and morals, and show convincingly that in spite of the turmoil of the time, they remain gloriously unchanged.

It is strange indeed that today one of the greatest praises that one can give a book is to say: it is sane. Indeed, we are living in the time described by St. Paul:

> "For the time is coming when people will not endure sound teaching, having itching ears they will accumulate for themselves teachers to suit their liking, and will turn away from listening to the truth and wander into myth. As for you, always be steady, endure suffering, do the work of an evangelist, fulfill your ministry." (Tim. 4-35)

These are the words which should be placed at the head of the present volume. Through the soundness of its doctrine, through the calm assurance that the Church is and remains the harbor of truth, it gives its readers the inner peace on which sound judgments alone can be based.

During the intellectual hysteria which has been reigning for a few years, it is so consoling to read a book which tells us that all this excitement (which has sent so many monks and nuns scurrying out of monasteries and convents) is a temporary illness which will pass, and peacefully recommends that we hold firm to the Rock of Peter.

One of the aims of the second Vatican Council was to "open windows." This is to be welcomed indeed provided that the windows opened allow us to breathe the fresh, clean, invigorating air of the heights, and not the pollution of modern towns which brings sickness and ailments in its wake.

This book is based on sound theology, sound philosophy, and carefully avoids the reefs of pseudo-sciences, like an unsound sociology, a doubtful psychology, and a "creative" theology. Like Kierkegaard, Father Miceli reminds us that sacred history cannot be reduced to profane history, (*Training in Christianity*, p. 36), and that the Holy Scriptures cannot be approached as one approaches a profane, empirical science. One's understanding of

Holy Scriptures should be based on prayer, on reverence, on an ardent desire to hear God's message, and respond to it adequately. Faith cannot be sustained without a deep prayer life, and just as plants cannot thrive without sun and water, so one's faith cannot be kept without practicing the attitude of little Samuel in the temple, when he said: "Speak, O Lord, Thy servant listens."

Alice von Hildebrand
Professor of Philosophy
Hunter College of the City University
New York

Contents

Part III — Philosophy

Introduction

Michel Montaigne, illustrious French essayist, wrote this pithy witticism, drawn no doubt from long experience: "No one is exempt from talking nonsense; the misfortune is to do it solemnly." The majority of essays in this work treat of what Horace, the Roman poet, called: *Mentis gratissimi errores,* that is, "Most pleasant fantasies of the mind." "We are," as Shakespeare writes, "such stuff as dreams are made of." And often, unfortunately, in our flights of fancy we are fascinated with the art of contradicting reality violently in futile efforts to force it to conform to our illusions. In such exercises we are not concerned with adhering to truth; we are rather determined to conjure up senseless visions from the depths of our rebellious wills and call them truths. Thus the head is ordered to proclaim as truths fantastic fancies of the heart.

Just such a high-flown delusion is the claim that women have a right to be ordained priests in the Catholic Church. Would that such ignorance, as the mother of prejudice, were restricted to this theological error! But as Ovid tells, and experience verifies: *Quantum animis erroris inest!* "O, how much error there is in human minds!" And so we are also forced to explode the following inflated fictions: Christ is a politico-economic revolutionary; Kung is a great theologian; Religious life should be secularized; Sisters make better religious without the habit; children are "unwanted beings"; the Catholic Church should advance to the perfection of being a classless church; the Humanist Manifestoes are the new gospels of salvation; communism is dedicated to establishing justice; the virtue of patriotism is passé; dialogue with Marxists is profitable for Christians; Heidegger and Bultmann are the great lights in philosophy and scripture today; Häring is our oracle in moral theology; vows are only meant to be temporary; transubstantiation has been displaced as a mystery by transignification; academic freedom is beyond the control of the Holy See; nuclear weapons are evil *in se;* violence is the road to social justice; detente is the sure path to peace; Christians can be Socialists or Marxists. These and other fiery fictions, emanating from the crooked wisdom of the world, are examined and rejected under the light of Catholic teachings.

But in the words of Cicero: *Nihil est veritatis luce dulcius:* "Nothing is sweeter than the light of truth." And thus there are other chapters which treat of what Seneca calls: *Veritas numquam perit*; the "Truth that never dies." Thus the reader should be inspired with the thoughts of such lovers of truth as St. Thomas Aquinas, Dietrich von Hildebrand, Gabriel Marcel, Pope Pius XII, Pope John Paul II, Rev. Joseph F. Costanzo, S.J., and others whose voices are heard here testifying to the fact expressed in Scripture: *Magna est veritas et praevalet:* "Great is the truth and it prevails."

This book declares that truth is the highest object of theology and philosophy. But unfortunately it is not always the highest object of theologians and philosophers. For truth to prevail in the words and deeds of men, there must exist in their hearts an intense love of the Author of Truth, God the Father, as known by reason through creation, and a zealous faith in the Revealer of supernatural truth, Christ the Son of God and substantial wisdom of the Father, as known in the scriptures and the teachings of the Magisterium of the Holy Roman Catholic Church. For in the words of the poet Byron: "Truth crushed to the earth shall rise again. The eternal years of God are hers." And as St. Augustine affirms: "The truth of the Catholic Church is ever ancient and ever new." It is also ever permanent and unchangeable for "the Church," in the words of St. Paul, "is the pillar and ground of truth."

Part I

Dogma

Woman and the Priesthood

In the present exaltation of total liberation, the class struggle is perverting even the natural distinction between the sexes. Understandably, women's liberation movements have operated successfully in the politico-economic sphere to throw off their supposed "inferiority" so as to gain social power and equality with men. Success in the secular sphere has spurred these women groups to fight another alleged "inferiority," that is, their exclusion from priestly positions in the ecclesiastical power structure. Such groups see the Church as a religious power structure similar to the State as a political power structure. According to them, the Church places religious power exclusively in the hands of a male clergy even as once the State placed political power exclusively in the hands of male statesmen. But the time has come to force the Church to advance to the level of progress made by the State. Liberated in secular society with an opportunity to attain all State positions, women now seek liberation in the Church, with an opportunity to attain ordination in all degrees of the priesthood.

The tragic truth at the heart of this view of the Church is that it is a surrender to secularism, the philosophy that rinses reality of God and religion. The Church, however one views her, is not a purely natural society. She cannot be reduced to the secular categories suitable to describe the State. For, like her Divine Founder, her Gospel, her sacraments, the Church is an ineffable mystery precisely because she and they are graces of God's infinitely gratuitous love for man. Applying *a priori* concepts to the Church — like democracy, civil rights, equality, power-structure, etc. — is an attack on her very essence. Such ideas mutilate her sacramental nature, her power, glory, beauty. They destroy her supernatural truth; they dissolve her transcendence before men's eyes, for they politicize her. Yet the truth is that the Church, in her essence, sacraments and structure, depends upon God's eternal Will, not on man's capricious desires. That is why this article hopes to convince the reader that the nonordination of women to the priesthood has nothing, *absolutely nothing* to do with any "inferiority" man or woman can imagine or concoct, no matter how plausible or pleasing the face of this falsehood may appear.

God does the calling

Now the plan of God for the ministry of the priesthood in salvation history is clearly delineated in Sacred Scripture. And the marvels of that plan are brilliantly revealed by the divine light which is dispersed through the prism of Christ's perfect priesthood. Writing to the Hebrews St. Paul teaches that the meaning of the Christian priesthood is centered in Christ, the High Priest. "For every priest taken from among men is appointed for men in the things pertaining to God, that he may offer gifts and sacrifices

for sins . . . And no man takes the honor to himself; he takes it who is called
by God, as Aaron was. So also Christ did not glorify himself with the high
priesthood, but he who spoke to him: Thou art my son; this day have I
begotten thee . . . Thou art a priest forever according to the order of
Melchisedech.''[1]

Several important truths are revealed in these statements of St. Paul.
First, God himself determines who will exercise the function of the priesthood in mankind's public liturgical relationship to himself. Men, neither
individually nor collectively, make this decision for themselves, nor ''take
this honor to themselves.'' Not even Christ, as man, takes the honor of
the priesthood to himself. And Christ, in speaking to his Apostles at the
Last Supper after making them priests like himself, reminded them of this
truth: ''You have not chosen me, but I have chosen you and have appointed
that you should go and bear fruit, and that your fruit should remain.''[2]
Second, God chose men exclusively to be his priests, both in the Old Testament as Aaron, and in the New Testament as Christ. Third, only men
are to exercise the ministerial priesthood, representing all mankind before
God in things pertaining to God. It is clear that St. Paul is speaking here
only of the ministerial priesthood, not of the common priesthood of all the
baptized. Further on we will consider the priesthood of the laity in which
all the baptized participate.

Chronologically Adam was created before Eve. Intelligent, free, an
image of God, he was head of the cosmic universe and animal kingdom
whose species he named at his pleasure. All creation intelligently sang God's
praises through the head and heart of this primordial priest. But God said:
''It is not good for man to be alone; I will make him a loving companion
like himself.''[3] And thus Eve, created from Adam's body, appeared as the
mother of all the living. And the whole human race was to adore and serve
God through the fidelity of its First Parents. Now Adam became the head of
Eve, his wife, and of the whole human race which was to be generated by
him through his wife. He now not only represented both the universe and
animal kingdom before God, but he also stood before the Divine Majesty
with prayers on his lips and presents in his hands in behalf of the whole
human family. Created in grace and holiness, both Adam and Eve were
called upon to return God's preferential love for them and their children
by an act of sacrifice, a sacrifice of their wills to God's holy Will. They
were to abstain from the fruit of a certain tree in response to a divine command. This act of sacrificial love would testify to their adoring self-donation
to God. Their reward would be, in time, an immortal confirmation of themselves and their children in holiness, in eternity, the unending enjoyment
of the beatific vision of the Holy Trinity. Thus Adam, the First Man, origin
and head of the human family, is the first official priest designated by God

through the primacy of his creation to offer gifts and sacrifices for the human family to God in things pertaining to God. Adam's priestly sacrifice entails an act of adoration, an act of grateful love and an act of petition.

Adam brought sin and death

When Adam rejected God, as first priest and representative of the human family he brought sin and damnation upon his whole family. Had Eve alone sinned and Adam remained faithful, the human race would not have fallen, for Eve was neither priest nor representative of her children or husband before God. Her sin would have been hers alone and what God's dispensation on her behalf would have been is hidden in the mystery of God's wisdom.

Had God decided to abandon fallen man as he did the fallen angels, all priesthood would have ceased. But God promised that the seed of woman would crush the serpent's head and redeem man. Thus in salvation history Adam continued to function as a priest, albeit a fallen priest seeking reinstatement in the friendship of God. Whereas before the fall his priestly functions fulfilled three essential exigencies of man — adoration, thanksgiving and petition — now Adam had a most urgent fourth reason for offering sacrifice. His gifts to God now had to signify man's petition to be rescued from sin and death, the death of the body and the death of the soul. Thus the blood of a lamb, the life of a heifer, were offered to preserve the blood and life of man. In the very lifetime of their father we find Cain and Abel imitating Adam as a priest. They too offer sacrifice to God in the role of priests and as representatives of their own families. Abel is accepted by God because he gives God the best of his flocks; Cain is rejected because he gives God "the seconds" of his harvest. And he who gives God second place, gives God no place, thereby sinning. As history proceeds and men universally fall into idolatry and violence, God determines to destroy them in the great flood. Only the just man Noah and his household are spared. The very first official act Noah performs upon leaving the Ark is to build an altar and offer sacrifice in thanksgiving to God for the deliverance of his whole family from the catastrophe of the flood. Once again only the men — the new Adams of the, as it were, new first family, Father Noah, his sons Shem, Ham and Japheth — act as the priests of ministry, the representatives of their families in sacrificial services to God.

When God first appeared to Abraham he ordered him to leave his country and travel to the land of Canaan. There he was to become the head, priest, father, prophet and patriarch of a special people that God was preparing for himself. Abraham obeyed. Arrived at Canaan, he built an altar to the Lord, offering sacrifice to his holy name. When Abraham defeated the kings who had captured his nephew Lot, Melchisedech, king of Salem and priest of the Most High God, brought bread and wine to sacrifice to God in joy over the victory. St. Paul sees in Melchisedech, offering a sacrifice of bread and wine, a true priest, the best type and forerunner of the perfect High Priest, Jesus Christ. Once again only by God's choice are certain men made priests of the Most High God for the good of their people in the things pertaining to God. Then God severely tested Abraham's faith and love. He ordered Abraham to sacrifice his only son Isaac on Mt. Moriah. Leaving Sara, wife and mother behind, uninformed of his mission, Abraham travels three days to the designated place of the sacrifice. At the moment of delivering the sacrificial blow with a knife, the angel of the Lord intervenes with a cry from heaven: "Abraham, Abraham, do not lay a hand on the boy; do nothing to him. Now I know that you fear God, since you have not withheld your only son from me."[4]

Christ's priesthood lasts always

St. Paul sees in Melchisedech a greater perfection of the priesthood than the priesthood exercised by Abraham. For Abraham, the patriarch, is blessed by Melchisedech and in return gives Melchisedech tithes of the best portions of the spoils he took in war. Paul writes: "Now beyond all contradiction that which is less is blessed by the superior."[5] In the fullness of time God the Father will fulfill an oath made from all eternity constituting his Incarnate Son the perfect priest after the order of Melchisedech. "The Lord swore and will not repent. Thou are a priest forever according to the order of Melchisedech."[6] Now to demonstrate the permanency and immutability of his will when he promises and performs his promises, God swears by his own unchangeable nature that Abraham will be blessed in his progeny, that his Son Jesus will be a perfect high priest forever. St. Paul writes: "For the others were made priests without an oath."[7] That is to say, the other priests were numerous and replaceable because they were prevented by death from continuing in office. But Christ continues forever, for he is ever living as eternal priest to make intercession for us before the throne of God. Now Christ, knowing his Father's will from all eternity and coming as a man to fulfill it most perfectly, shares his priesthood exclusively with men, those men known and chosen by him, his Father and the Holy Spirit from the foundation of the world. Already the exclusive bestowing of the priesthood on men from the moment of Adam's creation is the type and prefigure of the priesthood established in Christ and his Church by the heavenly Father. And since God is all-wise, never fickle nor inconsistent, he will never repent of nor contradict this divine ordination.

O.T. priesthoods fade away

As we progress from the history of Abraham, Melchisedech and the Patriarchs to the ratification of the Old Covenant between Moses and the People of Israel on the one hand and Almighty God on the other, we again witness God's explicit choice of men alone to function as the priests of this Covenant. While Moses was on Mt. Sinai, following the ratification of the Covenant, God gave him this command: "Aaron and his sons you shall anoint and ordain, consecrating them as my priests. . .to minister in the sanctuary."[8] Since Aaron was of the tribe of Levi, this priesthood was called the Levitical priesthood. Once again St. Paul reminds us that even the Levitical priesthood was imperfect, since under it the people of God received the Law which "brought nothing to perfection." Thus the priesthood according to the order of Aaron was mere copy and shadow of what was to come; it was only temporary, preparatory for that change from the Old Law to the Law of Christ which was promulgated by the Son of Man whose priesthood superseded all former priesthoods and is to last forever according to the likeness of the priesthood of Melchisedech. For the priesthood of Christ alone brings redemption, justification, sanctity, eternal life and glory to sinful man. All former priesthoods were absolutely incapable of achieving these divine accomplishments.

Upon coming into the world the Son of God, knowing that "it was impossible that sins should be taken away with the blood of bulls and goats," said to his Father: "Sacrifice and oblation thou wouldst not, but a body thou hast fitted for me; in holocausts and sin-offerings thou hast had no pleasure. Then said I: 'Behold I come — in the head of the book it is written of me — to do thy will, O God.' " St. Paul explains more fully: "In saying in the first place: 'Sacrifices and oblations and holocausts and sin-offerings thou wouldst not, neither hast thou had pleasure in them' (which were offered according to the Law), and then saying: 'Behold, I come to do thy will, O God,' he annuls the First Covenant in order to establish the second. It is in this 'will' that we have been sanctified through the offering of the body of Jesus Christ once for all."[9] Anointed high priest by his Father at the moment of his incarnation, Christ annulled the former priesthoods. At the Last Supper, having changed bread and wine into his Body and Blood as a sacrificial gift in preparation for his passion and death on the cross the next day, Christ annulled the old victims, becoming himself the eternal victim of sacrifice from mankind to his Father. Now all ancient priesthoods and victims are forever superseded; they had always been ineffectual anyway. And then Christ proceeded to share his unique priesthood and victimhood exclusively with men, his Apostles and their successors in his Church, when he commanded them: "Do this in memory of me."[10]

Adam is the figure of Christ

When we compare the priesthood of Christ with the ancient priesthoods we discover some profound truths concerning God's salvific plan for mankind. Adam, priest by primacy of creation, is the figure of Christ who is to come and become priest by incarnation and re-creation. Through Adam, the first priest, sin entered the world and death passed upon all men. All ancient priests offered victims for their own sins and the sins of the people. These priests were distinct from the victims they sacrificed. But the new Adam, Christ the Son of Man, as a priest is sinless; holiness itself is his essence. In his priesthood alone the priest and the victim are identified. Christ, the high priest, offers himself in sacrifice to his Father to redeem all men from their own sins. The new head of the human family, this unique priest, in a sense, becomes sin itself, destroying thus iniquity in himself upon the cross. In dying as personified sin, so to speak, Christ restores to man that superabundance of grace which achieves man's justification in renewed sonship and friendship with God. In the economy of salvation the first Adam and priest, as head of the human family, destroyed divine life in the souls of his children. His priestly sacrifices were incapable of restoring this life; they had to be superseded by the priesthood of Christ.

The Holy Trinity, beholding fallen Adam, again decreed: "It is not good for man to be alone. Indeed this time it is tragic for him if he remain isolated from us, fallen, supernaturally dead, the slave of Satan destined for hell. Let us make man a New Son, a new loving companion, a new head and Savior." So the Son of God volunteered to become the Son of Man. He took a body from a woman, Mary, so as to redeem the human family of which he was now the new Head. The original Adam came directly from the hand of God through creation, while Eve, created for love of him, came directly from the body of Adam. The new Adam Christ reversed the process. He came by the power of God alone from the body of Mary Immaculate. He came for the love of Mary and of all men. The first priest depended for his existence on the love of God alone. The perfect priest Christ depended not only on the love of God but also on the love, humility and obedience of the new Eve Mary for his existence as Man, Priest and Divine Savior. In the economy of divine mercy Christ, the new Head of man and always Head of all creation, restored divine life to his brethren through the death he offered once for all on the cross and the life he now lives forever unto God. By means of a woman a priest and man destroyed divine life in men. By means of another woman a priest and the Son of Man restored this life to men. The priesthood, therefore, from the beginning was irrevocably affixed to man who, as son of God, had been officially called from the beginning to give glory to the Holy Trinity through creation, incarnation and re-creation. The holiness the first Adam failed to preserve for his children through a priesthood of obedience, just such a holiness, raised to divine perfection, was won for all men by the natural Son of God made Man through a priesthood of obedience unto death, even unto the ignominious death of the cross. The Son of God, one of the persons of the tripersonal Godhead whom Adam offended now, as Son of Man and perfect high priest of the human family, introduces the source of divine sanctity into the Church, the communion of saints on earth, and restores men to the holiness and friendship of the Blessed Trinity.

Certainly from our soundings in Holy Scripture we can safely say that women are not called by God to the ministry of the priesthood. The entire Old and New Testaments are weighted against a female priesthood. Yet Catholics know that the Protestant principle *sola scriptura,* i.e., that the doctrinal sufficiency for the faith comes solely from scripture, is a false, indeed dangerous and often bankrupt principle. For Scripture must be interpreted by the living tradition of the ever-present teaching authority of the Church. Only then will it lead men to God in the fulness of truth and holiness. Now the Church has always seen the priesthood of Christ to be *incarnational, representative* and *redemptive.* The only begotten Son of the Father took on a physical particular human nature from Mary. That nature is male. He chose, ordained and sent out as his successors in the priesthood Apostles, all men. The Catholic Church, following the will and example of her Divine Founder, in a constant, clear, irreversible tradition, has chosen only men successors to these Apostles; every priest and bishop chosen by her for 2,000 years has been a man, representing and serving mankind before God. It is here that we begin to perceive the sublime role of woman in God's plan of salvation. Woman has the vocation of being man's historical God-bearer, Christ-Bearer (*Theotokos, Christikos*). Woman, in Mary, gives the Son of God the opportunity of becoming the Son of Man, of becoming the High Priest of God, the priest-representative, in a word, the priest-redeemer of men. For as God, the Son has no nature he can sacrifice to his Father. The one, unique, divine nature possessed wholly by the three divine Persons is impassible. But as God-Man he sacrifices his human nature on the cross. Other men, continuing on in the priesthood, always reflect the image of the Son of Man, the perfect priest. Other women, continuing to be Christ-and-God-Bearers to their children, reflect the image of Mary, the perfect woman and also the image of the Church as mother of all the living in God.

Priesthood is not a right

There is no question here of worthiness or unworthiness, of inferiority or superiority. We are in the presence of divine mysteries, of God's sovereign pleasure and inscrutable counsels. We are dealing here with grace, a pure gift of God. In the realm of salvation, in the Church everything is grace. And man's salvation from first to last is the gift, the grace *par excellence* of God. Changing God's plan to call woman priest and bishop can never be a matter of personal rights, human justice and equality. No one has any rights before God. And no one has a right to be a priest. The priesthood is not a profession left to one's option; it is a vocation freely bestowed by God and ratified by his Church. Moreover, God's choice of men for the priesthood was no accident any more than his decision to send his Son to become man and save each person was an accident. God does not act from whim or caprice. His choice of bread and wine at the Last Supper was no accident either. Accidents happen only to those who neither know nor can control all causes. But God knows and controls all causes. How appropriate were the elements of bread and wine to become the Body and Blood of Christ for the spiritual nourishment of men's souls. And perhaps, this side of eternity, that is all we can see in God's choices — their appropriateness. God's ultimate reasons are hidden in the infinite wisdom of his Godhead. Man is chosen to become a priest because man, as head and source of the human race, is a natural symbol of Christ, head and source of all creation. Woman is chosen to be God-Bearer because woman as mother of all the living is the natural symbol of Mary, Mother of the Church, and of the Church which begets all men in Christ. The special public vocation of man in the Church is to represent the Head, Christ. The special public vocation of woman in the Church is to represent the Church herself as Bride of Christ. Mary, Mother of the Church, is the perfect fulfillment of this vocation for she is also the mother of Christ and the Spouse of the Holy Spirit, the soul of the Church. Imitating Christ, the Son of God, we ought to accept God's Providence with complete joy and submission. "My food is to do the will of him who sent me."[11] Imitating Mary the Mother of God, we ought to magnify God's goodness to us with grateful humility. "My soul magnifies the Lord and my spirit rejoices in God my Savior, for he that is mighty has done great things to me."[12] "Behold the handmaid of the Lord, be it done unto me according to thy word."[13] We mere creatures do not know fully why God, who possesses together in an eminent manner whatever perfection there is to maleness and femaleness, thought it best to become one of us as a man-priest. But *de facto* that is what he chose to do. And it is wonderful in our eyes! Blessed be the name of the Lord forever for this most merciful dispensation.

Polls cannot change facts

Socrates warns seekers of truth to beware of those who have "more zeal than knowledge." Now in an age that is intellectually out of tune and morally off its hinges, rational arguments will not persuade irrational and emotionally exalted persons. Some women groups have already given fair warning that they will not be argued out of becoming priests. "We reject out of hand any arguments or efforts on theological or historical grounds,"[14] proclaimed the members of a Task Force chosen to study the status of women in a diocese in Pennsylvania. Nevertheless, following St. Paul's advice, the truth, however unpalatable, must be preached in season and out of season. And St. Peter advised Christians "to be always ready to give a reason for the faith that is in you." Moreover, agitating or screaming for change is not a Christian life-style. The intelligent Christian answers the arguments of marching masses by calmly, firmly reiterating the truth in love, trusting in the power of the living Lord and the efficacy of his revealed word as taught by the Church. For theological arguments founded on propaganda and slogans must be answered theologically lest such specious reasoning seduce simple spirits. Moreover, no polls, no mere vote-taking, can change salvation facts already decided by God. Such statistics have no theological decisional value whatsoever, though they may indicate the extent of the profound disorder in faith among Christians.

In the cacophony of confused arguments hurled about in this age of global revolution, it has been stated that Jesus was victimized by the customs and prejudices against women prevalent in his first-century society. Culturally conditioned as he was, Jesus bowed to iron-clad social pressures in choosing only men for the priesthood. In another age, under more liberal conditions, he would have also chosen women for the ministerial priesthood. Hence, Jesus would be all for women priests today. Their hour has arrived.

This argument is founded on a fanciful, when not invidious, fallacy, namely that Our Lord was a peaceful conformist. Moreover, the advocates of this shaky view, while absolutely convinced that they understand past "cultures," seem to be totally innocent of their own cultural "conditioning," of their own surrender to the "culture of liberation, class struggle and egalitarianism." They forget too that, since Christ appeared in the "fullness of time," the appropriate age chosen by God — to the embarrassment of the twentieth century which considers itself the standard-setter for all times — they are presumptuous to assume that the conditions of a different age would have caused God to change his plans for the salvation of men. The fact is that Christ often violently broke through the conventions of his surroundings. He vigorously cleansed the temple of accepted commercial conventions; he revoked the convenient custom of easy divorce, returning marriage to its pristine binding force; he scandalized many by speaking to Samaritans and especially the Samaritan women; he invited women to work with his band of disciples, something the Pharisees never allowed. Indeed the Pharisees themselves testified that Christ was no respecter of persons. They even accused Christ of breaking law upon

Levitical law, for Christ despised their legalistic customs. In the end they claimed they crucified him as a law-breaker. Was Christ unaware of women priests? In his time priestesses were far more common in idolatrous Semitic and Greek religions than they are today. It is unreasonable to pretend, in the face of overwhelming evidence to the contrary, that Jesus' choice of only men as priests was the one instance in his entire life when he committed an injustice for the sake of cultural expediency. The Rev. Dr. E. L. Mascall, commenting on this argument, writes: "If the supporters of women priests are right, then Our Lord in instituting an exclusively male apostolate, was doing something which has deprived half the members of the Church from their legitimate rights for nearly 2,000 years. And it would be difficult in that case to feel very confident of either his moral or his intellectual integrity. And then it is difficult to see why we should attribute any authority to him at all."[15]

In this push for women priests, St. Paul, through his letters, continues to function as the Prince of Polarization. Some "Women's Lib" members, recalling such statements to the Corinthians on women as: "For man was not created for woman but woman for man . . . Let women keep silence in the Churches; let them be submissive . . . for it is unseemly for a woman to speak in Church,"[16] stigmatize these thoughts of the Apostle as "time-conditioned, archaic, narrow-minded prejudices of a sexual neurotic." But then other members of these dangerously exalted movements gladly use St. Paul to justify the ordination of women. They quote his letter to the Galatians: "In Christ there is neither Jew or Greek; there is neither slave nor freeman; there is neither male nor female. For you are all one in Christ Jesus."[17] Consequently women have as much right as men to be advanced to all degrees of the priesthood.

Woman helps save man

Explaining the text "man was not created for woman but woman for man," even some sincere Christians misinterpret the phrase "woman for man." They say there is indicated in this Scriptural passage an essential superiority of the male over the female human. Thus they see in the "for man" that woman's role is to be an instrument, a means, an intermediate end for man's aggrandizement. Nothing can be further from the truth. Woman was created for man to save him from social isolation, to be his loving companion, wife and mother of his family. When he created woman God had in mind that both man and woman would find their social joy in their mutual surrender in love. The divine dimension of that surrender is found in the surrender Christ made when he became man *for* us, *for* our salvation, emptying himself and becoming a slave *for* love of us. Despite his loving surrender Christ always remains infinitely superior to us; he is our God. So Eve, though man's metaphysical equal, is yet socially man's wife, helper, mother. She is subordinate in loving obedience to his exercise of authority as father and responsible head of the family. Thus, the Church does not enslave woman to man; she enshrines woman in the place of love in the family as sweet counterbalance to the weight of authority emanating from the man.

Paul was no antifeminist

It is an act of self-deception to see in St. Paul's theology of women the prejudices of a neurotic man. No doctor of the Church more brilliantly presents the truly innovatory, sublime, revolutionary truth about women as revealed in the New Testament than does St. Paul. He led almost alone the struggle which made not only Gentiles the equal of Jews, but also women the equal of men in the Church. In his closing remarks to the Romans we read: "I commend to you Phoebe, our sister who is in the ministry of the Church at Cenchrae...For she has assisted many including myself...Greet Prisca and Aquila, my helpers in Christ Jesus who for my life have risked their own necks...Greet Mary who has labored much among you...Greet Tryphaena and Tryphosa who labor in the Lord...And Julia and all the saints who are with them."[18] Such valiant women are not second-class Christians for St. Paul. They are his sisters in Christ, saints of God. There is nothing antifeminist in these commendations. Elsewhere St. Paul is discovered improving on a sacred text so as to include women explicitly in its divine promise. In reference to 2 Sam. 7:14 — "I will be his father and he shall be my son," — St. Paul christianizes the text so as to present the full sweep of the liberty enjoyed by the followers of Christ: "And I will be a father unto you and you shall be my sons and daughters."[19]

As regards the text, "There is no longer either male or female, for you are all one in Jesus Christ," it must be stressed that this text is connected with baptism, not with holy orders. St. Paul precedes this passage with the words: "For all you who have been baptized in Christ have put on Christ."[20] It is also important to recall that this text has three parallels in St. Paul's epistles. To the Romans (10:12) the Apostle observes that since all men are saved who call on the name of Jesus, who confess with their mouth the Lord Jesus, and believe in their heart that God has raised him up from the dead, "there is no difference, no *diastole* at all between Jew and Greek." To the Corinthians (1 Cor. 12:13) Paul recalls that "we have all been baptized by one Spirit into one body, whether Jews or Greeks, whether bond or free; we have all been made to drink into one Spirit." Finally, to the Colossians (Col. 3:11) where St. Paul is describing the behavior proper to those who, being baptized, are risen with Christ, he teaches his readers that, since they have put off the old man as outgrown, and have put on the new man who does not cease to be renewed — in the light of perfect knowledge — after the image of him who created him, they must know that "there is no longer here either Jew or Greek, either circumcised, or uncircumcised, either barbarian or Scythian, either bond or free, but Christ who is all in all." Only the first of these four texts mentions that there are no longer male or female in Christ. But as shown clearly from the context, all four texts are intimately connected with baptism and have nothing to do with the ministry of the priesthood. Because baptism is sufficient for salvation since Christ's coming, circumcision is no longer needed. Women are no longer passed over by an initiating seal into the people of God. In what relates to their salvation they receive the same necessary rebirth in Christ and the Holy Spirit that men receive.

Christ preserved creation

In his theology of women Paul bases his teaching on the dignity and role of woman in God's plan of salvation not on the account of the Fall, but on that of Creation: "Man did not emanate from woman, but woman from man. Man was not created for woman, but woman for man."[21] This indicates that Adam, as priest, would always represent woman before God when offering sacrifice. When Christ, the New Adam, became man he did not change God's order of creation. Rather he saved Creation itself, with the exact order his Father put there. He did not come to save man from Creation. Christ, therefore, kept intact the kingly priesthood of man arising from his primacy of creation. This was the male vocation *par excellence*. Christ also kept intact the vocation of woman, to be the loving companion of man, his wife and mother of his children, to cooperate with man in the worship of God. Christ did not rescue man from the world-order willed by his Father; he rescued the world-order willed by his Father from sin. It is warped, diabolical thinking to take as a more perfect form of human liberty a revolt against God's plan for the diverse vocations to be fulfilled by the different sexes. The revolt of Satan from God's plan for the angels created devils and hell. For woman to reach out for the forbidden fruit of the priesthood against the will of God is for her to again succumb to the seductions of Satan. Redemption did not contradict Creation, nor overturn its order; it did not cancel out the vocations of the sexes. Rather it vindicated them and brought Creation, under its new Lord, the Son of Man, to an infinitely higher degree of sanctity and glory. In the history of the Church there were only the Marcionites and Montanists as heretics who denied that the Redeemer (who is also the Creator) willed a difference between men and women, a difference that would always remain to signify the diverse, though complementary, vocations of the sexes in the history of salvation. Because of these heretical notions, it comes as no surprise that the Marcionites and Montanists alone ordained women for the public consecration of the sacred mysteries and the administration of the sacraments.

What St. Paul's profound insights teach us is that sex is not an accidental characteristic of man and woman. A human person without sex is a strange abstraction. Sex entails the very identity of each person; sex plunges to the deepest mystery of each human person. St. Paul indicates this reality when he affirms that sexual sins involve persons up to the depth of their beings. He makes a sharp distinction between sins committed outside the body, i.e., outside the depth of one's being, and those committed against one's body, i.e., against what is destined for union with God as his temple and for resurrection and glorification with Christ. Hence the sexes, and the vocations pertaining thereto, are not interchangeable. Each person is called to serve God and his fellowman, accepting gladly the sex with which one is endowed and the vocation attached to that sex. The Dutch scholar Buijlendijk has expertly unmasked a modern error concerning the sexes. In his book *Woman* he says that it is only at an embryonic state of modern "feminism" that it is naively supposed that equality of women to men means women must do all things men usually do. This error fails to honor women for it neglects their positive, unique contribution to human society. Indeed, under the guise of advancing women to equality with men, this false principle makes a final attempt to subject women completely to the tyranny of purely masculine criteria.[22] Women cannot be made "copy-cat" men without degrading them by unnaturally robbing them of their femininity. A bogus masculinity does not honor or liberate women. Woman is honored and left free when she is genuinely accepted as an integral woman with all the characteristic charms of femininity. For woman contributes to human society what she alone can contribute with consummate excellence — the mothering, nurturing and training of the human family through tender love. It is the sin of sham modernity to subject women to the imperialism of the egalitarians. This would destroy the identity, the very humanity, of woman, both of which are linked mysteriously to her femininity.

Differences symbolize marriage

What St. Paul makes clear is that it is not in spite of nor without reference to their sexes that persons are called to serve God. Rather by accepting joyfully their very masculinity and femininity as an essential dimension of God's particular Providence, they attain their vocation to become saints and to bring others with them to sainthood. Perhaps the differences of the sexes attains its sublimest fullness in St. Paul when he teaches that this difference allows all men to enter more profitably into the "great mystery" of salvation. In Ephesians 5 St. Paul reasons with inspiration that the difference between the sexes is a symbol of marriage as restored by Christ in his Church. And this sacramental marriage is the symbol of the nuptial union between Christ and his Church. Christ, the Head, and the Church, his Body, are like husband and wife, distinct physically but united in intimate, permanent, mystical union. It is because the differences of the sexes assign men and women their vocations at their deepest levels of being, because these sexes and vocations are not interchangeable, that St. Paul can use this apt argument from analogy to hint at the inexhaustible mystery that is the Church as Bride of Christ. Thus the difference of sexes assigns men and women their places, their graces, their vocations within the Mystical Body. And these are not interchangeable but complementary in the fulfillment of God's plan for the salvation of the human family.

A final insight garnered from a reflective perusal of the New Testament's theology of woman gives a deeper appreciation of the significance and seriousness of masculinity and femininity. Despite its divinization of men and women through baptism which confers the common priesthood on all the faithful, the New Testament never grants women the graces of the ministry of the Holy Sacrifice, of the preaching of the word or of the discipline in the Church. These graces are reserved exclusively for men. Never is a woman chosen to be in public an authorized representative of Christ or his Church. To no woman does Christ ever make the promise to ratify in heaven what she has bound or loosed on earth. No woman is given the power of the keys. No woman is commissioned to perform the ministry of public preaching. Christ does not entrust the administration of the sacraments to women; neither does he commit the care of his flock to them. To no woman did Christ ever say: ''He who hears you hears me and he who despises you despises me.''[23] Moreover, consider the following historical incident. There were numerous holy women in the company of the Apostles who could have been chosen to succeed Judas in his bishopric. There was first of all Mary, Mother of God, holier by far than anyone in that company and who had already once given the Savior to the world. What worthier candidate could be available? Then there were Mary Magdalen, Joanna, wife of Chuza, Suzanna, the other Mary of Cleofa, etc., All of these holy women were more faithful to the crucified Christ than the men who abandoned him in his hour of need. Nevertheless, not one of these valiant women was even considered as a candidate. Two men totally unknown up to that time in the Scriptures were selected as candidates, Matthias and Joseph Barsabas. Why? Because this was God's will, Christ's dispensation that men alone function as priests in his Church. There is no disdain of women in his dispensation, no masculine obstinacy on the part of the Apostles who were only following their Master's commands.

Easter shows women important

The Easter events demonstrate the special importance women received from God in the New Testament. They are the last to leave the sealed tomb on that dark Friday, but the first to see the empty tomb on that glorious Sunday. The risen Christ appears first to these faithful women. They are commissioned not to tell the world about their risen Lord, but to tell the Eleven. They are to function as angels, messengers of the resurrection, the heart and essence of the Gospels, to the Apostles themselves! Nevertheless, those Apostles, often rebuked by Christ as "men of little faith," they alone, and their male successors, are officially commissioned by Jesus to announce publicly to the world all he had done and taught and to make converts of all nations.

The agitation for women to be ordained priests is a sterile venture, an exercise in futility. Why? Because, as we have seen, this project is of men, not of God. It will inevitably fail for its devotees are fighting even against God. The spirit behind the movement is one of prideful rebellion, of sitting in judgment on the ways of God. Such human self-centeredness founded on self-exaltation arises also from a naive, almost childish conviction that every revolutionary movement in Christian culture justifies a radical jettisoning of the entire Christian tradition. For today every novel trend, it seems, has to develop a corresponding novel trend theology. The theology for women priests is the logical conclusion of the theology of revolution, of liberation, of violence. Its spirit is one of coarseness and vulgarity, an affront to Christian courtesy and piety. Worse still, it is the diabolical fruit of the theology of "Christian Marxism." It can only destroy its enthusiasts, divide Christians and effectively kill charitable dialogue.

Speaking to rebels who questioned the justice of God in his day, St. Paul demanded: "Who are you, O man, that you argue with God, that you question him? Does the object moulded say to him who moulded it: Why have you made me this way? Or is not the potter master of his clay"[24] We must never forget that the Church of Christ is all grace and divine mercy. And the only holy Christian posture before God is one of joyful gratitude. St. Paul, of those who were ungrateful to God, again demanded: "What do you have, O man, that you have not received? And if you received it, why do you glory as if you received it not?"[25] In the reception of Baptism and Confirmation all men and women are made here and now partakers of the divine nature. They constitute a royal priesthood, a kingly people because they have been sprinkled and nourished with the Blood of Jesus Christ. This constitutes the essential priesthood of all Christians. Yet the institutional priesthood exists to maintain and expand this common priesthood. The priesthood of the ministry exists to make Christ present in a public way through sacrifice, sacrament and preaching. God has chosen men to exercise this function of the priesthood. If the bearer, the icon, the minister of this unique priesthood is man and not woman, it is because Christ came as a man and not as a woman. Why man? In the last analysis no culture, no sociology, no political philosophy, no theology and, certainly, no ideology can give an adequate answer. Only an ardent faith in the revelation of God's intimate love for his Creation, his Chosen People and his Church will render men ready to accept his Providence for salvation joyfully and unquestioningly. Finally, it should be remembered that the Church is not called upon to comply with any age in its fashionable prejudices; she is called upon to be faithful to the deposit of the truth possessed by her in her teachings and living traditions. It is not a question of progressive adaptation or reactionary obstinacy to ordain or refuse to ordain women. It is simply a question of obedience or disobedience to God's ordinances revealed in Scripture and the living traditions. The Church will remain faithful to God's ordinances for she is guided by the Holy Spirit. Hence in the Roman Catholic Church women will never be ordained priests. In the context of all the agitation over this question Our Lord's words, commenting on a similar trivial commotion, apply most appropriately here: "Martha, Martha, thou art anxious and troubled about many things; and yet only one thing is needful. Mary has chosen the best part, and it will not be taken away from her."[26]

Notes

[1]Heb. 5:1, 5.
[2]John 15:16.
[3]Gen. 2:18.
[4]Gen. 22:11, 12.
[5]Heb. 7:7.
[6]Heb. 7:21.
[7]Heb. 7:20.
[8]Ex. 28:41.
[9]Heb. 10:5 to 10.
[10]Luke 22:19.
[11]John 8:29.
[12]Luke 1:46.
[13]Luke 1:38.
[14]Cf. *Sexuality, Theology, Priesthood,* A Scholarly symposium on the ordination of women to the priesthood. Published by Concerned Fellow Episcopalians. San Gabriel, California 535 West Roses Road, p. 3.
[15]*Ibid.* p. 3
[16]1 Cor. 11:8; 14:34.
[17]Gal. 3:28.
[18]Rom. 16:1, 3, 12.
[19]2 Cor. 6:18.
[20]Gal. 3:27.
[21]1 Cor. 11:9.
[22]Quoted by Rev. Louis C. Bouyer, *Sexuality, Theology, Priesthood,* pp. 19, 20. This booklet was most helpful on this matter.
[23]Luke 10:16.
[24]Rom. 9:20, 21.
[25]1 Cor. 4:7.
[26]Luke 10:41, 42.

Reprinted from *Homiletic & Pastoral Review*, August-September 1976

Sisters as Symbols of the Sacred

A specific madness of modern society is its assault on the sacred. Suddenly the Secular City of Harvey Cox has degenerated into the Sacrilegious City of Jesus Christ Superstar in which the Son of God made man is reduced to being a moronic "hippie." And word comes from Denmark that the makers of the idols of the Sacrilegious City have some devilishly creative ideas they mean to immortalize in a new film. We read in *The Christian Science Monitor* for August 10, 1973: "Meanwhile, in Denmark protest is mounting over another film about Jesus (still in the making). Thousands of people from Europe, the U.S., Japan and Africa are expected to demonstrate in Copenhagen...against the film which, its director says, will portray Jesus as a bank robber and a lover. The state-controlled film institute has granted Danish director Jens Joergen Thorsen about $100,000 for the film."[1] On Sunday, August twenty-sixth Pope Paul VI, addressing a large gathering of the faithful, condemned the film with a holy zeal and anger: "We cannot remain silent and hide our personal sorrow about such an ignoble and blasphemous outrage which intends to deform the inviolable figure of our Savior, the supreme object of our faith and love....Christ is being made a laughing-stock, the victim of sacrilege and filthy lies: this is the reality! Where is our common moral and civil conscience? Can we allow our social existence to be degraded to such a point?"[2]

The forces of chaotic desacralization, though many, are at one in aggravating the spiritual sickness afflicting both lay and religious society today. Even before this plague had struck deeply within the bosom of the Catholic Church, the sense of the sacred was being eroded in society at large because of an escalating tyranny of technocracy in a world that was rapidly reducing persons and products to means for the attainment of mere profits and power. Exhilarating conquest of the natural universe was leading unnecessarily to the impatient dismissal of the supernatural kingdom. The overweening pride of self-glorification led man first to forget, then to deny and finally to assassinate the God of whom Holy Scripture writes: "He has made us and we have not made ourselves." Mammon, dressed in the shining, silver robes of technocratic progress, had become one of the new gods enthroned in the hearts of men.

But even as he was remaking his material universe so successfully under the direction of the god of technocracy, secular man felt impelled to remake his religious society as well. It seemed only logical that a technocratic revolution should be completed by a theological upheaval and that the result should be a remodelled, reconstructed Church. Thus the God of Revelation was to be replaced by the god of revolution. Secularist theologians determined to refashion the Church to the image and likeness of the new, humanistic man, now come-of-age with his brilliant discovery of a new way of life — that of scientific atheism. In the newly-constructed secularized religious society, dogmatic beliefs and moral practices were now to reflect the human needs of the times, with all their mutability, relativity and progressiveness. Such was to be henceforth the true meaning of the Gospels and it took scholars two thousand years to purify this truth from its mixture with myths and legends. From now on a traditional Church with permanent dogmas, fixed morals and an established teaching-ruling authority was to be considered as unfaithful to the true spirit of the Gospels and an obstacle to an evolving, progressing world. Henceforth evolving man was to be the center of religion, not a static God; theology was to become really sociology and anthropology, while the Catholic Church was to be seen for what it really was, a political rather than mystical entity.

The Catholic desire to join the world

At first the Catholic Church seemed impregnable to the assault of the forces of secularism. To outsiders she looked impressive, coherent, immense; they admired her clarity of doctrine, her sure guidance in morals, her firm authority, her unified counter-attack against spreading religious skepticism, savage totalitarianism and perverse hedonism. She was seen as the last and strongest bastion against the advance of organized, militant, atheistic barbarism. Moreover, a steady in-gathering of converts buttressed her fight against the forces of desacralization. Then the tower of truth and holiness began to topple from an earthquake within. Apparently there had been a hidden fault, a serious weakness down deep in the members of the Catholic Church. This weakness was found, it seemed, in the Church's leaders and especially among its prestigious intellectuals. It took the Council called Vatican II, the Council which, in the words of Pope John XXIII, was summoned to Rome "to bring the modern world into contact with the vivifying and perennial energies of the Gospel"[3]; it took this Council to discover that too many of its own members had been nurturing for a long time a secret desire to join the world and that now, abusing the Council itself as an authoritative pretext, such lovers of this world were opening the gates of the Church so as to bring the faithful into contact with the stultifying and deadly energies of neo-modernism. The result has been that the humanistic pretensions of the secular world have been vastly exaggerated for Catholics and the development of a serious inferiority complex has reduced many of them to confessing cravenly and obsessively nothing but Catholic depravities, as if the Church, instead of being the Mystical Body of Christ, had been in fact all along the sacrilegious body of anti-Christ. These "New-Church" Catholics had become scandalized over the Catholic Church's allegedly intransigent, dogmatic, authoritarian, rigid, anti-semitic, legalistic, intolerant, Constantinian, triumphant, Roman postures and policies. We have all heard these snide slogans flung against the Church as rocks for her stoning. Indeed, a fascination for the secular with a tendency toward the sacrilegious had already eroded the sense of the sacred in these "New-Church" Catholics. And under the influence of this fatal sickness, their hyper-critical, even delirious dialogue had reduced the number of conversions to the Faith significantly while increasing enormously the desertions of Catholic priests, religious and laity to the world of unbelief.

The tragic results of secularism's eclipse of the sacred among the "New-Church" Catholics are everywhere in evidence. There are serious divisions among Catholics on essential matters of faith and morals. Errors concerning God, the historicity of the Gospels, the Real Presence, infallibility, the resurrection, the nature of the Church and its salvational ministry and many others, too numerous to mention have divided and mutilated the flock of Christ. To the scandal and sadness of men of good will everywhere, even priests have cheapened the sacred convictions and holy places of the multitudes. They have violently occupied cathedrals, rudely interrupted holy liturgies, raucously challenged legitimate civil and sacred authority.

But the problem, of course, is not principally sacrilegious words and deeds. We must not mistake the symptom for the disease. The radical disease is a general loss of faith, a religious exhaustion which twists the souls of men from God and attaches them with enthusiasm to every clever and caustic criticism that corrodes the realm of the sacred and glorifies the city of the world. Religious sociologist, Harvey Cox, did not foresee that his brilliant Secular City would become that sacrilegious cesspool in which a decadently permissive society would exalt, in its novels, dramas, movies, paintings, liturgies and popular arts, savagery and sexuality. But you need not take merely my word for this social slide into spiritual sliminess.

In his book entitled *Trousered Apes,* Professor Duncan Williams wholeheartedly agrees with Leslie Fiedler that "there is a weariness in the West which undercuts the struggle between socialism and capitalism, democracy and autocracy, a weariness with the striving to be men."[4] Admitting that the news of God's death "has permeated, secularized and radically changed every aspect of Western thought and society," Professor Williams proceeds to document abundantly that, as a result of the banishment of God from society, "the Western world and its culture is saturated with violence and animalism. . . . We are teaching savagery and are naively appalled at the success of our instruction."[5] He demonstrates effectively how the literature of the times both reflects and provokes the escalating barbarism and defeatism that is creating the satanic society. Commenting on the Theater of the Absurd which degenerates into the Theater of Revolution and then into the Theater of Cruelty, Professor Williams writes:

What shocks an audience today will be acceptable tomorrow and thus the contemporary dramatist is constantly impelled to seek further excesses to gratify a warped taste which he has himself implanted in the public mind. . . . The whole modern cult of violence and animalism is in essence an admission of defeat. Since we cannot be men to any idealistic extent, let us lapse into barbaric animalism but, still clinging to vestiges of a past which we hate but cannot escape, let us clothe our defeat in high-sounding terms: "Alienation," "cult of unpleasure," "realism," and similar jargon. Yet all this fashionable phraseology cannot conceal the fact that the Emperor has no clothes. The literature of today lacks certain essential qualities. It no longer satisfies man's need for beauty, order and elevation, and to this extent it is incomplete and stunted. It contains, as Trilling has observed, an anti-civilizing trend, and to this is closely linked a cult of ugliness, a morbid concentration on the baser elements of life, a clinical obsession with the bizarre and with the grossly sensual and degrading aspects of human nature. . . . The contemporary playwright or producer might well take as his motto, *Apres moi, la secheresse* (After me, the draught), and congratulate himself that he is writing before a morbid public appetite demands scenes of such repellant realism that actors and actresses will have to be killed on stage in order to satisfy it.[6]

How do we recall a sacrilegiously sick society that functions on the fashionable fallacy that murder is the best therapy for the world's problems to the sanity and sanctity of the sublime? We, especially we Catholics and religious, must help man return to the nature and deep significance of the sacred. Only when men have grasped the nature, meaning and value of the sacred will they be equipped and willing to understand and confront the moral dis-values of their dying society. Truly an awareness of the sense of the sacred is a barometer that indicates the vitality of the religion, morals and culture of a people. A blindness to the nature of the sacred must be cured before a people can see the unearthly beauty of the holy and fall in love with it.

The sense of the sacred[7]

The sacred is a mystery. It heralds the presence here and now of the world above, the world of the divine, and it fills man with incomparable reverence. The sacred reveals that the religious sphere is set apart, wonderfully superior and distinct from the rest of man's existence. But this apartness, far from precluding contact between the religious and natural spheres of man's existence, is actually a pre-condition for their fruitful intercommunion. Sacredness is one of those ultimate data perceived in and by itself, unexplainable, indivisible, mysterious. Sacredness is a reality which does not exist solely outside man as a knower, but it invades and involves the whole man as a free person. The sacred seizes each man in his ontological, intellectual, psychological and historical developments.

Thus the sacred must be approached, not with curiosity the way we approach an objective problem, but with awe and trembling, the way we approach mysteries. For the sacred represents the divine call from above, forcing the man of good will, like Moses before the burning bush, like the three apostles before the transfiguration of Christ, to his knees in a prostration of adoration. The challenge emanating from the sacred is so powerful that man cannot remain indifferent to it. In the presence of God, the Source of Sacredness, man either adores with the prayer, "Thy Will be done," or rebels with the cry, "I will not serve!" Thus, God is the ineffable Someone at the summit of every experience of the sacred. This Summit of the sacred claims the first place in every intelligent being's life, angels and men. Religion is man's response to the sacred, to God, the Supreme, Prior, Independent yet ever present Other. The sense of the sacred presents man with these paradoxical experiences. God is presented as totally Other, transcending man, yet He is simultaneously experienced as being intimately present, nearer to man than man is to himself, filling man with awe and yet desiring to give Himself to man in intimate communication and communion. St. Paul tells us that "in him we live and move and have our being."

The sacred also brings man the experience of God's brilliance and luminosity. Thus man's response to God is his response to the numen or the numinous, that is, to the wholly illuminating, fascinating and ravishing Reality who is God. The experience of the *Mysterium Tremendum* suffuses the being of man with awe, a mixed feeling of reverence, fear and wonder, accompanied by an acute, grateful consciousness of one's creatureliness in the presence of an infinitely good Creator. In the experience of the sacred a "shudder" moves the whole person which, speechless, trembles to the deepest core of its being. The sacred presents God as the *Mysterium Fascinans* before whom the posture of prayer and adoration is the only adequate response called for by the whole of man's being.[8] Thus religion and the sacred always go together. Indeed, religion vanishes with the loss of the sacred, and vice versa. Religion flourishes with growth in the consciousness and love of the sacred. The moment the sense of the sacred diminishes in a people, it is a sure sign that the faithful are becoming secularized, materialized, paganized. For then they have lost an awareness of the presence of God and of His kingdom that descends from above.

The sacred applies not only to God but to all things that have a special connection with Him — angels, saints, miracles, churches, sacraments, etc. Moreover, there are sacred places and times. The Holy Land where Christ lived, died and redeemed man is a sacred place. Then too, sacred time reenacts, relives historically sacred events, e.g., Holy Week relives the events of man's salvation. But in all sacred instances, eternity is not pulled down to the level of time, rather time soars into eternity. For the sacred is above time, though inserted into time and capable of ransoming time. Thus, the sacred, as essentially related to religion, can redeem and blot out our faults committed in time. By transcending and transforming time through a life of faith in the true religion, the sacred does not obliterate time, but saves and sanctifies it. The Source of the sacred embraced man and his history when the Son of God forever embraced in His divinity the sacred humanity He received from Mary.

Man, therefore, is capable of transforming his domain of the non-sacred, of the profane, with the sense of the sacred or of degrading that domain and himself by obliterating in himself his love for the sacred. Man attacks the sacred when he rejects God and the true religion, thereby promoting himself and his affairs on earth as his only and ultimate concerns. Thus, in our times a social climate charged with hatred of God and the sacred has produced what even the atheist men of culture have sardonically referred to as the "Savage Sixties" and the "Sick Seventies." For once man rejects God, man becomes what Kierkegaard calls "the eternal zero." This is logical and necessary for, since his awareness of himself is founded on his awareness of God, the godless man, rootless and direction-less, is at sea in an absurd world. Of course, he has an identity crisis. And with his animus against God and the sacred, he becomes a menace and a plague to the faith and holiness of his fellow men. For when he breaks the sacred chains of love that bind him to God, he ends up breaking even the chains of civility and decency that should bind him to his fellow men. Moreover, it is not surprising that the man who has rejected God and the sacred continues to talk about God, religion and the Church. Now, how-ever, he speaks of these realities as being "interesting phenomena" in the ascent of man from infancy to maturity. Now this "uncommitted interest," this neutrality toward divine, sacred realities is a typical game of ridicule played by the spiritually defeated, atheistic, intellectual snob. Such spiritually exhausted "playboys," choosing to be smart and clever rather than sacred and celestial, refuse to realize that God, religion and the Church can never be merely interesting or amusing myths. The sphere of the sacred is really uninteresting in the shallow, cute sense of that term. For the sacred sector demands one's total self-donation to God, one's eternal salvation being jeopardized if one refuses to say "yes" to God. Trivial things and affairs can be the subject of interest and cleverness. But adherence to the sacred realm is a tremendously serious, ultimate, tragic affair. It is the awful, shuddering, one thing necessary for which all else must eventually be put aside, even life itself. When one jokes about the sacred, one is well on the way to participating in the sacrilegious.

For the rejection of the sense of the sacred as revealed in the dynamics of ridicule always degenerates into a dynamics of hate — hatred of God, of others and finally of oneself. Thus, in our times a social climate charged with hatred of God, poisoned with irreducible religious-moral-political tensions and with hourly seditious preachments bereft of all truth, of all objectivity, of all love is the logical, violent result of the loss of the sense of the sacred. A society sickened from its rejection of God and the sacred necessarily produces a sick culture. In a modern play, *Prometheus Unbound,* Prometheus, the Titan who stole fire from Zeus, the god of the gods, is confronted by the foul furies and asks them wonderingly: "Can aught exult in its own deformity?" Dostoevsky's Underground Man answers with a soul-searing affirmation: "I am a sick man. . . . I am a spiteful man. I am an unpleasant man." Underground Man then adds that he finds his only enjoyment "in the hyperconsciousness of his own degradation."[9] Today the post-Christian savage is idealized in philosophical, political, ethical, literary and theological works as the authentic man-come-of-age — the Rebel Hero of *Paradise Lost,* the Promethean Savior of a Cosmos Regained. From the heights of this hateful, over-weening pride such a man has created a culture in which he defines his fellow man as "that most precious capital," "that useless passion," "that walking bag of sea water." Sacrilegious man hurls these slogans against his fellow man from a rhetoric of hatred that delights in destroying the dignity, sacredness and divinity with which God has endowed men created and redeemed by His Son.

Sisters and the sacred

Earlier we had indicated that the sacred applies also to persons that have a special relationship with God. Now sisters, living the evangelical counsels of poverty, chastity and obedience, are a sacred people, for they have dedicated their whole lives to the service of God and their fellow men for the sake of the kingdom of heaven. It is true that sisters, like other Christians, have died to sin and have been initially consecrated to God through baptism. St. Peter reminds us that the whole people of God is "a chosen race, a royal priesthood, a holy nation, a purchased people. . . called out of darkness into his marvellous light."[10] Nevertheless, Vatican Council II, speaking of religious in its *Dogmatic Constitution on the Church,* reminds us that: ". . . in order to derive more abundant fruit from this baptismal grace, he [the religious] intends by the profession of the evangelical counsels in the Church, to free himself from the obstacles which might draw him away from the fervor of charity and the perfection of divine worship. Thus he is more intimately consecrated to the divine service. This consecration gains in perfection, since by virtue of firmer and steadier bonds, it serves as a better symbol of the unbreakable link between Christ and His Spouse, the Church.''[11] To the sister, then, who is a better symbol of the unbreakable link between Christ and His Spouse, the Church, these words of St. Peter are especially addressed: ''But as the One who called you is holy, be you also holy in all your behavior. For it is written: 'You shall be holy because I am holy.' ''[12]

Continuing to develop religious life as a special sign of divine life in a wasteland of secularism, Vatican II writes: ''The profession of the evangelical counsels, then, appears as a sign which can and ought to attract all members of the Church to an effective and prompt fulfillment of the duties of their Christian vocation. The people of God has no lasting city here below, but looks for one which is to come. This being so, the religious state by giving its members greater freedom from earthly cares more adequately manifests to all believers the presence of heavenly goods already possessed here below. Furthermore, it not only witnesses to the fact of a new and eternal life acquired by the redemption of Christ, it foretells also the resurrected state and the glory of the heavenly kingdom....The religious state reveals in a unique way that the kingdom of God and its overmastering necessities are superior to all earthly considerations. Finally, to all men it shows wonderfully at work within the Church the surpassing greatness of the force of Christ the King and the boundless power of the Holy Spirit.''[13] For the religious state and the sisters who live in this state, as signs of the sacred, belong inseparably to the life and holiness of the Mystical body of Christ.

In his ''Apostolic Exhortation on the Renewal of Religious Life,'' Pope Paul VI reminds religious of ''this special gift'' which enables those who have received it to be more closely conformed to ''that manner of virginal and humble life which Christ the Lord elected for Himself, and which His Virgin Mother also chose.''[14] In encouraging religious to seek God constantly through their undivided love for Christ, the Holy Father indicates a serious danger that would plague mankind if the witnessing to the world above, to the life in God by holy religious were to vanish. ''Without this concrete sign there would be a danger that the charity which animates the entire Church would grow cold, that the salvific paradox of the Gospel would be blunted, and that the 'salt' of faith would lose its savor in a world undergoing secularization.''[15] In warning religious against a spirit of naturalism in their attitude toward the life of the counsels, the Holy Father insists: ''In reality, the charism of religious life, far from being an impulse born of flesh and blood, or one derived from a mentality which conforms itself to the modern world, is the fruit of the Holy Spirit, who is always at work within the Church.''[16] In an age of irreverent iconoclasts, of sacrilegious image-breakers, of a society that seems to be preparing itself for the arrival of the Man of Sin, how can the sister recall this world to the sacred sense of life in men and nations? I suggest that the sister should turn her gaze to the Holy Mother of God and model herself into a living image, an inspiring icon which in imitation of that Holy Mother, virginally and totally consecrated to God's holy will, gives the world Christ and salvation through her self-effacing service.

Sisters as virginal, fruitful icons of the sacred

Mary, the Mother of God, is the perfect Christian and the supreme model for bringing the Son of God and His sacred humanity to save the world. Now when the Son of God became man, He chose to be born of this humble Virgin whose whole heart was ever dedicated to loving and serving God. Then too the Son of God as man lived a life of virginity while fulfilling His Father's mission of redeeming men. Sisters, consecrated to God in chastity, joyfully chose this sublime way of life, for they want to do God's work in Christ's way, in Mary's way. Mary became the perfect, holy vessel of salvation for mankind through Jesus, the fruit of her virginal womb. So in an analogous way, sisters vowed to God in chastity live ever more profoundly and fruitfully for their contemporaries because their hearts are given to their Lord in a preferential love of such intensity that, like St. Paul, ''they are in labor until Christ is born'' in those they serve. For their lives of chastity beget holiness in the sisters themselves and in the world they serve.

This is an age of ''ravaging eroticism,'' of ''savagery and sexuality.'' In such an age, chastity, lived out of love of the Lord and His brethren, must raise the hearts and minds of men ''to seek the things that are above, where Christ is seated at the right hand of God.'' The sister, through her decisively positive love and practice of chastity, demonstrates to the world that, with the grace of Christ, it is quite possible and indeed joyful ''to walk in the spirit so as not to fulfill the lusts of the flesh.'' It is true, chastity will continually present to the world the scandal and foolishness of the cross. But it will thereby challenge the world to change its evil ways and put its faith in its crucified Savior. Pope Paul VI tells us: ''When it is truly lived for the sake of the kingdom of heaven, consecrated chastity frees man's heart and thus becomes a sign, and a stimulus as well as a special source of spiritual fruitfulness in the world. Even if the world does not always recognize it, consecrated chastity remains in every case effective in a mystical manner in the world.''[17] The martyr and celibate priest Maximilian Kolbe, who freely substituted himself in place of a father of a family for death in a Nazi concentration camp, served and honored the family to the excess of perfect, Christ-like love. Thus too the sister, like Mary, is a sacred feminine symbol of a chastity totally dedicated in love to God and Man and endlessly fruitful for all men in the economy of salvation.

Chastity often enough has been chosen for the merely natural reasons of self-discipline, freedom to pursue a noble career, or for philosophical convictions. And those who practiced chastity for such honorable reasons received the respect and admiration of their fellow men. But there is nothing stoical nor career-like about a sister's life of chastity. She is not a mere dedicated social worker, educator or civic leader. Indeed, she is an ambassador of Christ's saving message and grace. For she is a praying, working, suffering, joyful witness to Christ. What makes her chastity sublime is its open, clear connection with the sacrifice of the cross. Our Savior's example and invitation have overwhelmed her heart. "If anyone wishes to follow me, let him deny himself and take up his cross daily and follow me. . . . He who loses his life for me and for the Gospel will save it."

The virgin sister wants to be identified with the Virgin Christ, with His Virgin Mother, so as to live, through her bearing of the cross they carried, "the mystery of the Church and her mission." Long ago the pagan savants Thucydides and Plato testified to the truth that the noblest manifestation of power is the ability not to use it, and the most courageous, meaningful victory is that over oneself. Now chaste sisters jolt a sex-maddened and permissive society out of its despairing surrender to the sinful enticements of sex. The very presence of sisters, dressed and living as virgins, reminds fallen man that there really exist people — normal, mature and busy — who actually live as virgins and are quite happy about it. Their virginity is seen then as something beautiful for God and inspirational for man. In the truest, even radical sense of the word, sisters as virgins are angels, i.e., messengers of God sent to lead men to the beatific vision, where all will finally be like the angels of God, for there will be no longer giving or taking in marriage, but God will be all in all. It is about time that men begin to realize that they need the help not only of invisible angels, but above all of visible angels like sisters who are vowed in chastity to the service of God and their fellow men. Like the angels who ministered to Christ in His agony in the garden, when His poor human friends slept, virgin sisters minister to men in their most tragic moments. For such sisters are found serving in orphanages, hospitals, maternity homes, leprosariums, ghettoes, old folks homes, schools at all levels, in missions in all parts of the world. Liberated from the temporal encumbrances of marriage and private families, like angels, sisters vowed in chastity seem to be everywhere ministering to Christ and His Mystical Body in all His brethren, but especially in the suffering and the needy.

Sisters as serene troubadours of the sacred

The religious sister vows to live in poverty in the use of this world's goods. Once again she does this out of a motive of love, to imitate Christ and His holy Mother in their complete dedication to the holy will of God. "I have a food of which you know not....My meat is to do the will of him who sent me." In imitation of their Lord, sisters seek to be liberated from temporal encumbrances. Their lives represent to a greedy world a joyful renunciation and detachment from earthly goods with a dedication, for the sake of Christ, to the eternal goods of the kingdom of heaven. "Seek first the kingdom of God and his justice and all these [temporal] things will be added unto you," is the rule and spirit of their lives. By their inspiring practice of the spiritual ideal of evangelical poverty, sisters warn men not to get bogged down in the banquet of the consumer society whose god is its belly, but to seek the great banquet of the communion of saints whose God is the ever-blessed Holy Trinity. The life of evangelical poverty reminds men that they must transfer their interests and energies from seeking gold and silver to striving for the better products of sanctity and glory.

But besides being indifferent to the material goods of this life as shown in the practice of the virtue and vow of poverty, sisters and religious aim at becoming indifferent also to the vanity of this world. They are also quick to give up those spiritual goods that tend to immortalize men in time. We are all tempted to aspire after fame, reputation and the credit of a great name on earth. We want glory; we want to survive in the memory of man, in history; we want to be immortal in the eyes of posterity even more than we want to work for immortality in the beatific vision. Too often history's hall of fame is more important to us than heaven's list of the saints. Our avidity for fame and glory is tremendous. It flows from a grotesquely secular greed and spiteful envy. The first murder in history flowed from this spiritual greed. Cain killed Abel not for land or cattle, but because Abel attained a position of preferential love in the eternal memory of God. Spiritual gluttony is a thousand times more terrible than physical voracity. The Spanish poet and philosopher Miguel de Unamuno writes on this subject: "If the so-called problem of life, the basic problem of food, were ever solved, the earth would be turned into a hell, as the struggle for [spiritual] survival would become even more intense."[18]

Now the sister who is poor with the evangelical spirit of poverty becomes the serene troubadour of the sacred in time, in search of the treasures of heaven. God, Christ and the heavenly kingdom are the theme songs of her daily life. Such a sister does not desire fame, nor the credit of a great name on earth. Her life is hidden with Christ in God. The Lord is her portion forever and she is willing to wait for the next life to enjoy Him with her glorified Savior in heaven. For the present she prefers, for the sake of her Lord, the cross and obliteration from the fame of this world. Like John the Baptist, prophet, son of the high priest Zachary and friend of the bridegroom Christ, she lives a life of such complete detachment from material and spiritual temporal vanities that she makes his spirit her own, "He must increase and I must decrease." And she allows the light of her good works to shine before men not from a motive of self-aggrandizement, but that they may glorify her Father who is in heaven. Thus the sister, untrammeled with the obsession for worldly status, would never dream of attempting to seduce the Absolute so as to satisfy an insatiable hunger for temporal immortality. Unlike the flamboyant Pharisees who sought their consecrated identity and fame in the eyes of the world, which can only judge from the surface, the simple sister seeks her identity in the sacred presence of God who sees into the secret depths of her nothingness and rewards her total trust in Him by "doing great things" for her, making her His spouse.

I fear that many radical Catholics — religious, priests and nuns — who publicly demonstrate for worldly causes and violently attack the Church, the faith and sacred authority, may be unconsciously seeking, through secular and sacrilegious notoriety, temporal fame and the credit of a great name on earth. Perhaps no longer believing in a life beyond the grave, they have decided to make sure of cheating death and personal oblivion by enjoying in time a thrilling, contestatory immortality.

In 1849, long before the marvelous, modern media of communications existed, John Cardinal Henry Newman exposed the idol of notoriety and castigated the lust for publicity as an evil that will bury its devotees in hell with Dives. In his sermon *Saintliness the Standard of Christian Principle,* Newman said:

> Wealth is one idol of the day, notoriety is a second. . . . Never could notoriety exist as it does now in any former age of the world, now that the news of the hour from all parts of the world, private news as well as public, is brought day by day to every individual . . . hence notoriety, or the making of a noise in the world, has come to be considered a great good in itself, and a ground of veneration. . . . Notoriety, or as it may be called, newspaper fame, is to many what style and fashion — to use the language of the world — are to those who are within the higher circles. It becomes to them a sort of idol worshipped for its own sake, and without any reference to the shape in which it comes to them. It may be an evil fame or a good fame; it may be the notoriety of a great statesman, or of a great preacher, or of a great speculator . . . or

of a criminal; of one who has labored in the improvement of our schools, or hospitals, or prisons, or workhouses, or of one who has robbed his neighbor of his wife. It matters not, [just] so that a man is talked much of, and read much of, he is thought much of; nay, let him even have died under the hands of the law, still he will be made a sort of martyr of. . . the question with men is, not whether he is great, or good, or wise, or holy; nor whether he is base and vile and odious, but whether he is in the mouths of men, whether he has centered on himself the attention of many. . . whether he has been [as it were] canonized in the publications of the hour.[19]

On the other hand, the sister, living the life of evangelical poverty in the daily presence of God, is an eloquent witness, for a world sunk in secularism, to the truth that man is called to grow in the love and attainment of the sacred, and simultaneously challenged to destroy in himself the lust for secular immortality. Free, unattached, liberated from human respect and the silly nostalgia for notoriety, the sister suffused with the sacred spirit of poverty directs her fellow men to the One Thing Necessary. She lives out the only correct answer to that most important question put by our divine Lord to all His listeners: "What does it profit a man if he gain the whole world but suffer the loss of his immortal soul? Or what exchange can a man make for his soul?" As a troubadour of heaven, the sister sings a paradoxical song. She celebrates the rigors and wonder of the spirit of poverty whose reward is, nevertheless, the immense freedom and riches of the divine prodigality.

Sisters as joyful victims of the sacred

Christian obedience, joyfully practiced under the bond of the evangelical vow, is an unconditional surrender which a religious makes of herself to the most holy will of God. Her mind, her heart, her will are submitted in total faith to the loving Providence of the Blessed Trinity. The obedient sister follows the teaching and direction of the Holy Church, of her congregation and of her superiors because she reveres God's holy will in them and wishes to adhere perfectly to His august authority. Almost as a natural rhythm of her life, the sister wishes to offer God a total surrender of her person so as to become a sacred sacrifice in loving imitation of Christ's total surrender to His Father's will. An obedient sister demonstrates to the world that liberty is not suffocated but sanctified and strengthened by obedience. Christ who was obedient unto death was the freest of men because He loved to an infinite degree. The obedient sister teaches freedom-loving man that obedience does not diminish the dignity of the human person, but rather raises man to the height of being a son of God in union with Jesus Christ.

In living out her joyful self-surrender, the sister, learning obedience through suffering in imitation of her Lord, submits her conscience to the objective norms of reason, to the sound teaching advice of her superiors and advisors and, above all, to the teaching of the Holy Father and the Magisterium of the Church. For the obedient sister, St. Peter's Chair, not the professor's, not the philosopher's, not the theologian's, is the guarantee of her faith, morals and practices for sanctity. She does not let herself be swayed by every theologian who happens to be in fashion and is lionized by the world because he is opposing the Catholic Church. For the obedient sister testifies that she is in love with the holy Word of God which the Church, like her Master, teaches infallibly with divine authority. Thus the obedient sister is not easily taken in by philosophers or theologians who superimpose private, gnostic ideologies on the Word of God. Pope Paul VI has warned the faithful about the defeatism which is sounding the death knell of true authority outside and within the Church. On July 14, 1965, Pope Paul said: "Today everyone knows how widespread this state of mind hostile to the principle of authority is. It manifests itself not only in temporal society, but also in various sectors of Catholic life itself. Obedience, that is to say, the welcoming and practical recognition of authority, is continually questioned as being contrary to the development of the human person, as being unworthy of free, mature and adult human beings. It is continually misunderstood as if it created weak and passive spirits, and perpetuated in modern times outworn principles of social relations. There are those who think it worthwhile to run the risk of a liberating disobedience and that it is a praiseworthy trick to confront authority with an accomplished fact...."[20]

The fact is that Christ taught us that the interplay between superior and subject should be a relationship of love. He constantly brings out this truth by using the familiar image of shepherd and flock. The pastor who has authority loves, serves and dies for his flock. The sheep love, obey and follow their pastor. Unfortunately, corrosive Catholic critics, who see in the Church nothing more than a human institution, have given this sacred relationship demeaning connotations. "Flock," despite its original sacred sense, has now been secularized to mean stolid masses ruled dictatorially from above. This wicked interpretation has engendered a false division within the bosom of the Church. The hierarchy or institutional sector of the Church is represented as being the enemy of the faithful, thereby introducing dialectical warfare in the Church, as if Christ can be divided within Himself. Is it any wonder that the seeds of distrust, resentment and disloyalty have been disseminated by secularists who have lost the sacred

significance of divine authority, especially as it descends from the Holy
Trinity, through the Pope and bishops, to the Holy Church? Think of the
marvelous faith the early Christians displayed when, following the advice
of St. Paul, they obeyed the divine authority that resided in such wicked
persecutors of the Church as Nero, Diocletian and others. Contrast this
holy faith with the abysmal lack of faith in many priests, nuns, theologians
and intellectuals in the Church who flagrantly oppose the authority of the
Pope and the Magisterium in matters of faith and morals. And God knows
the Holy Father and the Magisterium in the Church today have given
wonderful examples of personal holiness and total service to the whole world!
The truth is that God calls the faithful to obey His Son and the ruling
priesthood founded in and on His Son. It is sacrilegious to reduce the hierarchy to being a brotherhood of political bosses bent on maintaining despotic
power. Pope Leo XIII has taught us that "obedience is not servitude of
man to man, but submission to the will of God, who governs through the
medium of men."[21] If then our obedience to ecclesiastical superiors is
obedience to God, then our love for them is also part of our love for God.
In attempting to make us see what our love within the kingdom of the
Church should be, Fr. von Balthasar points to the perfect model of the
God-Man whose love we must imitate, for it was a demonstration of His
obedience unto death. "The kingship of God," writes Fr. von Balthasar,
"who reveals Himself as love, is shown to us in the humble obedience of
the Son to the Father, and so we are shown that this obedience is essentially
love. It is certainly the model for human love before the majesty of God.
But, more than that, it is the supreme image of the Divine Love itself
appearing."[22]

Miguel de Unamuno, Spanish poet, philosopher and one of the
strongest Catholic critics of the rationalistic atheism of the nineteenth
century, writes in his book *The Tragic Sense of Life in Men and Nations*
concerning the spirit of rebellion in the free thinker and the arrogant
intellectual, the following sagacious words most appropriate for our times:
"The real sin — perhaps the sin against the Holy Spirit, that ever mysterious
sin in Christian literature for which there is no remission here or hereafter
— is the sin of heresy, the sin of thinking for ourselves. We have heard
it said in Spain that to be a liberal, that is a heretic, is worse than to be
an assassin, a thief or an adulterer. The gravest sin is not to obey the
Church, whose infallibility protects us from reason."[23]

The sacred and religious dress

And one final friendly observation concerning the sacred and religious
dress. In my travels and conversations with all sorts of people from all walks
of life, I have found that people do not want a Modish Nun, nor do they

think that the "Mod Nun" is an inevitable wave of the future. They do not want the sister who meddles in the ordinary affairs and direction of their families. They despise the nun who tries constantly to adjust to the world. People do not see the essence of the religious sisterhood to lie in the humanitarian or social or political activity of religious. People are not seeking in the religious sisterhood an army of Florence Nightingales, wonderful as that army would be. Though they fully realize that the religious garb does not necessarily make the religious holy, nevertheless, people want a sister to be recognizable as a sister, i.e., they want a sister in religious dress so as to see in her always a servant of Christ who is a constant witness of a life other than that of this earth. People agree with Pope Paul VI who wrote: "While we recognize that certain situations can justify the abandonment of a religious type of dress, we cannot pass over in silence the fittingness that the dress of religious men and women should be, as the Council wishes, a sign of their consecration and that it should be in some way different from the forms that are clearly secular."[24] Perhaps Father Paul Crane, S.J., has treated this matter of religious dress and its sacred significance as well as any person who has put his pen to the problem. Father Crane writes:

> The mistake of clerics and religious, who discard priestly and religious dress, is, therefore, clear. It is that of angelism: the assumption that spirit, because of its purity, comes shining through irrespective of appearance, irrespective, therefore, of dress, which is at once its expression and its complement. A moment's reflection will show that the arrogance implicit in this assumption is awful. Religious who say they need no special mode of dress in witness to what they are, say really and by implication that their strength of spirit is such as to shine out on all in witness to what they are, irrespective of their appearance. Christ alone could say that because He alone was divine. Religious and priests are not. They are human beings made up of body and soul. Their appearance, therefore, must mark their witness — a thing impossible unless their dress does the same. The adoption, therefore, on the part of a religious of a distinctive habit or dress is not, as Progressives would have us believe, in aid of a bogus status, which priests and religious have taken to themselves. It is a sign rather of the deficiency they know to be theirs; of their inability as human beings to bear adequate witness to Christ without appropriate bodily aid. For the Emperor to call for his clothes is not a mark of pride, but of humility, an acknowledgement of essential dependence and a repudiation of self-

sufficiency. It is the same exactly with priests and religious in the Church who mark their calling with a distinctive dress.[25]

Here, then, is the serenely holy sister to whom the Church, the people of God, and indeed, the sacrilegiously sick would look for a witnessing to the sacred. It must be a witnessing of holy, valiant women who accept joyfully the abnegation of poverty, the total self-donation of chastity and the humble self-effacement of obedience. Such witnesses to the sacred are in love with the peace of Christ which they radiate to others because they are free from earthly compromise themselves, set on complete self-denial and exhibit a spontaneous, tenacious, strong, yet meek adherence to the faith. The sacred sister announces in her life the message about man's dignity, man who is called by his origins to live in communion with God and who becomes, through the redemption of Christ, a new creation, child of God, sacred by means of creation and redemption. As she leads men to Christ and through Christ to the Father in unity and love, the holy sister is attracting the whole human race to that tremendously serious, ultimate, awful, shuddering and tragic realm of the sacred, the realm that demands one's total self-donation to God, the One Thing Necessary for which all else must eventually be put aside, even life itself. Such is the sublime, sacred service the religious sister renders to God and man. For the sister, suffused with the spirit of the sacred, becomes in an especially efficacious manner what St. Paul said all Christians should become, a spiritual incense and a fragrance of sanctity: "For we are the fragrance of Christ for God, alike as regards those who are saved and those who are lost: to the lost we are a fragrance that leads to death; to the saved we are a fragrance that leads to life."[26]

Notes

[1]The Christian Science Monitor, Friday, August 10, 1973, p. 8.
[2]*L'Osservatore Romano*, English edition, September 6, 1973, p. 2.
[3]*The Documents of Vatican II*, Pope John Convokes the Council, Editor Walter M. Abbott, S.J., p. 703.
[4]Duncan Williams, *Trousered Apes* (New Rochelle: Arlington House, 1972), p. 43.
[5]*Ibid.*, p. 29.
[6]*Ibid.*, pp. 72, 40.
[7]Alice von Hildebrand, *Introduction to a Philosophy of Religion* (Chicago: Franciscan Herald Press, 1970), Chapter IV, pp. 32-39.
[8]Rudolph Otto, *The Idea of the Holy* (N.Y.: Oxford University Press), p. 6
[9]Duncan Williams, *Trousered Apes* (New Rochelle: Arlington House, 1972), p. 57
[10]1 Pt. 2:9.
[11]"Dogmatic Constitution on the Church," *The Documents of Vatican II* (Ed. Abbott), n. 44.
[12]1 Pt. 1:15.
[13]"Dogmatic Constitution on the Church," *The Documents of Vatican II* (Ed. Abbott), n. 44.

[14]Pope Paul VI, "Apostolic Exhortation on the Renewal of Religious Life According to the Teaching of the Second Vatican Council," (Boston: St. Paul Editions), paragraphs 2, 3.

[15]*Ibid.*

[16]*Ibid.,* paragraph 11.

[17]*Ibid.,* paragraph 14.

[18]Miguel de Unamuno, *The Tragic Sense of Life in Men and Nations* (Princeton University Press, 1972), p. 62.

[19]Quoted by Hilda Graef in her *God and Myself: The Spirituality of John Henry Newman* (N.Y.: Hawthorn Books Inc., 1968), p. 115.

[20]Pope Paul VI, Speech on Crisis of Authority, July 14, 1965, quoted in *Christian Order* (London, March 1972), Vol. 13, No. 3, p. 134.

[21]Pope Leo XIII, "Immortale Dei," Nov. 1, 1885, quoted in *Christian Order, Ibid.,* p. 135.

[22]Fr. von Balthasar, *Love Alone: The Way of Revelation* (London: Compass Books, 1968), p. 71.

[23]Miguel de Unamuno, *The Tragic Sense of Life in Men and Nations* (Princeton University Press, 1972), p. 79.

[24]Pope Paul VI, "Apostolic Exhortation on the Renewal of the Religious Life According to the Teaching of the Second Vatican Council" (Boston: St. Paul Editions, 1971), paragraph 22.

[25]Fr. Paul Crane, S.J., "Clothes and the Religious," *Christian Order* (London: November 1972), Vol. 13, No. 11, pp. 642-643.

[26]2 Cor. 2:15-16.

Hans Kung — Credible?
An Inquiry

In the world of philosophical, theological and biblical scholars the name of Hans Kung is a household word. This is especially true among Catholic professors who disagree ardently among themselves about the service or disservice being rendered theology, religion and the Catholic Church by the many publicized writings of this Swiss Catholic priest.

And now appears a new appraisal of this theologian's work, *The Historical Credibility of Hans Kung: An Inquiry and Commentary* by Joseph F. Costanzo, S.J., the Christopher Publishing House, North Quincy, Mass., 1979, Bibliography, Appendices A, B, C, Index of Scriptural Text and references, pp. 382, $12.95.

In this first volume of a prospective trilogy on the work of Kung, Fr. Costanzo carefully examines Kung's *Unfehlbar? Eine Anfrage,* in English translation *Infallible? An Inquiry.* He analyzes the work in depth, discussing it paragraph by paragraph, and indicates the topical referrals that Kung frequently multiplies within each paragraph.

Fr. Costanzo finds that from the opening sentence Kung's book is contaminated with an adversary spiritual and intellectual distemper. Thus intellectually mongrelized, the work *Infallible?* becomes a distraught attack, rather than a serene *Inquiry,* that distorts the subject of infallibility, the Vatican Council that defined it and the scholars involved in its development and definition. Kung prejudices and even politicizes in narration and perspective his own understanding of all that he had once affirmed by faith and theological research on the defined doctrine of papal infallibility.

In "A Candid Foreword" Kung reveals the flaming energy, *anima,* that has driven him to write this book. Unfortunately this intellectual life force is flawed by a fantastic, capricious twist of mind in the spirit of Hans Kung. His *animus* against Rome has driven his *anima* to falsify greviously Rome's teachings, intentions and acts of jurisdiction. Concerning this sad situation, Fr. Costanzo writes; "The pages (of the Foreword) ache intensely here (and not infrequently throughout the entire book) with teutonic neuralgia."

Hung up on 'Roman'

Kung never refers to the Pope as "the Vicar of Christ," but always as "Roman Pontiff," "Bishop of Rome." He never addresses the Pope as "His Holiness," with which title even the members of the diplomatic corps representing non-Catholic countries address the Holy Father. Kung's *animus* against anything Vatican and Roman appears to be obsessive. He writes of the "Roman ghetto," the "Vatican ghetto," the "curial ghetto," the "Roman central administration," "traditional curial policy and theology" (not Catholic theology), "The Roman curia," "Roman reaction," "narrow Roman theology and ideology," "not very ecumenical Romanism," "Roman system," "Roman textbooks" (even though many of these are by German and French authors), "Roman theology," "non-Roman readers," "Roman teaching," "Roman claim," "Roman-minded prelates," "Roman teaching office" (not the teaching office of the Catholic Church), "Roman mentality" (yet many of the professors of theology in Rome are non-Italians). The whole twisted bias of Kung's mind is that the realities represented by the words "Rome," "Vatican" and "Roman" have something evil and sinister about them, that it is a theological blight to teach according to the Bishop of Rome, the Roman Pontiff. The same denigrating procedure is applied to the Roman Church. The Catholic Church is called the "Church of the Roman Imperial Capital," "centralized, juridicized, romanticized." She is the Church of "Rome at the time of the Counter-Reformation," (*not* the Catholic Church), the Church that begets "Roman ecclesiastical policy and theology," the Church that causes the "polarization of German and Roman theology." (There is the rub!) She is the Church that is constantly "increasing Roman influence," "Roman ideas," "as an army in battle array under Rome's command," "romanizing the whole Church" with "Roman influences," "Roman absolutism," "Roman views" and so on and on *ad nauseam*. It is clear that Hans Kung reveals himself as suffering from an acute, all pervasive psychological alienation from the Roman Catholic Church. Fr. Costanzo proves this throughout his own study and states that this alienation has led to "an intellectual turning of the worm" in Kung's consciousness.

After studying the attack on Romanism, Part I of Fr. Costanzo's work goes on to analyze in depth some twenty-eight other resentments of Kung arising from theological and historical trifles that have prejudiced him against the Roman Catholic Church's positions on these matters. The many mental quirks blazoning forth from Kung's typewriter are addressed to a variety of subjects; some are old, worn-out, even discarded "chestnuts," like indulgences, Galileo, usury, secular power, Honorius, conscience, mixed marriages, liberty and law, the Photian affair. Others have gained prominence since Vatican II — Mary, Mater Ecclesiae, the Dutch Catechism, unhistorical saints, nuncios, Pope Paul VI's encyclicals, Papal Primacy, Scriptural exegesis, women religious orders, the Credo, the Rites controversy, celibacy, etc. Fr. Costanzo's analysis of each subject fills this section of the book with a wealth of accurate Church historical information. He reveals the simplicity or complexity of each problem; he studies it within its actual historical context. As philosopher and theologian of the first order, his dialectical reasoning is flawless, indeed profound; he separates foolish from true problems, prudential judgements from doctrinal teachings, naive solutions for perceptive and sophisticated wisdom. While demonstrating, in his own commentaries on Kung's resentments, genuine scholarship, he simultaneously unmasks the pseudo-scholarship of the author of *Infallible?* As an example we cite his scholarly analysis of Kung's list of "errors of the Ecclesiastical Teaching Office." Fr. Costanzo writes:

> A number of Kung's "errors of the ecclesiastical teaching office" are nothing more than the converse of Kung's own prepossessions on artificial birth control, mixed marriages, priestly celibacy, a latitudinarian ecumenism; others betray his ill-concealed aversion for the Roman curia, for indulgences and for theologians who teach according to "Roman" doctrine, that is, papal teaching. Others are frankly crude charges that Pope Paul VI has failed the faithful by his encyclicals on the Church *(Ecclesiam Suam),* on the Eucharist *(Mysterium Fidei),* on sacerdotal celibacy *(Sacerdotalis Coclibatus)* the *Credo,* Pope Paul VI's proclamation hailing Mary, *Mater Ecclesiae;* and still other "errors" are nothing more than an exploitation of uprooted history — usury, Galileo, Rites controversy and the problematics of modern critical-historical, biblical exegesis, Honorius, Eastern Church schism — not to mention his false antithesis between primacy of jurisdiction and primacy of service and, not least, his Lutheran interpolation of Pauline theology on law, the gospel and freedom, and perhaps thereby hangs the tale of Kung's ecclesiology and his acerbic assault on papal infallibility. Let there be no doubt about it — his book is not an *Inquiry,* despite his avowal to the contrary, as each reader may see for himself. Apart from Kung's credibility as a historian of fact and of theology, we cannot entirely foreclose two observations. First, these alleged errors are stated categorically without any of the intellectual inhibitions and incapacitations that Kung declares all propositional truths to be heir to. For Kung writes: "Propositions can be true or false — and propositions can be true *and* false." One would suppose that Kung's theory of cognition would have tempered his complete assurance on the "errors of the ecclesiastical teaching office." Secondly, it is this writer's considered judgment that it is more than highly questionable that these were really errors at all; they were certainly not errors *in any way* of the ecclesiastical teaching authority touching matters of revelation, doctrinal and moral.

In Part II of his study Fr. Costanzo seeks to determine what other obstacles are preventing Hans Kung's mind from having an "open road" to the "truth." The bad effects of Fr. Kung's studies point to the fact that there must be mental "knots" to be untied in his mind and obstacles to be removed in the very objects he is studying. Both the mental or subjective and the extra-mental impediments will have to be identified, acknowledged and rejected by Fr. Kung before he can have a truly open *Inquiry* leading to the attainment of truth in the religious matters he researches.

He divides the Church

Earlier Fr. Costanzo exposed two impediments in Kung's "state of intellect" and orientation toward truth. First, his acerbic resentment to all that is Roman in the Church. Second, his exploitation of an uprooted ecclesiastical history. These spiritual distempers have knotted up Fr. Kung's intellect and obstructed his road to truth. But in the process of pursuing truth, one intellectual sickness leads to complications with the appearance of other related spiritual breakdowns. Thus Kung's adversary state of mind disposes him to separate, to dichotomize what are integral religious realities, inseparable constitutents of Catholic dogmas. He disjoins the institutional from the charismatic Church; the Pope, the visible head of the Church, from the Lord of Glory, the invisible Head of the Church; the Pope from the Church; the Church from the Mystical Body of Christ; the Church's teaching office from the Divine Spirit of Truth. All this in open contravention of constant Church doctrine. Pope Pius XII in his encyclical, *The Mystical Body of Christ,* warned about the disastrous effects of that penchant in scholars to dichotomize integral religious realities.

> For Peter in virtue of his primacy is only Christ's Vicar; so that there is only one Chief Head of this Body, namely Christ. He never ceases personally to guide the Church by an unseen hand, though at the same time He rules it externally, visibly through him who is His representative on earth. After his glorious Ascension into heaven this Church rested not on Him alone, but on Peter too, its visible foundation stone. That Christ and His Vicar constitute one only Head is the solemn teaching of our predecessor of immortal memory, Boniface VIII, in the Apostolic Letter UNAM SANCTAM; and his successors have never ceased to repeat the same.
>
> They, therefore, walk on the path of dangerous error, who believe that they can accept Christ as the Head of the Church, while they reject genuine loyalty to His Vicar on earth. They have taken away the Visible Head, broken the visible bonds of unity, and they leave the Mystical Body of the Redeemer in such

obscurity and so maimed that those who are seeking the haven
of eternal salvation cannot see it and cannot find it.

Despite this teaching of Pius XII in 1943, Fr. Kung in *Infallible?* severs
apart the triune divine-human interrelationships of Tradition, Sacred
Scripture and the Magisterium, and he inserts arbitrariness among them.
Moreover, the clear passage to truth is effectively blocked by Kung's
selective use of primary and secondary sources. Fr. Costanzo demonstrates
how Kung misconstrues his sources. For example, the *False Decretals,*
Verardo's *Introductio Editoris,* St. Thomas Aquinas' *Contra Errores Graecorum.*
Then too Kung uses authors selectively to suit his purpose; he omits weighty,
scholarly authorities whose theology is supportive of papal infallibility.
Finally, Kung demands "proofs," "demonstrations," "substantiation,"
but he never explains what precisely would constitute "proof" in dogmatic
theology on an article of faith. Kung treats of ecclesiastical history, about
a supernatural history, scriptural exegesis, dogmatic theology, of
philosophical and theological propositions. Yet he never states what
disciplinary method, if any, is appropriate to each science he is following.
Another erroneous disjunction which Kung inserts into an integral
religious reality defined by the Church is his severing of the charism of
infallibility from the charism of indefectibility. Now the Fathers of Vatican
I and II understood that the original requirement and foundation, according
to the divine design, for the infallibility of the Church (and of popes and
councils) is that the Church is a *teaching Church of divine revelation.* Only to
an infallible Church could the sacred deposit of faith be safely confided.
Lumen Gentium of Vatican II states this clearly:

> The infallibility with which the divine Redeemer willed His
> Church to be endowed in defining a doctrine of faith and
> morals...This is the infallibility which the Roman Pontiff, the
> head of the college of Bishops, enjoys in virtue of his office, when
> as the supreme head and teacher of all the faithful...as the
> supreme teacher of the universal Church, as one in whom the
> charism of the infallibility of the Church herself is individually
> present, he is expounding or defending a doctrine of the Catholic
> Faith.

Thus the infallibility of the Church, of the Popes and councils is the
work of God; it is God's guarantee to preserve his teaching Church from
error in its presentation of doctrines of faith and morals. This unfailing
efficacy is from God. This very protection against error is no less a protection against speculative pontifical "arbitrariness" and "despotism" that
haunt Kung's mind. It is the divine Spirit of Truth that "directs" the popes
and councils in infallible definitions and not the popes and councils who

"direct" the Holy Spirit. In a word, the burden to preserve truth in the Catholic church is on God, so to speak. The Spirit of Truth exercises his counseling and guiding power not according to his pleasures, nor according to papal "absolutism." Rather, the unfailing assistance of the Holy Spirit prevents the Petrine and papal office (and councils) in its doctrinal decisions from introducing human inventions into the binding Apostolic witness to Jesus Christ. The Holy Spirit ensures that the Word of God, the message of salvation among men will be taught without error. Only by such a divine disposition can men know, through the obedience and certitude of faith, what has been divinely revealed and how it must be understood. We obtain the truth and remain in the truth, in the words of St. Augustine, "by the authority of truth and by the truth of authority."

Can Church teach error?

It is precisely at this point that Kung errs in *Inquiry*. Instead of contemplating the power of God to work through men as he wills, Kung concentrates on human capability for arbitrariness, on human intellectual limitations, on human liability to fall into error. Thus Kung's alternative to infallibility in the Church is indefectibility, which he explains as a "fundamental remaining of the Church in truth, which is not annulled by individual errors." But the astonished believer must ask: How can the Church maintain any truly "fundamental remaining in the truth" in divine mysteries and yet simultaneously be teaching error in Vatican I in its solemn definitions on papal primatial jurisdiction and magisterial infallibility? How can the Church have remained fundamentally in the truth when she repeated these same errors in Vatican II? How can the Church remain in the truth if her bishops throughout the world have taught, and still teach, these errors in moral unity unanimously for centuries, as even Kung admits? If, as Kung states, "propositions of faith participate in the problematic of human propositions in general," and "that they are rather fundamentally ambiguous" and this is so about all solemnly defined Trinitarian and Christological dogmas, then Kung has the burden of answering intelligently this reasonable question: "What good is your theological theory of the indefectibility of the Church? What good is an indefectibility that is severed from the charism of infallibility, and thus leads mankind into errors concerning truths to which it must adhere if it is to be saved?" On the contrary, the truth is that any truly "fundamental remaining in the truth" of divine mysteries and in the divine economy of salvation presupposes as absolutely necessary the charism of infallibility, if God wills that men know his word and live faithfully in it.

The Church endures in truth

Fr. Costanzo goes on to repair the rupture made by Kung between infallibility and indefectibility. He writes:

> There is indefectibility in the Church, but it cannot be severed from, much less opposed to, infallibility, as Kung maintains.
>
> Infallibility is the inner core of indefectibility. Indefectibility concerns the Church's Constitution, sacraments, etc., as well as its doctrine on faith and morals. In the latter area, it applies to the whole historical life of the people of God above and beyond the cases of strict infallibility (which it includes). It means the indestructibility of the faith upon which and by which the Church is built. The Church will remain to the end of time. Indefectibility is bound up with the notion of the Church as the new people of God and the final covenant between God and man. Heresies and schisms have assaulted the Church of Christ, at their worst, with Arianism and at the time of the Reformation. But despite these disasters His Church continued in existence, as foretold by Christ. Indefectibility comprehends failures, changes, reform, accommodation, and in merely disciplinary regulations, even reversals. But the nature, mission and sacraments of the Church as Christ ordained it endures.

In reality, then, infallibility is the divine assurance that when the successors of Peter and of the Apostles under Peter speak in Christ's name and by his commission that their teaching is true to his salvific message; they declare with a finality beyond all challenge and recall. Ecclesial and papal infallibility is above all a question of divine providence — whether God *can ensure* inviolably and intact the faithful and unerring transmission of the apostolic kerygma of Christ to all men, through all time, *whatever the failings of men in general and even of his own specially designated ministers.* Kung's perspective is in the reverse, namely, the limitations of men preclude such a divine ordination; the limitations of men limit the power and frustrate the will of the God-Man to grant infallibility to his Church and his Vicars. Fr. Costanzo's conclusion on this position unveils the utter irrationality of Kung's teaching.

> If then, according to Kung, there is no infallibility in the Church, neither of the popes nor of ecumenical councils in union and agreement with the Roman Pontiff, if indeed Scripture is not inerrant, to whom shall the faithful turn to know "the Way, the Truth and the Life?" Kung invites all his readers (including popes and the episcopacy) to rely on the collective expertise of learned

theologians rather than on a supposed magisterial authority in the Church. But the manifest evidence of ecclesiastical history is far from reassuring on this sort of recourse. The generality of heretics within and without the Church have been theologians from the days of Marcion, Tertullian, Arius, Nestorius, Luther, Calvin, the Modernists of the 19th and 20th centuries, the "prestigious" and non-prestigious theologues of our day.

In Part III Fr. Costanzo traces Kung's precedent faith in papal infallibility. He examines three of Kung's books that appeared before *Humanae Vitae,* and presents selective passages to show that Kung unambiguously supported the Petrine-papal office and its infallibility. Kung's *Council, Reform and Reunion* earnestly and repeatedly urges Protestants to reconsider and shed their opposition to the pontifical office and its infallibility. It unequivocally affirms the "infallible accuracy," "unalterable," "objective" truth of "dogmatic definitions," thanks to the "influence of the Holy Spirit." These definitions remain free from error, even as they are time-conditioned, imperfect, incomplete, as obviously any truthful affirmation of a divine mystery must be. Kung holds that primarily and principally it is not the human credentials but its divine credentials that make the Catholic Church infallible and credible. Here is a remarkable passage from that book:

> What is called for on the Protestant side is to consider whether the words of Scripture about the abiding rock, the guiding and ruling key-bearer of the Kingdom of heaven, the special possessor of the power of binding and loosing, the means of confirming the faith of others and the deputy shepherd over the whole of Christ's flock need to be understood more deeply, more powerfully, and with more relevance to the present day by Protestant Christians, to ask themselves whether the Apostolic Church, united in Peter, was not meant to go on, with the Petrine office continuing along with the pastoral office of the Apostles, for the sake of the Church (so that what was once *laid* as a foundation would continue to *function* as a foundation); whether it might not be possible to view the history of the popes, for all the dubious matters in it, in a somewhat more cheerful and understanding light; whether much disputing and bitterness could not now be forgotten, allowing us to recognize, across the barrier of all that is human, something which does indeed seem to be not the mere work of men but the work of our common Lord, promised to us and protected for us by the Word of God.

In his book *Structures of the Church* Kung gives indisputable evidence of his acceptance of office, structural order, principle of tradition and legitimacy, the authority of the institutional office, the Church's teaching office, the Acts of the Apostles, the Pastoral Epistles, the three principles of office, succession and primacy clearly discernible in the New Testament. He uses Scripture to establish that the whole New Testament is the Gospel, the message of salvation. At no time in this book does Kung question, much less disown, the universal, supreme, plenary primatial authority of the Pope Rather he explains, defends forcefully, persuasively, sincerely papal infallibility, focusing on the promise of Christ and the unfailing assistance of the Holy Spirit to maintain the Church and popes in truth.

In 1967 Kung published his book *The Church*. Here he still adheres to the official doctrine of the Church on papal primacy and infallibility, defending it as not being an arbitrary absolutism. True, there are in this book intellectual clouds containing doctrinal confusion which will become a full-blown heretical storm in *Inquiry*. The storm arrives in his book *Truthfulness: The Future of the Church* published in 1968. This book is a full-blown blast against the Catholic Church for every conceivable human failure. It contains half truths, exaggerations, misconstructions, antipathies, aversions. Kung sits in harsh judgment over ecclesiastical conduct, ecclesial authority, popes, bishops, priests, theologians, the Curia, canon law, the whole course of ecclesiastical history. Finally in 1970 appeared *Infallible? An Inquiry*. Fr. Costanzo stigmatizes this work as a pastiche, a theological melange of rhetoric, half truths, whole falsehoods, a misuse of Scripture, the denial of the human capacity for the formulation of propositional truths exempt from error, the indifference to the divine efficacy of the Holy Spirit of Truth to warrant an infallible declaration of revelational data, the implication of the futility of receiving Christian revelation as a secure human possession as Christ intended it to be, and finally, a dismal and cavalier confusion of partial, inadequate and imperfect knowledge with error and falsehood.

What caused Fr. Hans Kung to abandon his faith in papal primacy and infallibility in the short time of some two to three years? We all realize that the acceptance or rejection of the faith is ultimately founded on reasons shrouded in the mysteries of the grace of God, man's use of his freedom and the mystery of iniquity. These reasons are known only to God. Insofar as a human conjecture can be made from events following the close of Vatican II, Fr. Costanzo hazards several reflections, that persist in his mind, as possible answers. He writes: "If *Humanae Vitae* had never been promulgated or — *ex hypothesi impossible* — if a novel moral doctrine had been taught by Pope Paul VI that reversed the traditional moral teaching of the Church on contraceptives, would Kung have ever challenged papal infallibility? The second notion: Is it possible that Kung's ecumenical zeal has been protestantized at the sacrifice of the papal office?'' In other words, was it a Protestantized ecumenism and the ''new theology,'' with its rationalist criticism, that acted as catalysts in Hans Kung's fall from Catholicism to a latitudinarian Christianity?

Kung does not help his readers answer these questions. He is not accountable to himself nor to others. He never explains why his former faith lost its forcefulness on his ''state of intellect.'' Unlike John Henry Newman, he feels no compulsion to explain his change of faith to his former co-faithful. Kung feels no obligation to explain to his former co-religionists how and why he now reads the same material, the same revelational data, the same historical and exegetical evidences of the New Testament in opposite ways. No indication is given as to where he failed formerly and wherein lies the dogmatic correction. He never speaks of his former faith as do almost all converts. He never indicates the historical and exegetical weaknesses in his former faith that he had failed to discern, nor what is his new found strength that he had not known before.

Fr. Costanzo concludes his profound critique of Kung's *Infallibility? An Inquiry,* which lacks scholarly competence and true, extensive learning, with this important truth:

> A fallible Church patterned on an errant Scripture, with a fallible foundation and a fallible shepherd ''to feed and tend'' His flock cannot be an object of faith.

In conclusion, I hasten to indicate to my readers that this excellent work of Fr. Costanzo also contains, in appendices A, B and C, three brilliant articles of his which drew international praise from scholars and a high commendation from Pope Paul VI who warmly thanked our author in a personal audience to which the Holy Father summoned him. These articles are: ''Papal Magisterium and *Humanae Vitae,*'' ''Academic Dissent: An Original Ecclesiology,'' and ''Papal Magisterium, Natural Law and *Humanae Vitae.*'' For this reviewer these articles in themselves are worth the price of the book.

Reprinted from *Homiletic & Pastoral Review,* June 1979

Community in Chaos,
Community in Christ

Leon Bloy, a great French writer who was tireless in defending the Church and spreading devotion to our Lady, penned these immortal words: "There is but one real sadness: not to be saints." More recently in our chaotic times, Gabriel Marcel, philosopher of communion, has one of his dramatic characters exclaim in anguish: "There is but one sadness: to be alone."

These two poignant lamenations may, at first, seem to be completely different. But the soul with the vision that penetrates into what Marcel calls "the inexhaustible mysteries of Being" sees that there is a profound metaphysical bond between the sadness of not being a saint and the sadness of being alone. Jean Paul Sartre himself expressed only a half truth when he had one of his characters in the tragedy, *No Exit,* a play about people trapped in hell, cry out: "Hell is other people." The other half of the full truth which Sartre refused to see is that: "Heaven, too, is other people." And the essential difference between these two communities of people is that the group which constitutes heaven is united in love, a shared love for God and for each other in Christ, while the group which constitutes hell is divided in hatred, a shared hatred for God which isolates and divides the community in enmity with Christ and with each other.

Perhaps the melancholy collapse of many communities of religious women and men can be studied best by analyzing the "Tale of Two Communities: The Community in Chaos and the Community in Christ." Needless to say, no particular communities are being singled out here and indeed the two opposed communities often exist under the same roof. On the principle given to us by our divine Lord that "a house divided against itself cannot stand," and hence, all the more, cannot have a meaningful or successful apostolic ministry in the Church, we would hope to share with you truths which the Holy Spirit has once again poured out upon us through the apostolic exhortation of Pope Paul VI entitled: "On the Renewal of the Religious Life According to the Teaching of the Second Vatical Council." For it would be tragic not to realize that the renewal of religious life, and hence of community in Christ, is an absolutely necessary first requirement for the reflourishing of the apostolic ministry of religious women in the Church. For we must never forget our Lord's words and take them literally to heart: "Without me you can do nothing." They only echo the warning of the Holy Spirit given to the Chosen People in the ages of antiquity: "Unless the Lord build the house, they labor in vain who build it."

The community in chaos

Unfortunately, we *have* forgotten the Lord's warning and in too many cases religious communities have attempted to live and perform without Him. When a given life is severed from its central meaning and theme, that life becomes distorted, appears ridiculous and is often abandoned as being insupportable. The rising tide of flight from religious communities testifies to the reality that once a religious community leaves Christ, it is at once afflicted with the fate of those who attempted to construct the Tower of Babel without God. Such a community no longer gathers with Christ, but scatters, first its own members and then, through scandal, the faithful and other men of good will. When the Word of God is no longer the common language of love and labor among its members, then the religious community produces a cacophony of tongues, an unhinging of minds so drastic that former lovers are alienated and their apostolic labors annulled. Its results are chaotic: the dethronement of truth, the decadence of morals, the death of the spirit.

The new treasure of the community in chaos

"Where your heart is, there also shall your treasure be," our divine Lord reminds us. Now almost imperceptibly and surely largely in good faith, many religious communities have changed the dream of their lives, the treasure of their hearts. They have fallen in love with a humanistic heaven, a secularist visionary dream, a Utopia of this world, and, in doing so, they have lost sight of and faith in the Community in Christ which is the kingdom of Christ not of this world. Presently they are zealously bestirred building a new society on earth, tailoring Christianity so as to make it serve the exigencies of temporal happiness and the communion of humanist saints in the heaven of the Secular City. Personal and social fulfillment is to be attained here, not hereafter, they proclaim as the good news of the modern apostolate in the modern Church. Now what underlies this stupendous endeavor to create a self-contained world capable of rewarding its citizens with its own supreme temporal happiness is man's exhilarating adventure to free himself from his condition of being a creature. Man wants to deny his total metaphysical subordination to contingency, to disengage himself from all bonds with anything or anyone greater than himself. During the Renaissance this secularist dream was for a long time developing in the womb of man's consciousness. It came to birth in the Age of the Reformation and has grown to adulthood in our Age of Revolution. As far back as 1830, Lamennais, Catholic inheritor of the atheistic prejudices of the French Revolution, was challenging restored Christian monarchs and even Popes to create the eternal kingdom of a self-sufficient brotherhood of man on earth. In his "Essay on Indifference,"

Lamennais subordinated the Gospel and the Church to the role of being catalysts for the arrival of the secular kingdom and the attainment of its natural happiness through revolution. Needless to say, the Church, like her Master, refused to become the architect or king of a revolutionary, temporal secular Utopia. But the fascination for the world and the temptation to serve her interests, taste her power, attain her glory is never absent from the trials of the Church and her children. And so somewhat later we read this earthly ideal in the writings of Lacordaire: "The chief virtue of today is not faith but a sincere love of liberty." And, in 1863, Montalambert urged the Church "to make peace with the Revolution." To his eternal credit Pope Pius IX rejected these temptations. Then Marc Sangnier, with his movement known as "The Sillon," had another try at luring the Church into the construction of an egalitarian, fraternal, free City of Man based on the revolutionary gospel of 1789. This time St. Pius X stood firm. He refused to subordinate the kingdom of God to the contemporary secularism, convenience or happiness of self-centered man who was constructing his Modernist millennium.

Finally we arrive at our own times, the days since the Council, and we find that there are those who warn us that once again progressive intellectuals have challenged, indeed have almost buffeted the Church, into expending her energies for the creation of the promised land on earth. These latter-day zealots of an earthly ideology upbraid the Church for being pre-occupied with other-worldly visions and demand that she come down from her supernatural cloudland and help rebuild a new and abiding city of men on earth. The magic formula for the creation of this heaven on earth is contained in the charismatic slogan "democratic pluralism," which from experience is understood to be a sort of loving tolerance of all and any ideas, and an ecumenical indifference to all creeds and any churches. Despite the irreconcilable opposition of doctrinal and moral ideals, this democratic pluralism claims to be able to unite all men in a brotherhood guaranteeing them justice, friendship and peace. Not conversion to Christ with the whole heart, mind and being, but communitarian connection with cosmic man will assure the salvation of all. Today the Church is asked to accept and declare more or less sacred, perhaps even divine, this cosmic salvific society in which man is evolving to personal and social perfection on his way to an immanent, humanitarian paradise. The Church, in her document, *Mysterium Ecclesiae,* published by the Sacred Congregation for the Defense of the Faith on June 24, 1973, once again rejected the role of being a mere dynamic stimulator of secular progress in the project of constructing a messianic kingdom of self-reliant humanists. Commenting on this new dream and treasure that has captured the hearts of so many religious women and men, Father Paul Crane, S.J., editor of *Christian Order,* a monthly dedicated to promulgating Catholic social teaching, writes: "Rather rudely, I am afraid, I have described this dream city of man as a search for Disneyland on the basis of a Mickey Mouse theology" (C.O., Dec. 1973, p. 744). There is profound truth in this caustic humor.

The new tongues of the community in chaos

Our blessed Lord instructed us on another occasion that: "Out of the abundance of the heart, the mouth speaks." It was reasonable to expect, then, that once a religious community broke its bonds of love with Christ and fastened its heart on new and false love-idols, the language of affection had to change drastically within it. And so it has. Formerly authentic religious life was centered in communitarian dedication to Christ with a language of knowledge, adoration and love concentrated in unity on Him, shared in Him and put at the service not only of His brethren but of the whole human race for which He died. Today religious life is too often centered on pleasing the world, what Maritain calls, "genuflecting before the world." The members of such worldly communities, far from being united in Christ, are contending with each other, some to gain more worldly glory than others, while others are opposing the accommodation of their religious families to the spirit and ways of the world. Thus the language of competition has displaced the language of love. Divided communities have members seeking personal achievement, public recognition, worldly popularity, political relevancy, social salvation. Religious life has become for many a sort of athletic contest where only the victors are honored, and the also-rans, together with those who will not compete in this worldly farce, are pushed aside and despised. The result is there is no community of joy in the Lord, but rather hearts, atrophied from a lack of this divine love, are full of fear and bitter frustration. Commenting on this dismal situation, Von Hildebrand writes: "What in former times — that is holiness — was believed to be the result of religious formation is now considered to be the result of taking courses in sociology. What presupposes — that is total love of Christ — a heroic dying to ourselves and abandonment to God is now thought to be attainable by taking a degree" (New Tower of Babel, p. 17).

It is hardly surprising, then, that tongues of protest have displaced tongues of praise, and works of the world have displaced works of the Word. For when one changes the divine ideals of deeply unified communities in Christ for the ideals of the world, then the divisions of the world enter and disrupt the religious communities that go lusting after the world. Such religious communities have grafted themselves onto the worldwide Protest Society and they speak more of liberation and less of salvation; they prepare members more for careers in the world and less for holiness in the Church; they stress in their works more the solution of worldly problems and less participation in sacred mysteries; they prefer action to prayer; they exalt a distorted exercise of liberty at the expense of the true liberty of the children of God; they are forever demanding their rights and silent about their duties; they preach the political pabulum of endless progress but reject the folly of the cross; they function in an atmosphere of resentment instead of in a climate of reconciliation; they idolize equality and put it in the place of true charity. In this atmosphere of contestation the words of Aristotle are fulfilled in such worldly communities: "Here inferiors revolt in order that they may be equal, and equals that they may be superior." Finally such communities function in the shallow, trivial sphere of worldly publicity rather than in the profound, sacred silence of God's holy presence. Having lost sight of Christ as the secret gift of each dedicated soul, as the common bond and theme of all apostolic communities, such secularized communities have ceased to live and work in His love. They have lost their way because they have lost their life. They are on the road to anarchy and dissolution for, in attempting the impossible, they are tearing themselves apart. For they cannot be competitive handmaidens of secularistic humanism and simultaneously apostolic communities of love in Christ. They cannot reconcile the irreconcilable, serve God and mammon.

The spirit of the community in chaos

The religious community in chaos has accepted the principle of secularization which adapts its congregation to the spirit and forms of the world and exhorts its members to live by the norms of the world. Such a community has confused the claims of human dignity and those of divine authority, forgetting that "to serve God is to reign." The result is that some frightened superiors surrender to radical subjects who get their demands by threatening an appeal to the public, the press, the radio and TV, all of which are only too eager to champion a bogus democracy while revealing scandalous infighting within a religious community. Now when God-given human dignity is seen as conferring on subjects independence of thought and action, then God-given authority is degraded to a position of dependence on the consent of the majority for its valid exercise. Thus, a bogus democracy, founded on the mechanics of political factionalism, destroys religious unity in Christ. Now, other superiors, who are not so easily frightened by scruples or subjects and who are determined to have their ideas and power prevail, use this democratic process to create a majority of complaint voters. This they do by enforcing the legitimate principle of obedience selectively, using it as an instrument for the "spoils system," that is, favoring and advancing those who accept their ideologies, silencing and demoting those who would contribute a religious alternative to the process of secularization. Thus, under the facade of democracy, the tactic used to silence any reasonable critique of secularization, is totalitarian in its manner. It consists in hurling spiritually demeaning slogans against those with reasonable reservations. Such religious are stigmatized as being "rigid," "reactionary," "tradition-bound," "out-of-date," "stubborn" and "controversial." All this is equated with being disobedient. Indeed, in the general intolerance that is growing under such leadership, even deference to and reverence for the old and sick religious is fast disappearing. The new democracy and the new dynamism tends to sweep houses, where worldly religious predominate, clean of these old soldiers of Jesus Christ. Moreover, working from worldly models, religious communities in chaos have expanded their superstructures of power even while their subjects have drastically diminished. Thus religious subjects are placed under an escalating bureaucracy that leaves them depersonalized and isolated from easy contact with their religious superiors. Often they are treated like hired hands, being callously turned down for apostolates for which they are well prepared and told to go find jobs for themselves outside their congregations, and indeed outside the confines of the religious vocation to which they have dedicated their whole lives. The atmosphere of cold sufficiency suffocates the experience of deep, personal friendships in Christ. For the sublimely affective and effective power of the call of Christ is strangled by the cares of the world. Unable to find joy in the Lord within such communities of chaos, many religious seek it elsewhere, often at the cost of losing their vocations and even the Faith. For man cannot live a Faith or a calling that is totally divorced from his heart and affective life.

Then there is the infidelity of such communities to Christ's message as it is transmitted by the Church through the teachings of the Holy Father and the magisterium. Image-management techniques, calculated to make these communities acceptable to the intellectual world, foster a secularized, absolutist version of freedom and especially of academic freedom, a version which leaves the individual intellect and conscience the sole arbiter of revelational truth and morals. Moreover, a presentation and interpretation of history which represents the Church as the great oppressor of human liberty and cultural advancement is avidly imbibed by such religious communities which, ashamed of their Faith, have joined the world in its attack upon Christ and His Mystical Body. Indeed, progressive religious communities have proven themselves to be just as embittered in their authoritarianism, just as intolerant of opposing opinions and just as radical in their gnostic elitism as even the greatest enemies of the Church have been. Not long ago a provincial of an outstanding religious organization boasted of his secularist policy in his use of the sacred power of religious authority which had been entrusted to him by the Church. Here are his revolutionary words published in a national news organ of that religious organization: ''I happen to believe that social structures can only be improved by the nitty-gritty of elections, party organization, community pressures, pragmatic compromise and power struggles. There is nothing very holy or inspiring about it . . . .'' This desacralization and politicalization of religious authority degrades religious persons and communities to being merely pawns in a worldly power struggle, where each distrusts the other, with the result that diverse, opposing cliques are formed for the attainment of raw political power and for survival against religious tyranny.

Can the community in chaos perform an apostolic ministry?

The secularized community disrupts within itself its divinely established teleology of sanctification in Christ. It thus loses sight of this essential purpose of religious life and dissolves into a discrete mass of individuals with the self-interest of each as the starting point of all inquiry and activity. The organic nature and thrust of religious community in Christ gives way to a beehive of individuals who attempt to build a community out of their own desires. It follows that the attainment of greater individual liberty replaces the attainment of greater personal and communitarian sanctity. And the fuller satisfaction of private wants replaces the fuller dedication of service in the salvation of others. Naturally enough the new mission of the secularized community is reduced to being a *mere presence* in the world while working for a better and happier society. To attain these laicized goals, merely secular ideals and life styles are necessary. But by thus downgrading the uniqueness and sacredness of its original consecration such a community loses its own identity. In an attempt to rediscover its identity and achieve a new development, the secularized community runs for help to experience, sociology and psychology. But these sources being secularistic and non-sanctifying in themselves, it is small wonder that they erode even more drastically the sacred content of religious life. What has happened is that the secularized community has broken its ties with Holy Scripture, with the magisterium, with orthodox theology and with the Holy See as the true and only sources of its renewal as a community in Christ. The secularized religious community seeks an impossible revolutionary autonomy, as if it can live and thrive severed from the Vine that is Christ.

Now when we take account of the apostolic ministries these revolutionary communities are supposed to perform, a desolate scene of incalculable wreckage chills the soul. The results of the desacralizing divorce from Christ and His holy Church are disastrous. Communities are violently polarized; houses bitterly divided; dramatic defections decimate the ranks of religious; schools, missions and other apostolic works are closed down and abandoned on a large scale. And instead of *being a presence* for betterment to a secularist society, such communities have become camp-followers of that decadent world. Moreover, they have rendered religious life so forbidding and embittered that they repel rather than attract the young who dare not entrust their lives to groups swayed by maverick theologians, reckless renewalists, visionary progressives and liturgical peaceniks. The young are looking for the authentic vocation of religious communities which consists in cooperating with the Holy Spirit, under the guidance of the holy Church and the inspiration of approved constitutions, in the sanctification and salvation of their own and their neighbors' souls. Moreover, such secularized communities are by now infamous for their dissipation and waste of the enormous resources of all types donated by the generous faithful for the building up of Christ's kingdom in souls and in society. We must conclude then that secularized communities are incapable of performing apostolic ministries to save the world for Christ for the simple reason that they have joined the world in its fight against its Savior. Even their temporal ministrations for the world in social, political and economic activities are rendered sterile by a world that despises them for abandoning their transcendentally sublime vocation. Only God knows how much destruction of faith such religious communities in chaos have caused and are continuing to cause to followers of Christ inside and outside the Catholic Church.

But as if those evils were not enough, we come upon another strange phenomenon in these communities. With their passion for liberty emancipated, the acquisitive drive for all spiritual privileges, honors and functions becomes insatiable. Yet there is a strange inconsistency here. For if Christ is seen as no more than the greatest social reformer, and the needs of society are seen as being fulfilled by no more than a group of enlightened community leaders, then it should follow that sacraments, grace and the pastoral ministry are superfluous. Yet just at this juncture comes the insistent demand that women be admitted equally to all ministries, even to the fullness of the priesthood. Christ, it is argued, called only men to the pastoral ministry because He was conditioned by the prejudices and mores of His times which looked on women as inferior to men. Today, however, Christ would advance women to the role of the pastoral priesthood in a move to emphasize their equality with men. In answer to this arbitrary argument we quote the rejoinder of Jean Galot:

> "It seems to us that this way of reasoning is not in conformity with the mentality of Jesus. He made no concessions to the prejudices of His contemporaries about the inferiority of women, and He openly and clearly fought against these prejudices, recognizing woman's equality with man on many occasions. Thus He overcame all the conditionings of the environment in which He lived. If Christ reserved the priestly ministry to men, it cannot, therefore, be as a result of these prejudices, but by virtue of a

divine plan which desired for the Church the cooperation of men and women in different functions.

"What has contributed to distorting the problem has been the fact of considering the priestly ministry as a superior condition. Now, though involving a mission of authority, it is not a condition of superiority: it is a service. The fact that it is reserved to men does not in any way violate the principle of the equality of the sexes. In the Church, woman does not have a task that is inferior to that of the priest. She has a different and complementary task. Equality does not imply identity of function. . . .' (*L'Osservatore Romano*, Dec. 8, 1973, English Edition).

What we find most disturbing in these desupernaturalized demands is their arrogant spirit. A group of self-appointed religious agitators presumes to tell God, the Church and the whole world what they ought to do for women, what they ought to confer on women by way of privileges, ministries and honors. This spirit of demanding contradicts the very essence of religion. For it takes its own ego as its god and serves itself with a man-made religion, the religion of liberated humanism. Whereas the very essence of true religion is founded on the reverential adoration of God and humble obedience to His holy will. Could anyone ever imagine our Blessed Lady, model of all religious, ever agitating or demanding of God any privileges, least of all the towering privilege of becoming the Mother of the Messiah? One supreme aspiration ruled her whole life: to fulfill the holy will of God whatever that might be. Only when God called her to the honor of the divine maternity did our Lady even think of this possibility. And then she accepted the invitation only because God wanted to advance her to this role in the salvation of man, only because this advancement was to be accomplished in harmony with her totally chaste dedication of her whole being to God. Too often, the religious community of chaos apes, however unconsciously, the community of devils whose ruling principle of activity is Satan's battle cry: "I will not serve! I will rise above the throne of God." Of course this principle is couched in modern terms: "We will go beyond the Pope, beyond Vatican II. Eventually the Pope and bishops will see the light and catch up with us." But it is the ageless rebellion of the world, the flesh and the devil, the choice of the inflated ego over God and Christ. What secularized religious communities in chaos do not seem to realize is the truth expressed by Ruskin: "He who offers God a second place, offers Him no place." And in their hectic social ministrations to a decadent, secularist world, they do not take the prayer time to taste the truth of Shakespeare's words: " 'Tis mad idolatry to make the service greater than the God."

The community in Christ

But enough of the perversions of religious communities. Those religious communities which, like Lot's wife, have looked back to the allurements of the world ought to become pillars of pungent and salty wisdom to sober and season us in fidelity to communities in Christ. We have studied the tragic decay of religious life only to strengthen our fidelity to communities of persons who are gathered together with their hearts centered on the Lord, living and growing up together in the kingdom of the Son of God and the Son of Man. Here are persons called by Him who listen to Him, are charmed by His gracious personality, grow fond of Him and fall in love with Him. They want their lives to be like His, spent with Him and in His work. They want to be like Him, love like Him, pray like Him, behave like Him. In doing all this these disciples grow closer and closer to Him and to one another. They stand with Him in adoration, reverence and justice before His Father. His temptations and trials become theirs. In His humble heart and spirit they also patiently endure the rejection and hatred of the world. In all events of their lives they listen to and imitate Him, even as He listened to and imitated His Father, patiently waiting on His Father's will, accepting whatever humiliations His Father suffered to come His way. They do all this rejoicing in God's mercy and ever growing in grateful faith and love for God's loving Providence.

The treasure that is Christ

Religious life is a special gift of the Holy Spirit in which man lives out the primacy of his love for God. The real roots, the ultimate original source of religious life, are found in the poor, celibate, totally obedient communitarian life led by Jesus Christ, Son of God and Son of Man, with His band of disciples. "If you would be perfect," said Christ, "go, sell what you possess and give to the poor and you shall have treasure in heaven; and come, follow me" (Lk. 18:22). In a very real sense, a religious community in Christ, one following Him in love, striving to recapture, re-create and diffuse His *vita apostolica,* is already enjoying its treasure in heaven here on earth. For through its life in Christ, with Christ and for Christ, in the service of God's glory and man's salvation, this community in Christ is "more adequately manifesting to all believers the presence of heavenly goods already possessed in this world" (*Lumen gentium,* pp. 50-51). Did not the prophet Isaiah predict that when Christ came into time to save men, He would be Emmanuel, that is, God with us? "Religious life," according to Father Régamey, O.P., "is an affair of the heart . . . an affair of the heart in the Biblical sense of the word *heart,* that is, what is most intimate in man, deeper than our feelings, ideas, wishes, something imbued with the idea of the infinite, the absolute, our eternal destiny" (*L'Osservatore Romano,*

English Edition). And we can add that religious life is an affair of intimate love between the divine Heart of Jesus and the hearts of His close followers. The religious community in Christ constantly affirms before Christ, Gabriel Marcel's sublime insight about the nature of eternal hope: ''We hope in You for us.'' We hope to dwell forever with You. The You, that is, Christ, is the great treasure and guarantee of the union which holds *us* together. Christ holds me as an individual religious together integrally to myself against the temptation to go to pieces under trial, and He holds me to my fellow religious, my community, against the temptation to resentment, to succumb to the attitude of revolution against all light, against all goodness, against God, against my fellow men and my community. Christ holds us all together in His love against the temptation to agree with Sartre that ''hell is other people''; original sin is the arrival of others; others steal away my world, my reputation, my glory, my being, and cause my universe to leak away into nothingness, Christ, our treasure, holds us to God, to His father and our Father, to His Spirit and our Spirit, the Consoler, Advocate and constant Guest of our community of transcendent love living within the life of the Holy Trinity, the divine community of wisdom and love.

For what greater treasure do religious receive from Christ than His intimate love and friendship. ''No longer will I call you servants, because the servant does not know what his master does. But I have called you friends, because all things that I have heard from my Father I have made known to you. You have not chosen me, but I have chosen you'' (Jn. 15:15). And when He was interrupted while preaching to the crowds by a voice crying out: ''Behold, your mother and brethren are standing outside seeking you,'' Christ answered, stretching forth His arm towards the beloved community of His followers: ''Behold my mother and brethren! For whoever does the will of my Father, he is my brother and sister and mother'' (Mt. 12:46-50). For the love of Christ which is infinite and unfailing guarantees His beloved communities eternal life. Above the entire order and disorder of genesis, vicissitudes and death, Christ guarantees His communities victories over death: ''Amen, amen, I say to you, he who hears my word and believes him who sent me, has life everlasting and does not come to judgment, but has passed from death to life'' (Jn. 5:24). And St. Paul reminded the Romans of this tremendous truth: ''For in all things we have overcome because of him who has loved us. For I am sure that neither death nor life, nor angels, nor principalities, nor things present, nor things to come, nor powers, nor height, nor depth, nor any other creature will be able to separate us from the love of God which is in Christ Jesus our Lord'' (Rom. 4:38-39).

The tongues of fire

We know from reading the New Testament frequently that the religious community in Christ spoke a language of love with tongues of fire. In Christ and His Holy Spirit, they spoke a language of praise, of thanksgiving, of reverence and adoration. St. Paul writes: ''For whoever are led by the Spirit of God, they are the sons of God. You have not received a spirit of bondage so as to be again in fear, but you have received the spirit of adoption as sons by virtue of which we cry 'Abba! Father!' '' (Rom. 8:14-16) Notice we never hear the raucous cries of the Protest Society among the first followers of Christ; we never hear the constant howl for liberation — liberation from being poor, from being fishermen, from being oppressed, from their Galilean ghetto. The first followers of Christ were the freest of human beings because, in total love, they had given their lives to the freest of Masters, the God-man Jesus Christ. Generous self-effacement and total self-donation had created among them the communion and community of Christ. Only Judas, the traitor, took himself back from Christ, and he went on to self-destruction by his own hand. Nor were the first followers of Christ bound together by mere social contacts and pleasant conversation. People can apparently be enjoying such contacts while living in tragic isolation, in psychological solitary confinement. For social and cocktail party conviviality is often nothing more than a form of ersatz communion, a social and spiritual lie (Hild., *Art of Loving,* p. 52). In the religious community of Christ we notice that Christ knows only persons, unique persons, each chosen with particular love for creation, redemption and a special apostolic mission. The language of reverence suffused the first religious community. It radiated out from their prayers, from their struggle with Christ against the powers of darkness, from the tenderness of Christ's compassionate love for sinners, the sick, the abandoned sheep.

Now we have to remember that these men and women — the first followers of Christ and His religious family — were astonishingly like us — stubborn, ambitious, volatile, impatient, intolerant, even unpromising. Yet Christ revered and loved them for their *being,* for their being images of His Father, for the lovableness His Father had given each of them. Because of His Father's image in His fellow men, Christ loved and revered them even when they were sinners, even before they accomplished any good deeds or established any impressive credentials. For Christ set out to transform His followers into their true, full, mature selves, the persons His Father wanted to see them become, persons moulded and sanctified in the life and love of His own Son. ''This is my beloved Son,'' the Father announced to the world on two occasions, the baptism and the transfiguration of His Son. ''This is my beloved Son in whom I am well pleased. Hear ye him!'' But the language of reverence, praise and love never forces sinners to become saints. Rather, it gently, patiently but persistently attracts, persuades, purifies and inspires persons to respond humanly, gracefully and generously to its own overwhelming appeal and example of love. Pope Pius XII beautifully stated this truth when he wrote: "God with His love neither destroys nor changes nature, but perfects it" (Hild., *Art of Loving*, p. 67). How far removed is this language of reverence, praise and love from that Babel of confused tongues heard within communities in chaos, how far removed from what Pope Paul VI describes as "those disorderly outbursts which appeal to fraternal charity or to what one believes to be inspirations of the Spirit, but can also lead to the breakup of communities" (ET, p. 24).

The spirit of the community in Christ

Now the religious community in Christ is by no means exempt from trials and tribulations. "If they have hated me," says our Lord, "they will hate you; if they have persecuted me, they will persecute you." The disciple is not above his Master and even the friend of the Bridegroom preceded his Lord to martyrdom. The spirit of the community in Christ is best captured in watching it survive Satan's assaults on its existence. In the hours of darkness in which the powers of hell and the world crucified and buried its Master, the first community in Christ was in the throes of disintegration, on the verge of extinction. "Strike the shepherd and the flock shall be scattered," Holy Scripture had predicted. And so it came to pass. For the deathblow of every religious community is the betrayal of Christ and the removal of Him from its heart. When He was captured and bound that Thursday evening, the disciples, disillusioned, frightened and grieved, panicked and ran. Friday was the day of darkest disorder within that community, the apparent bitter end of all its hopes. The community had seen its beloved Lord hanging on the cross, mocked as a sorry impostor, pierced through the heart, hurriedly buried and sealed in a heavily guarded tomb. All meaning and purpose seemed to have gone out of the life of the sorrowing community; there remained nothing but mourning for their beloved Master. True, they vaguely remembered something He said about rising on the third day, and yet this flicker of hope against hope they dared not express openly. For whenever He was absent, and indeed often enough when He was present, these first followers were often too slow of wit, too dull of heart to comprehend and believe all the sayings the prophets foretold about Him. Thus, Friday and Saturday were days of hiding, of fleeing from a menacing world, of moving secretly behind barred doors. With love frustrated and meaning extinguished from their lives, the community began to suffer the disintegration that afflicted each of their spirits. Moreover, it was the third day and He had not returned. Why stay together any longer in the sterile activity of bemoaning a lost kingdom? Sadly two disciples left the community to return home to Emmaus. Thomas, one of the twelve, wandered off to brood in loneliness. The holy women seemed hysterically unhinged with deep sorrow. Understandably, the men would not believe their tales of seeing youthful angels and finally Him risen. Had Christ not really risen and returned to His religious community, this group would have certainly scattered, each returning to his home and his affairs, leaving perhaps not a single trace of its existence and experiences on the sands of time.

Yet one of the most amazing events in all history is the way in which a beaten, frightened religious community was transformed almost overnight into a community of souls on fire. ''Were not our hearts burning within us while he was speaking on the road and explaining to us the Scriptures?' And rising up that very hour, late in the evening, they returned to Jerusalem where they found the eleven gathered together and those who were with them saying: 'The Lord has risen indeed and has appeared to Simon.' And they themselves began to relate what had happened on the journey and how they recognized him in the breaking of the bread'' (Lk. 24:32-35). Our Lord had to rise quickly from the dead not only because the Scriptures predicted that the physical body of the Holy One of God would never see corruption, but also because the Holy Spirit would never allow His first religious community, His Mystical Body, to disintegrate in death. For the quick return of Christ to His brethren was the guarantee also of the outpouring upon them of His Holy Spirit, the vivifying soul of the Mystical Body. What a difference the living presence of Christ makes to religious communities! While He was dead and gone, the community was paralyzed with fear. When He returned with His Spirit, the community, instead of cringing before the world, went forth with tongues of fire to convert it to their Master. And the disciples went forth exultantly, knowing they would have to proclaim the Gospel to kings and princes, to learned and rustic, to friend and foe. Suffering and martyrdom were their certain fate, yet they rejoiced to be able to suffer something for the Name of Jesus. Humble but bold, weak but strong, they conquered the world for Christ by virtue of the love of Christ and of the power given them with the presence of the Holy Spirit, both of whom would abide with them forever. Moreover, they knew their authority and power. And they performed in the spirit of these incredible words of their first pronouncement: ''It has seemed good to the Holy Spirit and to us.''

The apostolic ministry of the community in Christ

Here they were, a group of unlettered men, become overnight prophets and messengers of God, teaching the word of God to all men in their own languages. Mosaic Jews to their fingertips, yet they are sent to convert the whole world. Everything was against their impossible mission. They had to fail, for they had no background in culture or education to equip them for success, and the world hated the simple. Yet the presence of Christ, the fire of the Holy Spirit in their hearts, sparked a response everywhere. Writing of the dramatic growth of the Church under the preaching of the apostles, St. Augustine testifies to God's marvelous work in His Son's first religious community:

> "What is really hard to believe is the way the world came to believe. The fishermen whom Christ sent out were men unversed in the liberal arts, with no skill in language, armed with no rhetorical power. Yet they landed fish of every sort, not excluding those rare specimens, the philosophers. Three incredibilities are involved. It is incredible that Christ should have risen; it is incredible that the world should have believed a thing so unbelievable; it is incredible that men so unaccomplished, so rude and lowly, should have convinced men of something so incredible and convinced them so conclusively. The skeptics, of course, will shy at the first incredibility; but the second they must believe; and if they reject the third, they have no explanation of a manifest fact" (City of God, Bk. XII).

Conclusion

We can only hope to rediscover the true meaning of religious life and to relive its apostolic commission if we keep our eyes reverently fixed and our hearts lovingly riveted on the Lord Jesus Christ. Unfortunately, the spirit of the world blurs our vision of the surpassing beauty of the beloved Son of God. Alas, too, the spirit of the world shrivels our hearts from communion with Christ to imprisonment within our own inflated egos. The daily apostolate of the community in Christ must be the apostolate of prayer, that is, the daily accomplishment of a real *sursum corda,* a personal and communitarian lifting-up of the mind and heart to God. The Holy Gospel gives us an incident in our Lord's life that can illustrate by way of analogy the sickness and cure of a religious community in chaos. St. Luke tells us that as our Lord was teaching in a synagogue one Sabbath, there before Him was a woman who for eighteen years had a sickness caused by an evil spirit. And she was bent over, utterly unable to look upwards. When Jesus saw her, He called her to Himself and said to her: "Woman, you are delivered from your infirmity." And He laid His hands upon her, and instantly she was made straight and glorified God. The poor woman was bound against her will, God allowing the devil to have his evil way in order to glorify His Son in His works of power and love.

But religious communities in chaos are bent over, stooped and cramped of their own free will. They have riveted their gaze downward, concentrating mind and heart on this world and its prestige. Their acceptance of the evil spirit of the world will not allow them to look heavenward, to discover the divine beauty in the face of Jesus Christ, to fall in love with the secret of His Sacred Heart, to glorify the magnanimous goodness of the Holy Trinity. Only the acceptance of the return of Christ among them can liberate them from their stooped paralysis. Only the teaching and the loving ministrations of the Son of God among them can liberate them from the degrading deformations they willingly suffer at the hands of the evil spirit of this world. Christ alone can straighten up these communities, lift up their vision, expand their heart and open their spirit to a joyful glorification of God in an apostolate of self-sacrifice and service.

In the beginning we stated with Leon Bloy that: "There is but one real sadness: not to be saints." Now the community in chaos cannot produce saints because it has lost Christ, the source of sanctity. Such a community only begets sad souls. A group of sad souls! Here is a hell on earth which is truly other people! Here is a community incapable of advancing the apostolic ministry of Faith in the Church. For such a community will wither and die in isolation and loneliness. Indeed, through the prophet Jeremiah the Holy Spirit predicted just such a dismal end for those who forget God: "Cursed be the man who trusts in man and makes the flesh his strength, and whose heart has departed from the Lord. . . . He shall dwell in the driest parts of the wilderness, in a land of salt, in an uninhabited waste land" (Jer. 17:5-6).

On the other hand, we can truly assert that: "There is but one supreme joy: to be saints." Now the community in Christ is already participating in the communion of saints. For Christ Himself is the source of its saintly joy. Behold, then, in this community a foretaste in time of that eternal heaven which is truly other people — the family of God, His angels and His saints. Moreover, this community in Christ has a most fruitful apostolic ministry in spreading the Faith. It produces saints, virgins, martyrs, doctors; it sends its angels of God to serve in orphanages, hospitals, schools, ghettos, anywhere that there is hope of God's greater glory and the alleviation and salvation of souls. For the community in Christ begets order, peace, civilization and sanctity in the lives of its own members and establishes these blessings in the lives of its neighbors. For the quality of its good works is often high in heroic sanctity. Through the same prophet Jeremiah, the Holy Spirit also predicted such a fruitful career for those who live with God: "Blessed be the man that trusts in the Lord for the Lord shall also be his confidence. . . . He shall be as a tree that is planted by the waters. . . . In time of drought he shall not be solicitous, neither shall he cease at any time to bring forth fruit" (Jer. 17:7-8).

Finally, it would be wonderful if all religious communities and all currents within these communities would heed the call of Pope Paul VI to work and pray for "reconciliation within the Church," within their communities, for that reconciliation in Christ which is the goal of the Holy Year. "We would like," wrote the Holy Father, ". . . to think that the loving teachings of the Church, aimed at reconciliation, will succeed in finding the art of reconstituting relations of association sufficient to strengthen interior and exterior communion so that the Church is seen to be what she is and must be: the social and Mystical Body of Christ. We would like the Holy Year to give us once more a new experience of this communion" (*L'Osservatore Romano*, English Edition, Dec. 6, 1973). But Vatican II explains the only way religious communities can achieve this union in communion. Its decree, "On the Adaptation and Renewal of Religious Life" states:

"Common life, fashioned on the model of the early Church where the body of believers was united in heart and soul (cf. Acts 4:32), and given new force by the teaching of the Gospel, the sacred liturgy and especially the Eucharist, should continue to be lived in prayer and the communion of the same spirit. As members of Christ living together as brothers, religious should give pride of place in esteem to each other (cf. Rom. 12:10) and bear each other's burdens (cf. Gal. 6:2). For the community, a true family gathered together in the name of the Lord by God's love which has flooded the hearts of its members through the Holy Spirit (cf. Rom. 5:5), rejoices because He is present among them (cf. Mt. 18:20). Moreover, love sums up the whole law (cf. Rom. 13:10), binds all together in perfect unity (cf. Col. 3:14) and by it we know that we have crossed over from death to life (cf. 1 Jn. 3:14). Furthermore, the unity of the brethren is a visible pledge that Christ will return (cf. Jn. 13:35, 17:21) and a source of great apostolic energy."

Here again the Holy Spirit, through the same prophet Jeremiah, relates how He will graciously reunite to God His wayward but chastened Chosen People and of course, His repentant religious communities that seek to return to their Father's house: "Behold the days shall come, said the Lord, and I will make a new covenant with the house of Israel and with the house of Juda. . . . But this shall be the covenant that I will make with the house of Israel after those days. . . I will give my law in their bowels and I will write it in their heart: and I will be their God and they shall be my people" (Jer. 31:31, 33). The presence of Christ in religious communities is the new law of love in the depths of their beings, the new covenant of reconciliation unto justification, the God who sanctifies His people.

Transubstantiation:
Anchor of Orthodoxy

Attacks on the dogma of transubstantiation have lately been mounted from several quarters, most notably from the Netherlands. Such attacks are to be clearly distinguished from other recent and valid efforts, regulated by orthodoxy, to redefine eucharistic theology.

That the traditional theology of the Eucharist came to be questioned at all is traceable chiefly to three factors. Firstly, modern phenomenologists began to investigate the symbol-creating activity of the sacraments and emphasized this activity, especially in the Eucharist, from an anthropological point of view. These theologians claimed that, whereas transubstantiation, in opposition to the errors of Luther, Calvin, Zwingli and Berengarius, stressed the physical presence of Christ in the Eucharist, modern theology would have to emphasize His sacramental presence. The physical presence was real, they said; but its full symbolism pointing to the unity of all Christians with Christ and among themselves, could be found only under the category of "sacrament-signs." These signs would stress the real *spiritual* presence of Christ as a corrective reaction to the crude "physicism" that spoke of a touching, breaking and grinding of the body of Christ in Holy Communion.

Secondly, the Aristotelian concepts of substance and accidents were challenged by the neo-scholastics. The distinction had been discredited by scientists for whom the appearances of a thing were equated with its reality. Modern philosophy had suggested, moreover, that a substance underlying accidents was unnecessary because it was never experienced. So the question arose: Did Trent in adopting the word "transubstantiation" accept as true Aristotle's theory of substances and, if so, did the acceptance make that theory an integral part of the Catholic faith? Karl Rahner and Schilebeeckx both claimed that transubstantiation affirmed nothing more nor less than the truth of Christ's words, "This is My Body." In a recent article Schilebeeckx asserts that the Tridentine fathers "while thinking in Aristotelian categories...intended to define dogmatically the reality proper to the eucharistic presence, *i.e.* our Catholic eucharistic faith, and not the categories which they used in discussing and formulating this properly eucharistic presence."

Thirdly, the new theologians argued that the scholastic formulation of transubstantiation tended to restrict the presence of Christ in the eucharistic liturgy merely to the one Real Presence under the appearance of bread and wine. Thus it failed to give Christians a full appreciation of the other spiritual presences of the Savior among them — as *host* in the person of the celebrant; as *teacher* in His word, speaking in the Scriptures, as well as in the reader, and the homilist; as *guest* praying and singing in His members at worship; and as *food* in the sacrament, feeding his flock and knitting it together into a community of love. The Protestant Reformers indeed denied the sacramental reality of Christ's real and proximate presence under the appearances of bread and wine at Mass; but then had nevertheless clung — and we should now follow them — to the ultimate reality of Christ's presence, seeking, in the primitive meal-character of the Eucharist, communion with Christ under the four social modes of His presence.

It is understandable that in trying "to speak a common language with Protestants and humanists," the new theologians should employ a terminology that stresses the multiple presence of Christ in the eucharistic liturgy, especially under the warm and loving symbolism of the family repast that brings the Savior into the midst of His brothers. Hence, in explaining the ontological change which is the reality of the eucharistic mystery, the terms "transfinalization" and "transignification" were substituted for "transubstantiation," with the hope that the historical and doctrinal differences between Catholics and their separated brethren over the latter term might be dissipated.

As matters worked out, however, the new terminology aroused confusion among Catholics and moved the Holy Father to write the encyclical, *Mysterium Fidei,* to remove confusion and strengthen faith.

> Indeed, we are aware of the fact that among those who deal with this Most Holy Mystery in written or spoken word, there are some who, with reference either to Masses which are celebrated in private, or to the dogma of transubstantiation, or to devotion to the Eucharist, spread abroad such opinions as disturb the faithful and fill their minds with no little confusion about matters of faith, as if every one were permitted to consign to oblivion doctrine already defined by the Church, or to interpret it in such a way as to weaken the genuine meaning of the words or the approved import of the concepts involved. (par. 10)

And the Pope went on to warn that "it is not allowable. . . to discuss the mystery of transubstantiation without mentioning the marvelous changing of the whole substance of the bread into the Body and of the whole substance of the wine into the Blood of Christ as stated by the Council of Trent, so that it consists in 'transignification' or 'transfinalization,' as they put it."

The Holy Father then carefully explained the orthodox meaning of the new eucharistic terminology. He showed that it could deepen and complete the explicit doctrine of transubstantiation by highlighting the intimate, interpersonal relationship that Christ effects between Himself and the communicant when He gives Himself under the signs of bread and wine and is accepted, as Himself, after the transmutation of the two material substances into His own substance.

In their very ontological change, Paul pointed out, the gifts of bread and wine, having become the Real Presence of the God-Man offered to man, undergo a *transfinalization* and an ontological *transignification;* their appearances now reveal Christ to be received as food and drink. In the reception of the sacramental food and drink a reciprocal presence is effected between Christ and the communicant. This is indeed a plentitude of presence for it completes the merely offered presence of Christ — who is really, physically there in the consecrated host and wine — by inviting Christians to take Him as food and drink. The eucharistic presence that is personally offered and personally accepted is the consummation of perfect presence.

Thus, the term "transfinalization" indicates that the purpose (*finis*) of bread and wine, originally meant to nourish man physically, is changed. For the appearances that now remain put the communicant into personal union with Christ through His real sacramental presence and effect the recipient's spiritual nourishment. The term "transignification" likewise must be understood as indicating not an extrinsic or peripheral change in man's gifts on the altar, but an intrinsic, profound, ontological mutation. The Pope wrote:

> After transubstantiation has taken place, the species of bread and wine undoubtedly take on a new meaning and a new finality, for they no longer remain ordinary bread and ordinary drink, but become the sign of something sacred, and the sign of a spiritual food. However, the reason they take on a new significance and this new finality is simply because they contain a new "reality" which we may justly term ontological. (par. 46).

Seven months after Pope Paul warned against those who "by careless use of words occasion the rise of false opinions regarding faith in the most sublime mysteries," Father Luchesius Smits, O.F.M. Cap., gave an alarming, six-and-one-half-hour interview to Mr. Patrick Riley, the National Catholic Welfare Conference's overseas news service reporter. Riley's seven page dispatch was given wide coverage in the U.S. Catholic press which, as a rule, followed the advice prefixed to the dispatch that "if published, it be used in its entirety to avoid the danger of misrepresenting Father Smits' theological views."

Fr. Smits, claiming to be a proponent of an existentialist theology of the Eucharist, proponded the following doctrine on the Real Presence:

Existentialist terms, he said, are "the new international language for speaking of the world and of man;" they are terms "that Protestants and humanists can understand." Man is a social being "because *his essence is being* together with other persons in a world."

St. Thomas and the Schoolmen, according to Smits, emphasized the person primarily as a being *in se,* only secondarily as a being in relation to others. This emphasis isolated, tended to destroy a person. A person standing alone is unintelligible, an impossibility, since "for us, the person *is* relation." Fr. Smits maintains that the dualistic body-soul, substance-accidents, system of thinking — ingrained in Christians through scholastic influence — begets a too objective, too physical, too depersonalized approach to receiving Christ as food and drink. This mental orientation encourages a physical as opposed to a spiritual interpretation of a very personal experience: "it makes the personal encounter almost impossible. Why? Because all I can meet is the accidents of bread. . . . True, they refer to Christ's body, but they also prevent me from meeting Christ immediately. The accidents are a barrier to the real encounter with Christ."

**The teaching of Father Smits . . . or
Trent and Mysterium Fidei**

Moreover, just as Scotus, as against St. Thomas, keeps Christ's whole human nature — essence and existence — in the hypostatic union, just so Smits argues: "I keep all of the Eucharistic bread in transubstantiation." For grace does not destroy, but perfects nature. And just as bread and wine in everyday family meals are an extension of the body itself as signs and gifts of love, so bread and wine in the Holy Eucharist remain as an extension of Christ, as signs and gifts of love from Him. "For me," Smits concludes, "bread and wine remain, yet in a way profoundly changed. In transubstantiation, nothing of the bread's nature needs to be destroyed in order to effect, *per modum assumptionis,* a change as deep as the change into Christ's human nature as extended." He adds that a full appreciation of the argument requires an understanding of the existentialist notion of the body as a full symbol, rather than as the empty, crass prison of the soul: one must understand "that an extension of the body is the body. The sacramental extension of Christ's glorified body in bread and wine makes of bread and wine a full symbol. . ."

How does Fr. Smits' eucharistic doctrine harmonize with the solemn proclamation of the Council of Trent? In condemning the heresies of the sixteenth century Reformers, the Council of Trent gave the Christian world a clear and unequivocal statement on the eucharistic dogma. "In the first place the holy Synod teaches . . . that in the precious Sacrament of the Holy Eucharist, after the consecration of the bread and wine, Our Lord Jesus

Christ, true God and true man, is truly, really and substantially contained under the species of those sensible things." *Truly, really, substantially* — each embraces a specific refutation of erroneous views concerning Christ's presence in the Eucharist. The *true* presence of Christ refutes Berengarius' notion that Christ is present only in symbol or power. The *real* presence of Christ refutes Zwingli's doctrine that Christ is present in figure only and as a representative image of the last supper and passion. The *substantial* presence of Christ refutes Calvin's teaching that Christ is only virtually present in the Eucharist, *i.e.,* only to the extent that He exercises his sanctifying powers. But Trent made clear that the Eucharist, unlike other sacraments, has the excellent and peculiar dignity that even before it is used, it contains the Author of Sanctity, while the other sacraments have the power of sanctifying only when one uses them.

But what, according to Trent, becomes of the bread over which the words of the consecration have been pronounced? Does the body of Christ mysteriously unite itself with the bread and wine? Does Christ permeate these substances with His own? Is Christ present in the bread, or with the bread? The Council answered these questions in the negative. Luther had taught the doctrine of consubstantiation or impanation, arguing that the bread remains together with the Body of Christ in the Eucharist. The Council, rejecting this teaching as heresy, declared that the substances of bread and wine no longer remain after the words of consecration: these elements are converted, changed, transmuted into the Body and Blood of Christ. Of the bread and wine there remain only the appearances. In fact Trent avoided the substance-accident dichotomy, and spoke of substance and appearances. "And because Christ our Redeemer declared that which he offered under the appearance of bread to be truly His own Body, therefore, it has ever been a firm belief in the Church of God, and this Holy Synod now declares it anew, that by the consecration of the bread and wine a conversion is made of the whole substance of the bread into the substance of the body of Christ Our Lord, and of the whole substance of the wine into the substance of His Blood; which conversion is suitably and properly called by the Holy Catholic Church transubstantiation."

It occurred to me, after several readings of the strange theological mélange in the Riley report, that no interviewer — however skilled and good-willed — could do justice in a news story to a theologian's six-and-a-half-hour disquisition on a mystery of the faith as profound as the Holy Eucharist. I therefore visited the N.C.W.C.'s offices on June 17 to find out how Father Smits had reacted to this rendition of his eucharistic views. I discovered that Father Smits had written a letter to Mr. Riley congratulating him on the accuracy of his report.

Let it be noted at once that throughout the lengthy story no reference is made, either directly or indirectly, to Pope Paul's encyclical, *Mysterium Fidei*. It is ignored — as though it had never been written. Is it possible that in his zeal to be a teacher to the universal Church Father Smits failed to take into account the official teaching of the first theologian among us, the Holy Father himself?

Father Smits' forays against Scholasticism imply that somehow Trent exceeded its powers in defining transubstantiation — that the Council made an ill-advised excursion into philosophy and permanently paralyzed the organic development of eucharistic dogma by entombing it in the strait-jacket formulae of the Schoolmen.

But of course it is not true that the Catholic Church's theology is so wedded to the Scholastic system of philosophy as to be *conditioned* by that system's terminology in its dogmatic pronouncements. The Church did not become Philonian when St. John the Evangelist borrowed and purified Philo's term, Logos, and applied it to Christ in order to make clear that, as God, Christ existed from all eternity in the bosom of the Father. In thinking philosophically about the mysteries of the faith theologians are forced to turn to one set or another of philosophical categories. In explaining, defending and spreading the Gospel, the Church has mined and refined its dogmatic terminology from remarkably divergent schools of philosophy — from Platonism, Aristotelianism, Stoicism, Augustinianism, Scotism, Thomism, Suarezianism — without ever becoming the slave of any one system. The truth of the Catholic Church is never a philosophical system; it is a faith in a body of revealed truth.

Transubstantiation is a philosophical term which is indeed associated with the system of the Schoolmen and their distinction between substances and appearances (accidents); yet it merely enunciates what St. Cyril and the early Fathers had always taught: "This seeming bread is not bread but the body of Christ." The inner reality of a thing, as contrasted with what the senses perceive, was called by the scholastics "substance"; therefore, the change of the substance of the bread into the body of Christ was aptly called *trans*-substantiation. Substances were said to exist in themselves, accidents to inhere in substances. Though forming a composite unity, they are, in reality as well as in thought, distinct. For substances are impervious to the senses; man gets at substances through their appearances.

Thus the eucharistic change is a change which escapes sense-perception because what is changed in the bread and wine is not their sensible appearances but their imperceptible substances. The Council of Trent called this conversion not only "miraculous" but also "unique," for no other change, natural or miraculous, is quite like this one. More than any other miracle, the Eucharist calls for unhesitating belief by the human soul in the omnipotence of God who changes whole substances from their ontological foundations.

Catholic mysteries are not, nor can they be, poured into philosophical categories that exhaust the meaning of the mysteries. In all philosophical discussions of the mysteries of faith, reason is being used to remove an apparent conflict with reason. Reason cannot comprehend these mysteries nor can reason's terminological tools perfectly express them.

St. Thomas' use of Aristotelian formulations does not pretend to *exhaust* the mystery of the Eucharist, but simply to affirm the real, actual presence of the Incarnate Word under the appearances of bread and wine. His use of Aristotelian terms, for that precise purpose, seems to me as valid in our day as it was in his. Thomas cannot be faulted for not going further — for not using a philosophical formulation unknown in his day that would draw attention to the interpersonal aspects of Christ's real presence. Moreover, while the Aristotelian categories do not explicitly indicate the social benefits of the Real Presence, it is unwise and unfair for Father Smits to imply that these categories somehow *deny* the communal aspects of Christ's real presence.

Existentialist revolt or Eucharistic sacrifice

In his preference for existentialist terminology, Father Smits rejects a system of thinking for a mood of thinking. E. L. Mascall in ''The Secularization of Christianity'' warns of this age-old habit of theologians:

> It has been a frequent trait in Christian theologians down the ages to commit themselves whole-heartedly to the fashionable philosophies of their day, while passing severe judgment on their predecessors for adopting precisely the same attitude. How close the Alexandrian apologists sailed to the wind of gnosticism is a commonplace among Church historians, and the Platonising or neo-Platonising of the Fathers has been a constant source of sorrow to biblical theologians, equalled only by their laments over the Aristotelianising of the medievals. Even such a great theologian as Charles Gore, while condemning the Roman doctrine of transubstantiation as a verbal encumbrance due to an inopportune intrusion into church doctrine of a temporary phase of metaphysics, substituted for it a doctrine explicitly based on a 'modern philosophy,' assumed to be incorrigible and immortal, which was in fact a contemporary version of Kantian idealism.

Now the existentialist mood is one of revolt; it stresses subjective, as opposed to objective, thinking. It forgets that philosophy is the clarification of two unknowns — the subject and the object. Impatient with abstractions, existentialists tend to become so subjective as to fall into subjectivism — the habit of imposing on reality what one wants to find there. I believe that, with the best of intentions, Father Smits *wants* the bread and wine to be totally changed; he *prefers* to emphasize the happy meal at which Christ entertains His family, thus stressing the human situation in which all Christians must live and work together in peace and love and joy with Christ. Proceeding from this true but only partial analogy between the Eucharist and an ordinary family meal, Father Smits insists that the bread remains after the consecration as a gift, an expression of love, an extension of the body of Christ. Because he wants to intensify the I-We relation between Christ and communicants and communicants among themselves in Christ, Father Smits insists that the gifts of bread and wine must remain as bonds of love in the family meal.

Obsessed with existentialist imperatives, Father Smits seems to have overlooked the Eucharist as sacrifice. He seems to have misunderstood the totally different needs of God and man in their intersubjective exchange of gifts. In the context of sacrifice, bread and wine are necessary extensions of men who want to give themselves to God, since creatures are incapable of giving themselves substantially. Their gifts, therefore, represent the lives of Christ and His members. In accepting these gifts at the prayer of consecration, God infinitely enhances them by transforming them into the Body and Blood of His Son. He then returns them as his gift of food for the eucharistic banquet. Now, in the context of meal, the appearances of bread and wine serve even more eminently as symbols of God's love for man. For in this return gift the Giver substitutes Himself and His Incarnate Son for the gifts of bread and wine. In the context of meal, therefore, the return gift not only does *not* remain bread as an extension of the body of Christ, but it *is* Christ Himself in an interpersonal communion that far exceeds in intimate love the initial offering of bread and wine.

It seems to me that Father Smits unwittingly achieves what he wants to avoid: he preserves a barrier between Christ and the communicant by keeping the bread in the Eucharist. His own expression of man's communion with Christ in the Eucharist has no advantage over St. Thomas' use of Aristotelian terms. In fact his explication obscures the most intimate dimension of this communion and offers grave doctrinal disadvantages.

God offers or extends Himself to man in an indirect and in a direct donation of Himself. Creation is an indirect Self-donation of God to man — the universe is an indirect extension of God to man. In the Holy Eucharist, however, we have a unique Self-donation of God to man. We have a direct giving of the God-man to man, even though this gift must be made under the appearances of bread and wine. For the unveiled possession of God in this life of pilgrimage is impossible for man. Thus, far from being a barrier to union with Christ, as Father Smits claims, the appearances or accidents of bread and wine are essential to the union because any confrontation between God and man in this life must be effected through a limited means. In Father Smits' explanation of the union between God and man, the divine extension is effected through the real, actual presence of bread which remains after the consecration. One is bound to ask Father Smits: What *is* the consecrated host? Bread or Christ? Or both? If it is both, has not Luther's impanation been resurrected in existentialist disguise? Would we not fall into idolatry if we paid the worship of latria to a host that remains bread?

It is evident that Father Smits' teaching arouses many doubts in the laity and clergy. Moreover, it is not only novel doctrine, but also fails to conform with either the defined doctrine of the Council of Trent or with the teachings of *Mysterium Fidei* on the dogma of transubstantiation.

Reprinted from *Triumph, September, 1966.*

A Forgotten Encyclical

Why not admit it openly? When it was published August 12, 1950, the encyclical *Humani Generis*,[1] "treating certain false opinions that threaten to ruin the foundations of the Catholic faith," caused consternation in the intellectual world, was not at all understood and, indeed, was resentfully rejected. Since then it has been relegated to the limbo of never-discussed, seldom-quoted and hardly-ever republished documents. Twenty-five years have flowed into past history since then. Does the severe lesson taught by that pontifical document have a chance of being better understood today? Have spiritual attitudes changed for the better so as to be open to its prophetic, warning message? We hope by explaining its background, its contents and applying its message to the confusion of today to make it more acceptable to Christians seeking a way out of the crisis of faith.

Just after the Second World War, an important segment of the Catholic intelligentsia in Europe, especially in France, experienced the need for a general renovation of thought. Often this need was expressed in a radical, extreme manner, with little or no attention being paid to established truths. These intellectual revolutions were not found merely in the initiatives of individuals, but above all in a movement of thought stemming from the new sensational study known as sociology. This movement was easier to describe than to define, so subjectivistic and undisciplined was it.

Looking back on it from the perspective of 25 years, one is struck forcefully by the irresponsible, impersonal aspect of the movement. In fact the encyclical scores the capricious tendencies of this movement. There are many dubious theological, philosophical, scientific, moral, biblical and ecclesiastical opinions in the movement. Not less remarkable in this movement was its passionate desire to have an opening to doctrines, values and traditions outside the Catholic and especially Latin milieu.[2] Now the encyclical, noting these trends, clearly states in its first part that the elaboration of religious and moral values free from error can never be accomplished without the aid of revelation. In its second part, the encyclical treats of the repercussions in certain Catholic quarters of erroneous ideas which have also caught the fancy of the contemporary world. After these two critical sections, a review of Catholic doctrine makes up the third part. And in the final part directives are given to ecclesiastical superiors and masters in the religious sciences on how to stem the tide running toward heresy and immorality. Well aware of the inclination of certain new teachers to minimize the teachings and acts of the Magisterium and of encyclicals, the Pope takes preventive precautions. Without calling on his supreme, *ex cathedra* infallible powers, but using only the infallible power of his ordinary Magisterium, Pius XII calls for interior and exterior assent to the teachings of the encyclical, quoting Our Lord's words: "He who hears you, hears me."

The Church esteems reason

In an age suffering a black-out of philosophy, we cannot fail to be struck by the importance given to philosophy in this encyclical. Pope Pius XII writes: "it would indeed be unnecessary to deplore these aberrations from truth, if all, even in the field of philosophy, listened with proper reverence to the Teaching Authority of the Church, which by divine institution has the mission not only to guard and interpret the deposit of divinely revealed truth, but also to keep watch over the philosophical sciences themselves, in order that Catholic dogmas may suffer no harm because of erroneous opinions." There is question here — and no one should deceive himself on the matter — of directing minds beyond the deadly either-or dilemma of choosing rationalism or irrationalism. The Pope finds some consolation in the fact that many non-Catholic historians and scholars, former adherents of rationalism, are returning to scriptural sources and the word of God, accepting them as the foundation of the sacred sciences. Yet the Pope deplores the fact that the more firmly certain of these prodigal scholars now accept the word of God, the more they diminish the value of human reason (K. Barth), and the more they exalt the authority of God the Revealer, the more severely do they spurn the Teaching Office of the Church, instituted by Our Divine Lord to preserve and interpret divine revelation.

Indeed such is the esteem for human reason in the Church that the encyclical assigns reason a quadruple sublime project: 1) Reason is to demonstrate with certainty the existence of a personal God. 2) It is to prove in a convincing manner from a study of the divine works of marvel, such as prophecies and miracles in human history, the rational and supra-rational foundations of the Christian faith. 3) Reason is to express with exactitude the moral law inscribed by the Creator in the hearts of men. 4) Reason is to explore the mysteries of the faith by prayer and study in order to render them more inspiring and fruitful in the lives of men. The Pope is telling the world that there is a crying need to get back to the study of true philosophy, if there is to be a return to the study of true Catholic theology. For the man of today, unfortunately, trusts more the scientific savant than the metaphysician or the Magisterium. The Pope writes: "It is well known how highly the Church esteems human reason . . . But reason can perform the four-fold functions mentioned above safely and well, only when properly trained, that is, when imbued with the sound philosophy which has long been . . . a patrimony handed down by earlier Christian ages, and which moreover possesses an authority of an even higher order, since the Teaching Authority of the Church, in the light of Divine Revelation itself, has weighed its fundamental tenets, which have been elaborated and defined little by little by men of great genius. For this philosophy, acknowledged and accepted by the Church, safeguards the genuine validity of human knowledge, the unshakable metaphysical principles of sufficient reason, causality, finality and finally the mind's ability to attain certain and unchangeable truth.''

Fads and fancies pass

The flight away from the true philosophy and revelation in order to find the meaning of life, pain and death in the strict and social sciences has led to a profound restlessness and anxiety among men. And this is quite understandable for the learned, ingenious mental constructions that have taken the place of true philosophy and theology distract man only for a moment; they are passing fashionable diversions, like dreams in a restless sleep. However skillful and apparently well systematized, they are founded on intellectual myths, not on the rock of reality. For a philosophy not based on a personal God as the beginning and end of all things removes all solid ground from under man's feet.

Is it any wonder that escalating dissensions and errors in religion and morality have created an age of atheism saturated with prejudice, passion, bad faith, fear and violence? The principal paths which the unwise learned, inside and outside the Church, have followed to this ''slough of despond'' are clear for all to see. ''Some, without prudence and discernment, admit and set up as the origin of everything the evolutionist system, despite the fact that this is not absolutely proved even in the field of natural sciences. They boldly adopt the monistic and pantheistic hypothesis of the universe being subject to continual evolution. The champions of Communism readily use this hypothesis to defend and propagate their dialectical materialism and banish from all minds every notion of God.''

Is nothing absolute?

The false statements of this evolutionism, by which everything that is absolute, certain and unchangeable is repudiated, have prepared the way for the errors of the new philosophy which, competing with idealism, immanentism and pragmatism, has taken the name *existentialism,* because, repudiating the immutable essence of things, it deals only with the ''existence'' of single individuals. What the Holy Father is challenging here is the proposition that there is a universal law in the whole of reality, a law that applies equally and unequivocally to the origin of all *cosmic entities:* the universe, the nebulae, the stars, the elements, life, *diversity of organisms, man's body,* his mind, *culture,* society, morals, religion, language and art. Fr. Raymond J. Nogar, O.P., in his book *The Wisdom of Evolution* writes: ''Strictly speaking, there is no universal law of evolution. . . . The supposition of a universal, causal, cosmic law of evolution is not a valid inference from

any of the known series of natural facts or laws established by science."
What Pope Pius XII is denying is that there is a shred of evidence from
the natural sciences to prove that evolution is a cosmic law that explains
the origin of all things, a law which repudiates all that is absolute, firm
and immutable while giving values only to events and their history. The
Pope rejects evolutionism, historicism and existentialism as fundamentally
identical expressions of different levels of being, e.g.: cosmic evolution as
evolutionism, mankind's evolution as historicism, personal evolution as
existentialism. These ideological expressions of evolutionism emerge from
two fundamental errors in scientific thought. First, the unrestricted,
uncritical use of the scientific device of extrapolation, i.e., concluding to
future or even present events beyond the known range of the evidence at
hand, but on the basis of certain variables within this known range. What
often appears in textbooks is a fanciful, unlimited use of extrapolation which
does much to gloss over the highly tentative nature of what look like evolutionary trends. The second error, more deep-seated theoretically and
practically, is what Maritain calls "*The gnosticism of history.*" It divides into
four capital, scientific sins: 1) over-simplification, a wanton, arbitrary
approach in the choice of materials to establish a cause historically and
scientifically; 2) a self-deceptive eagerness to establish an *a priori* explanation
of the pre-history and history of the cosmos; 3) a self-deceptive ambition
to get an all-inclusive explanation of the meaning of cosmic and human
history; 4) the ambition to be so scientific in one's method and explanation
as to give one's hypothesis that peculiar sense of aura of the scientific which
conveys to others the conviction that one's explanation of evolution enjoys
a kind of intellectual mastery over the subject-matter.[3]

    Fr. Nogar finds just such faults and rhetorical excesses advocating
evolutionism in the works of both Julian Huxley and Teilhard de Chardin.
Huxley, in his book *Religion Without Revelation,* presents his scientific
evolution not only as a new philosophy, but has it function also as a new
prophetic vision, a new religion to replace the old religions of supernaturalism and materialism (Marxist Communism). Huxley writes: "I
submit that the discoveries of physiology, general biology and psychology
not only make possible, but necessitate, a naturalistic hypothesis (for
religion) in which there is no room for the supernatural, and the spiritual
forces at work in the cosmos are seen as part of nature as much as the
material forces. What is more, these spiritual forces are one particular
product of mental activity in the broad sense, and mental activity in general
is seen to have increased the intensity and importance during the course
of cosmic time. Our basic hypothesis is thus not merely naturalistic as
opposed to supernaturalistic, but monistic as opposed to dualistic, and evolutionary as opposed to static."[4] Teilhard's rhetorical philosophy of

evolutionism has the same starting point as Huxley's, namely, faith in a vision that exceeds the scientific evidence at hand, a faith that is extremely subjective, apologetic, ideological, personalized and, though presented in the name of science, is really a religion filled with the obvious gloss of analogy, metaphor, neologisms and equivocation, with Time, eons and eons of it, being the Magical Agent which synthesizes all levels of being in onward and upward evolution towards a millennium in progress. Listen to Teilhard in his *The Phenomenon of Man:* ''Is evolution a theory, a system or an hypothesis? It is much more; it is a general condition to which they must satisfy henceforth if they are to be thinkable and true. Evolution is a light illuminating all facts, a curve that all lines must follow.''[5] Here is mandatory science at its highest level of dogmatic faith! Working from the intuitive idealism of Bergson and French phenomenology of science, Teilhard intended to arrive at the Divine Alpha and Omega, at the Cosmic Christ in the religion of the Meta-Christianity. The point is that his evolutionism stems from assumptions, hypotheses, ''intuitions'' which lie outside the domain of scientific evidence; they do not arise as inferences from scientific facts. In his method Teilhard's approach is not unlike that of Marx and Huxley, though he wants to arrive at the Cosmic Christ, not at the classless society of Marx nor at the atheistic humanism of Huxley. Yet all three of these utopias are non-realities; they are science — and theology — fictions. Thus when it comes to the matter of evolution *Humani Generis* teaches two things: 1) There is no question of the origin of man's soul; its origin is not a matter for discussion for it is directly created by God. 2) As for the origin of man's body, all Catholics, whatever their personal opinion on the matter, are forbidden to teach as an established fact that man's body was evolved from pre-existing living matter.

We reject polygenism

As regards the theory of *polygenism,* namely that there existed here on earth real men who were not descended by natural generation from Adam as the forefather of all men; or else that Adam represented groups of many forefathers, the Church and the faithful cannot embrace these errors. ''For these theories cannot be reconciled with what the founts of revelation and the teachings of the Authority of the Church proclaim about original sin, which comes from a sin committed individually and personally by Adam, and which, transmitted to every man through generation, is an inherent property in each man'' who has lived (Mary alone excepted), is alive today or will be born.

When we come to the historical sciences, the Pope finds that, just as in the biological and anthropological sciences, there are Catholic scholars who audaciously overstep the limits and precautions set up by the Church.

Particularly deplorable is a certain system of interpreting the historical books of the Old Testament too freely. Misinterpreting a letter of the Pontifical Commission for Biblical Studies, some rash exegetes deny that the first eleven chapters of Genesis are real history. The Pope corrects these errors as follows: ''This Letter, in fact, clearly points out that the first 11 chapters of Genesis, although properly speaking not conforming to the historical method used by the best Greek and Latin writers or by competent authors of our time, do nevertheless pertain to history in a true sense, which however must be further studied and determined by exegetes. The same chapters in simple and metaphorical language adapted to the mentality of a people but little cultured, both state the principal truths which are fundamental for our salvation, and also give a popular description of the origin of the human race and the chosen people. If, however, the ancient sacred writers have taken anything from popular narrations (and this may be conceded), it must never be forgotten that they did so with the help of divine inspiration, through which they were rendered immune from any error in selecting and evaluating these documents.''

Therefore, as Vatican I defined, God is the Author of Holy Scripture, and that opinion has often and must again be condemned which asserts that immunity from error extends only to those parts of the Bible that treat of God or of moral and religious themes. Certain exegetes even wrongly speak of a human sense of the Scriptures, beneath which is hidden a divine sense and this divine sense alone is the infallible meaning. In interpreting Scripture, false exegetes often reject the analogy of faith and the Tradition of the Teaching Church, attempting to decipher the Bible with the key of pure human reason, instead of explaining Holy Scripture according to the mind of the Church which Christ Our Lord has appointed guardian and interpreter of the whole deposit of divinely revealed truth.

'Who hears you, hears me'

Unfortunately, Christian scholars who are lovers and advocates of novelty pass easily from contempt of scholastic philosophy and theology to contempt for the Teaching Authority of the Church itself. They paint the Magisterium as a hindrance to progress, as an obstacle in the way of science, as an unjust restraint on the reform of the discipline of theology. Often they ignore this Authority as if it did not exist; they intentionally, habitually overlook what is expounded in encyclicals by the Pontiffs about the character and constitution of the Church, saying that, since encyclicals do not define doctrine, they are not binding on minds and wills. Then too they play off the teachings of the Ancient Fathers, especially the Greeks, against the teachings of the Popes. But Pope Pius XII in answer to this tactic of evasion reasserts the binding force on consciences of papal encyclicals: ''Nor must it be thought that what is expounded in encyclical letters does not of itself demand consent, since in writing such letters the Popes do not exercise the supreme power of their Teaching Authority. For these matters are taught with the ordinary Teaching Authority, of which it is true to say: 'He who hears you, hears me'; and generally what is expounded and inculcated in encyclical letters already for other reasons appertains to Catholic doctrine. But if the Supreme Pontiffs in their official documents purposely pass judgment on a matter up to that time under dispute, it is obvious that that matter, according to the mind and will of the same Pontiffs, cannot be any longer considered a question open to discussion among theologians.''

In calling upon the faithful to give interior and exterior assent to encyclicals when they treat of matters of faith and morals, the Holy Father asked Catholics to remember this most important truth. There is no real, substantive difference between truths touching matters of faith and morals that have been solemnly proclaimed by *ex cathedra* definitions and truths that have been constantly, universally taught by the Roman Pontiffs and the Magisterium without *ex cathedra* or *conciliar* definitions. It would be a mistake to conclude that because a truth of faith or morals has not yet been formally defined, it may not be true at all; or it may be fallible and therefore one can ignore in conscience the call of the Magisterium to accept it. Really, the infallibly defined doctrines of the Catholic faith are merely the small, sharp face of a massive glacier of Christian truths extending backward through the valleys and mountains of salvation history throughout the ages.

The Magisterium's authority in teaching the whole deposit of the faith faithfully is exercised with diverse degrees of solemnity and diverse styles. The Magisterium may choose to define *ex cathedra* in the person of the Pope alone, or in the person of the Pope together with a general council. Or the Magisterium may choose to use its ordinary teaching style, in a pastoral manner, in the person of the Pope writing encyclical letters, or in the person of the Pope and a general Council publishing pastoral documents on faith and morals as was done in the Second Vatican Council. What is most important to remember is that the infallibility of the truth proclaimed does not derive from the *ex cathedra* definition. It arises from a deeper, permanent source — the Petrine commission bestowed upon the Teaching Church by Christ and guaranteed by the guidance of the Holy Spirit. Remember, the very conception of the requirements for an infallible pronouncement is modern, dating only from Vatican I in 1870.

What does 'defining' add?

The Fathers, Doctors and theologians of the past and present, scanning Church teachings for centuries, have traditionally acknowledged an infallibility functioning in the ordinary Magisterium of the Church, guaranteed by the abiding assistance of the Holy Spirit who sustains the Church as "the pillar and ground of truth." As Fr. Joseph Costanzo, S.J., during the uproar over *Humanae Vitae* wrote: "The technical formality of an *ex cathedra* definition would not add to the intrinsic validity, that is, its certitude, and the obligatory force of *Humanae Vitae*. The Magisterium of the Church is no less 'put on the line' by its constant and universal ordinary teaching than by the solemnity of a formal decision. Surely, no one would suggest that the papal teaching authority was in abeyance in matters of faith and morals for four centuries prior to the solemn definitions of the Council of Nicaea (325)."[6] Hence there is more fanfare than substance in claiming an intrinsic distinction between the infallibility of an *ex cathedra* definition and the infallibility of the authentic, authoritative ordinary teaching of the Roman Pontiffs. A truth that has been defined by the Magisterium was just as true when it was being taught by the ordinary Magisterium without formal definition. After its *ex cathedra* definition, it received only an extrinsic added solemnity and a graver legalistic binding force, with now an excommunicating sanction usually attached against Christians who continue to reject this truth despite its solemn definition by the Magisterium.

The controversy over *Humanae Vitae* of Pope Paul VI would never have scandalized the entire world and brought so much evil on Christian families if the teaching of Pope Pius XII in *Humani Generis* on the binding force of encyclicals was heeded by bishops and laity and priests. As it was, many dissident theologians, even bishops, dismissed the doctrine of *Humanae Vitae* as erroneous and the moral perfection it called for as impossible of attainment. They advised Christians to do as they pleased on the matter of contraceptives, suggesting that they follow their consciences instead of the law of God as upheld in the teaching of the encyclical. But, thank God, wise scholars have been heard from to offset the avalanche of error and sin. Dr. P. Cremin, member of three Vatican II commissions, including one on marrriage, stated: "In my opinion the Pope's teaching on unlawful birth control is infallible."[7] Fr. Joseph Costanzo, S.J., wrote: "I am personally persuaded that the theological note of *Humanae Vitae* is infallible from the ordinary magisterium of the Church, irrevocable and irreformable as to its substantial mutability."[8] And Charles Cardinal Journet asserted: "The theologian who will reflect on the gravity of the matter, in the light in which it has been clarified, on the precision and certitude with which the response is given, will even be able to conclude that he is in the presence of a point of moral doctrine which could be later defined and accepted in the future with an assent of divine faith."[9] Monsignor Lambruschini, reporting to the Associated Press in the name of the Holy Father when the encyclical was published, said: "The decision has been given and it is not infallible (*ex cathedra*). But it does not leave the question of the regulation of birth in a state of vague uncertainty. . . . The decision binds the consciences of all without ambiguity. In particular, it can and must be said that the authentic pronouncement contained in the encyclical *Humanae Vitae* excludes the possibility of a probable opinion, valid on the moral plane, opposed to this teaching.''[10]

He condemns errors

Back to the encyclical *Humani Generis,* the Holy Father also condemns Christian scholars who deny the existence of angels as persons, who reject the essential difference between matter and spirit, who reject the super- natural order, grace and the beatific vision as purely gratuitous gifts of God, but would instead make these gifts natural to man. The Pope also rebukes the Christians who pervert the concept of original sin and the redemption performed for us by Christ. He laments the fact that certain theologians, rejecting the Church's terminology of transubstantiation and her doctrine on the Real Presence, reduce Christ's presence at the consecration and in the Holy Eucharist to being merely symbolic, not real and substantial, with the Body, Blood, Soul and Divinity of our Divine Lord being physically present under the species of bread and wine.

Here are some of the causes the Holy Father enumerates for the spread of these errors: Many of these false teachers are moved by imprudent zeal and a love for false science. Others are inspired by a false irenicism, a spirit of false peace and good will at any price, even the price of truth. They attempt to level the barriers between truth and falsity, goodness and wicked- ness by acting as if there were no difference between them, trying, in the name of a false and impossible ecumenism, to reconcile contradictory positions. The love of novelty and the idolization of pure reason and science drives others on to oppose the Church and cause scandal by written works which they clandestinely circulate among the young clergy to the detriment of their vocations and the authority of the Magisterium.

In conclusion, perhaps no better advice can be taken to avoid the errors the Holy Father speaks of here than that found in C.S. Lewis' brilliant book *Miracles:*

> When you turn from New Testament to modern scholars, remember that you go among them as sheep among wolves. Naturalistic assumptions. . . will meet you on every side — even from the pens of clergymen. This does not mean (as I was often tempted to suspect) that these clergymen are disguised apostates who deliberately exploit the position and livelihood given them by the Christian Church to undermine Christianity. It comes partly from what we may call a 'hangover.' We all have Natural-

ism in our bones and even conversion does not at once work the infection out of our system. Its assumptions rush back upon the mind the moment vigilance is relaxed. And in part the procedure of these scholars arises from the feeling which is greatly to their credit — which indeed is honorable to the point of being Quixotic. They are anxious to allow to the enemy every advantage he can with any show of fairness claim. They thus make it part of their method to eliminate the supernatural wherever it is even remotely possible to do so, to strain natural explanation even to the breaking point before they admit the least suggestion of a miracle. . . .

In using the books of such people you must therefore be continually on your guard. You must develop a nose like a blood-hound for those steps in the argument which depend not on historical and linguistic knowledge but on the concealed assumption that miracles are impossible, improbable or improper.[11]

For the laity fidelity to the authentic teaching of the Magisterium on faith and morals will guarantee salvation from heresy and moral wickedness by the attainment of truth and holiness.

Notes

[1]Pope Pius XII, *Humani Generis,* St. Paul Editions.
[2]Olivier Lacombe, "L'Encyclique 'Humani Generis' in *La Vie de L'Eglise Sous Pie XII,* Recherches et Debates, No. 27.
[3]Nogar, Fr. Raymond J., *The Wisdom of Evolution.*
[4]Huxley, Sir Julian, *Religion Without Revelation.*
[5]de Chardin, Fr. Teilhard, *The Phenomenon of Man.*
[6]Costanzo, S.J., Fr. Joseph F., "Papal Magisterium and *Humanae Vitae,*" *Thought,* Vol. XLIV, No. 174, Autumn 1969.
[7]Cremin, Dr. P., in *Times,* London, in *Atlas,* Oct. 1968.
[8]Costanzo, S.J., Fr. Joseph F., *Thought,* Autumn 1969.
[9]Journet, Charles Cardinal, in *L'Osservatore Romano,* English Edition, August 8, 1968.
[10]Lambruschini, Monsignor, in *L'Osservatore Romano,* August 8, 1968.
[11]Lewis, C.S., *Miracles.*

Reprinted from *Homiletic & Pastoral Review,* June 1976

Modernism and the Priesthood

A priest is a bridge-builder between God and man. He is the reconciler between creature and Creator. This truth finds its perfect fulfillment in the eternal High Priest par excellence, Jesus Christ.

From the moment of his conception in his immaculate Mother's womb, Christ brought together in himself God and man in a unique union, called hypostatic because it unites Christ's perfect human nature with the Divine Logos, the Second Person of the Blessed Trinity, in an ineffable, mysterious unification that will last forever. Thus, Christ is in himself not only the bridge-builder, but he is the only priest who is the bridge itself that unites God and man for all eternity in the temple of his Sacred Humanity. For Christ alone is anointed a priest *by nature*, conceived and born a priest by the mandate of his heavenly Father and the power of his Holy Spirit.

Upon coming into the world, the Son of God, knowing that "it was impossible that sins should be taken away with the blood of bulls and goats," said to his Father: "Sacrifice and oblation you would not accept, but a body you have fitted for me. . . Then said I: 'Behold I come — in the head of the book it is written of me — to do your will, O God.' "[1] The heavenly Father expressed his will with an oath taken on his divine nature: "You are my Son, this day have I begotten you. . . The Lord has sworn and will not repent. . . You are a priest forever according to the order of Melchisedech."[2]

All other Catholic priests are Christ's priests by delegation, ordination, participation. They are his priests by the grace of vocation, by a privilege bestowed by Christ, ratified by his Church. All other priests can recall a certain date when they passed from the lay to the priestly state forever. Hence, men will appreciate the essence and purpose of the Catholic priesthood by reflecting often and prayerfully on the priesthood of Jesus Christ. The purpose, therefore, of the priesthood of Christ is to reconcile fallen man, not only in his being but also in his activities, to the Being and Holiness of God. We shall consider one of the fundamental functions of the priesthood of Christ, namely, that of being the bridge to God for man's attainment of revealed truth through the gift of faith.

The event is history

It is a fact of history that God the Son took flesh of a Virgin Mother and became the God-Man whom we know as Jesus Christ. It is an event of history that he delivered his doctrine by word and miracles to his Apostles, and that they did the same to the body of believers. This is Revelation for Catholics — notice it is not private religious experience nor private visions — but something external, coming to man from without, from above. In its effect, of course, revelation produces profoundly internal resonances, enlightening the mind, attracting the will, gaining ardent adherence. But in its origin Faith is from without, transmitted by the Oracle, the High Priest of Truth, Jesus Christ, so as to bring ignorant, fallen man into communion with the Family of Truth, the Holy Trinity. And Christ commissioned his priestly Magisterium to speak in his name and share his truth with all nations.

Moreover, Christ himself constituted the believers of his truth into a body which he called his Church. He gave that body a priestly sacrifice, a hierarchical form of government, with Peter and Peter's successors, endowed with the fullness of Christ's priesthood, having the required powers and authority to support his teachings. This is Christ's Church as Catholics correctly understand it.

Supernatural aid is needed

Now the doctrines revealed by Christ, either directly or through his Church, are often truths beyond the power of reason to discover or comprehend. Naturally, then, supernatural aid is required to accept such truths. This aid is called the gift of faith. For faith is a supernatural gift of God for the acquisition of truth in the supernatural order, just as reason is a natural gift of God for the acquisition of truth in the natural order.

Moreover, as these supernatural truths are proposed to believers by the Church, then, if they are to believe at all, they must believe on the word of God made known by his Church. For Christ appointed his Church to teach all men, in an infallible manner, those truths beyond reason necessary for man's salvation. It is, therefore, on the basis of authority that the faithful believe, the infallible authority of God and of his Church. And when speaking in the name of Christ, the Church speaks as he did, plainly, with clear statements, with definite, precise sayings. *Truths* thus formulated by her are termed dogmas, that is, permanent substantially unchanging, though organically developing truths which call for clear, permanent, unchanging, though strongly growing *faith* among believers. Hence Catholics should have clear, precise notions on such subjects as Revelation, the Church, Faith, Authority, Dogma which, taken together, constitute a brief, though always inadequate but correct, summary of Christianity.

Nevertheless, Catholics are more confused about their faith today than ever before. Why? A look at Modernist thought will give the fundamental reasons.

Man knows 'appearances'

Modernism is that heresy which dissolves the coherency of the faith by clandestinely proposing profane novelties, couched in Catholic terminology, as the New Christianity. The Modernist teaches that man knows with intellectual knowledge not reality as it is, but only its appearances; not things but phenomena. Here is the metaphysical and epistemological foundation for the Agnosticism of the Modernist, the road leading straight to atheism. It follows that man cannot know with intellectual knowledge God or the supernatural. But since man speaks of God so often, he must attain God by other means.

The Modernist holds that man reaches God by religious experience, by religious sentiment. "Man feels within himself instinctively the need of the divine. That need excites a corresponding sentiment, 'the ceaseless palpitation of the human soul panting for the divine,' in the words of Buisson."[3] That religious sentiment is God; it is Revelation; it is Faith uniting the soul with God. Thus in the Modernist sense, Revelation, God, Faith are wholly internal and subjective in origin, the result of psychological experiences in the soul. Revelation is not an object of faith; it is not truth addressed by a transcendent God to the human intelligence, but truth addressed to the feelings by an immanent God. The Modernist practically makes his own Matthew Arnold's definition of religion: "Morality touched with emotion."[4]

For the Modernist dogmas are tentative, provisional formulas, the outcome of on-going religious experience, as changeable as that experience itself.[5] The Collective Conscience of the many sharing similar dogmas forms the Church. And Church authority originates from the Collective Conscience. Christ, therefore, did not directly establish the Church nor directly endow it with divine authority. True, Christ inspired believers to form the Collective Conscience and to center authority in that Collective Conscience. Thus, for the Modernist, "the entire Collective Conscience is the true and immediate vicar of Christ."[6] The Church, as a consequence, is not hierarchical, but democratic; its authority does not derive from Christ, but from the Collective Conscience which rules over the individual. We have here not a reformation but a transformation of Christianity; not a renewal of but a revolution against the Catholic Church as we know it.

Now what happens to the person and priesthood of Christ in the New Theology of Modernism? Jesus must be refashioned to suit the mentality of the age which is agnostic and today atheistic. Since man's knowledge cannot transcend the facts of experience, and since the God-Man is not a fact of experience, then Jesus as God is incapable of being known intellectually. Yes, Jesus of Nazareth existed; he was a man, a prophet "mighty in deed and work," of exceptional goodness. The phenomena prove this; he was a historical figure. But to say he was God, that he possessed divine knowledge, worked miracles, rose from the dead, is to speak about things that transcend man's experience. And the Modernist explains thus: Jesus is the object not only of intellectual knowledge, but also of faith.

As object of intellectual knowledge, Jesus is a mere man in the natural order of things, the Jesus of history. But as object of faith, Jesus becomes a different character. Faith divinizes him as the Christ, immanent in the experiences of believers. Subjective faith builds legends about him until he becomes God, conquers death, gives his flesh and blood as food, performs miracles demonstrating his absolute power over creation. But is he *really* God? Did he really rise from the dead? No, he is only God and does these wonders in the belief of Christians.

Christ, the High Priest, the God-Man, is not a reality of history. He must be carefully distinguished from the Jesus of history. The historical Jesus is a fact of history; the Christ of faith is merely an idea of man's consciousness. Modernists do not hesitate to call the Christ of faith an idea. Fr. Tyrrell called him "the incorporation of an idea."[7] Thus the God-Man is merely a legend, myth, creation of religious sentiment, revealing himself progressively to the private and Collective Conscience. He is not a fact, a reality of history; nor are his miracles, teachings, priesthood. The Modernists have done what St. John the Evangelist predicted Antichrist would do: "They have dissolved Jesus (into the Jesus of history and the Christ of faith). . .And every spirit that severs Jesus is not of God, but is of Antichrist, of whom you have heard that he is coming and is now already in the world."[8] And again: "Who is a liar save him who denies Jesus is the Christ?"[9] The spirit of Modernism is not of God; rather it is a lying spirit of Satan who was a liar and murderer from the beginning. In denying the dogmas of the Catholic Faith, Modernism necessarily subverts the redemptive priesthood of Christ.

Thus, in the time of Pope St. Pius X, Modernist views corrupted a large number of younger, more adventurous spirits among the clergy. The Pope's energetic action brought about the rout of its forces. In July 1907 he published a syllabus, *Lamentabili,* in which he condemned sixty-five of its most distinctive errors. On September 8 of the same year, the Pope struck again with his famous encyclical *Pascendi Dominici Gregis,* in which he condemned the whole system of Modernism, root and branch, calling it the "synthesis of all heresies." What the Holy Father did was to tear away the mask from Modernism and expose it to the world in its true colors as subversive of the whole Christian Faith.

Today Modernism has returned in a more virulent, updated form. Posing as progressivism, it has infected ecclesiastical circles with a flood of foolishness and an infinite series of errors and deviations. It is once again leading astray vast numbers of adventurous spirits in the ranks of clergy, sisterhood, theologians and philosophers. We can identify three trendy activities through which Modernism daily is worsening the already abnormal religious situation within the Church. All three activities are founded on a false, though seductive, understanding of liberty. The activities are: 1) Moral permissiveness; 2) uncritical dialogue; 3) irrational ecumenism.

Evils are visible

Today everybody knows the deplorable state into which Catholic seminaries have fallen. Many have closed; many are almost empty. Many still functioning have become hothouses of heresy or training grounds for Christian Marxism. With today's Church in ruins, what future can there be for a Church soon to fall into the governing and teaching power of clerics tainted with heresy? The Modernists planned their demolition of the Church shrewdly. Under the guise of responsible liberty, they introduced a moral permissiveness that reduced religious discipline to worldly laxity. Under the slogan of intellectual openness, they reduced academic standards and placed heresy on the par with the Truth of Christ. Their pluralism in doctrine has dethroned truth and advanced indifferentism and atheism. In the fields of liturgy, pastoral theology and seminary training, their uncritical, uprooted, antihistorical reformism has gravely wounded the Church. The evils are there for all to see. Catholic morality has degenerated, in the words of Fr. Cornelio Fabro, theologian to the Holy See, into a ''pornotheology''[10] that strives to justify a happy and unbelievable exaltation of free love, free abortion, free drugs, free homosexuality. And all this is promoted by Catholic Modernists without any protest or condemnation from ecclesiastical authority which looks on with folded arms, helpless, inarticulate, tongue-tied, incapable of taking any steps to protect the truth and morals of which it was called by God to be the official guardian. Indeed often matters are even worse, as, for example, when the authorities submit their clergy to the teachings of roving bands of Modernist theologians, sociologists, philosophers and psychologists; when they permit desacralized liturgies; foster general absolutions without sufficient reason or guarantee of later private confession; encourage women to continue agitation for the priesthood despite the Holy See's official teaching that it is not in God's economy of salvation that women be ordained; and demote their own religious authority by working openly with Modernists for the attainment of a democratic, classless Church.

Is truth relative?

Dialogue is another bridge over which the perverted concept of liberty travels to infect Catholics. It has become an expedient means for every form of contestation, bereft of all Catholic identity or orientation. It has induced in Catholics a timid, progressive denial of the faith with the result that many think Catholic truth is relative and changeable according to the needs of the times. Thus many Catholics no longer believe in the Church; they have renounced their identity; they oppose all Catholic tradition; they go outside the Church to find truth and salvation. Such has been the tragic itinerary of so many Catholic groups, so many priests, so many religious, so many seminarians.

Unfortunately, the dialogue with non-believers and atheists was not understood by Catholics to be an opportunity to share Catholic truths with them, but rather to be a progressive, uncritical absorption of their ideas into Catholicism. The result has been that youth in the tens of thousands have left the Church to join the Party.

Then there is the false concept of ecumenism in which all ideas are considered relatively true. It has been the bridge over which many Christians have crossed to atheism. Shaking-hands, cocktail-sipping, back-slapping with militant atheists, while cynically remaining silent about their heinous doctrines and crimes against humanity, is a betrayal of the Catholic Faith. For in such an atmosphere, where the sin of servility is rampant among Catholics, ecumenism becomes the equivalent of atheism. Tolerance of doctrinal deviation and moral wickedness ends up becoming Catholic backing of Communist crimes. The time has come to call a halt to this systematic betrayal of the faith, to denounce traitors with courage and firmness.

The whole Christian world must pray for a hierarchy alert to the plague of Modernism and prompt to crush it, in imitation of the courageous St. Pius X. We need bishops, priests, sisters, Catholic teachers who understand their office better and who are profoundly conscious of their solemn duties to the flock of Christ, especially that of never scandalizing his little ones.

We pray for bishops, priests and Catholic teachers who, whenever the need arises and Catholic truth is challenged, above the confused babel of conflicting tongues, will be able to proclaim the truth adequately and refute error decisively. The tactic of temporizing out of fear of the world's contempt or of compromising, economizing and minimizing the faith must be abandoned, if the Catholic Church is not soon to become a deserted Church.

The only solid, indestructible bridge to God in truth, faith and holiness will ever be the High Priest, Jesus Christ, true God and true man. Modernists attempt to destroy that priestly bridge in Christ's other priests. They then attempt to build their own bridges to the Kingdom of this world. But a priesthood of agnostics and atheists crossing bridges of moral permissiveness, doctrinal pluralism and irrational ecumenism is a perfect example of the blind leading the blind into the pit of hell. Bishops must always remember that Christ did not commit the supreme teaching authority to experts, theologians or the Collective Conscience, but to him to whom, and to whose successors, he said: "I have prayed for you, that your faith fail not. . . Strengthen your brethren."[11] Not from the professor's chair do Catholics accept Christ's teaching, but from the *Cathedra Petri* — the Chair of Peter, himself high priest, Pontifex and bridge-builder to God with the same priesthood of Christ.

A priesthood totally loyal to the teachings and guidance of Peter and the Magisterium can never be subverted into becoming a sort of organized Freemasonry of Modernists leading a revolution to create a Catholic Church acceptable to the World. The loyal priest rejects Modernist doctrine with scant ceremony. Following St. Paul, he avoids their "vain babblings, profane novelties. . . that contribute much to ungodliness. . . which some have professed and have fallen away from the faith." Rather the faithful priest lives the advice of St. Paul: "Beware lest any man spoil you through philosophy and vain deceit. . . Guard the deposit."[12]

Notes

[1] Hebrews 10:4-8.
[2] Hebrews 5:5,6; 7:21.
[3] George Tyrrell, *Through Scylla and Charybdis*, p. 305.
[4] Quoted by Fr. Bampton, S.J. in his *Modernism and Modern Thought*, p. 39.
[5] *The Life of Fr. Tyrrell*, p. 202.
[6] *Ibid.* p. 191.
[7] *Ibid.* p. 397.
[8] 1 John 4:3.
[9] 1 John 2:22.
[10] Cornelio Fabro, *L'Avventura della Teologia Progressista*, pp. 15, 16.
[11] Luke 22:32.
[12] 1 Timothy 6:20.

Modernism Revisited and Updated

Modernism, the perennial heresy, is rampant in the Christian Churches today. In this article we hope to demonstrate how the "new theologians," now called in Europe "pornotheologians," because of their espousal of "the liberating function of Marxism and even greater liberating extremism of Freudianism," are in the vanguard of rampant neo-Modernism.

Child of the Protestant Reformation and the French Revolution, Modernism leads straight to atheism. "The essential error of Modernism," wrote Fr. A. Vermeersch, S.J., "is nothing less than the perversion of dogma, the critique of supernatural knowledge according to the false principles of contemporary philosophy." The Abbe Loisy, the Father of Modernism, agrees. "In reality all Catholic theology, even its fundamental principles, the general philosophy of religion, divine law, and the laws that govern the knowledge of God, come up for judgment before this new court of assize." In his classic work on the heresy, Prof. M. Perrin of the University of Louvain wrote in *Modernisme Dans L'Eglise*: Modernism is that humanitarian movement whose ambition is to eliminate God from all social life."

Following St. Pius X who stigmatized "Modernism as the synthesis of all heresies," we hope to expose some basic errors of this vast congeries of falsities. Led by agnostic philosophers, Catholic Modernists accept immanentist, evolutionary explanations of God, religion, dogma, the sacraments, Scripture, the Church and its Magisterium. All faith is subjected to science and personal experience. Divine revelation is imperfect and therefore subject to continual, indefinite progress corresponding with the progress of reason. Prophecies and miracles of Scripture are the poetical imaginings of men. Dogma is merely man's approval of his refined formulas on religious experience. As experience changes and evolves so must dogma take on new, even contradictory, historical meanings. All religions arise from experience and lead to salvation; the advantage of one over another rests merely in the liveliness or vividness of its formulas. Indifferentism follows with the result that it is considered divisive to make converts to the Catholic faith.

The first aim of Modernists is to convert the Church of Rome and then the universal Church. Modernists insist that "the Roman Pontiff can and ought to conform with contemporary progress, liberalism and civilization." Really, they seek a Church in their own image and likeness — a small, Gnostic, elite Church of worldly-wise intellectuals. Scandalized that Christ founded his Church for all men, especially for outcasts, it is small wonder that Modernists exhibit an indifference to official Catholic teaching and express an irreconcilable animosity to the custodian of this truth, the Magisterium.

Today Modernism has regrouped its forces under such titles as "Catholic Opposition," or "Catholic Dissent," or "Christian Critics." On November 17–18, 1973 the Christian Critics held an international assembly in Lyons, France. At the end they proclaimed the "New Christianity." Here are its 5 main characteristics: 1) *Anthropocentrism:* Man not God is the center of religion. God is found solely in the face, functions, fortunes and future of man. God is loved and served solely in man. The primacy of man is identified with the primacy of God. 2) *Immanence in the World:* The kingdom of God is here not hereafter. Salvation means liberation from social sin, i.e., from ignorance, hunger, underdevelopment, political oppression, economic exploitation. Personal sin is no longer relevant in today's historical context. The new Catholics, enlisting under Socialism's banner, must achieve the kingdom of God by destroying Capitalism. 3) *The New Evangelism:* The true meaning of the Gospels is economic not spiritual, arising from service to the poor. For the Gospels belong exclusively to the poor; only the poor and their socialistic champions can understand them. The Magisterium has misinterpreted the meaning of the Gospels, using them to exploit the poor and remain in power with the mighty of this world. 4) *The New Ecclesiology:* The Church is part of the world; she does not exist for herself, but to serve the world. Hence, she must dissolve all her own institutions. In her liturgical life, any members may function as priests.

In her jurisdictional life, local churches must be autonomous, for all authority comes from the faithful who share co-responsibility. 5) *The New Passion for Christ:* But this love is not for Christ the God-Man. Rather it is for a Christ who is only human — the Man-for-others, the friend, the defender, liberator of the poor. Indeed, the revolutionary and Grand Subverter, aiding the poor to overthrow all corrupt institutions, the traditional Church included.

Replying to these errors it must be noted: 1) A religion of man must deny God and produce a decapitated love for man who is lovable only because God loves him. 2) The strait-jacket of immanence prevents salvation from entering man's history, denies the eschatological kingdom and reduces religion to being a mere political ideology. 3) The Gospels belong exclusively to the Catholic Church because she alone possesses the Holy Spirit as the Author, Inspirer and Source of Scripture. 4) The Church, as the unique creation of Christ and the Holy Spirit, is in but not of this world. 5) The Christ of the Modernists is a non-historical fiction, tailored to push Marxist propaganda.

Professor George Santayana, famous agnostic of our era, in his book *Winds of Doctrine* made a trenchant critique of Modernism thus: "Modernism . . . is the love of all Christianity in those who perceive that it is all a fable. It is the historic attachment to his Church of a Catholic who has discovered that he is a pagan...The Modernists are men of the Renaissance, pagan, pantheistic in their profounder sentiment, to whom the hard and narrow realism of official Christianity is offensive just because it presupposes that Christianity is true...As for Modernism, it is suicide. It is the last of those concessions to the spirit of the world which half-believers and double-minded prophets have always been found making; but it is a mortal concession. It concedes everything; for it concedes that everything in Christianity, as Christians hold it, is an illusion." And remarking wrily on the modernists' opposition to Rome, Santayana writes: "The modernist feels himself full of love for everybody...except for the Pope."

Here then is updated Modernism, the new-styled cradle of religious revolution. It is militant, socialistic, revolutionary, Marxist. It advocates a theology of violence, a morality of total sexual permissiveness. The sure way of destroying this disease is that of total dedication to the teaching of the Apostolic See of Rome. "He speaks in vain," wrote St. Maximus in the sixth century, "who tries to persuade me of the orthodoxy of those who refuse obedience to His Holiness the Pope of the most Holy Church of Rome."

And Cardinal Newman, prophet and doctor of our times, warns us not to follow ourselves in matters of faith and morals, but Christ and his Church. He writes: "Be our mind as heavenly as it may be, most loving, most holy, most zealous, most energetic, most peaceful, yet if we look off from him (Christ and His Church) for a moment, and look towards ourselves, at once these excellent tempers fall into some extreme or mistake. Charity becomes over-easiness; holiness is tainted with pride; zeal degenerates into fierceness; activity eats up the spirit of prayer; hope is heightened into presumption. We cannot guide ourselves. God's revealed word is our sovereign rule of conduct; and, therefore among other reasons, is FAITH so principal a grace, for it is the directing power which receives the commands of Christ, and applies them to the heart."

Now the modernist is a person who trusts in himself alone; he has lost his faith in Christ, in his Church and her doctrines, but cannot steel himself to admit it. Therefore, he has to fill the traditional dogmas with new content. He uses the right words, God, Christ, the eternal life, kingdom, sin, salvation. But he empties them of all Catholic meaning. For him the more a thing changes, the more it remains the same.

Written by Fr. Miceli, The Editor of the newsletter *Confraternity of Catholic Clergy*, April-May 1975

Permanent Consecration: Anchor of Religious Community

At some time in her life, every religious has seen a vision. The look of Christ has flooded her fantasy. His call to communion has reverberated in her soul: "Come, Follow Me!" The charm of His infinitely gracious person has suffused her memory. His knock on the door of her heart has driven her to sally forth so as to abide with Him, to share His fortunes and His fate. The Master's incredible invocation to the religious to enter into the promised land of intimate, divine communion with Himself reveals the stupendous love in the Redeemer, a love that strives to fulfill the insatiable hunger in the creature for a life of total mutual self-donation to God.

When the religious said: "Yes" generously in word and deed to the appeal of the Incarnate Christ, she engaged her whole being, her entire person, her "I," not her ego in a total commitment to her Master. She dedicated this commitment to a life of love and fidelity with the Divine "Thou" of the Son of God. This acceptance of a total, permanent commitment to Christ, her divine Redeemer, lifted the religious from the dull anonymity of being a mere somebody, another person, individual unconscious of divine realities and sublime moral values, to becoming a real person, revivified in grace, awakened to the vibrant presence of God and eager "to grow up," in the words of St. Paul "with that mind and heart in her which were in Christ Jesus."

But the life of intimate communion with Christ has to be won by the violence of faith. It demands the totality of throwing oneself into God's arms even when all seems darkness. In the words of Kierkegaard. "Man must make a leap into the darkness totally trusting God even though he does not see the future." And only persons of a generously violent faith and love will succeed in this magnificent project.

When the Apostles James and John sought, through their mother's intercession, to be enthroned on either side of their Lord in the kingdom of His glory, the divine Master challenged them thus: "You do not know what you are asking. Can you drink from the cup which I am about to drink? Are you willing to be baptized with the baptism with which I am about to be baptized? Since James and John truly loved the Lord, they could reply: "We can." Their answer to their Lord's challenge with its willingness to "venture all on Christ" demonstrated their zealous love of Jesus. This "venturing for the Faith," as Cardinal Newman calls it, demonstrates the complete trust of these saints in Christ. Their whole lives, their fortunes, their destinies were totally committed to the Heart of Christ, even though, humanly speaking, they were in ignorance of the future and could not be certain of their own fidelity. But Christ was their guarantor of success.

Marvelling at this unconditioned generosity, Cardinal Newman analyzes the full commitment of James and John thus: "Success and reward everlasting they will have who persevere unto the end. We cannot doubt that the ventures of all Christ's servants must be returned to them at the last day with abundant increase. This is a true saying: 'He returns far more than we lend Him and without fail.' "[2] But I am speaking of individuals like ourselves, says Newman. No one among us knows if for certain he will persevere, yet every one among us, to give himself even a chance of persevering, of success, must make a venture. With regard to individuals, then, it is quite true that all of us must for certain make a venture for Christ and for heaven. Yet without having the certainty of success in this venture. This is indeed the very meaning of the word venture, for that would be a strange venture which had nothing in it of fear, risk, danger, anxiety, uncertainty. Yet so it certainly is, and in this consists the excellence and nobleness of faith. This is the very reason why faith is singled out from other graces, and honored as the special means of our justification, because its presence implies that we have the heart to venture everything on God's goodness.[3]

St. Paul in his epistle to the Hebrews, clearly explains the nature of the venture made by those fully committed to follow the vision of faith. He first exhorts the imitators of Christ not to lose heart in the following of their Master. "Do not, therefore, lose your confidence which has a great reward, for you have need of patience, that doing the will of God you may receive the promise. For a very little while He who is to come will come and will not delay."[4] Then comes Paul's famous scriptural quotation: "Now my just man lives by faith, but if he draws back he will not please my soul."[5] The apostle then closes with a note of encouragement for his fellow Christians: "We, however, are not of those who draw back unto destruction, but of those who have faith to the saving of their souls."[6] And to make sure that his readers understand the nature of full commitment to God and Christ, the commitment that this faith entails, St. Paul enters into the heart of the definition of faith: "Now faith is the substance of things to be hoped for, the evidence of things that are not seen."[7] Thus faith is the living realization of things promised by God to his followers. It is the ground of proof, the evidence of these realities which are not yet seen. For faith makes present here and now, the unseen realities of God. It does this in such a manner that the believer acts on the mere prospect of these realities as if they were already possessed. Thus the man who lives by faith stakes today his present worldly possessions, his ease, his wealth, his relationships upon the chance of having fulfilled in the future the promises that God has made to him today. And in order to emphasize the reality of this truth, St. Paul presents a cloud of Old Testament witnesses who attained God's approval because in the full commitment of their faith to Him, they kept looking for that city with fixed foundations, of which city the builder and the architect is God. For without faith it is impossible to please God. The Apostle insisted on this truth as he exhorted the Christian Hebrews to put away every encumbrance and sin entangling us, and to run with patience to the fight set before us, looking toward the author and finisher of our faith Jesus, who for the joy set before him, endured a cross despising the shame.

Now if faith is the essence, the foundation necessary for the fulfillment of religious life, it follows that the truly committed religious will permanently risk everything in following Christ. What the religious now has or what she could have in the future, all this and more she will risk on the promises of Our Lord to be her reward. Moreover, the religious risks all in a noble and generous manner, not at all rashly or lightly. Thus the religious surrenders to Christ without knowing every detail entailed in this total sacrifice. Nor does the religious know the total reality of what she shall gain as a reward. The religious makes this "leap of faith" even though she is still uncertain about victory in this life-long struggle to remain faithful to her gift of total self-donation to her Lord. Yet in all the trials of this life-long sacrifice unto death, the religous leans upon, waits upon Christ, trusting Him to fulfill His promises, trusting Him to give her the strength to fulfull her vows faithfully. Never does she trust in herself. And thus the religious always progresses in intimate communion with Christ without excessive fear. The lack of fear is not irrational because it is based on the divine fidelity of Christ to fulfill His promises.

Thus Abraham, the religious Father of the Chosen People, trusting in God completely, went out from his native land at God's command, not knowing where he was going, but convinced that God would keep His promises, give him a land flowing with milk and honey and progeny as numerous as the stars. Many of the other saintly patriarchs, prophets and judges served the Chosen People at God's command and died having received the promises of God, but as St. Paul tells us "having seen these promises from afar." For even though they did not experience the fulfillment of God's promises in their lifetime yet they were convinced of their reality; they embraced them in faith; they confessed that they were strangers and pilgrims on this earth and they looked for God's City of Joy in the next life. Every religious who accepts the Will of Christ is daily saying, in effect, to Our Divine Lord: "Yes, we are able; we are willing to drink of your cup of sufferings, to be baptized with the baptism of your Passion." Every religious plunges herself, as the Apostles James and John did, into the fidelity of Christ, to go all the way in this life with Christ, even to the baptism of martyrdom if that be God's holy will. They keep before themselves the words of Christ, "You believe in God, believe also in Me."[8] With St. Thomas the Apostle called the Twin, the religious in order to remain with

Christ in life and death, willingly cries out: "Let us also go with him to Jerusalem where they are seeking to stone Him, so that we may also die with Him."

Though the religous life, in which three evangelical vows are professed, is a high road to sanctity, it must not be considered the only road to perfection. The laity are also called to sanctity; their vocations are also means to holiness. Total Christian commitment to Christ is also an obligation for them in the way of life to which the Holy Spirit has called them. The Holy Spirit distributes His gifts to each one according to His will. Yet he does give the special gift of evangelical perfection to certain chosen souls. But there is no reason why these souls should glory in this special gift for any personal motive. "I have chosen you, you have not chosen me," Christ reminds his apostles. "And to whom much has been given, from him much will be demanded."

Thus holiness can be attained even outside of religious communities. Witnesses to this reality are the many saints of the Old and New Testaments who are publicly honored by the Church who, as faithful parents fulfilled God's call to holiness. But what we are emphasizing here is this truth, namely, that the primary purpose, the central ideal of religious community, is to aim at the achievement of constant intimate communion with God. Its purpose is to train the mind, the soul, the heart, the spirit of its members to the work of pleasing God in all things. For who more than a religious should be able to apply to herself the marvelous statement of St. Paul? "I live now, not I, but Christ lives in me."[9] Though all this be true, yet the masters of theology, St. Thomas Aquinas, St. Bonaventure, supported by the brilliance of St. Augustine, teach us another aspect of this truth, namely that a life of total commitment to God will not ordinarily possess the stability of virtue, the habitualness of an organic way of supernatural life, unless vows are taken. And these vows are to be lived in community life so as to make this commitment to Christ intact forever. Religious need one another so as to live out their commitment to Christ together as a family of Christ.

That is why religious bind themselves to perpetual vows of poverty, chastity and obedience. They hope by this means to persevere bravely unto death in following Christ as the Way, the Truth and the Life. They want to follow the Lamb wherever He goes, to sing the new canticle for Him forever, the canticle which no one else can sing as the Apocalypse informs us.

Now there is a grave crisis in religious commitment today. The idea of the part-time religious is becoming a fashion everywhere. One astonished non-Catholic remarked: "By Jove, these part-timers enter religious life and after a few months or years, they leave seeking self-fulfillment in some secular project. And they call this process "maturing" in their vocation."

But in the eyes of the world this is called the "cop-out" process summed up in the words of our Lord: "He who puts his hand to the plow and turns back is not worthy of Me."[10]

Now when such persons give their credentials later on as they seek new positions in the world, they put down "premarital religious life," as if this stay in religious life were to be a unique experience, one that qualifies them for any new undertaking. Experience not fidelity is their new criterion of mature personhood.

Is it any wonder that we are living in an era when religious communities are disintegrating. Permanent commitment to God is slowly vanishing. It does no good to ignore or gloss over this tragedy. Now the disease that is attacking religious life in its very essence is the madness for change. This frenzy is a fever that rises from metaphysical instability and theological rootlessness. Behind the plague of instability lies the loss of the sense of the sacred, the sense of vocation. The call of Christ is drowned out by the blare of the sirens of the world calling to a life of ease, a life that is sated with the lust of pleasure, notoriety and the credit of a great name on this earth. In the life of the religious of the day the new enthusiasts for secularism have caused the consciousness of God to fade and the consciousness of man to take God's place in the heart of man. Hence the call to a vocation from God tends to be obliterated and the call to serve this world in a secular humanistic profession takes its place. The Abbe Loisy, the father of the heresy called Modernism, analyzes the spiritual disease that is destroying religious life thus: "In reality all Catholic theology, even its fundamental principles, the general philosophy of religion, divine law, and the laws that govern the knowledge of God, come up for judgment before Modernism's new court of assize."[11] And Fr. A. Vermeersch, S.J. writes: "The essential error of Modernism is nothing less than the perversion of dogma, the critique of supernatural knowledge according to the false principles of contemporary philosophy."[12] The child of the Protestant Reformation and the French Revolution Modernism leads straight to atheism. Man not God has now become the center of religion. God is found solely in the face, functions, fortunes and future of man. The primacy of God is identified with the primacy of man. Thus the providence of man supplants the Providence of God. And, of course, the only account of his stewardship that man has to render, is the account he gives to himself, to his fellowmen. This is his purpose, his "career" in life.

Thus the basic sense of vocation has succumbed to the assault of a practical atheism, an implicit atheism contained in a philosophy of life known as secular humanism. The mission of man is likewise degraded. Whereas in Christianity the mission of man is to cooperate with Christ in liberating man from Satan, sin and death, thereby restoring man to membership in the Divine Family of the Trinity, now the secularized mission of man aims at liberating humanity from ignorance hunger, underdevelopment, political and economic oppression, thereby leading man into the promised land of a temporal Utopia. The mission of man is no longer to sanctify, to divinize one's fellowman and the social atmosphere in which man lives. Now the naturalistic mission is to make progress and to humanize the environment. Thus in concentrating his efforts on making humanitarian progress, man has rejected God's Will for the human race. "This is the Will of God, your sanctification... Now is the time of salvation.... Today if you hear His voice, harden not your hearts." Man is now shielding himself from the challenge of the cross by plunging himself into the delirium of utopian change.

"Changing society for the better" is the rationalization put forward by many religious families for abandoning the religious life. They have now "expanded their life-styles" to include in their midst uncommitted singles, married couples, persons of non-Catholic religious persuasions. But this rationalization is but a sop to the consciences of those striving to justify the process of disintegration they have introduced into what used to be celibate, permanently committed and genuinely religious communities. Changing society is an empty, plausible slogan, dinned into the ears of the unwary so as to cloak the betrayal, the surrender of religious communities to the spirit of rebellion against God that is abroad in the world today. Indeed, even Holy Scripture is pressed into service to ratify this pastiche in the religious melting pot. This madness for the melange of the wedded and the celibate under the same roof is the smoke of Satan that has blackened the beauty of the religious life dedicated to the service of Christ and His Church.

Of course, there are plenty of false exegetes presenting private interpretations of Scripture, exhibiting personal charisms and claiming personal revelations that prove that the novelty in religious life comes from the Holy Spirit who, as a result of Vatican II, is leading the Church and the world to a better understanding of what true religious life and commitment is. Commitment now means that each religious does her own thing. This is the Holy Will of God for her. But, of course, the meaning now given to commitment is temporal, secularistic and relativistic. The word fidelity seems to have lost all meaning, to have dropped out of human usage. The fickleness of man and woman, their changeableness is the virtue of the age. One must not be too rigid, too dogmatic, too steadfast; maturity indicates the ability to change, even to call back one's promises and vows made to God.

Religious communities are dying because they are adapting to the mores of a religiously sick society, whose designs have so twisted the human heart and turned the human head that many so-called consecrated communities are ablaze with the lust for irrational freedom. They have fled from God to the world in a wild search for unlimited liberty. Religious life is threatened by the principle of self-direction. Being a fully committed religious has become a hazardous vocation today. Yet the attack on religious life, strangely enough, does not come primarily from external enemies; it comes from the religious themselves who have decided to live their own lives in their own fashion. Even many religious superiors are following the wisdom of the world after abandoning the wisdom of God. They rule their communities as if they were merely secular corporations, seeking in their policies security and efficiency instead of poverty and sanctity. They have wavered in their faith in God. St. James, in two graphic analogies, describes the evil effects of this faltering faith. "For he who hesitates is like the wave of the sea, driven and carried about by every wind. Therefore, let us not allow such a person to think he will receive anything from the Lord, being a double-minded man, unstable in all his ways."

Then too, religious have forgotten who they are, and who they must be, namely persons totally consecrated to achieving the Holy Will of God in themselves and in the people of God. In the people of God they must achieve this holy goal by a life of constant prayer and self-effacing service. Instead, they have become too often hearers of the word, but doers of the wisdom of the world. The prophet's complaint can be made against them: "This people honors me with their lips, but their heart is far from me."[13] Hence they often suffer from an illusionary, schizophrenic relationship with God and religious life. This attitude has created in many a severe identity crisis. Whole communities have become so disoriented that thousands of religious have abandoned their consecration to God as being a way of life that was insupportable, that pulled them apart in many directions, that they could no longer endure for any length of time if they were to save their sanity. St. James once again describes this spiritual sickness: "But be doers of the word, and not hearers only, deceiving yourselves. For if anyone is a hearer of the word, and not a doer, he is like a man looking at his natural face in a mirror. For he looks at himself and goes away, and presently he forgets what kind of man he is. But he who has looked carefully into the perfect law of liberty and has remained in it, not becoming a forgetful hearer but a doer of the word, shall be blessed in his deed."[14]

Really, permanent religious commitment is that way of life which embodies what St. James calls the "perfect law of liberty." No one is as free as the religious; no one was as free as the Apostles. They gave themselves totally to the freest of human Masters, Jesus Christ, the God-Man. And when one attains the perfect law of liberty, it is found to consist in total consecration to Christ. For to serve God is to reign. And to serve God to the best of one's ability is to reign with the greatest of power, the power of God. Such a commitment of total consecration can only be lived faithfully when the religious adheres not to her own will, but solely to the Holy Will of God. "Sanctity," St. Augustine tells us, is "*adhaerere Deo*", namely "to cling to the Will of God." And this is the state of perfect liberty.

The crisis therefore today in religious life is one of fidelity to the word and Will of God. Fidelity is perhaps the most important virtue needed in religious life. The habitual attitude of faithfulness is founded on the Faith. Faithfulness forever. Here we are speaking about faithfulness to God through the consecration of one's whole life to Him by means of the evangelical vows. Here we are also speaking of fidelity to Christ as the heavenly spouse of the Sister religious. Yes, sisters are human beings like the rest of men and like them they differ in spiritual depth. Alas some of them are a bundle of disparate impressions, of confused inter-locking experiences. They live in the moment without a deep reverent memory. We all forget so many of God's gifts to us, or just take them for granted. We forget the continuity of love Our Lord established when He said at the Last Supper: "Do this in memory of me." We forget too often our roots of holiness in Christ, the Apostles, the millions of martyrs and confessors, in the Motherhood of God with Mary. Our loss of our sense of our spiritual roots and culture, of our membership in the communion of saints often leads to our disorientation and identity crisis. We must regain through prayer that deep reverent memory which makes it easy for us to connect harmoniously the Christian past with the present, and of projecting both into God's divine future. We need the holy capacity of maintaining a Christlike continuity with the Church Triumphant, Suffering and Militant. We need the vision of the prophets, of the saints, of Christ, of Divine Providence, to see always "*sub specie aeternitatis*," that is, all history in the light of eternity. Alas! Too many religious aping their secular brethren are living only for the moment. That is why they are wandering, disoriented and lost. The present fashion is all powerful, overwhelming for them. The holy past is despised because it is the past. Apparently there is something evil about the past. I've never seen such a terrible attack on tradition and the past as is taking place in modern times. Some event that has taken place only a week ago is immediately despised as a past event. Our modern secularists refuse to learn from the past; only the present has meaning for them. This hatred of tradition comes from the godless philosophy of Marxism. It teaches that all that took place before Marx is pre-historical; history began with Marx and is now in full victorious swing toward the godless, classless society. Many Christians are infected with this propaganda, I'm afraid; even nations, with political and religious leaders, have fallen for this false philosophy of man, society and history.

Many religious today are like butterflies, always on the move emotionally, winging their way from fragile flower to fragile flower. Concerned with feeding merely on the bright, fragrant, sweet blossoms of this life. Dr. Dietrich von Hildrebrand, in his book *The Art of Living*, explains the futile floating through life thus: "Such religious are like a sieve through which everything runs and nothing is contained. Though they can be good, kindly and honest, they elude one's grasp; they are incapable of having deep relationships with Christ, with other people, because they are incapable of having deep relationships with anything. They do not know responsibility because they know no lasting bond, because one day does not reach into the next one. Even though their impressions are strong, they do not penetrate down to the deepest level in which we find those attitudes which are over, above, and perdure beyond the changes of the moment. They do not plunge to the depths where the realities of God exist, where Christ tells us to look to find the kingdom of God within ourselves. Such persons honestly promise one thing one moment, and in the next their promise has completely disappeared from memory. They make resolutions under some strong impression, but the next impression blows these resolutions away. For such persons weight and value are not the preponderant factors determining their interest in things, but only the liveliness of an impression created by the actual presence of things. What makes an impression upon them is the general advantage of liveliness, the excitement of things happening, presenting situations that blot out the memory of things of the past."[16]

Unfortunately, such fickle persons never experience the holy paradox which is expressed for us by the Psalmist when he prayed with joy to God: "With you, O Lord, one day is as a thousand years, and a thousand years as one day." Here we have a certain experience of eternity in living with God. Now often enough the unstable religious is a person of deep feelings and even of deep convictions. The core of such a religious is not void of serious spiritual aspirations and commitments, as witness how many of these religious have remained many, many years in consecrated religious life prior to abandoning it. Nevertheless, the novelty, the excitement, the thrill, the whole storm of a fresh situation, of a new movement suffocated their deeper aspirations and commitments, while the glow or gloom of new events asserting its powerful magnetism of attraction or repulsion moved such inconstant religious to abandon their first loves. They dismissed from their hearts their original commitments. They became, in a sense, fugitives from their own higher, better selves, fugitives from Christ. In a way, they have become, without being conscious of it, material traitors against themselves, others and God. For them the new situation has changed everything. They advance this new situation as the reason for breaking off their former bonds of sacred promises and vows. It thus becomes apparent that their spiritual temple was built on the sands of selfishness, not on the rock of selflessness. Their spiritual castle has collapsed before every wind of trial, storm of doubt, hurricane of heresy or invasion of worldly enticement. Had such religious really dedicated themselves in constant love to God and Christ, they would have remained faithful to their vows over the opposition of worldly allurements. Christ has predicted the opposition of the world against all who would follow Him in evangelical perfection; he also predicted the serious temptations that his followers would have to overcome. But He encouraged his followers to rely solely upon Him for their victory: "Have confidence, I have overcome the world.!"[17]

Jesus testified to the great love and fidelity of His Apostles, even though they were weak in spirit, with these words: "You are my friends for you have continued with me in my trials."[18] Because of this fidelity the weak, frightened Apostles were able to be formed by the Holy Spirit into bold, courageous martyrs who rejoiced to suffer for the name of Jesus and indeed to die as his faithful witnesses. Unfortunately, because of their infidelity many religious have been blown away like chaff, separated from the corn in the divine granary. Seduced that every change in the Church was a forward march to improved religious life, such fickle persons, like reeds shaken by the winds, abandoned their permanent center Jesus Christ. Hypnotized by the novelty of the latest, most advanced renewals, they marched under the tyranny of fashion straight off the mountain of prayer and holiness into the wilderness of the world where their tremendous potential for serving God and saving souls was cut off and short-circuited to the advantage of the enemy of souls.

In order to be moved to great fidelity to God, we ought to contemplate God's fidelity to us. Moreover this would lead us to contemplate Mary's faithfulness to us, for Mary is the model of all Sister religious. Let us reflect then for a moment on God's permanent fidelity to us. Thus we may be moved to heed the advice given us by the Holy Spirit: "If today you hear His voice, harden not your hearts." The astounding truth is that God does not call us to His service through total consecration only once. His call is incessant, enduring every moment of our lives. Every instant His appeal is arriving and sounding in our souls. If we would but listen. The original call is in Baptism, notarized with an indelible seal; this call daily presents us with grace upon grace. Whether we remain faithful to this call or not, God continues to shower his graces upon us endlessly. He calls us from grace to grace, from sin to holiness, from holiness to higher holiness while life here lasts. Abraham was called out of Chaldea, Peter from his nets, Matthew from his coins, Elisha from his farm, Nathaniel from his fig tree. Never does God cease calling us. On and on come his invitations in a million different variations. That call is beamed from one creature to another, always reaching its destination our chosen souls. The call of God to religious is especially intimate and especially insistent. It invites friends to come up higher, to exchange gifts, to exchange themselves forever in love. It invites lovers to work together, to suffer together, to die in the same divine cause and finally, to rule together from the same divine throne for all eternity. God calls these favorites of His again and again in order to justify, sanctify, glorify and reproduce His Divine Son in them perfectly for all eternity.

Now every call accepted invites a greater and higher call, leading the consecrated soul higher and higher to the mountain of its transfiguration in Christ. Our Lord was constantly complaining to His Apostles: "O You of little faith, why did you doubt?" Why do you not trust my goodness completely? My plans for your sanctification are limitless; my plans for your success in my Father's project to save souls, for saving the world are beyond your wildest dreams. It is only your lack of faith, your lack of generous response to my call that puts restrictions on the outpourings of my blessings, on my Will to divinize you and, through you, the souls of millions.

If only religious would appreciate this truth in depth. God loves them as favorites, unconditionally, permanently. God has sent His Son to live permanently among them as their spouse. And this beloved Son is also the incarnation of God's call to His favorites. It is true, God cannot sanctify nor glorify anyone without their cooperation. Nevertheless, His love for them, His call to them remains forever. For God never falls away, never falters in His faithfulness. When religious, or for that matter when any soul, leaves God, they leave Infinite Love Unchanged behind. But notice, it is Infinite Love that never takes back its invitation. Judas abandoned a sublime call that was never revoked by the God of Love. For God is the God of eternal Faithfulness and there is no shadow of change or alteration in Him.

Unfortunately, religious do not always grasp the truth that God is calling them constantly no matter how long they have been in religious life. For now is the acceptable time, now the time of salvation, now the time to come up higher and sup with the Divine Master. In this ignorance, they do an injustice to the wonderful plans of God in their own regard. For God wants to do great things to and in them, but they do not believe this truth. Nor do they look for this special, enduring, loving Providence in their own cases. They forget that God dwells in an Eternal Now, even though He is also immanent in time and human history, though never possessed nor limited by time. God is in history with us, for us. But He dwells in an Eternal Now without past or future and it is both there and in time that His invitation to religious to come up higher is one with His Eternal, changeless choice of love of them from all eternity.

Religious should realize that they can apply to themselves the scriptural oath God the Father took concerning the priesthood of His Divine Son. They can adapt this oath to their own religious life. "The Lord has sworn

and will not repent: Thou art my Spouse, my Consecrated One forever.''
On this matter too Cardinal Newman has composed a prayer that can
instruct and inspire us: ''Give me, O Lord, that purity of conscience which
alone can improve thy inspiration. My ears are dull so that I cannot hear
thy voice. My eyes are dim so that I cannot see thy tokens. You alone can
quicken my hearing and purge my sight, and cleanse and renew my heart.
Teach me like Mary to sit at thy feet and to hear thy word. Give me the
true wisdom which seeks thy will by prayer and meditation, by direct intercourse with Thee more than by reading and reasoning. Give me the discernment to know thy voice from the voice of strangers, and to rest upon it
and to seek it in the first place as something external to myself. And answer
me through my own mind, for I worship and rely on thee as being above
and beyond me and yet ever within me.''[19]

And now let us consider the faithfulness of Mary. In an age of infidelity,
when too many priests and religious are abandoning the vineyard of the
Lord to work in private careers under godless overlords, in an age in which
formerly consecrated persons are now running after intellectual, political,
financial, legal and even military power, religious souls should consecrate
themselves to God with greater fervor and zeal. To do this they should
contemplate Mary, the holy Mother of God, and take her as their model
of total, irrevocable faithfulness in a sublime vocation to God. In response
to the Angel Gabriel's invitation to serve God by becoming the Mother
of His Divine Son, Mary, though troubled and puzzled about the future,
nevertheless surrendered with an irrevocable consecration to the Holy Will
of God. ''Behold the handmaid of the Lord. Be it done unto me according
to thy word.'' Mary was not directing herself; she accepted God's direction.
Mary is thus seen as the Woman of perfect faith. Unlike Zachary, holy
man that he was, Mary never faltered, never doubted. And Elizabeth, allud-
ing to the contrast between her husband's response to the angel and Mary's
response, exclaimed in praise of Mary's conduct: ''Blessed art thou among
women, and blessed is the fruit of thy womb, and blessed is she who has
believed, for the things promised her by the Lord shall be accomplished.''[20]

Even as she accepted God's plan, Mary felt deeply her own inexpressible unworthiness. After all, she was an unknown, humble girl. In the eyes
of the world she was really a nobody. But she had what God loves in his
dedicated creatures — purity and innocence of heart. Her bright vision of
faith produced a total and confiding trust in the goodness of God. When
she presented Jesus in the temple and Simeon predicted a future sword would
pierce her heart on account of this child, Mary did not panic. She did not
look back, rather she prayed and pondered over these prophecies in her heart.
So anxious was she to enter into the mystery of God's holy Will in her regard
and to fulfill perfectly her role in God's plan for man's salvation.

When she lost her son for three days, there was only one preoccupation, one concentrated activity, to seek, find and be reunited to him. And when she found him and heard his explanation for remaining in the temple in the service of his heavenly father, though she did not fully understand, Mary nevertheless gave herself up to prayer, so as to ponder over God's ways in her heart. She does not only accept God's will; she grows in it to full holiness. Mary thus is a model for the religious in faith and fidelity to God's holy will, no matter what obstacles she must overcome to follow perfectly the ordinances of that holy will.

To Mary, model of perfect fidelity and permanent faithfulness to God's holy will can be applied the words of St. Paul when he is describing his own fidelity to his beloved Corinthians:

> Now is this my intention, did I show fickleness? Or are my plans made according to the flesh, so that with me it is now "Yes" and now "No"? God is my witness that our message to you is not both "Yes" and "No." For the Son of God, Jesus Christ, who was preached among you by us . . . was not now "Yes" and now "No," but only "Yes" was in Him. For all the promises of God find their "Yes" in him; and therefore through him also rises the "Amen" to God unto our glory."

Can we not literally say that all the promises find their "Yes" in Jesus Christ, because they first, at least chronologically found their "Yes" in the holy Mother of God, the faithful Mother of the Most Faithful Son?

And when we contemplate Mary in her greatest sorrow, when we behold the sword in her heart as she stands at the foot of the cross, we are moved to the depths of our being. For Mary the Mother of God remains the valiant woman in full resignation to the will of God. She accepts with her son the ignominy, torture, and death as a criminal on the cross because that is the Holy Will of God and of her divine Son: Moreover, in St. John the Evangelist, she welcomes, at her son's command, the whole human race as her children. This family she will nurture, protect, guide for the kingdom of her dying son, even though she fully understands that this very family has been the cause of the criminal crucifixion of her divine son. In the end Mary united herself with complete love and reverence to her son's farewell prayer: "Father, into thy hands I commend my spirit." For the vocation of Mary was to complement the vocation of her divine son, to consummate perfectly, faithfully the divine plan for the sanctification of man. Mary's fidelity to God is a perfect replica of her divine son's fidelity to the Father's will — total, unreserved, unconditional, unchangeable surrender of herself to God.

The faithfulness of consecrated religious

The more sublime a reality is, the greater is the danger connected with its abuse. Now the superb gift of freedom implies the risk of infidelity to God. For all men are tempted to fall back upon themselves as autonomous centers, asserting rights on things from others or breaking off intimate relations. But the religious communion and community is a gift from God. No mere human effort could achieve this social masterpiece. Plato tells us that people grow wings when they fall in love. And, as we saw in the beginning of this article, men and women who caught the vision of Christ left all things and flew after him. But, unfortunately, as the trials of life beset even the best of us, we seem to get used to God's indescribable gifts. One of the weaknesses of the "We-Community", the community of "You" and "I," is that it is a sort of bodiless community without any visible organs proper to it. But the community only catches hold of us and thrives within us, as it were, across the spiritual space and mysterious presence that exists between the "I" and the "Thou." In this particular case the "I" happens to be the individual religious and the "Thou" has to be Christ. If they are not together in love and fidelity, the whole community and its members will disintegrate.

Now St. Paul reminds us that all men suffer from the ambiguity of the divided will. This disjointed articulation of the will is one of the basic mysteries in man, the mystery of iniquity. And this disjunction tears man in opposite directions, now towards self isolation, now towards communion. And the press of our daily preoccupations, changes, events tends to engross the mind and will of man in what he calls the real, practical life. However, little by little man gets wrapped up in his work, likes, dislikes, fantasies, failures, successes, friends, enemies. In a word, man gets wrapped up in himself, herself and falls from communion to self-fascination. Shakespeare expressed this fall from communion and the ecstasy of love when he wrote: "Men are April when they woo, December when they wed." Many religious have become December in their religious lives. The dust of life and time has taken off the wonder, the shine of their marvelous vocation.

Our Divine Lord expressed this fall from enthusiastic faith in the parable of the Sower. The fickle who at first received the word of truth with eagerness fell back into the sleep of infidelity because they were choked by the cares and deceits of this world. Now the religious life and community when dulled by habit, or shaken by suffering, disillusionments and bitterness does tempt many religious to fall back upon themselves. They move to save themselves by abandoning a collapsing society. This flight into mediocrity, of course, will wear the garments of reasonableness. "I can serve God better in the world, closer to the people, uncluttered by the obsession of my own sanctification, unrestricted and isolated by my religious habit. Moreover, the Vatican Council has counselled letting down the bars, the walls of the convent, opening the windows and letting in the air of freedom. And anyway we religious have a right to happiness.''

Judas is an example of one who jumped a sinking ship and went on to self-destruction, though he was convinced at the time that he was saving himself. Let us analyze an historical example that will bring us strength. We have in the situation of St. Peter, confronted by the servant girl over his tie with Christ, an elucidation concerning the ontological role of permanent fidelity. ''You also were with Jesus the Galilean.'' As a matter of fact, Peter was with Jesus in the richest, most spiritual meanings that can be wrung from this intersubjective expression of communion and community. Yet Peter fled. He denied the bonds of knowledge, of co-presence, of collaboration, of natural and supernatural mutual love and communal living that had been enjoyed by him in the company of Christ. Peter swore he did not know the man. Formerly these bonds has riveted the two, Peter and Christ, to each other in the communion of sublime love. Now Christ, Peter's friend, needed Peter more than ever, for Christ was abandoned and on his way to execution. But Peter, seeking to save himself from a similar death, flees back to himself: ''I swear I do not know the man.''

Fidelity on Peter's part called for his public avowal of his ties with Christ. Permanent faithfulness demanded his prolongation of the presence of his friend in himself. Indeed it demanded an open defense of his friend and the manifestation of the many benefactions of his friend to himself and others. Had Peter performed, which he later on would do in a heroic degree, these acts of permanent fidelity, had he defended his friend faithfully and courageously in his trial, he would have participated in the very faithfulness of the Son of God, who was willingly giving himself up to death in order to obey and glorify His Father.

Peter's fidelity would have creatively multiplied and deepened within himself, while testifying before others to the unfathomable goodness of his friend, the presence and the goodness of the one who chosen him on the day he enlisted and eloped with Christ. For Peter's communion with Christ, his ardent reassertion of his ''We'' fellowship with Christ, originally rested on the instant he first crossed over to Christ. This intimate communion could only survive and wax strong on the instant to instant renewal of his confessing of Christ before men under fair or foul circumstances. For all fidelity is founded and constructed on a certain deeply felt commitment to indefectibility. Come what may, ''God must increase and I must decrease,'' in the words of the utterly faithful John the Baptist.[22] Even though religious know their own feebleness, even though they know that others often enough increase their own weakness by their defections, for this very reason the religious maintains the vows of consecration with constant prayer for strength. Would that Peter has heeded his Master's exhortation: ''Pray, lest you enter into temptation.''[23] Nor will the religious of permanent consecration allow the apparent extinction of death to tempt her to infidelity in her vows or obligations. Many flee religious life for a fling with the world in their middle ages, fearing that approaching death will put an end to the last chance to enjoy the world and thus end everything. Gabriel Marcel delineates the fidelity that conquers death in this splendid passage:

> Fidelity asserts herself never more truly than when she is challenging, defying, confronting an absence, when she is triumphing over this absence and, in particular, when she is conquering that absence that presents itself to us, doubtless falsely, as absolute absence — the absence known as death.[24]

The spouses of Christ living in the family of religious community are really living like the angels in heaven, with their fidelity. They neither marry nor are given in marriage. They have dedicated themselves to God in consecrated virginity. This is not a state of proud independence, nor of dreary selfishness, nor of notorious careerism, nor of crushed affections. This is a life of sublime freedom, of overwhelming love of God which draws men and women to rival the angels in their spousal dedication without ceasing to be human. This is the gift of ruling with God.

Let us close then with Cardinal Newman's words of wisdom to those who consecrate themselves irrevocably to God unto death:

> Just as the very idea of matrimony is possession, permanent, total possession, so too is the life of marriage to Jesus. It means to possess Christ totally, forever, with an indissoluble tie. It means to be His while he is ours, to go wherever the Lamb goes, to be marked with his sign, to wear his ring, to sing his special canticle, to be clothed in his spotless wedding garment. It means to participate in that wonderful sacrament, which united him to his Blessed Mother, I am my beloved's and my beloved is mine. He pastures his flock among the lilies. What a towering condescension, that the son of God should stoop to be ours, ours in a most intimate, most enduring way!... The Son of God becomes ours to love, ours to console, ours to converse with, ours to suffer with, ours to die and to reign with, ours so fully that it is as if he had none to think of but of each one of us personally and individually.[25]

In a life that is doomed to death, separation and bereavement, the religious permanently consecrated to Jesus are assured by their fidelity, that the day of the solemnity of their marriage to the Son of God is not far off and will last for eternity.

Notes

[1]Matt. 20:22.
[2]Newman, John Henry, *Parochial and Plain Sermons,* Vol. IV, p. 295.
[3]Ibid.
[4]Hebrews, 10:37.
[5]Ibid. 10:38.
[6]Ibid. 10:39.
[7]Ibid. 11:1.
[8]John, 14:1.
[9]Galatians, 2:20.
[10]Luke, 9:62.
[11]Rev. A. Vermeersch, S.J., "Modernism" Catholic Encyclopedia, 1913.
[12]Ibid.
[13]Isaias, 29:13.
[14]James, 1:25.
[15]Newman, John Henry, *Parochial and Plain Sermons,* Vol. II, pp. 278-79.
[16]Dietrich and Alice Von Hildebrand, *The Art of Living,* pp. 13 etc.
[17]John, 16:33.
[18]John, 15:14, 15.
[19]Newman, John Henry, *Meditations and Devotions,* pp. 521-22.
[20]Luke, 1:14, 15.
[21]2 Corinthians, 1:17-20.
[22]John, 3:30.
[23]Matt. 26:41.
[24]Gabriel Marcel, *Du refus a l'invocation,* p. 199.
[25]*Newman the Oratorian,* edited by Placid Murray, O.S.B., Sermon on the Occasion of Nuns Taking their Vows.

Children As Blessings

Blessed are you who fear the Lord who walk in his ways!...Your
wife shall be like a fruitful vine.... Your children like olive plants
around your table. Behold thus is the man blessed who fears the
Lord....May you see your children's children.

Psalm 128

This song is an outburst of joy that celebrates the blessings of family
life. The Psalmist congratulates the father of a family to whom the Lord
has given a fruitful wife and many sturdy children. He foresees as the climax
of this family's blessings a long life of prosperity and peace.

Time was when the birth of a baby in a Christian family was celebrated
as a "blessed event." Family, friends, Church and city gathered together
to rejoice over the new arrival in a liturgy of religious solemnity and musical
banqueting. The center of adoring attention was the bawling baby
announcing its presence as the new person, the radiant witness to the
conjugal love of its parents and to the faithful protection of its civic family.

The meaning of blessing

What is the meaning of blessing in Holy Scripture? If we trace the
notion of blessing from the beginning of sacred history through the Old
Testament, through the New Testament right up to the Lord's second
coming, we can see the connection between God's loving goodness and
his efforts to share that goodness by bestowing being and life on his chosen
creatures. Blessing comes freely, ultimately from God; it is God's choice
of a creature he wishes to make fruitful. On the fifth day of creation God
bestowed his blessing on the living creatures in the waters: "And he blessed
them, saying: 'Increase and multiply and fill the waters of the sea; and
let the birds be multiplied upon the earth.' "[1] But the Lord, the source
of all blessings, also bestows his favors on lower creatures as tokens of the
greater blessings he will pour out upon man, his favorite creature.

Examples of blessings

Thus on the sixth day, after he created man in his own image and
likeness as male and female, as man and wife, God blessed Adam and Eve
saying: "Increase and multiply and fill the earth, and subdue it, and rule
over the fishes of the sea and the fowls of the air and all the living creatures
that move upon the earth."[2] In this blessing God bestows on man a
participation in his own power of governing; he gives a special power to
man whereby man has the authority to call down blessings on the very
creatures he will use for his journey toward union with God. Thus Scripture

reveals that in the name of God a father can call down blessings upon his children. God blessed Abraham and Abraham blessed his son Isaac all in connection with God's plan for the generation of Isaac and the formation of the Chosen Race. The kings of Israel called down blessings upon their subjects; the priests of God called down blessings upon the Chosen People. Today the Catholic Church, founded by Jesus Christ, calls down blessings upon the whole universe, upon all men, especially upon all the faithful. Moreover, after all things had been created and found "good" by his loving providence, God blessed the seventh day on which the universe was completed, the day of his own repose. We have here God's blessing upon man's day of rest, the day of contemplation in which man was to participate in the divine serenity through union with God in liturgical prayer within his own family.

Now although God also blessed inanimate things, he did so only in relation to increasing and fructifying the life of man. Recall Christ's blessing of the five loaves and two fishes in order to feed his five thousand hungry, travel-worn listeners, he repeated this miracle on another occasion, blessing a scanty amount of food to feed, again unto satiety, four thousand, for all blessing is directed to living beings and they can multiply, can fructify inanimate realities which normally retain their measured beings only in order to revitalize the life of man.

Blessings and maledictions

Now God blessed living things with the special power of generation. For living things contain a secret source of life which flows from the mysterious gift God placed within their natures from their very beginning. It is to this mysterious capacity for creating new life that God's blessings are most often applied. In his physical realm God's blessings on man often increase the vitality of his body, spirit, mind and heart. In the realm of man's spirit God's blessings produce marvelous fruits in the intellectual and supernatural life of man. God's graces — another word for blessings — create mystics, martyrs, saints, doctors of the Church, holy heroes from mere men and women from all walks of life. For blessings stir the inner depths of the soul, unsealing hidden springs and resources for mighty feats of vitality and holiness.

Let us see how God's blessings are applied for the increase and growth of human life in its physical and spiritual dimensions. From the very moment man sinned, he worked to destroy the blessings of God. For the loving God who blesses being and life is the same just God who curses the nothingness of sin and death. Man sinned and God cursed him and with him the earth, its fruits, all his labors, even his wife's womb. "Dust you are and unto dust you shall return." Malediction is barrenness; it chills and locks the earth into petrifaction. It binds the fertile world into a thorn-encrusted, thistle-entrapped wasteland that runs to weeds. God's curse rendered life harsh, work brutal, nature sterile. Recall for a moment Christ's curse upon the barren fig tree which represented God's judgment on the spiritual sterility of Israel brought on the whole nation for its refusal to accept his Son's teachings and produce the fruits of holiness. The following day the Apostles were astonished at the sight of the dead tree which was withered to its very roots. "Rabbi, look!" exclaimed Peter, "the fig tree you cursed has withered up."[3] The curse of sin begets famines, floods, earth-quakes, tornadoes, hurricanes, plagues, wars — all the malevolent forces that threaten man with universal chaos.

Now since the blessing of God was frequently granted to bestow on man the special power of procreation, it is no wonder that among the Chosen People, indeed even among pagan peoples, a barren wife was thought to have been cursed by God. Rightly or wrongly, her sterility was considered to be a divine punishment for sin, for God's favors were seen to be poured down upon wives who begot many, healthy children. One of the promises God made to Abraham while his wife was still childless was that his offspring would be as numerous as the stars. And Abraham, hoping against hope, put his faith in God's promise to visit him with the blessing of a procreative fruitfulness that would challenge the stars in their infinite ubiquity. Thus God's blessing was seen as the power that released the fertility of a family and brought that family to a prosperous fulfillment in the Chosen People.

Thus the blessing of the child Isaac which God granted to Abraham and Sarah in their advanced old age was a miracle in answer to their prayers. Sarah exclaimed in her joy: "God has given me cause to laugh, and all who hear it will laugh with me. Who could have told Abraham that Sarah would nurse children in her old age?" Abraham was one hundred years old when Isaac was born. An angel had previously promised this blessed event: "Is anything too marvelous for the Lord to do?"[4]

Moses had predicted to the Israelites, on the eve of their entrance to the promised land, the blessings or curses they would experience depending on their fidelity to their God:

> Here then, I have today set before you life and prosperity, death and doom. If you obey the commandments of the Lord, your God...loving him and walking in his ways, and keeping his commandments, statutes and decrees, you will live and grow numerous, and the Lord, your God, will bless you in the land you are entering....If, however, you turn away your hearts and will not listen, but are led astray and adore and serve other gods, I tell you now you will certainly perish; you will not have a long life.... I call heaven and earth today to witness against you: I

have set before you life and death, the blessing and the curse.
Choose life, then, that you and your descendants may live by
loving the Lord, your God, heeding his voice and holding fast
to him.[5]

Then there was the wife of Manoah. He and his wife were a God-
fearing couple who lived when the Israelites were under the domination
of the Philistines. An angel of the Lord appeared to her and said: "Though
you are barren and have no children, yet you will conceive and bear a
son.... This boy is to be consecrated to the Lord from the womb. It is
he who will begin the deliverance of Israel from the power of the
Philistines."[6] That son was the mighty Samson who ruled and judged the
Israelites for twenty years and defeated the idolatrous Philistines.

In answer to Hannah's tearful prayers for a son, God removed her
sterility, and she begot Samuel who became a great prophet. Hannah then
broke out into a canticle of ecstatic thanksgiving which strongly resembles
in beauty Our Lady's Magnificat.[7] In the New Testament Luke relates
the blessing God bestowed on the aged, childless, sterile couple, Zechariah
and Elizabeth. An angel announced to the high priest Zechariah: "Do not
be afraid, Zechariah, your prayer has been heard. Your wife Elizabeth shall
bear a son whom you shall call John. Joy and gladness will be yours and
many will rejoice at his birth."[8] That child was John the Baptist, prophet
and precursor of the Messiah, Jesus Christ. At John's birth Zechariah,
filled with the Holy Spirit, broke out into a canticle of praise and prophecy
that also approaches in sublimity the Magnificat of Mary.[9] Here we see
how God's beneficent interventions made fruitful some holy but sterile
women who became mothers of sons famous in salvation history. God's
blessings always beget joy, grace, and the music and perfume of holiness
through the new lives he creates for spouses that are faithful in his service.

Jesus: fullness of blessing

But our consideration of the notion of blessing and its special relation
to the power of procreation leaves us so far merely on the periphery of
this inexhaustible mystery. Not until the angel Gabriel appears to Mary
do we even begin to suspect the profound meaning of blessing. Not until
the Incarnation and birth of Jesus Christ do we really appreciate the divine
connection between blessing and generation. All the blessings that God
showered upon mankind since the fall and before the advent of Christ merely
foreshadowed the ineffable blessing of the Incarnation and birth of the God-
Man. All blessings before, during, and after the temporal existence of Christ
were given to prepare for the human generation of Christ in the flesh and
for his final coming in power and glory when he will return redeemed
creation to his Father in heaven. For all blessings that have ever or will

ever be bestowed upon mankind and his universe are focussed in Jesus Christ, the Messiah, the Blessed One to whom "all power is given in heaven and on earth." He alone is the living fountain of salvation from whom all blessings stream. "I have come," exclaimed Christ, "that they may have life and may have it more abundantly."

The angel Gabriel indicated this to the Holy Virgin: "Blessed are you among women....Do not fear, Mary, you have found favor with God. You shall conceive and bear a son....Great will be his dignity and he will be called the Son of the Most High." When Mary, pregnant with God's and her own son, visited her cousin, who was also pregnant with John the Baptist, "Elizabeth, filled with the Holy Spirit, cried out in a loud voice: 'Blessed are you among women and blessed is the fruit of your womb.' " Then the Mother of God in her own ecstatic canticle of thanksgiving, the Magnificat, prophesied thus: "All generations shall call me blessed, for God who is mighty has done great things for me."[10]

Jesus Christ, the new Adam, begotten of Mary, the New Eve and Mother of all the living, is indeed the greatest "blessed event" God could have bestowed upon the human family. "Is it possible," exclaims St. Paul, "that he who did not spare his own son but handed him over for the sake of us all, will not grant us all things besides? If God is for us, who can be against us?" The sacrifice of Christ on the cross and at daily Mass is a blessing that guarantees our reconciliation, justification, predestination and glorification in God. Christ, our Blessing, has cancelled the curse of God caused by man's sin; he restores both man's physical and divine life; he blesses bread and wine daily and transforms them into man's super-natural nourishment; he begets, strengthens, and multiplies the family of the communion of saints; his whole life and being is one infinite blessing whereby he transforms sinners into saints, children of the earth into children of God, sons and daughters of his heavenly Father. The blessed life of Christ opens up mankind to a fertility undreamed of in this world, a super-abundance of divine life that comes solely from his own redemptive love; for now where once the death of sin abounded, because of him the life of grace superabounds; where once the curse of Satan tormented men, now the blessings of Christ sanctify them.

Christ and children

In chapter ten Mark describes how children are brought to Christ for his blessing. The Lord is indignant at those who would chase them away from him. "Let the little children come to me, and do not hinder them, for of such is the kingdom of heaven." When the children are brought to him, he embraces them, lays his hands on their heads and blesses them.[11] Without a doubt Christ blesses them in their physical and emotional development, in their earthly destinies. But, above all, his blessing penetrates to the core of their beings, deeper than their merely corporal well-being, or warmth of heart, or earthly success. Jesus' blessing centers their whole beings in the profundity of the Godhead which is the fountain-head of all personal holiness, for, as St. John writes to the early Christians: "God's love was revealed in our midst in this way; he sent his only son to the world that we might have life through him."

The rejection of children

Unfortunately, today the new birth that used to be hailed as a "blessed event" is too often stigmatized as "an unwanted baby." There is an appalling degradation in society's unconcern for the sacredness and dignity of human life. More and more spouses are seeking "liberation from the tyranny of having to beget and raise children." In the words of Ashley Mòntagu: "It is necessary to be unequivocally clear concerning the distinc- tion between sexual behavior and reproductive behavior. Sexual behavior may have no purpose other than pleasure, without the slightest intent of reproducing....Orgasmic pleasure and interpersonal affection have now become the most important meaning and end of human sexuality."[12]

The result of this self-centered separation of the amative from the procreative dimension of sexual intercourse has been an alarming increase in the number of divorces, a raging escalation in the scourge of abortions, a wide-spread recourse to sterilization and a growing approval of all forms of unnatural sexual life styles — homosexuality, lesbianism, incest and even bestiality. Such a sterile, malevolent, barren, contraceptive, anti-life mentality is leading a decadent world down the road to social suicide. All over the world, but especially in the so-called Christian nations of the West, millions upon millions of fetal babies are legally slaughtered each year. Their cadavers are thrown back into the face of the God of love who created them with this message for the Author of their lives: "We reject these unwanted, unloved biologial appendages of our sexual activity!" Everywhere the curse of Cain is attempting to obliterate the kiss of Christ.

Because of such a cruel, anti-life mentality millions of couples are refus- ing to share in the procreative blessings that are bestowed on them by the love of their own Creator. They are rejecting God's call to a free, respon- sible cooperation with him as our universal Father in the transmitting of the gift of human life to their children. They are willfully blocking the fun- damental purpose of family life, the actualization in history of the original blessing of the Creator — that of transmitting by procreation the divine image from their own persons to the persons of their offspring, for in the beginning, "God blessed them, and God said to them: 'Be fruitful and multiply, and fill the earth and subdue it.' "

Pope John Paul in his Apostolic Exhortation, *Familiaris Consortio* (The Role of the Christian Family in the Modern World), exposes the taproot of this wicked flight from family responsibility:

> At the root of these negative phenomena there frequently lies a corruption of the idea and the experience of freedom, conceived not as a capacity for realizing the truth of God's plan for marriage and the family, but as an autonomous power of self-affirmation, often against others, for one's own selfish being.[13]

The explosion of licentiousness in sex is creating a heartless, affection-less society, in which nobody cares for anyone but himself, or for anything but instant self-gratification. Today there is a demand for sex without love, for violence just for the fun of it; we are blunting sensibility and are well on the way to legalized slaughter through abortion and euthanasia. Rome before Christianity was both profligate and brutal; the Christian West is living in a post-pill paradise; it has created a venal, coarse, heartless quality of life addicted to limitless hedonism in a vain attempt to enjoy an otherwise meaningless life. Sex has become by turns the toy, the glue, the trauma, the therapy, the hope, the frustration, the revenge, the narcotic, the main line of communication, the sole pitiable shield against the awareness of death. Increasingly secularist in outlook, sex-ridden and selfish, the new post-Christian barbarians have created a society dominated by harsh greed, insatiable sex, delirious violence and colossal pride. Such is our society, that only knows how to solve social problems with the policy of murder.

Children: the blessings of marriage

God the Creator, modelling the human family on his own divine family of Father, Son and Holy Spirit, ordained married life as the principle and foundation of domestic love and community. He willed that from the mutual, holy love of benevolence between the spouses the human family would be founded, increased, and multiplied. Children were to be the loving, radiant witnesses of the faithful love of their parents. Nay, even more, children were to be at the same time, the blessed witnesses of God's eternal love for the human family. Pope John Paul expresses this truth in a sublime fashion:

> According to the plan of God, marriage is the foundation of the wider community of the family, since the very institution of marriage and conjugal love are ordained to the procreation and education of children, in whom they find their crowning.
>
> In its most profound reality, love is essentially a gift; and conjugal love, while leading the spouses to the reciprocal "knowledge" which makes them "one flesh," does not end

with the couple, because it makes them capable of the greatest possible gift, the gift by which they become cooperators with God for giving life to a new human person. Thus the couple, while giving themselves to one another, give not just themselves but also the reality of children, who are a living reflection of their love, a permanent sign of conjugal unity and a living and inseparable synthesis of their being a father and mother.

When they become parents, spouses receive from God the gift of a new responsibility. Their parental love is called to become for the children the visible sign of the very love of God, ''from whom every family in heaven and on earth is named.''[14]

Conclusion

It is always salutary to remind the human family, especially when it is tempted to dethrone God and turn its institutions against him, that ''unless the Lord builds the house, then in vain do the workmen labor.'' The mission of being the primary, sacred cell of society has been given to the family by God himself. This mission can only be accomplished if the family, by the mutual affection of its members, and by family prayer presents itself as a domestic sanctuary of the Church. These then are the blessings God wills for the Christian family — loving offspring, permanent conjugal love and fidelity, and the holy Sacrament of Matrimony whereby the family participates in the Church's sanctifying liturgical worship and receives the grace to practice the spiritual and corporal works of mercy.

For those unrepentant, fallen away Christian families who have reduced marriage to being a sterile exercise for refining the pleasures of the flesh, it is absolutely necessary to remind them that God's providence for bestowing blessings and imposing maledictions will continue until the end of time. Eventually eternal blessing or eternal malediction will seal the destiny of every person. On those families who have believed in the name of Christ and have tried to live the love of Christian family life, Christ their Brother will bestow his final blessing: ''Come blessed of my Father, take possession of the kingdom prepared for you from the foundation of the world.''[15] But on those families who have rejected the name of Christ and closed themselves to the love of Christian family life, Christ their Judge will impose their final curse: ''Depart from me, Accursed One, into the everlasting fire which was prepared for the devil and his angels.''[16]

Notes

[1]Gen. 1:20.
[2]Gen. 1:24.
[3]Mark 11:12-21.
[4]Gen. 21:6; 18:14.
[5]Deut. 29:15-29.
[6]Judges 13:2-5.
[7]I Sam. 2:1-10.
[8]Luke 1:13-15.
[9]Luke 1:67-79.
[10]Luke 1:46-55.
[11]Mark 10:13-16.
[12]Ashley Montagu, *Sex, Man, and Society*, pp. 13-14.
[13]Pope John Paul II, *Familiaris Consortio*, No. 6.
[14]Ibid. No. 14.
[15]Matt. 25:34.
[16]Matt. 25:41.

Reprinted from *Fidelity*, June, 1983.

The Church and the Family

If you split the atom, the smallest unit of matter, tremendous physical disaster results from the explosive forces released. If you split the family, the smallest, sacred unit of society, tremendous social disaster results from the explosive passions released. If you split the Church, the only unit of salvation, tremendous, eternal disaster results from the satanical forces released. Now there is no law against splitting the atom. But God Himself forbids the splitting of the family: "What God has joined together, let no man put asunder." From the very beginning the Creator has decreed: "...A man shall leave his father and mother and cleave to his wife, and the two shall become one flesh." And the Son of God Himself, founder and head of the Catholic Church, says: "He who is not with me is against me; and he who does not gather with me, scatters."

Thus God has planned that the peace and holiness of the family should consist in a unity of mind, heart, soul and body between spouses and their children. And this peace should be expressed, or be the fruit of the mutual love of the family members for each other, a love founded on their love for God. But the marriage house in which all families are to be sanctified in permanent faith and love is to be the divine house built on a rock in which house of the living God, all Christian souls and families, united by the bond of faith and charity, would become citizens and saints of the Catholic Church. Such is the marvelous, loving plan of God for the family of mankind. But, unfortunately, today sin has struck at the family of man and of the Church.

Today the family is under violent attack. Some deny the sacramental character of marriage; some deny the unity and permanence of the marriage bond. Others deny the true purpose of marriage — the mutual love of the spouses, their generation of children and their education of the children to Christian virtue. Instead marriage has been thoroughly secularized where it has not been paganized and perverted. The purpose of marriage is said to be recreation, pleasure, or position, or power or money. As a result the divorce courts, the birth-control clinics and the abortion mills give blood-curdling evidence of the moral decay that has already sapped the spiritual fiber of our generation. One out of every two marriages in the U.S. ends in a broken home. Easy pre-marital sex, begun as a habit on the campuses of universities, has led to a massive escalation in mere cohabitational unions. In an age that is experimenting with sex, unnatural lesbian and homosexual marriages have been legalized by the laws of so-called civilized and Christian nations. Even the marriage courts of certain Catholic dioceses in the U.S. are handing out annulments on such a large scale that the Holy See had to make investigations to see whether the whims of disenchanted spouses are being catered to rather than the sacredness of the marriage bond being protected.

Things have gotten so bad world-wide on the level of family life that the British *Observer Color Magazine* had to make the enquiry: "Are We the Last Married Generation?" In its inquiry, the editors wrote: "Now for the first time marriage itself is being eyed for its possible unsuitability to human nature. . . . Marriage will have to disintegrate. It's too demanding and crippling. And children are really self-sufficient at fourteen. . . ."

Commenting on the survey as a whole in the *Observer* of Oct. 1, 1967, Katharine Whitehorn wrote:

> At one time at least (in Victorian times) the whole social framework did ensure that once you had taken the plunge and got married you were stuck with it: as you made your bed so did you lie in it — or at worst had a bed made up in the dressing room. Nobody said, "There, there, dear, it was just a boyish mistake," and you got out of it; nobody thought that if you shut your eyes and took a deep breath your wife and children would simply disappear like spots before your eyes. Yet that is often what I feel the softies of the modern age expect.
>
> . . . They are liberal enough to sympathize, when talking about a distressed friend or criminal, with the problems of children of broken homes — and then go right ahead and organize a broken home for their own. . . .
>
> . . . I would like, just once, to hear someone say of a man who has left his wife and four fat babies in the middle of the kitchen floor, *not* that he's been through a hard time lately, or that his mother was a very complicated woman, or that he's worried about his job, or that he married very young; but simply, "You louse."

The explosion of licentiousness in sex is creating a heartless, affectless society, in which nobody cares for anyone but himself, for anything but instant self-gratification. Today there is a demand for sex without love, for violence just for the fun of it; we are blunting sensibility and are well on the way to another Auschwitz through the legalized slaughter mills of abortion and euthanasia. Rome before Christianity was both profligate and brutal; the Christian West living in a Post-Pill paradise, has created a venal, profligate, coarse, heartless quality of life addicted to limitless hedonism in a vain attempt to enjoy an otherwise meaningless life. Sex has become by turns the toy, the glue, the trauma, the therapy, the hope, the frustration, the revenge, the narcotic, the main line of communication, the sole, pitiable shield against the awareness of death. Increasingly secularist in outlook, sex-ridden and selfish, the new post-Christian barbarians have created a society dominated by harsh greed, insatiable sex, delirious violence and colossal pride. St. Paul described the contemporary post-Christian West when he wrote to the Romans. Little did he know that the wheel would come full circle and his words, directed against pagan pre-Christian Rome, would apply even more forcibly to a decadent, post-Christian West which had once known and loved the Gospel of Jesus Christ. Here is what he wrote to the pagan Romans:

> ...Although they had the knowledge of God, they did not honor him or give thanks to him as God; they became fantastic in their notions and their senseless hearts grew benighted; they, who claimed to be wise, turned fools, and exchanged the glory of the imperishable God for representations of perishable man, of bird and beast and reptile. This is why God abandoned their lustful hearts to filthy practices of dishonoring their own bodies amongst themselves. They had exchanged God's truth for a lie, reverencing and worshiping the creature in preference to the Creator (blessed is he forever, Amen); and, in return, God abandoned them to passions which brought dishonor to themselves. Their women exchanged natural for unnatural intercourse; and men, on their side, giving up natural intercourse with women, were burnt up with desire for each other; men practicing vileness with their fellowmen. Thus they have received a fitting retribution for their false belief.
>
> And as they scorned to keep God in their view, so God had abandoned them to a frame of mind worthy of all scorn, that prompts them to disgraceful acts. They are versed in every kind of injustice, knavery, impurity, avarice, and ill-will; spiteful, murderous, contentious, deceitful, depraved, backbiters, slanderers, God's enemies; insolent, haughty, vainglorious; inventive in wickedness, disobedient to their parents; without prudence, without honor, without love, without loyalty, without pity. Yet, with the just decree of God before their minds, they never grasped the truth that those who so live are deserving of death; not only those who commit such acts, but those who countenance such a manner of living.

How modern society was undermined

How was modern society so undermined spiritually that it could create not only the Secular City of Man but now the Sacrilegious City of Satan? The downward course is based on man's rebellion against God and the divinization of himself in place of God.

The Protestant Revolution broke the harmony of the Catholic family. It rebelled against the dogmatic, moral, sacramental teachings of the Church and substituted the revolutionary principle of "private interpretation" in matters of religion. Thus God's revelation was left to the judgment of the individual, not to the authority He established in His Son and St. Peter together with the bishops of His Church. Religious revolution led easily to political revolution and to philosophical revolution.

The French Revolution of 1789 was launched ideologically by Rousseau and the Encyclopedists, deists and enemies of the Church, who idolized man's individual liberty into an absolute autonomy. For them man was no longer bound by the natural law, nor political, economic, religious nor social bonds. Self-interest was his ruling motive for action, replacing justice. This revolution quite naturally led to the horrible Reign of Terror which ruled men through the violence of the guillotine. Liberty, Justice, Equality were divinized as goddesses in a religion of idolatry. Natural humanism led to man's inhumanity to man.

Then the 19th century socialists, now openly-confessed atheists, pushed absolute freedom for man in another direction — the social, utopian, egalitarian dimension of man. Following Fourier and Saint Simon, Proudhon set revolution in opposition to revelation; the secular society he pitted against the Church. For him collective reason, created and formed in the dialogue of Socialism, would guide mankind to happiness. The Church, theology, religious life, religion itself would have to be dissolved in the interests of the socialized revolution. Proudhon was not only an atheist; he was an active enemy of God and of the Church; he was an anti-theist.

Enter Karl Marx with his militant atheism of the masses. His revolution is economic; man must be freed from capitalistic and religious exploitation. Man's hope for happiness lies in the revolution, the class warfare conducted by the proletariat. The dictatorship of the proletariat, once having destroyed all bourgeois governments and the established religions, would develop into the abolition of all classes, into the creation of the happiness of the classless society.

We come finally to the complete individual and social liberation of man by his fullest revolution against God. Freud taught man to liberate himself from sexual repressions which are at the root of his fears and failures. Religion and God are the causes of the collective neurosis of man. The sexual revolution will dissolve these causes and thus break down the collective neurosis. Then Wilhelm Reich went further in proclaiming the necessity of a sexual revolution which will create "a revolutionary morality of sexual drives," one freeing man from capitalistic morality, the repressive morality of the dominating class. Aiding this cultural and sexual revolution of man will be the widespread use of contraception; the right to free and financed abortion; the right to trial-marriage; the right to experiment in sexual experience; the right to homosexual, lesbian activities and marriages; the right to beget children technologically in test tubes. Only through these means will man attain his right to total liberation.

Thus for revolutionary man the meaning of world history is not the salvation of man by God-become-man, but rather that meaning is the creation and salvation of man through his own human work. Indeed man, as his own creator will be finally totally free when he conquers or escapes utterly from *time*. For Marcuse, a contemporary Marxist, tells us that "the fatal enemy of man's lasting gratification is *time,* the inner finiteness." Claude Lanzman, another disciple of Marx, affirms the same thought, not in terms of internal finitude, but in terms of man's final end and goal. "In transcending the limits the world imposes upon us, man conquers both the world and himself ....Man's will has become the very reason for his existence. Thus there is no end for man higher than himself. There is no other end for man than man himself. Man is his own beginning and end, his own Alpha and Omega." Man has escaped into eternity, the timeless freedom from all dependence, pressure, subordination. This is the final cult, the only religion, the idolatry of man. His total liberation now is no longer merely individual, not even social, but his complete liberation now is metaphysical, ontological. Totally liberated man is no longer individually, socially, economically, politically, physically or materially or even spiritually dependent on anyone. He has ceased to be a creature. He has escaped all subordination and dependence. He is at once his own creator and his own god.

Now man's social attitudes on the fundamental relationship of family life, his just claims and moral obligations therein, are determined by his care or carelessness about his relationship with God. As a rebel against God, man then turns all his institutions, especially his family, against God. In dethroning God, he degrades his own family life. Even atheist Socialist Proudhon had to marvel at how all human problems, especially political and social ones, were assumed into theology. In his *Confessions of a Revolutionary,* Proudhon wrote: "It is a cause of wonderment to see how in all our political problems we invariably stumble up against theology." But Donoso Cortes, in his essay "On Catholicism, Liberalism and Socialism," commenting on Proudhon's wonderment at God's presence everywhere in politics, wrote: "There is nothing here that should cause surprise except the surprise of Proudhon. For theology, by the very fact that it is the science of God, is the Ocean that contains and embraces all the sciences, just as God is the Ocean that contains and embraces all things." And it was the great St. Augustine who said that in its roots every serious political or social problem has a causal nexus with faith or lack of faith in God. The Psalmist long ago had written: "Unless the Lord builds the house, they labor in vain who build it." This is a truth that applies to families, nations and to the Church.

What God wills for the family

God the Creator, modelling the human family on His own divine Family of Father, Son and Holy Spirit, ordained the human family as the principle and foundation of domestic love and community. He willed that from this pure, holy love the human race would increase and multiply. But when the family of man fell into sin, God sent His Son as a man to raise the sacred, though now sinful, family of man, to the rank of a truly sanctifying sacrament of the New Law. He promoted the human family to a degree of honor beyond its original sacredness, making it now a doubly-divine institution, first as issuing from God's love in creation, second as rising from the death of sin in the Son of God's love in re-creation or redemption. Moreover, God now, through the will of His divine Son-made-man, entrusted all the care and discipline of the family to His Son's spouse, the Catholic Church.

The Second Vatican Council clearly explains the sublime vocation of Catholic spouses; "Christian couples are for each other, for their children and for their relatives, cooperators of grace and witnesses of the faith. They are the first to pass on the faith to their children and to educate them in it. By word and example they form them to a Christian and apostolic life; they offer them wise guidance in their choice of vocation, and if they discover in them a sacred vocation, they encourage it with all care."

The Council continues: "To give clear proof in their own lives of the indissolubility and holiness of the marriage bond; to assert with vigor the right and duty of parents and guardians to give their children a Christian upbringing; to defend the dignity and legitimate autonomy of the family: this has always been the duty of married persons; today, however, it has become the most important aspect of their apostolate. They and all the faithful, therefore, should collaborate with men of good will in seeing that these rights are perfectly safeguarded in civil legislation; that in social administration consideration is given to the requirements of families in the matter of housing, education of children, working conditions, social security and taxes; and that in emigration regulations family life is perfectly safeguarded."

"The mission of being the primary and vital cell of society has been given to the family by God Himself. This mission is accomplished if the family, by the mutual affection of its members, and by family prayer presents itself as a domestic sanctuary of the Church." These then are the blessings God wills for the Christian family — loving offspring, conjugal faith and fidelity and the sacrament of Matrimony whereby the family takes part in the Church's sanctifying liturgical worship, receives the grace to practice the spiritual and corporal works of mercy, is moved to adopt abandoned children, receives loving strangers, helps in the running of schools, supports adolescents with advice and help, assists engaged couples to prepare well for marriage, shares in the teaching of catechism to children and non-Catholics, supports married people and families in material or moral crises, and aids the aged in every way possible.

The church and the family

Now outside Christianity all is not corrupt, far from it. All is not corrupt, but what does not remain childlike is always in peril of going astray because of the weakened condition of mankind produced by original sin — the darkening of the intellect, the weakening of the will, the revolt of the passions, the pride of life, the concupiscence of the eyes and the concupiscence of the flesh. Outside Christianity nothing attains its end. However high it climbs, it moves without Christ towards its ultimate collapse. For the only end towards which all human endeavors, all human desires, even if unknowingly, are in movement *is the embrace of God in Christ.* This is especially true of the movement known as the human family. As the most admirable, most widespread and the most vigorous of human endeavors, the human family absolutely needs to be impregnated with Christianity, if it is to bear permanent temporal and eternal fruit. The Church is therefore necessary for the moral rectitude and supernatural sanctity of the human family. Without the Church, the human family becomes a great void crying out for the plenitude of peace, joy and holiness that only God can give it through His Church. Outside Christianity, humanity tries to collect its members in family or state unities. Throughout the centuries this powerful instinct to live together compels mankind to avoid the chaos of isolation, dispersal, conflict, collisions, competitions, wars and to strive for social integration, harmony and a common life in peace and trust and security. But left to itself humanity cannot overcome all the opposing forces which are everywhere at work, forces within itself and outside itself, always at work to destroy individuals and the society of men. Cities expand, yet are always closed societies; they combine together but only to fight more bitterly with one another, and beneath their outward unity, there is always the personal enmity of souls within them. "Unless the Lord builds the house they labor in vain who build it."

But only the Church is that divine house built upon a rock. She is the marriage house in which men are permanently joined to each other in peace because she is the marriage house in which heaven is joined to earth in justice and sanctity. The Church, Spouse of Christ, is the household in which all men are gathered together to eat of the Lamb; to offer the true sacrifice to God. Hence the Church is the household where the family finds moral rectitude, spiritual peace, holiness and divine nourishment. Only in the Family of Christ, the Church, can the human family bring its divine mission to eternal fruition. It is only through the leavening of the Gospel within the Catholic Church and by the aid of the Holy Spirit that the human family can be established in the peace of Chirst as the Beloved One of God.

Conclusion

It appears that the post-Christian paganized West has lost its transcendent motive for "fighting the good fight for the faith," for finishing an honorable course. Not having kept the faith within its own soul, its institutions — and especially its families — are now morally paralyzed with the rot of infidelity and moral perversion. The West is incapable of projecting a cogent program for family and political peace with dignity and sanctity. When will it cease being unfaithful? When will it come back as the prodigal son and accept God's grace as the only cure for its spiritual exhaustion? With the escalation of violence, crime, confusion, licentiousness, wars and rumors of wars emanating from religious apostasy, family infidelity, political intrigue and disengagement, the stage seems set for the coming of the Antichrist, the final enemy of the human family of mankind. True, his name and his time are known only to God. But the portents of his nearness are evident everywhere in the general desertion of the faith. Still agnostic and atheist sophisticates will smile patronizingly at our prophecies of doom concerning the Antichrist's coming in a pestilence of heresies, preternatural heroics and cosmic wars. Of course, progressist Christians will join the intellectual scoffers. It was thus in the days of Noe who was laughed to scorn as he built his ark of salvation. It was thus in the days of Abraham as he pleaded fruitlessly with Sodom and Gomorrah to give up their sexual perversions and return to God. It was thus in the days of Christ as He wept over the city of Jerusalem. All these unfaithful skeptical societies were wiped out violently. It will be thus at the end of time. For the wicked societies and depraved families are too proud to accept and follow the ways of God.

Catholics must invite Jesus and Mary and Joseph to their weddings. Their homes and families must always be founded before and upon the altars of God, in the presence of His ambassadors to whom Christ said: "And when you enter a house, salute it saying, 'Peace be to this house.' " This peace is begun in the sacrament of Matrimony. It is continued in the home at the family prayers and rosary, the dedication of the family and home to the Sacred Heart of Christ. The Christian home must love and rear its children, in the words of St. Paul, "in the discipline and service of God." Catholics must use every moral, political and legitimate means to fight contraception, birth control, abortion, euthanasia and all sexual perversions permitted by a corrupt society. Catholics must be convinced that marriage and family life in the Church — a life in Christ, with Christ, through Christ — is for husband, wife and children the high road to heaven and sanctity. Christian family life is a sublime vocation, a call from God to serve Him and our fellowmen, to do good in society for the peace of Christ for all men. Pope Pius XII has said: "The Christian home must be preserved — that rock on which is raised the fear of God, unbroken fidelity, temperance, love, the peace and holiness of Christ. To save the Christian family is the chief task of the Catholic" (Italian Cath. Action, Sept. 7, 1947). For the Christian family can save society from committing social suicide both spiritually and physically.

Indeed only saintly Christian families can give the example and inspiration needed for a universal reconciliation of mankind with God and His Church. Such faithful Christian families will form little islands of holiness everywhere, but especially in their homes which, *as domestic sanctuaries of the Church,* will surely but slowly re-Christianize a neopagan society, even as the little band and family of Jesus Christ — the early Church in its own disciples — first Christianized the pagan Roman Empire. The secret, most effective weapon of the Catholic Church for saving the world is the Christian family living the life of Christ in modern times of perversion. The Christian family is the light of the world, the salt of the earth, the leaven of salvation.

Hence the motto of every Christian home should embody these sentiments:

Christ is the unseen Head of this home
The Welcome Guest at every meal
The silent inspiration and listener to every conversation.

Reprinted from *The Church and the Family,* 1979

Christ As Blessed Event

"For in truth He did not take on the nature of Angels, but He took on Himself the seed of Abraham." (Hebrews 2:16)

No single event rejuvenates more a human family than the birth of a child. The Psalmist sings the blessings that flood the family that fears the Lord. "Blessed are you who fear the Lord, who walk in His ways... Your wife shall be like a fruitful vine...Your children like olive plants around your table...May you see your children's children." (Psalm 128)

Clearly children are blessings because they are loved and created by God. Time was when the birth of a baby was celebrated as a "blessed event." Family, friends, church and city celebrated with liturgical solemnity and civic banqueting. The center of adoration was the bawling baby announcing its arrival as a new person, a radiant witness to the conjugal love of its parents and the creative love of God. For all blessings come freely, generously from God. Blessing is God's choice of creatures, His Will to call them into existence from nothingness and to make them fruitful beings He plans to sanctify and glorify.

St. Augustine was flabbergasted before the mystery of God's love of preference in creating some beings and not others. "Why me and not many others He knew, could have chosen but did not?" His answer is: "Because God is good I exist." But the mystery involved is: *loves does such things.* And there is no fathoming the "Why?" of the infinite Love of God. Before this love the heart of man is aroused, inflamed while his mind bogs down in an intellectual impasse. For the greatest blessings spring not from the intellect but from the heart; the first and final word of the whole of creation is not "I know you," but "I love you." God's love is His own mysterious, incomprehensible divine nature. The awesomeness and glory of this truth is so overwhelming that to anyone who will not gratefully accept this love as the only absolute point of departure of all created blessings, the manifestation of any blessings must seem the most senseless folly.

But our consideration of the notion of blessing and its special relation to the generation of children leaves us only on the periphery of this inexhaustible mystery. Not until the birth of Christ do we even begin to suspect the profound meaning of blessing. Christmas gives us a real appreciation of the divine connection between blessing and the birth of children. For all the blessings God showered upon mankind since the creation and the fall before the birth of Christ merely foreshadowed the ineffable blessing of the Incarnation and birth of the God-Man. Here again the understanding is stymied by the incredible love of God. Here is a father who sends his son into human history to take up human nature in a humiliating fashion as a slave and to sacrifice it in an ignominious death as a criminal on the cross. The blessing of this death revives man from the death of sin to the life of grace. And there is more joy among the angels over the rebirth of one sinner in the life of grace than over the continued life of grace in the ninety-nine just. Such is the blessed event of the birth of a sinner into the life of God. *Love does such things.* All the blessings ever bestowed or that will be bestowed on man are given to prepare for the birth of Christ in the flesh and for His coming in power and glory. For all blessings are focussed in the Christ Child. He is the Messiah, the Blessed One par excellence to whom "all power is given in heaven and on earth." From this living fountain of all blessings issues the truth: "I am come that they may have life and may have it more abundantly."

Thus as we Christians rejoice in our annual liturgical flashback to the Crib of Christ, we should strengthen our faith by reflecting on the marvelous realities that God reveals in the birth of His Son. The Child in Mary's arms is the Son of God; Mary is the Mother of God and the New Mother of all the living. The Child is also the Son of Man for by assuming human nature He took up the nature of every one of us. As the Son of Adam He is our brother. Nay more, He is the New Adam who restores our fallen brotherhood in His own Sacred Humanity and raises it to a divine brotherhood in the family of the Holy Trinity. "For He took not hold of angels, but He took hold of the seed of Adam, of the offspring of Abraham." For from all eternity Divine Love decreed that "the Word" should be "made flesh." Thus the God-Child in the manger is the greatest "blessed event" that could possibly be bestowed upon man. "Is it possible," exclaims St. Paul, "that He who did not spare His own Son but handed Him over for the sake of us, will not grant us all things besides?" Only Divine Love is capable of granting such mind-boggling blessings. Let us remember that the Child in the crib condescended in ineffable love to empty himself of the trappings of divinity. He accepted trials and temptations in the condition of His human nature. He became one of us in all things, sin alone excepted. And though He was and remained God from all eternity, as the Only-begotten Son of His Father, yet He took within Himself the thoughts, affections, infirmities of each of us, thereby, through the fullness of His divine nature, raising these thoughts and affections to His Father and Our Father, and destroying our infirmities in His expiatory death, a death which resuscitated man from his own death in the history of the fall and raised him to a higher life in the history of his divine recovery.

The Child in the manger assumed our human nature in order to redeem it; He redeemed it by subjecting it to suffering in His own Divine Person; He purified it in His own expiatory sacrifice; He first sanctified it in Himself, made it holy, made it acceptable to God by wholly submitting His life to the Will of His Father and then shared that Sacred Humanity with us. He took it, consecrated it, broke it, and said: "Take and eat, take and divide it among yourselves." And thus by the Son of God becoming man, men, through communion with Him, through brotherhood with Him, became as gods. The new Child in the stall of Bethlehem is a human being, with a human brain and limbs and heart and soul. And yet He is also God. Those who claim that Christ did not know He was God, but only gradually came to such a realization, are maintaining an impossible intellectual posture. For all acts of intelligent beings are acts of the person. *I* know; *I* think; *I* love. But there is only one Person in the Christ Child, the Second Person of the Blessed Trinity, the Word, the Only-begotten of the Father. Now is it possible that a Divine Person be ignorant of Who He is? To claim so is to perform the mental gymnastics of trying to unite, to make reasonable a metaphysical contradiction. A Divine Person is always all-knowing; but Christ is always a Divine Person; therefore, Christ always knew who He was and is, namely a Divine Person, i.e., God.

The Christ Child came to manifest the Will of His Father, to proclaim sacred tidings, to stir mankind with the power of God, to establish a New Covenant and shoulder the sins of the world, expiating them with infinite love and raising mankind through the degradation and death on Calvary, through the victory of the Resurrection, into a new creation and new birth in the divine life of grace. In this accomplishment alone lay the self-perfection of Jesus, the Son of Man. In this accomplishment alone lay the redemption and perfection of His brethren. The fulfillment of His mission achieved the perfection of His Sacred Humanity and of the human nature common to every child of Adam. He is the First Born of many brethren, the First Infinite Blessed Event of every other blessed event in the communion of saints. Christ Himself points out how His sufferings perfected His and our humanity: "Did not Christ have to suffer these things before entering His glory?" And we His brethren must also ask: "Do not the brethren of Christ have to purify their human nature in His cross before they can rejoice in His crown of glory?"

He who created the cosmos occupies a crib. This birth of the Son of God as a man is so profound a mystery of love that the angels remain in stunned and awed ecstasy at it for all eternity. And that is why we humans are happy on this blessed night. Even though we may be poor, or tired, or fearful over the threat of war for our loved ones; even though we may not be in the best of health; even though we may be worried over the cares and trials of life, yet on this wonderful night there dwells deep within our hearts a sense of joy, of peace, of happiness. And we are happy because we are living an old story, a story as ancient as the hills, yet as new, fresh and scintillating as the most recent brilliant sunrise. And we are happy not merely as isolated individuals. Far from it. We are joyful as members of a family. For tonight a son is born to us. Jesus Christ, who is born of the Father from all eternity, is born into our human family today. Ages ago, Isaias foretold this blessed event: "A Child is born to us and a Son is given to us. And government is upon His shoulders. And His name shall be called Wonderful Counsellor, Mighty God, Father Forever, Prince of Peace."

Yet tonight there is something wonderfully strange about this youngest son. Unlike our other children, upon whom we parents bestow life and all the blessings of body and soul, this marvelous Child appears within our midst as the Giver of all good gifts to his new family. He delights men with the gift of divine life, of divine sonship, of divine friendship, of divine inheritance. In His birth human persons have become partakers of the divine nature, a royal priesthood, a holy nation, heirs of heaven destined for the intimate unveiled embrace of the Holy Trinity for all eternity. For today God the Father makes all things new in His and our divine Son. Thus the angels break through the vault of the heavens, singing and heralding not merely an old story, but an up-to-the-minute story, a scoop that is happening today, at this instant. St. Leo the Great writes: "Today there is shining upon us a day of new redemption, a day restoring that which was lost long ago, a day of bliss unending." And the Church sings at Holy Mass: "A day of salvation, a day sanctified by mystery, a day full of divine and sanctifying power is shining upon us. Alleluia, Alleluia."

The saints of all ages, gazing lovingly, even as we do now, upon God in our flesh, enthusiastically tell us over and over again with St. Cyprian that "what man is, Christ wished to be that man, in his turn, might be what Christ is." Or as St. Augustine so forcefully expresses the same truth: "God has become man that man might become God." Or as St. Cyril exclaims: "Christ is called the New Adam because by sharing in our nature He has enriched us all unto happiness and glory. Thus by dwelling in one human nature Christ dwells in all so that His one human nature, being made the Son of God in power, the same dignity now passes to the whole human race. For as Christ became man by putting on our flesh, so we become God by being incorporated into His flesh."

Christmas teaches us that Christianity is not so much a body of doctrines as the revelation of a mystery. And a mystery is a divine action of love leading men into the bosom of God, into intimacy and communion with the Three Divine Persons. Now this mystery lays upon all Catholics a grave debt and obligation. We who have received the gift of Christ are obliged, are pressed from within by the overwhelming intensity of love that has been heaped upon us, to make known the love of the Divine Savior to the ends of the earth. Christ is born to us, O Christians, that He may appear through us to all who do not yet know Him. Today is the day of his birth within us, but everyday must be the day of His manifestion through us. "It is as impossible," says St. John Chrysostom, "for a true Christian not to radiate Christ as it is for the sun not to send forth its rays of light and warmth."

But there is a graver truth concerning the Child in the stall. "This Child is set for the rise and fall of many, and as a sign of contradiction," predicted the prophet Simeon as he blessed the infant in the temple. Indeed the Child was born into a world under the power of Satan, a world of violence, a world of baby-killers. King Herod, Satan's agent to thwart the plan of God for man's salvation, sent his soldiers to kill the Christ Child. Foiled by an angel of God, he nevertheless slew all the male holy innocents from the age of two and under in the town of Bethlehem. Today the Christ Child is born again into a world of escalating violence, into a world that hates human life, that legally murders millions of innocent, defenseless babies in the womb. Now the Child in the stall is the Creator and Lover of all children. He identifies Himself with every human child, especially with the innocent, defenseless. This Child in the manger is also the severe Judge of the living and the dead. He is the Judge of all the Herods of history who kill babies out of lust for pleasure, money and power. He will render justice in the cause of the millions of "unwanted children." It were better for those Herods if a mill stone were placed around their necks and they were drowned in the depths of the sea, than that they should hear one day this malediction from Christ's mouth: "Depart from me, you accursed, into everlasting fire prepared for the devil and his angels, for I was an infant, a child in the womb and you murdered me." To prove our love for the Christ Child we Christians must fight in word and deed against the Satanic scourge of abortion. May this resolve to champion the lives of little babies be our gift to the Christ Child for Christmas.

Reprinted from *The Remnant*

The Humility of God

"My delight is to be with the children of men."

The Christmas liturgy unveils a stunning, magnificent, ultracosmic arrival from the divine world of the Savior of mankind in these beautiful words: "For while all things were in quiet silence and the night was in the midst of her course, thy Almighty Word leapt down from heaven from thy royal throne..."

This passage is brimming with the wonder and mystery of the Incarnation. It overwhelms the spiritually alert with the instantaneous speed and the sacred stillness of the Christ-Child's arrival in the womb of Mary. And the birth of Christ in the manger at Bethlehem also reveals that God's greatest acts of love are accomplished in humility and silence, not in the glamor, glare or display characteristic of gaudy, superficial, worldly spectaculars.

On the other hand, when man soars in transcendence to conquer the stars, he requires years of preparation to create the technological machines that are wonders of the world for their complicated precision, accurate performance, safe blast-offs and re-entries. There are tremendous explosive rockets, exciting sonic booms and long furious trails of bursting flames that launch giant sky-labs hundreds of miles above the earth amid the breath-holding anxieties and frenzied cheers of multi-millions around the globe. But when God plummets from the heights of eternity to the depths of time all creation is awed into a wondrous stillness. For the silent forces of God are the strongest in existence; they are the forces that stream from all eternity from the heart of divine love. How different are the ways of God in his secret, self-effacing descent, powered by love and humility, toward the littleness of man from the ways of man in his spectacular, self-inflating ascent, powered by pride and ambition, toward worldly greatness, wealth, power and fame.

What a sublime panoramic scene could be conjured up in man's imagination if he would silently reflect on the background of the stupendous Christmas event. The Holy Trinity would be seen gazing below at its own marvelous creation. Before it would gleam the universe composed of myriads and myriads of galazies, suns, stars, planets and other heavenly bodies, all moving silently at tremendous speeds, now basking in golden light, now plunged in cold darkness. And somewhere in the depths of those oceans of galaxies would be seen a grain of sand spinning, immersed in the colored spectrum of a cloudy atmosphere. That grain of sand is the planet earth. Those tiny creatures at work and play on that planet are fallen lords known as men. And, *mirabile dictu,* it is this pygmy planet and those wayward creatures inhabiting it that have attracted the heart of God. God is consumed with his love to descend in person and become a child of man's family.

Why would God do this for such worthless creatures? The answer is found in words on every page of Holy Scripture. The answer throbs with life in the heart of the Christ-Child in the manger. God is a God who loves. He is *Love Itself*. Love does such unfathomable things, deeds that soar beyond reason, that overturn the normal standards of usage. When the God of love enters history in the person of Jesus Christ, he shatters all traditional forms of existence and rational conduct. Yet the awed human mind asks: ''How can such behavior in the God-Man be reconciled with the genuine Godhead?''

The answer is hinted at by another mystery that dwells in the heart of God. God is a humble God. The Child in the manger in his charming feebleness shouts this truth to the whole universe. St. Paul touches on this ineffable truth of God's humility when he says of Jesus: ''. . .who though he was by nature God, did not consider being equal to God a thing to be clung to, but emptied himself, taking the nature of a slave and being made like unto men. . .'' Humility consists in the movement of a superior being downward to a lower being out of respect for the very helplessness and sacred defenselessness of that lower being.

God is humble because, in his love for helpless man, he moves downward towards man's very weakness and defenselessness. God hungers for this descendence because in his kindness and gentleness he would stoop to conquer the enemies that prey on man's weaknesses — the tyrants known as Satan, sin, temptation and death. God humbles himself in order to liberate man from these tyrants and to restore man to the divine grandeur in which He created him. Humility begins only where divine greatness bows before one who is not great. There is something sacred in puny fallen man that attracts God's condescension. That something sacred is the defenseless image and likeness of God in which man was created. Moreover, that something sacred is the very love of God for man that still resides at the root of man's nature. Because the Holy Trinity created man in its own image and likeness, it sent the Son of God to become a man and man's defender, redeemer, advocate and sanctifier. This humble God lowers himself to serve his beloved creature; he lowers himself wholeheartedly because he loves man with an everlasting love. Man's very metaphysical and moral nonentity has attracted God downward to fill up the human deficiency and weakness created by sin with his own grandeur and holiness. That is why Christ exhorts men ''to be holy as your heavenly father is holy.''

The Christ-Child in the womb of Mary is but the first awe-inspiring, secret and silent example of God's stooping in love towards that which in his eyes scarcely exists. The Christ-Child in the manger, with his winsomeness and fragileness, is a more visible, attractive example of God's humility. That child will grow up to be a man, meek and humble of heart, to choose simple fishermen as his companions, to eat with sinners and publicans because they need his care as a physician of souls. That child will become the Teacher *par excellence* spreading the good news of God's love and humility toward men. He will courageously unmask the hypocritical Pharisees and yet willingly succumb to the hatred of this caste of politically ambitious theologians for the sake of man's salvation. This Teacher will sing a paean of praise to his heavenly father because "thous didst hide these things (the wonderful mysteries of revelation) from the wise and prudent" and "didst reveal them to the little ones." This humble God-Man will invite all persons to imitate him not because he is omnipotent, omniscient, or omnipresent, but because "I am meek and humble of heart." This God-Man will at the Last Supper kneel before his disciples and wash their feet, not so much to debase himself as to reveal to them, through this humble action, the divine mystery of God's loving humility. And wonder of wonders, this God-Man will so humble himself as to give his body and blood to be the food and life of men's souls.

God himself is humble because in him — the eternal, omnipotent, glorious One — burns a love that is ready to prostrate itself before the tiny scrap of being known as man, made in the image and likeness of God. There is no explanation for this divine conduct; there is no reasoning to this madness of God's love; it is the mystery seemingly of a divine folly of love. "Because God is good, I exist," exclaims St. Augustine. Because God is humble and utterly in love with man, the Christ-Child exists and is lying in the manger this Holy Season of Christmas. Because God is humble, his Divine Son has become my brother and my Savior. All we can say with Mary and Joseph is: "My soul does magnify the Lord and my spirit rejoices in God my Savior because He that is mighty has done great things to me, and Holy is his Name." All we can sing with the angels, the shepherds and the Magi is: "Glory to God in the highest," and in the lowest, "and on earth peace to men of good will." All we can repeat for ourselves over and over again in wonderment and gratitude is: "Love does such things, spontaneously, profusely, endlessly." For Divine Love, in its overwhelmingly tender humility, performs feats of holiness in favor of man which only the Omnipotent Goodness of God could ever imagine or achieve. St. Paul testifies to this truth thus: "Eye has not seen, ear has not heard, nor has it entered into the mind of man to conceive those things God has prepared for those who love him," and we may add for those whom God loves. The Christ-Child in the manger at Bethlehem demonstrates eloquently the truth of this relevation. May his peace and love remain with you always.

Reprinted from *The Remnant.*

The Evangelization of the United States

From the moment she was enveloped by the roaring wind and fiery tongues of the Holy Spirit on that great Pentecost day, the Church's task was to make all nations disciples of Jesus Christ by drawing them into herself, the one, true fold founded by her Divine Master. This task of the Church will never change until the end of time. Throughout the ages fainthearted Christians — Churchmen and laity — have rationalized, with the aid of slogans and syllogisms, their abandonment of this vocation to convert the churchless millions, but the Church can never be seduced into abandoning this sacred mission.

In an allocution given on July 2nd, 1975, Pope Paul VI scored Christian devotees of detente in the field of evangelization:

> In practice many people who call themselves Christians think so [i.e., that the field of faith can be separated from that of activity], believing that the adherence to religion does not involve other duties than some specific observances, such as Sunday Mass and the fulfilling of the paschal precept. We must note, in fact, a certain allergy on the part of modern Christians to action qualified by their own religious sentiments, owing to a misrepresentation of so-called pluralism, as if every docrinal opinion were admissible, and therefore it was not worthwhile to propose as necessary one's own faith to others; or because of an exclusive authority attributed to subjective conscience, to the detriment of the objective principle that must inform conscience itself.[1]

The people of the United States are today in greater need of the whole truth of Jesus Christ, i.e., the whole teaching of the Catholic Church than they were a century ago. Then they were at least Christian; they took part frequently in Christian activities; considerable numbers of them attended Christian churches. In fact in those days, Orestes Brownson, himself a convert to Catholicism, remarked enthusiastically about the prospects for the Faith in America thus: "Never, since the going forth from the upper room in Jerusalem, has the Church found a national character so well-fitted (as the American) to give her civilization its highest and noblest expression."[2]

And Bishop Spalding of Peoria could add in 1880:

> An observer who a hundred years ago should have considered the religious condition of this country could have discovered no sign whatever that might lead him to suppose that the faith of this little body of Catholics was to have a future in the American Republic; whereas now there are many reasons for thinking that no other religion is so sure of a future here as the Catholic."[3]

And indeed, in the United States, Roman Catholics have increased and multiplied from 30,000 at the time of the Revolution to almost 49,000,000 as recorded in the *Official Catholic Directory* for 1976. That number amounts to 22.78 percent of our population today. Yet within the last couple of decades, the number of believing and practicing Christians has declined ominously and the number of churchless people has increased alarmingly.

What is causing this decay which is rapidly corroding the Catholic spirit of America? The enemy of the Catholic religion in America is a so-called liberalism or neo-modernism which fosters in Christians a secularist attitude, one that rinses God from reality and creates an *animus* against the Faith. Factors our forebears never so much as dreamed of have entered the body of the Catholic Church in America changing it for the worse. Broadly speaking, we can indicate the entrance of the principle of religious rebellion, of private interpretation of dogma, of a licentious permissiveness in morals which tolerates all sorts of natural and unnatural sins, of an all-pervading indifferentism that spurns the splendor of philosophic and evangelical truth, of a spirit of bitterness against the Church and the Faith, a bitterness which begets such a blindness in men that they no longer see the Faith and the Church as essential gifts from God for the creation of civil and saintly citizens of Earth and Heaven.

Some specific evils spawned by this neo-modernist sickness are: In the doctrinal field, the resurrection in a most virulent form of the heresy of Americanism against which Pope Leo XIII in January of 1899 wrote his apostolic letter *Testem Benevolentiae*. This American style of modernism was based on the spirit of American independence, taken from its political sphere and applied to the Catholic religion. The propositions condemned then are quite flourishing today. They state that: In an age of liberty, spiritual direction is less necessary. The Holy Spirit alone is needed to guide souls, not the Church. Natural virtues are to be preferred to the supernatural, active virtues to passive. Thus humility, charity, and obedience are to be downgraded, while personal initiative, efficiency, hard work and humanitarianism are to be exalted. Naturally, religious vows are outmoded. And finally, new methods suited to the times are needed in spreading the Faith. This was interpreted as a whittling down of doctrine to make Catholicism more acceptable to non-Catholics. In rejecting this game of doctrinal and moral detente and accommodation, Leo XIII wrote:

> We cannot consider altogether blameless the silence which purposely leads to the omission or neglect of some principles of Christian doctrine, for all the principles come from the Author and Master, "the Only Begotten Son who is in the bosom of the Father." . . . Concerning this point Vatican Council — says: "All things are to be believed with Divine and Catholic Faith which are contained in

the Word of God, written or handed down, and which the Church, either by solemn judgment or by her ordinary and universal Magisterium, proposes for belief as having been Divinely revealed.'' Let it be far from anyone's mind to lessen or to suppress for any reason, any doctrine that has been handed down. Such a policy would tend rather to separate Catholics from the Church than to bring in those who differ. There is nothing closer to our heart than to have those who are separated from the fold of Christ return to it, but in no other way than the way pointed out by Christ.[4]

At the time Leo XIII wrote this letter, Americanism was no more than a theological bugaboo created out of whole cloth by the French Abbe Maignen's hatred of America. This was so true that the Abbe Felix Klein easily exposed it as a fraudulent nightmare in his book *Americanism: A Phantom Heresy.* Today, unfortunately, that phantom has acquired bone, blood, muscle, and clout. Leo's letter is far more pertinent to our times than it was more than half a century ago.

In the moral field, post-Christian paganism is peddled by many self-styled progressive Catholic theologians and sociologists. These neo-pagans promote the pill, easier divorce and remarriage, premarital intercourse, the legitimization of homosexual relationships, abortions, euthanasia sugared over as ''death with dignity'' and, of course, women's lib free-for-alls in profane and sacred places. All this aims at destroying the Christian family, that necessary sacred cell for the building and development of a sane civil and ecclesiastical society. In the field of liturgy many hot-brained progressives pose as reformers. Actually with iconoclastic exaltation they strip churches of holy statues, priests of sacred vestments, the Mass of its mystery, the temple of its atmosphere of prayer. All this is done in the name of ''evangelical simplicity,'' for they have the Manichean's hatred of the incarnate aspect of Catholicism, of the Word made flesh and dwelling among us. They despise that wonderful art, music, symbols and gracious atmosphere which testify eloquently to the ineffable gift of God in the flesh, a God Who daily sanctified His children through Holy Sacrifice and sacraments. Instead, the liturgical storm-troopers insist on herding the faithful into group activities, organized to prevent the faithful from experiencing the warmth and color of such devotions as Benediction of the Blessed Sacrament, the Rosary, Holy Hours, sacred processions, novenas to the Sacred Heart, to Mary, to the saints. Organized, enforced togetherness, not the sweet indwelling of the Holy Trinity is their God.

Some statistics

We must report, then, that in America there is a drastic drop in practicing Catholics. The Church is divided from within; the Catholic school system is rapidly declining. Statistics of universal deterioration never make pleasant reading except to one's enemies. But facts must be assessed if evangelization is to be undertaken intelligently. Figures show that about 3,100 Catholic elementary and high schools have closed in the past decade, that enrollment has dropped from 5.6 million in 1965 to 3.5 million in 1975. Some 35,000 American nuns and 10,000 priests have left their vocations and, at times, even the Church. This is an alarming exodus and the end is not in sight. Then too seminary enrollment, at a high of nearly 49,000 in 1964 fell to a low of 17,200 in 1975. With such few priestly replacements, it is no wonder that conversions are way down.

In its good years, some three decades ago, the Church would harvest about 120,000 converts a year. Today its convert increase does not make up for its losses through the spreading malignancy of desertion. What is even worse and scandalous, many priestly and lay parties within the Church discourage the making of converts, foster mixed marriages, and the participation in the liturgies of false religions. Driven on by a fascination for exaggerated ecumenism, these parties undermine the apostolic mission of the Church. Really, this "wild cat" ecumenism is the identical twin to indifferentism. Is it any wonder then that the great majority of the people in the United States have lost faith in organized Christianity? They are not interested in an ecumenical religion that flattens out all doctrinal and moral differences, makes no demands of self-sacrifice and thus renders religion vapid. Many Catholics too have become apathetic through reading in the Catholic press what they know to be dilutions of the deposit of the Faith and the ideals of sanctity. We are faced, then, with the fact that America is ceasing to be a Christian, even Protestant, country and is fast becoming a pagan nation. For, unfortunately, the United States has turned its attention from Americanizing its masses of Christian and Catholic colonists and immigrants to paganizing them along with the rest of its natural citizenry.

In an age of escalating agnosticism and atheism the whole of the West, and especially the entire United States, has become missionary territory. Roman Catholics must once again become the leaven of this pagan mass; they must awaken or be awakened to their obligation to engage in genuine evangelization which is basically the practice of Christ-like charity towards their fellowmen. And the primary action of this love consists in the effort to share their greatest treasure, the holy Faith and the true Church, with all who do not possess it.

But any attempt to evangelize will fail in so far as it fails to revive in bishops, priests, religious, and laity the conviction that the Church must go out in an organized way full of faith and zeal, even as the college of the Apostles did, to preach the entire truth of Christ as handed down by

His Apostles and taught by the living Magisterium. The Catholic hierarchy, with priests and religious, must cease preaching only the social gospel and those truths which are popular or ecumenically acceptable. They must also preach Christ crucified, sin, repentance, penance, Satan and Hell, all the truths unpopular to a hedonistic world. If they do this, they will win first the admiration of sincere men and finally their allegiance to Christ. Like Christ they will be proclaiming the good news of the Kingdom of God. For with the priestly power and authority of Christ given them, that is what they were sent to do. And the message they must preach in season and out of season Pope Paul VI indicates in his apostolic exhortation *Evangelii Nuntiandi:*

> The message is indeed necessary. It is unique. It cannot be replaced. It does not permit either indifference, syncretism, or accommodation. It is a question of people's salvation. It is the beauty of the Revelation that it represents. It brings with it wisdom that is not of this world. It is able to stir up by itself faith — faith that rests on the power of God. It is truth. It merits having the apostle consecrate to it all his time and all his energies, and to sacrifice for it, if necessary, his own life.[5]

The meaning of evangelization

We can only give an inadequate definition of so complex and mysterious an activity as evangelization. Being the work of God and man in co-operation, it must ever be a thrilling and awesome adventure. We can say, however, that this sanctifying activity proclaims Christ to those who do not know Him, preaches the Gospel to them through catechesis and missionary sermons, confers Baptism and other scraments and tirelessly exhorts converts to scale the heights of sanctity. Jesus Christ, Himself, the Good News of God, was the very first and greatest evangelizer. He proclaimed an absolute Kingdom of God, making everything else relative. He proclaimed salvation, namely liberation from sin, Satan, death, a liberation that bestowed upon sinners returned to God grace, resurrection in immortality and glorification in the triune God. He proclaimed the price man must pay for his salvation, namely that men must gain Heaven by violence, i.e., through a life of penance, toil, and suffering accepted in the spirit of the Suffering Servant of God. And above all He proclaimed that man must undergo that interior renewal which the Gospel calls *metanoia,* that is that radical change of heart and mind which destroys "the old man of sin" and creates "the new man of grace."

Now evangelization is not an extracurricular Christian activity, a sort of hobby-like avocation for Catholics. Rather, true followers of Christ can and must communicate the good news of Christ to their fellowmen. "It is as impossible," writes St. John Chrysostom, "for the true Christian not to radiate the light of Christ as it is for the sun not to send forth its own rays of light." The Savior's words apply to each member of His Mystical Body according to his position and function in that Holy Body. "I have come to cast fire upon the Earth and what will I but that it be enkindled." As members of the communion of saints, therefore, the Holy Spirit calls each member of that communion to draw new converts to Christ. And St. Paul adds: "Not that I boast of preaching the Gospel, since it is a duty that has been laid upon me. I should be punished if I did not preach it." Moreover, Christ reminds His followers: "He who is ashamed of Me before men, of him I will be ashamed before My Father Who is in Heaven."

Obstacles to evangelization

St. Thomas Aquinas teaches that three things are necessary for a soul to find, follow and embrace Christ. First, a person must know what he ought to believe. Second, he must know what he ought to desire. Third, he must know what he ought to do. Now *ignorance* is the first great obstacle to evangelization. Catholics, therefore, should grow in a profound knowledge of their Faith through a constant reading and reflection on the Gospels and a faithful following of the teachings of the Magisterium. Only thus will they come to appreciate the Catholic Faith as a gift of God that is true, good and beautiful. They will then be moved by the Holy Spirit to bring non-Catholics to share this gift from God with them. The Holy Spirit will aid them to expound its truths with simplicity, conviction, and sincerity.

A second obstacle to evangelization is the failure of Catholic schools to teach the Faith. Catholic children of today should be trained and formed to be the Catholic apostles of tomorrow. Formerly a flood of vocations to the priesthood and sisterhood came out of genuinely Catholic schools. Today that flood is hardly a trickle. What has happened? Catholic education has become secularized; it discovered John Dewey and the world and has joined them. Catholic education, which is only a death mask of what it used to be when alive and well, has given up the task of training apostles of Christ for all walks of life.

The tragic fact is that in many, many Catholic schools not only is there no attempt at apostolic formation but deliberate opposition to any such attempt being made. Catholic teachers in large numbers have joined the ranks of the secularists and harsh critics of the Church. Vagrant theologians are frequently invited, lionized, and paid fat fees to teach doctrine opposed to the teaching of the Magisterium. And this on Catholic campuses where thousands of unwary youth are seduced into error. Today Catholic theology has been downgraded to being just one form of religious subject among hundreds of others. The very scientific study of Catholic philosophy and

theology on the university level is substituted for by a Program of Religious
Studies or Religious Sociology or Comparative Religions in which all
philosophies and theologies are laid out smorgasbord style and the student
is invited to take what he likes, since apparently no one philosophy or
theology is truer or better than another. The result is that doctrinal disputes,
ideological polarizations and mutual condemnations rend Catholic communities, scandalize students, parents, faculty and infect the public at large
with confusion and the disease of relativism and indifferentism.

Much of what we here say of the schools is true also of the Catholic
seminaries where the level of learning and discipline has dropped drastically
and neo-modernism along with religious laxity corrodes the Faith and ideals
of aspirants to the priesthood and Religious life. Now a mediocre grade
of priests not only will not aid the evangelization of America but will actually
prevent the conversion of America to Christ. Priests and Religious who
are carriers of heresy can only spread heresy. An infected, mediocre grade
of priests has always been a disaster to the Church. One need only recall
what happened after the Black Death in the Middle Ages when anybody
was ordained who presented himself as long as he knew some Latin. Today
even the Latin is not needed.

"*The Christian Mind*," Mr. Harry Blarmires writes in his persuasive
book of the same title, "has succumbed to the secular drift with a degree
of weakness and nervelessness unmatched in Christian history. It is difficult
to do justice in words to the complete loss of intellectual morale in the 20th-
century Church."

Sir Arnold Lunn, famed Catholic convert and apologist for the Faith,
conqueror of the Great White Slopes, inventor of the Slalom and author
of a score of books on explaining, defending, ransoming and rebuilding
a weakened or lost Faith, wrote in a brilliant article for *Triumph* magazine
entitled "Apologetics Without Apology," these words of wisdom pertinent
to the work of evangelization: "Only a minority has the courage to defy
the tyranny of fashion...of a widespread will to disbelieve in the supernatural.... There should be nothing apologetic about the statement of the
case for Christianity.... To become a competent apologist a sound basis
of study and research is essential, but it is as true of Christian apologetics
as of boxing that the art cannot be mastered from books. Sooner or later
you will have to get into the dialectical ring.... It is in the schools that
a beginning must be made to counteract the moral defeatism which is
infecting all the churches. In an increasing secular society the Christian
who wants to be 'with it' is tempted to regard his religion as a purely private,
if not secret, affair, and to rationalize his reluctance to influence his non-
Christian neighbors with such formulas as: 'Nobody is ever converted by
argument but only by example.' A Catholic member of the British Parlia-

ment informed us that for the educated 'apologetics and polemics are out.' It is apparently a suitably educated thing to canvass for a political party, but uneducated to canvass for Christianity. . . .

"The hope of the future is a militant ecumenism, not the kind of pacifist ecumenism which consists in swapping pulpits and compliments in the catacombs, but an effective alliance to defend the basic Christian beliefs and the Christian code against the concerted and so far successful attempt of secularists to impose their code and culture on countries which still retain some traces of Christian influence" (*Triumph,* Nov., 1966, pp. 1517).

We are told by Algernon Cecil: "The morals of Christianity survive dogmas by one generation, but no more. If the creed goes, the moral standard follows after."[6] Unfortunately, with our superb mass-media communication-systems the date for moral corruption after the flight from dogmas has been advanced. Moral degradation now takes place in the very generation that rejects dogmatic truth. Rampant immorality is a third obstacle opposing the work of evangelization. Since conduct flows from convictions, once Catholics cancel their creed from their lives, their conduct inevitably becomes depraved. Is it any wonder that students and their parents are disturbed, disoriented, and depressed? The decay on all sides of Christian morals makes it not only difficult for Catholics to bring in those outside the Church, but even to stay in themselves and hold their fellow Catholics within the Church. In a real, tragic sense we are creatures of our environment. For new dogmas, new morals convince so-called new Catholics that it is convenient and permissible to discard the old religion as an unnecessary cramping of the new Catholic lifestyle. Theodore Maynard writes: "Some Catholic theologians and leaders imagine that American independence means freedom in every department of life, especially independence of any hierarchical control except that of their own choosing. They see papal control of faith, morals, and liturgy as foreign control."[7]

Finally, *the spirit of the world* is the fundamental, all-inclusive enemy of true evangelization. For it is the implacable enemy of the Holy Spirit, of whom Jesus spoke when He applied to Himself, at the beginning of His public life of evangelization, the words of the prophet Isaiah:

> The Spirit of the Lord is upon me because He has anointed me to bring the good news to the poor; He has sent me to proclaim to the captives release and sight to the blind; to set at liberty the oppressed; to proclaim the acceptable year of the Lord, and the day of salvation.[8]

Now the spirit of the world is made up of many erroneous currents of thought and wicked winds of volition. Some of its modern thought movements are: agnosticism, immanentism, pragmatism, idealism, existentialism, humanism, and atheism. They sow the seeds of dissension, disbelief, and the destruction of the Faith. Some of the modern winds of willfulness are: hatred for Christ and His Church, contempt for the true and the sacred, a decision to cooperate with the Prince of Darkness in this world and with his demons, a frenzy for power and possessions, a lust for pleasure, an enthusiasm for notoriety, a conniving for a great name and place on Earth. All these evil spirits daily wage war on Christian values and attempt to establish the tyranny of Satan in souls. Insofar as Bishops, priests, and laity are infected with these intellectual atmospheres and moral attitudes, the evangelization of America will be neglected or half-hearted and assuredly a failure.

We Americans are accused of being materialistic, despite our generosity and helpfulness. Why? Because "the American way of life" usually means a fat, opulent, pleasure-full existence chock-full of convenient machines, gadgets, and entertainment palaces bestowed on us by the God of Technocracy who is, in reality, our own genius. When, therefore, we have no other God than our own Technocracy, how can we fail, enraptured by our own marvelous scientific achievements, being God unto ourselves? Thus, the Godless, humanitarian humanism of America is driven on by an imprudent zeal and idolization of science. It is also inspired by a false irenicism, a spirit of false peace and good-will at any price, even the price of abandoning Christ and His Church. Its attempt to level barriers between truth and falsity, goodness and wickedness, as if there were no radical difference between them, in the name of pluralism, ecumenism, and Americanism, is the insane attempt at playing the role of a super-God. For not even the true God is beyond good and evil, nor could He reconcile such contradictory realities.

Aleksandr Solzhenitsyn, the prophet of our times who was spewed up upon the shores of the West, like a modern Jonah, by the Leviathan of militant Atheism, daily cries out to the conscience of America by his writings, lectures and interviews the following message: "America, you are attempting to exist in a spiritual vacuum bereft of the Christian God. It is not easy to discern any essential difference between your post-anti-Christian humanism and the murderous atheistic humanism of Communistic countries. You are both tyrants for you both reduce man to being a mere economic animal and you impose on this image of God the seal of Satan. Your policy of detente is your decision to abandon to the fate of permanent slavery the nations caught beyond the iron and bamboo curtains." We know that Ninevah listened to Jonah, was converted to God and saved. So far America refuses to hear the cry of the new Jonah. Indeed he has been shunned and snubbed by our political leaders.

Means for the re-evangelization of America

Unfortunately, the fact is that the Church in the United States, instead of being the crusading, courageous, evangelizing society Christ founded it to be, has become a cream-puff chaplaincy to the converted — and because of this attitude is failing to hold on even to these. This posture is also deplored by sincere members of other Christian churches and apostolic communities. How are we to stir up again the spirit of evangelization? Pope Paul VI in *Evangelii Nuntiandi* gives us our marching orders:

> On us particularly, the pastors of the Church, rests the responsibility for reshaping with boldness and wisdom, but in complete fidelity to the content of evangelization, the means that are most suitable and effective for communicating the Gospel message to the men and women of our times.[9]

We mention here just two basically important means. America needs saints. The time has come for bishops, priests, and Religious, demonstrating that boldness and wisdom advocated by Pope Paul VI, to cease using half-measures and making compromises that allow false teachers to ravage the flock of Christ. The moment has come for ecclesiastical authority to attack abuses more firmly, even vigorously. Now is the time of salvation. The advice of St. Pius X to bishops in his famous encyclical against Modernism *Pascendi Dominici Gregis* must immediately be enforced.

> Truly there is no road which leads so directly and so quickly to Modernism as pride. When a Catholic layman or priest forgets the precept of the Christian life which obliges us to renounce ourselves if we would follow Christ and neglects to tear pride from his heart, then it is he who most of all is a fully ripe subject for the errors of Modernism. For this reason, venerable brethren, it will be your first duty to resist such victims of pride, to employ them only in the lowest and obscurest offices. The higher they try to rise, the lower let them be placed, so that the lowliness of their position may limit their power of causing damage. Examine most carefully your young clerics by yourselves and by the directors of your seminaries, and when you find the spirit of pride among them reject them without compunction from the priesthood. Would to God that this had always been done with the vigilance and constancy which were required![10]

The one absolutely prime requirement, therefore, for true evangelization is that zeal for the salvation of souls should once again dominate the thinking of all Catholics, but above all, of bishops, priests, and Religious. This is the mind of Christ for all of us. "Let that mind be in you which was in Christ Jesus." How can we have the mind of Christ, if we are not determined to work zealously to share the treasures of His Church with those who are ignorant of them or have rejected them? The first means of evangelization is, therefore, and will ever be, the imitation of the life of Christ. But Jesus began to do and to teach. Hence the witness of a holy life in Christ is the first means. But following holy conduct must come holy, authoritative teaching. For how are people to believe in Christ, if they never hear the preacher talk of Him? How are they to attain truth if they hear only false teachers?

At this point, allow me to make a useful suggestion to bishops, priests, and Religious. Faith comes from the Word of God that is preached and received. And the Word of God is powerful in itself to effect conversions. For the Word of God is not bound, not even by the so-called scientific mentality. Hence why not liberate as many bishops, priests and Religious, who have been given the grace of vocation to preach effectively, why not liberate as many of these as possible from stuffy offices and meeting rooms to preach to the people? How many millions of Americans are pleading for their words of life? How many millions of Americans know nothing of the work of Redemption continued in the Mass, of intimacy with Christ in Holy Communion, of the comfort of forgiveness in the Sacrament of Penance, of the sacramental nature of marriage, of the sureness of the dogmatic and moral guidance offered by the infallible teaching voice of the Church, of the example of the lives of the saints, of the help to Christian living supplied by the liturgy, of the accumulated wisdom of Catholic doctors — male and female — concerning the life of the spirit and the ways of prayer, of the consolation of being able to help departed loved ones, of the benefits of a tender devotion to the Blessed Mother of God.

We Catholics, unfortunately, take all these blessings for granted. But the charity of Christ, His compassionate love, should urge us to share these treasures with the poor multitudes who wander like sheep without a shepherd. This is what evangelization is all about! Hence it would be wise to liberate bishops, priests, and Religious from the bureaucratic walls that too often imprison them in commissions, committees, congresses that meet with such concatenated frequency that these men of God are hindered from preaching to the world about the things of God. The twelve Apostles converted a pagan empire by preaching; we do not read that they were forever meeting among themselves, much less with experts. They met in general Council but once. Yet Scripture tells us that their word went forth to the ends of the Earth because they brought that word there in person and produced great fruit, i.e., immense conversions. American clergymen and Religious would do well to heed the advice of the late Cardinal Heenan on this matter:

> Whenever the need for urgent action is admitted, a committee usually called a commission is formed or a conference is arranged. Clergy and especially bishops can spend a major part

of their time at meetings. There are parish councils, deanery councils, diocesan councils of administration, schools' councils, liturgical commissions, ecumenical commissions, senates of priests and pastoral councils. I seriously believe that much of our pastoral effort is being stifled by the growing number of meetings, discussions, conferences to which bishops and priests are subjected. I look for a radical curtailment of meetings and conferences. I sincerely believe that, in addition to sapping physical energy, the present burden of talk produces a weariness of spirit, leading to narcissism and the neglect of personal prayer. People who talk excessively rarely pause to listen to God in prayer.[11]

When many more of our bishops, priests and Religious build up their apostolate on the solid foundation of constant prayer and the pure love of God, then we can begin to look hopefully for a mass return of men to God and for many conversions. What is of first importance in the apostolate of evangelizing the United States is that Catholics of America reverse their outlook from naturalism to supernaturalism and reduce as well as subordinate their works of hustle and bustle in the service of a sick society to the prayerful deeds needed to change that sick society into a society of saints. What is of utmost importance to convert America is that all American Catholics put on the whole mind and heart of Christ and His Church. For the deepest source of the power American Catholics will exercise over their times and fellowmen will be the completeness of their own surrender in love and loyalty to Christ and His Church.

Notes

[1]Pope Paul VI quoted in *Faith* magazine, September-October, 1975, by Francis J. Ripley in an article "The Evangelization of Great Britain," p. 3.

[2]Maynard Theodore, quoted in his book *The Catholic Church and the American Idea,* 1953, p. 292.

[3]*Ibid.,* p. 292.

[4]Leo XIII in his apostolic letter *Testem Benevolentiae* reproduced in English translation in Abbe Felix Klein's book *Americanism: A Phantom Heresy,* 1951, p. 315.

[5]Pope Paul's apostolic letter *Evangelii Nuntiandi* translated by Daughters of St. Paul, Boston and New York, 1976, par. 5, pp. 4-5.

[6]Quoted by Theodore Maynard in *The Catholic Church and the American Idea,* p. 214 from Cecil's book *A House in Bryanston Square.*

[7]Maynard, Theodore, *ibid.,* p. 54.

[8]*Luke* 4:18; *Isaiah* 61:1.

[9]Pope Paul VI's apostolic letter *Evangelii Nuntiandi,* English translation by Daughters of St. Paul, Boston, N.Y., 1976, par. 40, p. 23.

[10]St. Pius X's encyclical *Pascendi Dominici Gregis,* On Modernism, English translation by Daughters of St. Paul, Boston and N.Y., par. 40, p. 52.

[11]Quoted in *Christian Order* by Fr. Robert Nash, S.J., in article entitled "To Whom Shall We Go?" February, 1976, p. 111.

"Arise and Anoint Him"

Each year in the solemn commemoration of the feast of Sts. Peter and Paul on 29 June, the Church joyously chants this antiphon: "While they lived they established the Church by shedding their blood; they drank the chalice of suffering that their Master had drunk; in their lifetime God chose them as His friends."

Holy Scripture is full of examples that demonstrate God's preferential love for men and women imbued with the spirit of zeal. Even when the zeal of some of His friends or enemies is misdirected in good faith, God remains on friendly terms with such generous spirits. His abundant grace enlightens, inflames and eventually guides the zeal of such generous souls to fight for the better gifts — the greater glory of God and the salvation of souls through a life of perfect charity.

What is this virtue of Christian zeal? St. Thomas Aquinas writes: "Zeal arises from the intensity of love. For it is evident that the more intensely a power tends to anything, the more vigorously it withstands opposition and conquers enemies. Since, therefore, love is a movement toward the object loved, as Augustine teaches, an intense love or zeal moves single-mindedly toward the beloved, removing in its progress every obstacle that obstructs the path to communion with the beloved. Thus, the distinctive note of zeal is the *vehemence* and *intensity* of love in the lover for the beloved."

Now love is basically divided into two main species — the love of concupiscence and the love of friendship. Naturally, zeal too is manifested in two main types — the zeal of envy or of *egoism* and the zeal of unselfish concern for the beloved or of *altruism*. By the love of concupiscence persons desiring something intensely for themselves fight off all obstacles hindering the possession and enjoyment of the object loved. Thus lovers fight off competitive suitors; husbands fight off prowling lovers. And they do so with the zeal of jealousy or envy of which it is written: "Be not emulous of evildoers, nor envious of those that work inquity." On the other hand, in the love of friendship, zeal does not seek primarily the lover's enjoyment or peaceful possession of the beloved, but the good of the friend. Thus the intensity of love for one's friend rejects everything that opposes the good and glory of the friend.

A person is said to be zealous on God's behalf when he endeavors to the best of his ability with the means at hand to repel whatever is contrary to the will and holiness of God. Thus we read in Kings: "With zeal have I been zealous for the Lord of hosts." And St. John in his Gospel writes: "The zeal of thy house has eaten me up." John is relating how Christ, ablaze with holy zeal against the profanation of the temple, cleanses the House of God with a whip that drives out the desecrating merchants and money-changers.

Christian zeal, therefore, is that intensity of the love of friendship which strives for the greater glory of God and the salvation of souls. It is that ardent desire for God's honor and man's salvation which drives a person to perform not only ordinarily good deeds, but even heroic, adventuresome feats, and this in the teeth of what seem to be insurmountable obstacles. Total adherence to God and God's plan is the essence of Christian zeal.

When the prophet Samuel was sent by God to choose a new king in Israel to succeed the unfaithful Saul, he examined seven of Jesse's sons — all of them tall, handsome, broad-shouldered, perfect specimens of young manhood. But God rejected them all, saying, "Look not on the countenance, nor on the height of the stature because I have rejected them; nor do I judge according to the look of man, for man sees those things that appear, but the Lord beholds the heart." Finally, the eighth son, David, a ruddy boy, comely of features, was fetched from his sheeptending, and God said to Samuel: "Arise and anoint him, for this is he."

What had God seen in David that he had not discovered in his brothers? He saw a youth zealous for the honor of the Lord God of hosts, a man after the heart of God Himself, And indeed, it is David, stone and slingshot in hand, ignoring the fearful advice of his brothers, of his friends, of King Saul himself, who unflinchingly challenges the giant Goliath, that Philistine who dared to curse the armies of the living God. While all Israel quaked with fear, David taunted Goliath: "You come to me with a sword, a spear and a shield, but I come to you in the name of the Lord God of hosts, of the God of the armies of Israel...He will deliver you into my hands and I will slay you." And David destroyed the enemy of God's people. Elias, prophet of the Lord, before the assembled Israelites, slew the prophets of Baal in his zeal for the glory of the One, True God. Judith, a peaceful wife, yet zealous with the zeal of God, beheaded the mighty Holofernes and routed the immense army of the Assyrians who were threatening the chosen people of God.

What is this vigorous virtue of zeal which drives friends of God to heroic deeds? Christian zeal is an essential religious quality to be found in the very concept of a religious person. It is inherent to being a man or woman of God. No one can be serious in religion, or earnest in living the faith and serving God, until he magnifies his God and Saviour. A zealous Christian consecrates and exalts God, indeed the very thought and Name of God, in his heart. God is the supreme, ineffably good Thou, the three most lovable Persons whom he praises, adores and rejoices over when They are honored and over whom he grieves when They are dishonored. Indeed a zealous person is eager to avenge the honor of God either by routing the enemies of God in battle or by offering himself as a victim of reparation. For zeal is that religious temper expressed best as loyalty to God under all circumstances. A religious, loyal person does not merely obey God, but he or she obeys with promptness, energy, enthusiasm, with total disregard of personal inconveniences or fatal consequences.

Christian zeal is an essential qualification in the very notion of a servant of God. It is the source of holy action in religious services that manifest love of God and of neighbor. Christian zeal signifies that a person loves God above all things, above all men, above one's dearest, most intimate beloved ones. And Christian zeal partakes of a priestly quality, for it signifies the consecration of God's servants to the office of rendering sacrifice and adoration to God. Thus the baptized are initially sealed and anointed as children of God; the confirmed are doubly sealed and anointed as soldiers of God, while the ordained are triply sealed and anointed as priests of God. Thus the zeal of friendship with God in the priest should be three times the intensity found in the initially baptized, which is to say, priestly zeal should aspire to the intensity of Christ's zeal for His Father's glory and the salvation of souls.

Our Blessed Lord, the great High Priest, began the manifestation of His divinity with two acts of zeal for His Father. To be sure, His whole life was a continuous history of zealous love and service for His Father. But we choose just two events of that life for contemplation at this moment. When twelve years old, Christ's dedication to the service of His Father, led him to leave Mary and Joseph and remain in the temple. He wanted to discuss with the religious leaders in Israel the prophecies concerning the Messiah. When Mary and Joseph found Him after three days of sorrowful search, He answered their parental complaint: "How is it you went looking for me? Did you not know I must be found in my Father's House, about my Father's business?" The Father is served and loved above His beloved parents.

When He began His public life, Christ found the temple desecrated by a rabble of merchants, buyers and sellers. He made a scourge of cords, drove out the sheep and oxen, overthrew the money-changers' tables and chided the Pharisees for tolerating the profanation of the temple: "My Father's House is a house of prayer, but you have made it a den of thieves." It was as they saw Christ in this zealous fury that the Apostles remembered the prophecy foretold about Him: "The zeal of thy house has eaten me up."

Consumed by zeal Himself, is it any wonder that Christ chose His Apostles, those with whom He would share His divine Priesthood forever, from among the zealous? James and John, whom He called Boanerges, sons of thunder, had flaming hearts. On one occasion they wanted to call fire from Heaven to avenge a Samaritan snub against their Master. Peter was so upset at his Lord's prediction of His passion and death that he took Christ aside and,in mistaken zeal, tried to talk Him out of submitting to the humiliation of the Cross. But Christ rebuked His mistaken zeal: "Get thee behind me, Satan, for you are a scandal unto me; for you do not mind the things of God but those of men." Peter was even more upset in the garden of Gethsemani at His Lord's arrest; he cut off the right ear of one of those seeking to seize Christ, in a zealous but vain attempt to rescue his Master. Simon was called Zelotes, the zealous one, for he belonged to a Jewish sect which professed extraordinary devotion for the law.

Then there is Thomas, the doubter, who in his ardent love for Christ, said to the others, when his Lord decided to risk His life in a return to Judea in order to raise Lazarus from the dead: "Let us also go that we may die with Him." We have too the example of Philip who, in ardent expectation, cried out to Christ: "Lord, show us the Father and it is enough for us." He was hoping thereby to see and adore the divine Face of Holiness itself.

Extraordinary is the example of St. Paul. He is perhaps the most zealous of the Apostles. He violently fought Christ and the infant Church whom he saw as enemies of the Old Covenant of God and of the Chosen People. But he did so in good faith, from earnestness, from, in his own words, "being zealous toward God, though blindly so." A Pharisee's Pharisee, he was convinced he had to do away with the name of Jesus and His followers. So he arrested, jailed and killed Christians. But he was spared by God because his false zeal, unsuspected by himself, was driven by ignorance of Christ and unsound judgments toward wicked ends. Christ, in His compassionate goodness, knocked Paul from his horse near Damascus, enlightened, converted and redirected Paul's zeal to a life of sublime service to God and the conversion of the Gentiles. The new Paul, no longer lived his own life but Christ lived in him. And now in his ardent love for Christ, not only would he never hurt or kill others, but he would fain be condemned to Hell, if he could thereby save Israel. Paul writes: "I bear them (the Jews) witness they have a zeal for God, but not according to knowledge", meaning here, not acording to the excellent knowledge of Our Lord Jesus Christ, the substantial Wisdom of God whom they tragically rejected.

What God loves about the zealous is that they are serious about religion, salvation and the glory of God himself. At times the zealous may be innocently ignorant of the true revelation; they may even be culpably adamant in rejecting the truth that has been revealed to them — witness Thomas and the other Apostles on the fact of the Resurrection. Even so, as long as they remain zealously concerned about the things of God, they win a certain mercy from God and there is hope of their conversion. To be fighting God is, at least negatively, the virtue of being seriously concerned about the One Being necessary in one's life, the Alpha and Omega of one's existence and destiny.

Zealous persons are not scoffers. They are not like Gallio, the Roman proconsul of Achaia, who is recorded in the *Acts of the Apostles* as "caring for none of these things", these religious matters over which Jews and Christians fought. For to such haughty scoffers it mattered not whether God existed, nor whether they worshiped this idol today or that one tomorrow. The prophet Samuel reports how God abominates such religiously neutral indifferentists: "Our Holy Lord honors them that honor him, while they that despise him are lightly esteemed". God is nauseated by the lukewarm and the disloyal. He proclaimed a severe judgment against the spiritually anemic in His complaint against the Church of Laodicea through John the Evangelist: "I know your works that they are neither hot nor cold. I would that you were cold or hot. But because you are lukewarm, I am vomiting you out of my mouth". Wholehearted, zealous opposition to God is less odious to God than the clever temper of the man of "uncommitted interest" in religion, the man who writes and discourses about "the phenomena of religion" in an olympian fashion. The new Gnostic religion of our times consists precisely in this neutrality toward revealed, sacred realities; in this game of ridicule played by those who hold that one religion is as good as another; in this refusal to take God at His word, to consider seriously His revelation and to order one's life in accordance with His plan of redemption.

In this age of atheism, the Church of God on earth is being greatly reduced before our eyes by the steady desertion of clergy, religious and laity. For the last fifteen years a national and international band of roving theologians has been subverting the doctrinal foundations of the Catholic Church. Lionized in the packed halls of the universities, in parish councils and even in seminars for updating bishops, these teachers of novelties deny or question their Church's official teaching concerning the infallibility of the Pope, the indissolubility of the sacramental marriage bond, the objective graveness of the evil of masturbation, the wickedness of extramarital sexual intimacy, the sinfulness of artificial contraception and many, many other dogmatic and moral truths. In fact, just about the whole deposit of the Faith and of Christian morality is thrown up for reexamination. Such teachers have gone so far as to reject the ordinary and extraordinary teaching of the Magisterium, putting themselves in the chair not of Moses but of Peter by their own abitrary wills.

This subversion of doctrine and morals has produced a widespread professed indifference to any particular form of Christianity, Catholicism included. The pretense for justifying this erosion of faith and morals is the birth of a new spirit expressed in a universal, ecumenical toleration of all religions. What the new teachers never tell their fascinated audiences is that their tolerance of every sort of fable does not arise from the spirit

DOGMA 153

of Christian charity or forebearance, but from a loss of faith and from a hunger to join a world that is set on undermining Catholicism by multiplying and encouraging rival religious doctrines and sects. Indeed things have so deteriorated for the Church that governments, formerly friendly to religion, now give protection to no religions, but rather give preferential treatment to atheistic humanism as the new religion of liberated man. Such governments have already embodied in their laws and policies the false principles and immoral practices of this godless sect. Small wonder the nominal Christians in the hundreds of thousands are deserting the Church for the permissive pleasures of state humanism. Unfortunately, before and after they leave, many of these deserters insult the Magisterium, vilify public worship and abuse their fellow Catholics because it is no longer in fashion or popular with public authorities to be a practicing Catholic.

Satan's strategy is to attack the unity of Catholics in Christ and His Vicar the Pope. Satan acts to split up and divide the faithful, to create a false class struggle. The Magisterium is presented as the enemy of the theologians: the theologians are the protectors of religious liberty against the authoritarian Magisterium; the college of bishops is pitted against the Pope in the protection of their episcopal rights; priests are pitted against priests, bishops and the laity; Christian Western culture is pitted against Christian Eastern culture. The tactic of Satan is gradually to dislodge the faithful from Peter, the rock of their strength, and then assault the super-structure of authority. Is it any wonder that Catholics are splintered in all regions of Christendom, that the Church is divided within, reduced to internal schism and weakened from a high running fever of heresy and infidelity?

Surely in this crisis, when a kind of bastard, syncretist Christianity, that juxtaposes Christian and anti-Christian elements, is creating an age of unbelief, rebellion, license and violence, bishops and priests must no longer keep silence nor remain inactive. If the religious leaders continue to show themselves dumb, sleepy dogs that have forgotten how to bark or bite, they will be failing in the terrifying duties of their priestly office to protect the flock of Christ against the wolves of Satan. They must not any longer give themselves up to the ease and comfort of an attitude that "sees no evil, hears no evil and speaks no evil". The Master will demand of them an accounting of every soul lost as a result of their pusillanimity. In an age of craven accommodation to falsity and immorality, must it remain the dismal fact that scarcely anyone any longer openly dares to defend the Church against the powers of this world? Newman reminds us that it is the clergy and scholars who usually introduce heresy and religious chaos into the Church. Analyzing the Arian heresy and violence which infected more than eighty per cent of the bishops in the Eastern Church, he writes:

"The laity as a whole revolted from Arianism in every part of Christendom. It was an epidemic of the schools and of theologians, and to them it was mainly confined. . . The classes which furnished martyrs were in no sense the seat of the heresy''.

Yet it is only the bishops, aided by their priests, who can individually and collectively liberate the Church from the scourge of heresy. Many religious friends, not of our faith, but who seek in the Catholic Church the maintenance of the high moral values and stability in doctrine, lament the fact that the Catholic Church is suffering from lack of leaders and, in the words of one of my Protestant friends, "from a clergy in which the proportion of the mediocre is unduly high". In humility we must admit that the spread of atheism and hedonism reveals that we have been less than adequate in repulsing the evils of the day. Confession and contrition are the first steps to conversion. Moreover, Our Lord told us: "Without me you can do nothing". Even when we have done our best in His service, Christ has taught us to call ourselves "unprofitable servants" for having done what we should have done. We know that in the work of building up the Mystical Body, Paul plants, Apollo waters, but God alone gives the increase. With such insights, let us examine the causes of priestly mediocrity.

Some priests begin to lose their zeal when their vision strays from the Person of Christ and concentrates on themselves and their own ambitions. This spiritual disease is known as *careerism*. Its evil effects are numberless. We merely mention the following: blurred spiritual vision progressively approaching spiritual blindness; a running to and from sanctuary to the world with consequent confusion about divine and worldly wisdom; the development of an appetite for the secularized tastes, opinions and habits of the children of this world; the concentration of the heart and its energies on the attainment of worldly fame, rank or station, wealth, ecclesiastical promotion to a bishopric or cardinalatial princedom; finally a loss of loyalty to the cause of the Church.

Other priests develop a special species of this same spiritual disease. It is known as *professionalism*. This new disease is found in myriad types of hyphenated clerics spawned in the murky interpretations of the Second Vatican Council. The priest-sociologist, priest-psychologist, priest-politician, priest-professor, priest-artist, priest-guitarist and so on endlessly, is generally so engrossed in his secular speciality that the hyphenated tail of his profession vigorously wags the corpus of his priestly vocation. Usually such persons have lost interest in their priesthood or feel they are failures as priests but a success as professionals. They prefer to be known as experts rather than as priests, or even as Catholics. Moreover, in playing up to their professional peers, many of these schizophrenic types declare their independence of the

Church's authority in doctrine and morals. They do this so as to create the public image of being open, unfettered, mature, liberated. Slowly, almost imperceptibly, they develop an affectation of refinement and an almost idolatrous fascination for the powers of reason. Usually they arrive at a contempt for the Church, her Magisterium, her sacramental system, her doctrines and those religious devotions popular with the poor and lowly.

These new gnostics attain a habitual self-esteem and an utter ignorance of the number and heinousness of the sins of pride which cry out against them. Careerist and professionalist priests seek and preach themselves; they no longer seek or preach Christ of whom they are now ashamed. St. Paul warned the Philippians about this breed: "For they all seek their own interests, not those of Jesus Christ". They live by that false zeal of concupiscence, that zeal of envy which arises from an excessive love of self, security, financial luxury, comfort, notoriety, the world, the lust for the credit of a great place and name on earth. Their mission is no longer one of salvific service to God and souls, but one of clever maneuvering for personal advancement against competitors. The escalation of careerist and professionalist priest in the Church today accounts for the wide diffusion of an arrogant, ungodly, falsely liberal and worldly spirit among youth. It is certainly one of the main reasons for the lack of vocations to the Priesthood and religious life. For the Holy Spirit does not attract youth to imitate self-seeking priests or religious!

Finally, many priests, though fundamentally loyal to Christ and the Church, become mediocre because of a blackout of their faith with a consequent failure of hope and loss of nerve and heart. Witnessing the hurricane of neo-Modernism and hedonism, such priests deeply bewail the ruin these are spreading in God's kingdom. The very enormity of the spiritual demolition weakens their faith and shatters their hope. Their courage quakes and vanishes; they passively, almost fatalistically, resign themselves to inevitable disaster. This is the disease of *naturalism*. Such priests forget that Christ has overcome the world, that He expects to win this present war with their zealous cooperation. Here we have the suffocation of the zeal of friendship, of altruism, not by the selfish vice of the zeal of concupiscence, but by the faithless timidity of pusillanimous souls. One's intense love for God and souls, instead of being ablaze to a roaring pitch by the escalating impieties of the day, flickers and fades under the paralyzing fear of the howling storm. Thus like Peter, walking with Christ on the waters, one looks away from Christ to the wild elements, begins to tremble at the winds and waves, and to sink into oblivion.

Total, single-minded love of Christ and His Church is a basic temper of the soul on which priestly zeal must be founded. Such a self-effacing love was expressed by St. John the Baptist, son of the high priest Zachary, when he witnessed to the Messiahship of Christ: "Behold, the Lamb of God who takes away the sins of the world. He must increase, I must decrease". St. Pius X in *Haerent animo* wrote of the needs of the priest: "There is one quality which indisputably links man and God and makes him a pleasing, not unworthy dispenser of His mercy, namely sanctity. If this, which is but the supereminent knowledge of Jesus Christ, is lacking in a priest, all things are lacking".

St. Augustine defines sanctity in a most felicitous phrase: Sanctity is *adhaerere Deo:* sanctity is to cling to God, with one's whole mind; it calls for continuous prayer with one's whole soul; requires daily Mass and sacramental communion; with one's whole strength it demands a permanent dedication of one's talents to doing God's holy will; with one's whole being it requires profound adoration and total surrender to God's Providence. This perfect love expressed in the first commandment will flow over into openhearted love for all men for whom Christ died. Total self-effacement and the permanent enthronement of Christ and His Church in the place of primacy in the heart of a priest begets the virtue of Christ-like zeal. "You are my friends, if you do what I command you".

Loyalty to the commands of Christ is inseparable from loyalty to the commands of the Church He founded, of which He is the Head and with which He identifies Himself. Priestly zeal and loyalty to the Church are twin virtues; they always will be present in the priest whose life is totally dedicated to Christ. In his book, *Christ Is Passing,* Fr. J. Escriva de Balaguer, founder of Opus Dei, reminds the careerist and professionalist priest of the primacy of their Priesthood: "A priest should be exclusively a man of God. He should reject any desire to shine in areas where other Christians do not need him. A priest is not a psychologist, not a sociologist, nor an anthropologist. He is another Christ who has to look after the soul of his brothers".

What a scientist, philosopher, doctor, perfect omnicompetent genius, Christ, the substantial Wisdom of the Father, could have revealed Himself to be! But His food was to do the will of His Father, to be the Suffering Servant of the Lord, the Word sent to preach to the poor, the Savior sent to redeem all. We are not saying that priests should not develop their other talents and use them in the service of God and man. What we are saying is that their professional talent must never downgrade or eclipse their Priesthood. Frank Sheed, speaking to a group of American seminarians, advised them: "Make up your mind whether you are preaching Christ or yourself. If you are preaching yourself, heaven help you, for the better you do it, the worse it is". Now the priest, whose career and profession come before his priestly mission, is actually preaching, pushing and exalting himself, not Christ.

For those of us who tend to lose heart, let us remember that perfect zeal is founded also on deep faith. Frightened Peter sinking in the waves cried out: "Lord, save me!!" "Lord", the father of the possessed boy cried at another time, "I believe, help thou my unbelief". The Lord upheld and confirmed Peter and cured the child. James and John, ambitious for high places in Christ's kingdom, boldly accepted Christ's chalice: "We are able to drink it, Lord". The priest of deep faith never aspires to be above or unlike his Master. Strong faith points out the goal toward which zeal should be directed; it guides priests in choosing the right means to arrive at that God-given goal. Strong faith will preserve bishops and priests from the pose of "prudent inactivity" when attacks on faith and morals call for courageous interventions to protect the flock of Christ. Strong faith will give bishops and pastors the zeal to cleanse the schools where teachers are disseminating errors as Catholic doctrine. Such organizational and ideological walls as tenure, faculty unions, accreditation associations, academic freedom and development of doctrine will not be allowed to frustrate Church authorities in their mission to preserve and spread the deposit of the Faith. For priestly zeal arising from strong faith and ardent charity will never shrink from facing up to its sublime responsibilities.

"Evil flourishes", wrote Dante, "because good men do nothing". And so in the Church today impieties are rampant because good bishops and priests, intimidated by the opinions of the world, do nothing. What Our Divine Lord complained about so much in His Apostles and His generation is true of us: "O you of little faith! Why do you doubt? O evil and perverse generation, how long must I bear with you?" What strong faith does for priestly zeal is to give it the eternal dimension of *patience, resignation* and *perseverance* in cooperating with the holy will of God. Strong faith continually reminds the priest that mere nature cannot conquer spiritual enemies, that God is always with His Church controlling the storm, that, in the words of St. Pius X, "we are not divine Providence", but we look to the Son of God with the eyes of servants toward their Master, of captains toward their General for orders and inspirations to perform the zealous deeds that guarantee Christ's final victory in and through His Church.

Strong faith sustains the priest in zealous activity by reminding him that God in His own time will reap the harvest of his good deeds. Hence he should never become discouraged, never disillusioned if he does not attain instant or reasonably quick success. Strong faith reminds the zealous priest never to accept salvation from the world, but to seek it where Paul found it: "I can do all things in him who strengthens me."

The priest who is zealous with the zeal of Christ will be attacked not only by the world but by false brethren within the Church. His zeal will be labelled intolerance; his earnestness, madness; his constancy, stubborness; his fidelity, backwardness; his virtue, stupidity; his defense of truth, contentiousness; his piety, mawkishness; his traditionalism, rigidity; his orthodoxy, superstition. But in response to the litany of calumnies, the zealous priest rejoices in his magnanimous dedication to Christ; he has no inferiority complex over belonging completely to Christ and His Church; he suffers no identity crises; he rejoices to be considered a fool for Christ. As long as his conscience is clear and his heart riveted on God, he is ready to suffer all for Christ. He is a fulltime priest, free from earthly compromise, set on self-effacement, exhibiting a spontaneous, tenacious, audacious yet meek adherence to the faith and moral law of His Church.

Zealous, loyal priests are the salt of the earth for they sharpen man's appetite for sanctity and preserve his virtue from corruption. They are the light of the world, never intimidated from allowing their good words and works to shine before men for the glory of God. It was to Timothy and all bishops and priests that Paul spoke when he wrote: "I admonish you to stir up the grace of God which is in you by the laying on of my hands. For God has not given us the spirit of fear, but of power and of love and of prudence. Do not be ashamed of testimony for Our Lord." "O Timothy, guard the trust and keep free from profane novelties in speech and the contradictions of so-called knowledge, which some have professed, and have fallen from the faith". "But do thou be watchful in all things, bear with tribulation patiently, work as a preacher of the gospel, fulfill the ministry".

Moreover, it was of himself and of all zealous Christians that Paul spoke when he wrote: "For we are the fragrance of Christ for God, alike as regards those who are saved and those who are lost: to the lost we are a fragrance that leads to death; to the saved we are a fragrance that leads to life". Like their Master, like the first priests, the Apostles, zealous priests will always be signs of contradiction, set up by their own dedication to God and His Church for the rise and fall of many. But they will be signs of contradiction because the zeal of their Father's Church has eaten them up, and because they fight to save even those children who insist on destroying their souls by rejecting Christ and his Church.

Reprinted from *Friar*, October 1976.

Part II

Morals

The Taproot of Violence

He (Satan) is your father, and your will is to do your father's desires. He was a murderer from the beginning and was never grounded in the truth. . .for he is a liar and the father of lies. (John 8:44)

We are living in an era whose atmosphere is saturated with the flames of hatred. It is an age of violence whose tempo of disruption is so rapidly escalating that there is scarcely a city anywhere in the world where humans can be assured of normal, physical security. In an age of irrational aggressivity, Pope John Paul II, a spiritual leader dedicated to peace, was gunned down in Rome and nearly killed; in Washington, D.C., the newly-elected president of the United States of America was felled by gunfire; in Cairo, a presidential statesman, winner of the Nobel Peace Prize for his successful efforts in attaining peace between Egypt and Israel in the inflamed Middle East, was assassinated. Within the totalitarian nations the litany of the liquidated has risen to such astronomical figures that only God knows the exact number. Within the so-called "Christian" nations of the West the myriad millions of helpless, innocent children murdered in their mothers' wombs boggles the imagination. The violence-explosion at present is so horrifying that it is stupefying the minds of men all over the world. Indeed hundreds of thousands have already constructed underground survival hideaways to escape what they see will arrive in the near future, the Age of Violence Unlimited.

Future historians will be sorely taxed to explain the unparalleled international crescendo of savage assaults in all forms of intimidation, vandalism, kidnapping, bodily brutality and guerrilla massacres against persons and institutions. For the explosion of violence represents a demonic reality similar to a Hydraheaded serpent. It is a persistent, ever-increasing plague with many sources and causes. Indeed the apologists for the new barbarism are not merely, nor even primarily, demonically sick individuals, but rather organized groups who have raised nihilistic anarchism to the status of a religion whose fundamental dogma seems to be: "I kill, therefore I am."

Inspired and sustained by this metaphysics of murder, centers of organized revolution have mushroomed in every nation. They seem bent on demonstrating the truth of Oscar Wilde's aphorism: "Moderation is a fatal thing. Nothing succeeds like excess."[1] Moreover, they enthusiastically strive to experience both the subject and the object of Shakepeare's truism: "Violent delights have violent ends."[2]

"New" immorality proclaimed

Nietzsche is the prophet who foresaw and foretold the coming of the beast of violence. Indeed, he proclaimed its greatest commandment whose faithful practice would create a society of savages. "The time has come," he wrote, "to oppose morality with immorality, to call what priests call good, evil and what they call evil, good. The time has come for the transvaluation of all values."[3] This prophet of modernity, of revolutionary society and radical thought was a champion of extremes. He also wrote: "We moralists do not even need to lie. . . . We would come into power without the truth. . . . The magic that fights for us is the magic of extremism."[4] Nietzsche, who accepted with pride the description of himself as an "aristocratic radical," was used by Marx and his followers to create citadels (Russia, Red China, Cuba, Nicaragua, the Eastern Satellites) as camps for the training of armies of proletarian radicals. These centers of organized revolution radiate out to the whole world the call for violence and rebellion. This call is beamed everywhere twenty-four hours a day, for these centers, and their apostles of hatred everywhere in the world, effectively, ceaselessly and secretly work, like the law of gravity, to pull down to destruction every civil and religious community striving for social justice and peace. Now both Nietzsche and Marx foresaw the public victory of the extreme side of their thinking. This gave them both the experience of triumphant power. There is a hypnotizing fascination in their fanaticisms. Their chaotic excesses, their iron wills, their high voltage writings have attracted millions over the last hundred years to fly with suicidal enthusiasm and madness into their incandescent ideologies. Nietzsche was forever knocking down things and taking wild delight in their destruction.

> O My Brothers, am I cruel? But I say: What is falling we should still push. Everything today falls and decays: Who would check it? But I — I even want to push it. Do you know the voluptuous delight which rolls stones into deep depths? These human beings of today — Look at them! How they roll into my depth! I am a prelude of better players. O My Brothers! A precedent! Follow my precedent! And he whom you cannot teach to fly, teach to fall, faster! . . . To this mankind of today I will not be a light, nor be called a light. Those I will blind! Put out their eyes, O Flash of my Wisdom![5]

We are living in the days of Nietzsche's better players who, ecstatic with "the voluptuous delight which rolls humans into deep depths," keep pushing society to the brink of social chaos and suicide. Yeats in his poem "The Second Spring," reveals the murderous zeal of Nietzsche's modern ideological offspring:

> Things fall apart; the center cannot hold
> the blood-dimmed tide is loosed and everywhere
> The ceremony of innocence is drowned.

The best lack all conviction, while the worst are
Full of passionate intensity.
Surely some revelation is at hand;
Surely the Second coming is at hand.[6]

The word *violence* is derived from the Latin verb *violare* which means
to use force so as to injure an innocent person in his physical and spiritual
welfare. To be more specific, this force is often used to subdue, dominate,
rob, rape or kill the innocent, perhaps too, even his family, friends and
properties. When such attacks of force were made against institutions, then
the violence engendered took on more heinous proportions because of its
social and religious aspect. For the Greeks and Romans, and for us their
cultural heirs, violence against sacred persons was a sacrilege, against
temples a profanation, against the state treason, against oaths perjury. Such
violent acts were seen as acts of irreligious contempt for law, a dishonoring
of the gods, barbarian attempts to overthrow religion, the holy empire and
its emperor gods. Though used today more often in its first, predominantly
secular meaning given above, violence still retains its profane, sacrilegious
dimension especially when sacred persons, places and things are the victims
of its onslaughts. And this onslaught on sacred beings is occurring more
frequently today as violence becomes a worldwide, universal phenomenon.
Popes, ministers, rabbis, nuns, priests, temples, mosques, synagogues and
churches have been frequently and flagrantly assaulted within the last fifteen
years. And there is no end in sight for today's violent offspring of Nietzsche,
Marx and the atheist humanists, are determined to destroy not merely the
secular but, above all, the sacred.

It suffices to look at some of the ruins. The universities, once centers
of Christian wisdom, are now very often training grounds for post-Christian
pagans. In the cities mass confrontation has degenerated into guerrilla warfare. In the Churches clergymen and clergywomen, seeking notoriety,
proclaim the ''new morality'' of hedonism and engage in the burning of
property, the supplying of rebels with lethal weapons. In the media, under
the rubric of liberty and reform, the role of traitors and violent protesters
is romanticized. Thus, factories, schools, theatres, civic halls and chapels
have become launching pads for the projection of violence into the
surrounding peaceful communities.

Our laws are under siege

Concerning television as an agent in the spread of violence we now
have a scientific report that proves this to be true. On May 6, 1982, the
National Institute of Mental Health published a Federal Report, the result
of 10 years of careful research, on the relationship between violence in everyday human behavior and violence on the television screen.[7] The report

concluded that there is now "overwhelming" scientific evidence that "excessive" violence on television leads directly to growing aggression and violent behavior among children and teen-agers. The report states: "In magnitude, television violence is as strongly correlated with aggressive behavior as any other behavioral variable that has been measured." Children, teen-agers and even adults who heavily viewed violent programs were found to be often in conflict at home, fighting on the streets and in aggressive delinquency at play. "Television has become a violent form of entertainment." Why? There are at least four reasons. 1) Frequent visual violent behavior rubs off on youngsters the way language, cultural and social skills are learned and imitated from parents and friends. 2) Violent attitude postures and changes are induced by the heavy violence witnessed on the screen. Viewers become distrustful, suspicious, unruly, antisocial after the characters they are constantly viewing. 3) Violent episodes often arouse physiological reactions leading to violent deeds. 4) The too frequent viewing of violent scenes is often used by viewers to justify their own aggressive conduct, especially when these viewers eagerly identify with their favorite television stars on violent programs.[8] Because violence has been idolized, romanticized, fantasized, viewers want to participate in it. Thus television has become an occasion of violent sins for the unwary, untrained, easily seduced youth of the nation, while the channels, the producers and actors of the programs rake in millions from the unconcerned advertisers who could care less what happens to the nation's youth as long as they rake in their multi-millions too.

In politics, ideological sloganizing develops the proclivity for violence in the intellectually rootless and spiritually depersonalized masses, fashioning them into willing storm-troopers bent on overturning legal and peace-keeping institutions with neither thought nor care about what to put in their places. And the courts, having usurped legislative power and become sociological agents bent on advancing the general will for corruption disguised as progress, deliver the worst blows against man's civil and religious liberties. For the Justices seem to consider themselves as movers and shapers of the country's destiny rather than as impersonal spokesmen for the law. The decision in *Roe v. Wade* converted the crime of murder against innocent, helpless humans in the womb into the folly and madness of a permanent law. British historian Edward Gibbon wrote in *The History of the Decline and Fall of the Roman Empire* that "the discretion of the judge is the first engine of tyranny."[9] This is especially true today when judges see themselves not as faithful interpreters of the law but as social reformers who make the law mean what their own sociological prepossessions want it to mean. Is it any wonder that today the courts are coddling criminals while betraying the fundamental rights of innocent victims? For they who do violence to the law perpetrate violence against the citizenry that must be judged by the law. The Justices, the judges and the courts may be today the greatest agents of violence against the greatest number of helpless, innocent American children who should be the greatest resource that the nation has for its future. A nation under judgment by Justices, judges and courts that have slipped their legal moorings in order to usurp legislative power is headed for shipwreck on the shoals of legalistic imperialism. Such is the violent, tragic state of affairs in the United States at the present moment.

The West has opted for sin

What is the taproot which is causing such growth in the delirium for violence which is rampant today? It is the attack against God. *It is hatred of the truth.* Behind the metaphysic of murder lies the metaphysic of hatred of the created order. "I refuse to accept this order of things. I will not serve, therefore I am." Refusal to serve God was the cry under which Satan brought violence and rebellion among the angels as they stood trial in the vestibule of heaven. Christ told his apostles: "I saw Satan like lightning falling from heaven."[10] Elsewhere we read: "Satan and his wicked demons were drawn down by infernal ropes into the depths of hell."[11] Christ himself testified that this "father of lies was a murderer from the beginning," thus making the connection between hatred of the truth and the lust for violence. He warned the Pharisees that men who reject God's plan for their salvation will imitate Satan's deeds.

As a matter of history, the religious leaders of the Jews were looking for a Messiah who would be a conquering hero, a military Savior who would subject the Gentiles to the service of the Chosen People and thus usher in that worldly, materialistic utopia which the leaders had falsely fabricated from their misinterpretations of the Scriptures. When king Herod heard of the birth of the king of the Jews in Bethlehem, he sent soldiers to seek him out and kill him as a threatening rival in political power. So secularized had the notion of the Messiah become among the Jews. But God, ever faithful to the revelations he gave his prophets, sent his Son as the Suffering Servant to save all nations through his humiliation and death on the cross. Instead of a terrestrial kingdom of pleasure and power, the Son of God established a supernatural kingdom of sacrifice and sanctity. This plan of God, this humble Messiah scandalized the Pharisees. They rejected Christ, fought against his kingdom, plotted his death. If they could not have their own type of Messiah, neither would they accept God's. To make sure the Jewish people would not be seduced by Christ, they plotted the death of Christ and trapped the Romans into doing their dirty work for them. And then, as if this hatred of God's truth were not bad enough, in the presence of their Roman masters, whom they despised, they justified their violence against Christ by shouting out, in a frenzy of mob madness, this sacrilegious lie: "We have no king but Caesar!"

We live in an age of violence because we live in an age of organized and spreading atheism. In the West, nations that have rejected absolute Christian values and truths, that have dissolved God into a series of harmless abstractions, that have disestablished and secularized religion, that have fostered permissiveness and favored heresy, are living lives pleasing to that "murderer from the beginning." Such a pseudo-Christian civilization is trying to live off the vanishing perfume of Christianity, having abandoned its substance long ago. In coming to terms with lying, fornication, adultery, divorce, sexual perversion and mass abortion, the West has opted for a life of sin — the source of every violent way of life. Such a decadent civilization cannot any longer attract its citizens to work for the ideals and virtues it has long betrayed. On the contrary, corrupt nations inflame men to violent rebellion because of their betrayal of these values and of their hypocrisy in still posing as champions of Christianity.

Betrayal arises in man's heart

Our modern atheistic Leviathans with their amazing advancement in technical progress have, nevertheless, turned men into machines, destroying their sense of personal dignity and responsibility. True, they have afforded man much upper middle class affluence. But even this, because it lacks religious roots, has only excited the passions of greed and pleasure, has riveted man to an earthly, ruthless competition for more wealth and power and has suffocated his spiritual, humane aspirations. The revolutionaries of today are striking in blind hatred against this system of post-Christian hedonism. For nations that have nothing to peddle but facts and things, that attempt to solve social problems with an anti-life policy of legalizing and financing contraception and abortion, that can no longer throw light on the spiritual dimension and destiny of man, are being violently vomited out of the stomach of an enraged mankind.

Falsity is the heart of immorality, and hatred of truth is the taproot of criminal violence. Unfortunately, men take violence for granted as an ugly fact of life and seldom attempt to plumb the metaphysical and theological roots of its nature and existence. We are all aware of the tremendous role of violence in the unfolding history of human events. But what is not realized is that the apparent arbitrariness and haphazardness of violence can be and ought to be seriously and precisely analyzed from the philosophical and theological point of view. The need for a thoroughgoing treatise on criminal aggressivity is testified to by the rising flood of objective evils perpetrated by individual and organized agents of violence.

Many are tempted to be untrue

As we saw earlier, violence entered creation from the rebellion of Lucifer. This rebellion arose from the heart of pride. But the sin of pride is the offspring of the vice known as hatred of truth. Hatred of truth is the result of the creature's attempt to rearrange God's hierarchy of beings and values into an order which the creature prefers to the plan of God. This attempt immediately produces the violence of disorder, the chaos of falsity and immorality. For hatred of truth is really hatred of God who creates all things wisely and governs them lovingly. Lucifer, the Morning Star, was instantly deformed into the Prince of Darkness because he attempted to live a lie. He wanted to dethrone God and become God himself. Here is Scripture's account of the event:

> How art thou fallen from heaven, O Lucifer, who did rise in the morning? How are you fallen to the earth, that did wound the nations? And you said in your heart: I will ascend into heaven; I will exalt my throne above the stars of God; I will sit in the mountain of the covenant, in the sides of the north. I will ascend above the height of the clouds. I will be like the Most High. But yet you shall be brought down into hell, into the depths of the pit.[12]

And St. Peter relates the divine vengeance that hatred of truth drew down upon demons and evil men alike:

> For God did not spare the angels when they sinned, but dragged them down by infernal ropes to Tartarus, and delivered them to be tortured and kept in custody for judgment. Nor did he spare the ancient world, but preserved (with seven others) Noe a herald of justice, when he brought a flood upon the world of the impious. And he condemned the cities of Sodom and Gomorrah to destruction, reducing them to ashes, thus making them an example to those who in the future should live impiously.[13]

St. John the Evangelist in his Apocalypse sees in a flashback vision the violence that broke out between the demons and the holy angels:

> And there was a battle in heaven; Michael and his angels battled with the dragon, and the dragon fought with his angels. And they did not prevail, neither was their place found any more in heaven. And that great dragon was cast down, the ancient serpent, he who is called the devil and Satan, who leads astray the whole world; and he was cast down to the earth and with him his angels were cast down . . . Woe to the earth and to the sea, because the devil has gone down to you in great wrath, knowing that he has but a short time.[14]

St. Thomas starts with the truth taught by Christ to his apostles that all evil issues forth from an evil heart and bad will. ''But the things that proceed out of the mouth come from the heart, and it is they that defile a man. For out of the heart come evil thoughts, murders, adulteries, immorality, thefts, false witness, blasphemies. These are the things that defile a man. . . .'' In his discussion of violence St. Thomas lists five elements that constitute the nature of violence and describe its context. 1) Violence is that which causes any being to act contrary to its nature or natural inclination. 2) The agent of violence is always extrinsic to that which is violated. 3) The natural inclination of a being is always prior to the violence and is presupposed by an act of violence. This constituent of violence recognizes the fact that man as an agent or efficient cause cannot, strictly speaking, create anything, but always presupposes the existence of that with which he works. Man, at best, is the cause of becoming, never the cause of being. In fact it is precisely the existence of natures with their intrinsic inclinations that renders the violent act possible by the extrinsic cause. 4) The intensity of the violence is in proportion to the severity in which a being's natural inclination is removed from attaining its natural end. 5) Evil is always related to violence and vice versa.[15] In this connection power must not be confused with violence, for power — physical or spiritual — is morally neutral, not evil in itself and becomes evil only when used for evil purposes or under evil circumstances, e.g., in acts of aggression.

In summary then, violence is an attempt by an external agent to force natures to perform actions contrary to their intrinsic, essential inclinations. Although these essences with their inclinations are conditions without which violence itself would be impossible, the intensity of the violence and of the evil effects produced by it are in proportion to the severity in which the natures are rendered incapable of attaining their ends. Thus violence can be understood as a creature's attempt to rearrange, redefine, indeed, almost recreate, a being and direct it away from its divinely appointed end towards an arbitrarily selected end that leads to the convenience, the pleasure and even self-glorification of the violent agent.

Firm convictions needed

We can imagine the tremendous violence that must have burst forth in the war between the faithful angels and the demons. Being pure spirits, far more intelligent and powerful than men, that war in heaven must certainly have dwarfed all the most violent wars in human history taken together. Scripture relates that just one angel, passing over the sleeping army of the Assyrians who were besieging Jerusalem, killed in one night one hundred and eighty thousand soldiers. Moreover, an indication of the power of the angels is suspected when one realizes the enormity of the act of

violence which Satan and his demons planned to perpetrate in heaven. They
were to dethrone God and become God with their own power and on their
own terms. They were to demote God from Creator to creature and advance
themselves to Almighty power and honors. Such was their hatred of God
and the order of creation that Satan and his demons would have destroyed
both if they could. Indeed in their attempted violence Satan and his demons
even violated their own natures, chose for themselves a goal contrary to
their natures and a destiny that has made them eternal failures hardened
in iniquity. And when Satan and his devils were ''cast down to the earth,''
Scripture tells us that they continued their violence by being the agents
''who lead astray the whole world.'' ''Woe to the earth and the sea,'' a
voice from heaven cries out in the vision seen by St. John in the Apocalypse,
''because the devil has gone down to you in great wrath, knowing he has
but a short time.''[16] That ''short time'' is the last days, or the time between
the Ascension of Christ into glory and his Second Coming. St. Peter tells
mankind how these demons are using this short time. ''For your adversary
the devil goes about like a roaring lion seeking whom he may devour.''[17]

From the above study we must conclude that violence involves one
in a special metaphysics whose first principle is this: To be is to be willed;
or to be is the effect of a creature's free decision. The real is what a creature
wants it to be. Truth is what men want truth to be. We have here the
philsophical attitude of violence known as subjectivism, i.e., a personal
hatred of existing truth posing as the creator of new truth, a world of lies
fabricated in the fantasies of aggressively rebellious creatures. Because this
voluntaristic, irrational intentionality nurtures irrational violence it is intrinsically evil even before the external act of violence is committed. Eve
sinned before she took a bite out of the apple; she sinned when she took
the word of the serpent over the word of God and decided the serpent's
version of reality was the version she wanted to experience — to become
godlike on her own terms, not on God's terms. And so she chose death
instead of life. ''In the day you shall eat of that fruit you shall die.'' Thus
arrogant voluntarism is the mother of criminal violence, for it proclaims
the lie that the creature's whims take precedence over the divine natural
law which is incarnated in creation and stamped on the conscience by the
God of creation.

Shakespeare, with a poet's profound, prophetic vision, demonstrates
in the tragic destiny of Macbeth that, when hatred of the existing order
of truth is incarnated in voluntaristic attempts to change that truth, such
hatred produces bloody deeds which create that murderous nothingness
known as sin, that working of the mystery of iniquity which would destroy
God, but succeeds only in destroying sinners, in this case Lady Macbeth
through madness, Lord Macbeth by the sword. Macbeth himself, in a

profound soliloquy, sensed the tragic finale of his violence as he nurtured the temptation to rearrange the order of kingship in the kingdom of Scotland to his own and his wife's aggrandizement:

> This supernatural soliciting
> ...cannot be good:....
> If good, why do I yield to that suggestion
> Whose horrid image doth unfix my hair,
> And make my seated heart knock at my ribs,
> Against the use of nature? Present fears
> Are less than horrible imaginings:
> My thought, whose murder yet is but
>   fantastical,
> Shakes so my single state of man, that
>   function
> Is smothered in surmise; and nothing is
> But what is not.[18]

In our endeavor to disclose the intelligible features of violence we have restricted our scrutiny to the taproot of violence — hatred of truth. There are other roots of violence which can be studied in relation to other relevant attitudes of the person, such as, pride, vanity, covetousness, distrust, suspicion, infidelity, envy, revenge, lust, anger, greed. The study of these relationships to violence would help to sharpen and deepen our insights into the nature of the abyss of violence. An investigation of this sort would involve us in a discussion about the cure or treatment of this curse of criminal aggressivity which constitutes a terrible plague in our times.

An allied, though external reason for the escalation of violence today is the failure of authority — that spiritual power — to exercise itself as a bulwark against criminal violence. This failure is due to the weakened adherence to truth and the loss of faith of both civil and religious authorities. The poet Yeats so well expressed this problem endemic in our days. "The best in society lack all conviction, the worst (the criminals) are full of passionate intensity." For violence proliferates with the breakdown of authority. And authority breaks down when Christian convictions are denied in theory or betrayed in cowardly conduct. When governors, superiors, lawmakers, administrators and teachers cease to believe that they have a body of truth to teach and a code of Christian holiness to live up to, inculcate into others and, yes, even die for, then the community is abandoned by its leaders and left a prey to professional inciters of murder and rapine. For once bereft of effective Christian leadership, the masses are pathetically prone to heed the siren call to revolution. When authority is confused, apathetic, fearful of performing its duty, then society falls into the hands of the most cunning and powerful who are usually organized and proceed to amalgamate ruthlessly communities into communes. When authority is weak it often succumbs to blackmail, thus becoming a catalyst to fiercer attacks of the revolutionaries. For successful violence inevitably calls forth greater, bolder, more frequent violence. What civil and especially religious authorities must realize is that the apologists for organized violence know no loyalty, reverence, reality but their own selfish goals. They are neo-nihilists, spiritually famished, deprived of mature personhood by self-idolization. They are the waifs of a materialist, godless civilization that seeks a utopia here and now. What they need is not coddling but discipline. What they admire and respond to is not capitulation but firm convictions and adamant enforcement of doctrinal, moral and civil laws. When authorities, civil and religious, are eaten up with a zeal for truth and holiness, when they show a courage that is the fruit of deep Christian convictions and conduct, when they demonstrate a love for wandering souls that stops at no sacrifice to bring them back to the Good Shepherd of all souls, then the rising tide of criminal violence will begin to fall to a low ebb. Then the spiritual starvelings who are fascinated with the violence of gangsters and of hucksters of false ideologies may be won back to the violence known as intensity of love, that zeal which conquers the kingdom of heaven and leads to a life of truth, holiness, peace and joy with God and man. "The truth will make you free," says Christ. And to be sure a society founded on adherence to truth and holiness will enjoy a peace and a freedom that are immune from the plague of criminal violence.

Notes

[1] Oscar Wilde, quoted in *Roget's Thesaurus* under *violence.*
[2] Shakespeare, *Romeo And Juliet,* Act II, scene 6.
[3] Friedrich Nietzsche, *Thus Spake Zarathustra,* p. 144.
[4] Karl Jaspers, quotes Nietzsche thus in his *Nietzsche and Christianity.*
[5] Nietzsche, *ibid.,* p. 321.
[6] Yeats, *The Second Spring.*
[7] *New York Times,* May 6, 1982, "An Overwhelming Violence-TV Tie."
[8] *Ibid.*
[9] Edward Gibbon, *The History of the Decline and Fall of the Roman Empire.*
[10] Luke, 10:18.
[11] 2 Peter, 2:4.
[12] Isaiah, 14:12-20.
[13] 2 Peter, 2:4-7.
[14] John, Apocalypse, 12:7-9.
[15] St. Thomas, Summa Theologica, Par. II, Q. 6, a.5; Contra Gen. 1, 13, 19, 39. Cf. article by J.J. Califano in Divus Thomas, 1975, a. 78, "Technology and Violence."
[16] John, Apocalypse, 12:7-12.
[17] 1 Peter, 5:8.
[18] Shakespeare, *Macbeth,* Act 1, Scene 3.

Reprinted from *Homiletic & Pastoral Review,* December 1982.

Christ and Revolution

Just when a flood tide of liberation theology is inundating churches and campuses in the U.S.A., attempting to suffocate the Christian faith of millions, Marcel Clement's brilliant exposé comes to the rescue from across the Atlantic. *Christ and Revolution* is expertly translated from the French by philosopher-scholar Dr. Alice von Hildebrand, author of *Greek Culture: the Adventure of the Human Spirit* and of *Introduction to the Philosophy of Religion.* Marcel Clement, a prominent French Catholic layman, was professor for more than 15 years at the School of Business Executives of Christian Patronage. He has travelled all over the world on professional missions and, besides being the Director of *L'Homme Nouveau,* a prestigious bi-monthly journal, he has authored: *Socialism; Social Philosophy; Woman and her Vocation* and *The Joy of Loving.*

Liberation unto sanctity

To the question: "Is there a social message implied in the Gospels?" Marcel Clement responds that the most powerful, most efficacious, most universal social message ever presented to man is found in the teachings of Jesus Christ. But it is not the social message put forward by the liberationist theologians — Catholic and non-Catholic — under the banner of a "revolutionary" Gospel. Christ did not come primarily to renew society as found in history. He came to liberate men spiritually, to rescue them from serfdom to sin and Satan. Christ preached a baptism of repentance for the remission of sin; his is a mystical liberation even today, a work of mystery in the interior, silent, prayerful, penitent recollection of the soul with God. Christ redeemed men through the sacrifice of the cross, unchaining them from original sin as well as from all personal sins sincerely repented of. At the same time this supernatural liberation ushers man into the holy life of God through grace. Of course, persons thus freed had to cooperate in their redemption and sanctification; they had to die to themselves, to reject utterly Satan and all his works and pomps; they had to make sacrifices for the brotherly community founded in Christ, to sustain their brethren in daily trials, to carry the cross after Christ and to strive to live a daily life of faith, hope and charity. Now this fraternal, supernatural life is essentially the fruit of the interior, mystical life of prayer and the exterior sacramental life of communion with God in Christ. Here is the social message in the Gospels, the charitable cooperation of each member of the Mystical Body with each other and with their neighbours so that all may come to know and grow up in Christ the Head of the Body.

Liberation into serfdom

But the liberationist theologians discover a different social message in the Gospels, founded not on the dialectics of repentance, love and reconciliation in the cross but on the dialectics of revolution and class struggle. Marcel Clement, however, cleverly tracks down this new liberationist Gospel and traps it in its atheistic lair where it was born and raised to its present menacing stature. Rousseau and the Encyclopedists made an idol of abstract liberty, guaranteeing men absolute autonomy or individualistic liberation. This autonomy only liberated the masses and their governments into serfdom to nineteenth century economic dinosaurs. Then in a dialectical antithesis to Manchesterian serfdom, the socialists guaranteed absolute liberty to the masses if the masses would revolt against their masters and agree to live in an egalitarian collectivity dominated by an omnicompetent State. But Prudhon revolted against this collectivity. He undertook to liberate man totally by setting revelation and revolution in complete opposition. His "religious" Socialism sought to demote, desacralize and destroy the Catholic Church and thus open the way to a revolutionary morality founded on the organ of collective reason. This organ was said to be present in groups formed to discuss ideas and promote world-wide justice.

But then Marx rejected this utopian Socialism of "petit bourgeois" Prudhon. Yet, like Rousseau and Prudhon, Marx accepted revolution as a precondition for the liberated state. Rousseau placed his hope for human salvation in the "general will" of the sovereign people; Prudhon hoped in world-wide justice attained by discussion groups. Marx placed his hope in the "proletariat". Though transitory, the dictatorship of the proletariat would, using class struggle and revolution, abolish all classes, realize economic liberation through Socialism, wipe out religious alienation and liberate men from God, religion, churches. But this fertile tree of liberation was to produce new fruits. Freud, following Marx and deeming religion to be a collective neurosis which psychoanalysis had the mission to break down, taught man to liberate himself from his sexual repressions, the root of his fears and failures. Wilhelm Reich then went further seeking a sexual revolution capable of establishing "a revolutionary morality" of sexual drives, a morality of the dominating clerical class. Thus today sexual liberation has become the pivot of a cultural revolution and in the name of total liberation every type of sexual immorality and perversion is justified. Finally, Marcuse is seeking the ultimate freedom — metaphysical liberation; he is trying the impossible, to liberate man from his human finitude, from his contingency, from his time-space dimensions, indeed from his very creaturehood. In the end the gospel of liberation makes man his own God. Man's will has become the reason for his being; he is his own God; he is his own Alpha and Omega. As a result of this ontological liberation, man's cult is the cult of himself. In self-adoration, imitating Satan seduced by his own beauty, man strives to express in his private, political, family, economic and cultural life his ontological independence of God.

The dialectics of ideological detente

Now what Marcel Clement so expertly demonstrates is that many Catholics, moved by a sincere desire to save mankind from the "sin of the world," namely economic injustice, have — some wittingly, others unwittingly — baptized Socialism and Communism, having accepted even their methods of class struggle and revolution in the quest for man's total liberation. Influenced by the rhetoric of these salvation systems, such naive Catholics have made it their mission to plunge the Church into the class struggle. They aim at degrading the Church's apostolate of redeeming men from sin and Satan to an apostolate of liberating men first from poverty and eventually from every ontological, moral or divine law. Their entrapment in this sterile adventure has been cleverly achieved by their atheistic friends. In a dialectic of friendly *detente* with the militant forces of atheistic Socialism, many Christians have surrendered to the spirit of the world. They have succumbed to the seductions of non-believers and followed after false, double-minded prophets. Theirs has been a fatal concession, the whole of the deposit of the faith and the treasury of Christian morality. They have been persuaded to interpret Christianity according to Socialist-Marxist principles. These so-called "Christian Socialists" or "Marxist Christians" are now teaching a new understanding of the faith, of the Gospels, of the Church, a new way of living in harmony with the Marxist vision of history. And so they proclaim insistently that they are liberating the Gospels and the Church from the ideological superstructures of a decadent, capitalistic society. They emphasize that they are returning both the Gospel message and the Church's mission to their true, original, revolutionary inspiration and vigour. Unfortunately, ideas have consequences and violent ideas have violent consequences. Thus these Marxist Christians have been infected with more than the ideology of their atheistic friends. For in a hostile dialectic of confrontation with their fellow-Christians, they attack the Church with an animus of a prosecutor accusing a man in the dock of criminal activity. Infected also with the activist dialectics of the class struggle and violent revolution they go beyond dialogue to distortion and anathema against the faith, the Magisterium, the whole Church. Such is their furor against the Church that, in opposing her teaching, they eviscerate the authentic Gospel revelation, demote Christ to the level of a mere man, the Church to the level of a mere natural institution and render Christianity meaningless.

Final judgment

Marcel Clement gives a profound final judgment on these seducers of the spirit who attempt to arrange a marriage between Christianity and all forms of Socialism. Pope after pope has condemned this attempt, demonstrating how Christianity and Socialism are hopelessly incompatible partners, not only psychologically but above all ontologically. And no matter how often or expertly Socialism has its features lifted through the slick art of "new Christianity" surgery, it will never acquire the beauty of a human, much less Christian face. For it denies man's divine origin and destiny; it strips man of the exercise of his liberty, initiative and creative intelligence. Moreover, its appeal to the masses to revolt against established institutions under the trumpet call from a Christ burlesqued as the Great Liberator and the Grand Subverter, is sheer sacrilege and religious demagoguery.

Marcel Clement concludes in the name of his fellow-Christians thus: "I know for a fact that my reaction to the 'new Christianity,' cast in a Marxist-Leninist mould, is not isolated! The silent majority of the Christians in France, in the name of the Word of God, *choose* the social doctrine of the Church, for there is one. It, and it alone, is the perfect way to communion with God who has come to live among us." This powerful little book, which expounds so well the social doctrine of the Church and unmasks so completely the Marxist caricature of Christianity, is *must* reading for bishops, priests, religious and all lay leaders who are zealous about sharing, in love with their fellowmen, the authentic revelation in the Gospels of Christ the Son of God and of His Mystical Body the Church.

Reprinted from *L'Osservatore Romano,* November 20, 1975.

The Morality of Nuclear Weapons

In *Nuclear Weapons: A Catholic Response,* five distinguished British university professors discuss the morality of those weapons. Four of them are philosophers and all are Catholic; but, despite different personal emphases, all of them agree that the best Christian counsel is non-violent resistance.

The editor of the symposium, Walter Stein, calls for a "policy of unconditional disarmament" together with willingness in the West to oppose "the ultimate weapon of meaningful suffering to Communist invasion; the future can safely be left to God." Professor Anscombe deplores "double think about double effect." Nuclear weapons, he maintains, have obliterated the distinction between the intended killing of combatants and the accidental killing of the innocent. Professor Markus asserts that making, holding, and exploding such weapons is morally wrong in any circumstances. He encourages "our representative to throw caution to the winds. . . . Mr. Khrushchev has offered complete mutual disarmament. There is no excuse for not taking him at his word." Professor Geach contends: Granted that Communist domination intensifies allurement to apostasy, should Christians expect immunity from severe temptation? Professor Smith claims that papal and episcopal documents brand as immoral every use of nuclear weapons, even testing.

Despite the prestige of these professors, I am unconvinced by their reasonings. The authors are "relative pacifists." They hold, not that war is an intrinsic evil, but that today it can never be justified because of the uncontrollable effects of nuclear weapons. This premise is both unproven and erroneous. Thomas E. Murray, formerly of the AEC, assures us that "a nuclear war can still be a limited war." On April 12, 1956 he proposed to the Senate Subcommittee on Disarmament a program for "rational nuclear armaments" that would set a limit to the number of bombs, develop only bombs of low-order destructiveness and restrict testing to underground sites. This program is rational because "it is consistent with the moral principles of the civilized tradition in waging war and it is adapted to the military necessities of the nuclear age."

On September 10, 1954 Pius XII said: "One cannot, even in principle, raise the question of the liceity of ABC (atomic, bacteriological, chemical) warfare except in the case in which it must be judged indispensable for self-defense in the conditions indicated."

The conditions indicated are the traditional seven that must all be fulfilled for a war of self-defense to be deemed justifiable. The war must be 1) undertaken in a just cause; 2) waged by lawful authority; 3) directed with a just intention; 4) resorted to as the only means remaining to check unjust aggression; 5) engaged in with morally permissible means; 6) assured of a reasonable hope of success; 7) directed toward attaining a good that outweighs the evils it brings about.

The contributors to *Nuclear Weapons* admit that in Communist aggression against the free world the first four conditions are fulfilled. The last three, however, are not, they insist, because nuclear weapons are never morally permissible; no side ever succeeds in a nuclear war and no good can ever outweigh the evil of annihilation.

What none of the authors has been able to see is that some day nuclear war may be indispensable for self-defense and that its conduct need not be uncontrollable or immoral so long as governmental policy guarantees its limited use. Intelligence, good will and fear can do this. Neither misuse of nuclear weapons in the past nor the probability of misuse in the future is proof that any use of these weapons is immoral. The last contention begets the spiritual posture sloganized in the dilemma of defeatism: *"Lieber rot als tot."* Fr. John Courtney Murray has exposed the fallacy in this pernicious dilemma.

"The choice, of course," he has written, "is between the desperate alternatives, either universal atomic death or complete surrender to Communism. The Catholic mind, schooled in the traditional doctrine of war and peace, rejects the dangerous fallacy involved in this casting up of desperate alternatives. Hidden beneath the fallacy is an abdication of the moral reason and a craven submission to some manner of technological or historical determinism." (*Morality and Modern Warfare,* p. 84.)

The belief in unconditional, unilateral disarmament that abandons the future to God and settles down to passive suffering in the present is a political Quietism that will guarantee the very fate the relative pacifists hope to avoid: self-annihilation and passive absorption into Communism. Perhaps many adults can suffer individually unto a meaningful death. The history of persecutions testifies that many would defect and suffer uselessly.

And what would become of the children? Communists completely cut the lifeline between parents and children, between priests and people. How meaningful can be the suffering of adult Christians who, because they meekly surrendered, must stand by and helplessly behold the inevitable transformation of their children into incarnate devils?

There are no catacombs in Communist countries where Christians may hold secret services to preserve and hand on their faith. The secret police are everywhere and a scientifically efficient system of spying and violence pervades every place and person. How does a parent teach his child the Sign of the Cross when the child must report this religious act as a political act of treason? To surrender unconditionally to the Communists without a fight is to cooperate by default in their program. Christians who fail to witness in deeds to the primacy of spiritual and supernatural values leave the present and future of their children to the annihilation of moral slavery, a condition infinitely worse than the merely physical death and destruction threatened by all-out war.

Pius XII, who never allowed his horror of nuclear war to blur his vision or weaken his will, in an address to military doctors upheld "the absolute necessity of self-defense against a very grave injustice that touches the community, that cannot be impeded by other means, that nevertheless must be impeded on pain of giving free field in international relations to brutal violence and lack of conscience." He knew that resolution to defend the right at all costs is the strongest deterrent to unjust aggression. Non-violent resistance may be laudable against a grave injustice that touches the individual alone. It is irrelevant, dangerous, and immoral against very grave injustices that touch the community in political and religious matters.

In the tragic aftermath of the Hungarian Revolution, when the brutal deeds of Communist violence shocked a complacent world, Pius XII wrote:

> "...when the threat is made to use atomic arms to obtain concrete demands...it becomes clear that...there may come into existence in a nation a situation in which all hope of averting war becomes vain. In this situation a war of efficacious self-defense against unjust attacks...cannot be considered illicit."

I accept Fr. Murray's conclusion as the only valid Catholic response to the threat of nuclear war: "One cannot...uphold the simple statement that atomic war as such, without further qualifications, is morally unjustifiable, or that all use of atomic weapons in war is, somehow in principle, evil." (*Morality and Modern Warfare*, p. 79.)

Humanitarian pacifism is naturalism in soft garments. It evaluates tragic events with a sentimentalism that implies that physical survival and materialist progress are absolutes. A truly Catholic response to nuclear warfare never downgrades the supreme human goods that transcend the temporal; it embraces the divine life of the Faith as that "pearl of great price" for which any chalice of sorrows must be drained to its dregs, even to the lees of nuclear war. Clear-minded and resolute in a wilderness of incoherent whimpering, the valid response rejects a trembling-reed posture before the atomic winds of Communist hatred.

Reprinted from *National Review,* October 9, 1962.

Abortion: God's Viewpoint

"My Delight is to be with the Children of Men." (Prov. 8:31)

Things do not just happen in human lives; they are brought about by intelligent causes. The Roman poet Virgil wrote: *Felix qui potuit rerum cognoscere causas.*[1] "Blessed is he who has been able to discover the causes of things." Thus, when friends sing out with joy: "Happy Birthday, Dear Maria! Happy Birthday to you!" they are not only rejoicing over the presence in life and love of Maria, they are also paying thankful tribute to the agents of Maria's birthdays — her parents and God. They are joyful that God chose, in an act of love from all eternity, to give Maria existence in the womb of her mother. They are also grateful that Maria's parents loved her enough to bring her into the world and to raise her up in the friendship of her family and friends. All our birthdays are gifts of God and of our parents who cooperated in divine and human love to welcome us to the banquet of life.

Unlike humans whose desires are often sterile, God's desires are always creative. Thus He does not just say his "delight is to be with the children of men." He creates the fruitfulness of this desire by sending His Son, the Second Person of the Holy Trinity, God from all eternity, to become a child of man by assuming a human nature from the Virgin Mary. Thus the Son of God becomes the Son of Man through the marvelous condescension of the Incarnation. His "delight" is really to become a child of man, to live among the children of men, like them in all things except sin.

From this action of God we can deduce God's relationship of love to human children. From all eternity God loves each human person that he has chosen to create. Why? There can be no reason for this love in the persons loved, for they were, prior to their creation, no-thing, nonentities. St. Augustine exclaims in wonder: "Why do I exist and not millions of others whom He knows and could have created?" He answers: "Because God is good, I exist."[3] But the mind still demands a reason for this goodness to me. In what does this divine goodness towards each created person consist? Here we are forced to go beyond reason; the heart not the intellect must speak. *Love does such things!* We are in the presence of the mystery of God's preferential love for each one of us. "I have loved you with an everlasting love, therefore, have I drawn you (out of nothingness) taking pity on you." "Before you were formed in the womb, I knew and loved you," is the divine message each person's existence is proclaiming to himself and to the world. Is it any wonder that the human mind is flabbergasted, at a thought impasse, before this mystery of divine, prodigal, unsolicitable, unmerited love? There is no fathoming the "Why?" of such ineffable love. Knowledge is nothing compared with loving. The fact is that God's greatest blessings spring not from the intellect but from the heart. The first and final word of the whole of creation is not "I know you," but "I love you." *Love does such things!* And God's love is His mysterious, incomprehensible divine nature. From all eternity, then, God has been and still is enamoured of every human child conceived in the womb. The awesomeness and glory of this eternal reality is so overwhelming that anyone who gratefully accepts and lives by this love, as the only absolute point of departure of all created blessings, will certainly become a saint, a hero of God in heaven's hall of fame. Whereas anyone who rejects this love will live a life of the most senseless folly, destined to eternal damnation.

Divine love is the inexhaustible source of all blessings. Blessing is God's choice of creatures. It is His love that calls creatures into existence from nothingness and endows them with the capacity to grow, to become fruitful, to cooperate with Him in His plans to sanctify and glorify all creation. Clearly, then, from God's point of view, children are, from the instant of conception, God's benefactions to themselves, to their parents and to the whole human race. For they are forever loved, chosen, created, bestowed by God. Creatures receive, but God bestows blessings. That is what the Bible means when it says: "It is more blessed to give than to receive."[4] Children come from the heart of God freely, generously. That is why the birth of a child in Christian civilization is celebrated as a "blessed event." The center of society's adoration is the new bawling baby announcing its arrival as another person, a radiant witness to the conjugal love of its parents and the creative love of God.

The intimate love of the parents for each other cooperates with the omnipotent love of God who creates the human soul at the moment of conception. The child is at once the image and likeness of God and of its parents. As spirit it reflects the Infinite Spirit that God is; its faculties of soul — intellect, will, memory — are imitations, inklings of the three divine persons in the family of the Holy Trinity. As a human nature, body and soul, man reflects the parenthood of God, for the capacity for fruitful procreation found in man and woman descends from the Father above, from whom all paternity arises. Thus men and women as parents are created shadows of the perfect parent, God the Father; and fathers, mothers and children as families are echoes of the Divine Family of the Holy Trinity. That is why human persons in the loving union of matrimony are blessed with the fertility of procreation. God in His love wills to share with them not only the benefaction of existence, of life, but also that of paternity and parenthood. *Love does such things!* God in an ecstasy of divine love within the bosom of the Trinity delights to beget His Divine Son from all eternity and to create man in time. Man in an ecstasy of love with his bride delights to procreate his children. And Mary, the Virgin, in an ecstasy of love with the Holy Spirit delights to conceive and give birth to the Most Blessed Event in all history — the God-Man, Jesus. *Love does such things!* For "it is more blessed to give than to receive."[5] God sees children only with the eyes of a divine lover who is forever giving Himself in more vigorous life to others.

The inspired Psalmist witnesses to this truth in his famous apostrophe to God: "What is man, that Thou are mindful of him, or the son of man, that Thou art concerned about him? Thou hast made him a little less than the angels; Thou has crowned him with honor and glory; Thou hast given him power over the works of thy hands; Thou has placed all things at his feet."[6]

But our appreciation of God's love for the children of men would have remained merely on the periphery of this mystery, if God had not revealed the blessing of the Incarnation. Not until we have meditated on the birth of Christ do we even begin to suspect the fathomless depth of God's affection for the children of men. The birthday of Jesus, the God-Man, gives man a supernatural appreciation of the connection of birthdays with divine benefactions. Every blessing, every birthday — past, present and future — merely foreshadows the blessing of the Incarnation, the birthday of the Son of God in time. The message of billions of human birthdays proclaims that God wills to share with men His goodness, His life, His fertility, His Family, His embrace in the beatific vision. And the message of the Incarnation with the birth of Jesus proclaims that God wills to share not merely human but also divine life with men. For God so loved the world that He delivered up His Son as a victim to redeem men and bring them back from a sinful death to a rebirth in the banquet of the divine life of grace. "I am come, says Christ, "that they may have life and may have it more abundantly."[7] *Only divine love does such things!*

Thus all blessings are focussed in the Christ Child, the Blessed One, par excellence, the Most Blessed Event in all history. God loves children because His Son, as man's son, is the First Born of many brethren, the exemplary event of all other blessed events begotten in the communion and family of saints. The Angels remain in awed, stunned ecstasy at God's presence as a child among men. "For, in truth, He took not hold of the angels, but of the seed of Adam, of the offspring of Abraham."[8] From all eternity God's love decreed that "the Word" should be "made flesh." The God-Child is the greatest blessed event that could possibly be bestowed upon man. "Is it possible," writes St. Paul, "that He who did not spare His own Son, but handed Him over for the sake of us, will not grant us all things (all blessings) besides?"[9] *Divine love grants such mind-boggling graces!*

St. Augustine tells us that "God became man that man might become God."[10] And St. Cyprian writes: "What man is Christ wished to be so that man, in his turn, might become God."[11] Or as St. Cyril proclaims:

"Christ is called the New Adam because by sharing in our nature He has enriched us all unto happiness and glory. Thus, by dwelling in one human nature, Christ dwells in all so that His one human nature being made the Son of God in power, the same dignity now passes to the whole human race. For as Christ became man by putting on our flesh, so we become God by being incorporated into His flesh."[12] Indeed so ardent and unchanging is God's love for the human family that the Father has exalted His Son in His Humanity, welcoming our human nature in Him into the bosom of the Holy Trinity for all eternity. And a human person, Mary the Mother of God, has been raised above all the angels as the Queen of heaven and the universe in an exaltation that enthrones her forever at the right hand of her Divine Son.

We are now in a position to appreciate somewhat God's appraisal of the heinous crime of abortion. The abortionist squads in effect tell God: "You have loved this child in the womb from all eternity. Well, we don't want it; we hate it! Here is its cadaver. As a child it was an inconvenience, an embarrassment, a menace to us. It threatened our freedom to attain pleasure, treasure, happiness. We will not allow it to enjoy any birthday in human history. Moreover, we are the masters of the life of man; we decide who lives, who dies, who is wanted, who is unwanted and is expendable. We have the unlimited right to control the human body. Hence the surgeon, following our command, has agreed to terminate this pregnancy. Then too the judges of our nation have legalized this type of extermination of human life."

What is God and all God-fearing persons witnessing here? Creatures rebel against their Creator; they usurp God's power over life and death. They commit a crime that is never allowed under any circumstances, for the murder of the innocent is an intrinsic evil. They repay love with hate, blessings with curses, mercy with murder, fertility with sterility, joy with sadness, generosity with selfishness, humility with pride and life with death. Against the joyous command of God to male and female "to increase and multiply and fill the earth," the abortionist squads impose the malevolent maledictions upon man "to decrease and die and lay waste the earth."

The abortionist squad

The abortionist squad is usually made up of doctors, lawyers, psychologists, nurses, friends and yes, very embarrassed parents who surround confused, frightened pregnant women pressuring them to enter baby-killing clinics. These permissive storm-troopers are the apostles of a murderous way of life. For the most part they foster in society what Kingsley Amis calls "the unexamined abortion-divorce-homosexuality-censorship-marijuana package."[13] They act from an evil spirit that corrupts the heart and rivets it to human conduct that concentrates the powers of man on self-love, self-conceit, self-reliance. As persons who have neglected or denied God, these predators on human life have endowed sexual permissiveness with the solemnity of infallible dogma and they explode with irrational rage when God-fearing persons suggest reasonable, legal, cultural or even any self-imposed restraints. They seem to be all for the degradation of mankind for they have silenced their consciences which would trouble them over their cult of fetal murders. Having abolished Almighty God, the abortionist squad has set up Almighty Man in His place. But when Almighty Man becomes his own God, he devours his fellowmen. Of course, he justifies his inhumanity to man with high-sounding scientific, humanistic rationalizations.

God's judgment

What is God's judgment on the abomination of abortion? "Thou shalt not kill!"[14] the Lord thundered from the smoke and fire of Mt. Sinai. This command was aimed at protecting all innocent lives, especially the lives of defenseless children born or unborn. Again through the mouth of Moses God warned the Chosen People thus: "I call heaven and earth to witness against you. I have set before you life and death, the blessing and the curse. Choose life that you and your descendants may live by loving the Lord...If, however, you turn away your hearts and will not listen, but are led astray and adore other gods, I tell you now you will certainly perish."[15] This was spoken to a People who would fall into idolatry and sacrifice their children to the idol Moloch. Today's idol that devours children in abortion mills is the god Libido, the god of wanton desire and caprice.

St. James in his letter to the Church rebukes those "whose desires are at war in their members." "You desire and you do not have, so you kill... Do you know that friendship with the world is enmity with God... Or do you suppose it is vain that Scripture says: 'God is jealous and He is unwilling to lose the spirit which He has placed within us?' "[16] Jesus became indignant at those who would chase children away from Him. "Let the little children come to me and do not hinder them, for of such is the kingdom of heaven."[17] On another occasion He warned those who scandalized children of the wrath of God and of the jealousy of their guardian angels who always see the face of their Father in heaven. "Whoever leads one of these little ones who believes in me to sin, it were better for him to have a great millstone hung around his neck, and to be drowned in the depths of the sea."[18] How much more terrible will be the punishment of abortionists who prevent children from being born into the world, thereby removing the possibility of their coming to belief in Christ through rebirth in Baptism and their being incorporated into His Mystical Body as His members in the communion of saints!

Christ, children and Herod

The Son of God at His own birth in time felt the hot breath of the baby-killer. He was born into a world under the power of Satan, a world of violence and of baby-killers. Satan dispatched his agent Herod to kill the Christ Child. Foiled by the Guardian Angel of God, Herod in a rage slaughtered all the male children in Bethlehem from age two and under. Today, Christ, the lover of children, is again being crucified. For we live in a world of exploding violence, where an increasing number of medical merchants of death are annually murdering millions of innocent, defenseless babies in the womb. But Christ is ever the Creator, the Redeemer and Lover of all children. He identifies Himself with every child whether intact, deformed, wanted or unwanted, illegitimate or highborn. Whatever is done to them He takes as being done to Himself. He is also the severe Judge of the living and the dead, of all the Herods in history who kill babies out of lust for pleasure, treasure or power. He will render justice in the cause of the millions of murdered ''unwanted children.'' These innocents have suffered for justice sake in the brilliant light of Christ's teaching, in the exquisite laser beams of His life, passion and death, in the splendor of His resurrection. These children are being unjustly murdered despite the loud, world-resounding protests of Popes, of holy people like Mother Teresa and of millions of pro-life apostles. Surely they will certainly attain the kingdom of heaven as predicted by Christ for those who suffer persecution for justice sake. Satan may snatch their physical, bodily lives, but the compassionate love of their Savior will glorify their souls and eventually their bodies. It is not possible in God's economy of salvation that Satan could be allowed to snatch so many millions of innocent souls from the pierced Heart of Christ, their Creator and Redeemer.

Woe to abortionists

But woe to those who perform abortions, who cooperate in their performance, and to those who, being in positions of authority to oppose this infamous plague, tolerate its spread with specious reasonings. These latter who compromise by saying they are personally opposed to abortions, but must follow the law that legalizes them, these latter, I say, are imitators of Pontius Pilate who, after declaring Jesus innocent and washing his hands of his condemnation, then ordered his crucifixation as though he was a convicted criminal. Such hypocrites will have to suffer the wrath of God. Dante expressed his ardent contempt of such moral pygmies when he wrote: ''The hottest places in hell are reserved for those who, having the power and responsibility to oppose evil, did nothing to extinguish it.'' As for the hardened abortionists, they too will hear from the lips of Christ, the Champion of Children's rights, this eternal malediction: ''Depart from me, You Accursed, into everlasting fire prepared for the devil and his angels, for I was an infant, a child in the womb, and you murdered me." "For as long as you did it to the least of my little ones, you did it to me."[19]

The abortionist quarrels with God's plan for the procreation and redemption of man. Like Satan he is a rebel against the loving Providence of God for the increase of life and love among the members of the human family. Speaking to rebels in his times who questioned the plans of God for man's life and destiny, St. Paul made a demand which is most appropriate now against the merchants of death: "Who are you, O Man, that you argue with God, that you question Him? Does the object moulded say to him who moulded it: Why have you made me this way? Or is not the Potter master of his clay?"[20] And again: "What have you got, O Man, that you have not received? And if you have received it, why do you glory as if you received it not?"[21] Abortionists should daily meditate on this warning from Holy Scripture: "It is a fearful thing to fall into the hands of the Living God!"[22]

Notes

[1]Virgil, *Roget's International Thesaurus,* New Edition, Thomas Y. Crowell Company, New York, 1950, Word 153 Footnote.

[2]Proverbs 8:31.

[3]Augustine, *The City of God,* Image Books, N.Y., Doubleday & Co., 1958, p. 228.

[4]Acts 20:35.

[5]Ibid.

[6]Psalms 8:5-7.

[7]John 10:10.

[8]Hebrews 2:16.

[9]Romans 8:32.

[10]Augustine, Sermo 13 de temp; Sermo 128; Patrologia latina; XXXIX, 1997.

[11]Cyprian, De idolorum vanitate, c. 11; Patrologia latina IV, 579; Corpus scriptorum ecclesiasticorum latinorum, III, I, 28.

[12]Cyril, quoted in *The Mysteries of Christianity,* Matthias Joseph Scheeben, pp. 381-382.

[13]Kingsley Amis, Article in *Sunday Telegraph,* London, July 2, 1967.

[14]Exodus 20:13.

[15]Deut. 29:15-29.

[16]James 4:i, 4, 5.

[17]Mark 10:13-15.

[18]Luke 17:1-2.

[19]Mt. 25:41-46.

[20]Rom. 9:20, 21.

[21]1 Cor. 4:7.

[22]Hebrews 10:31.

Reprinted from *Homiletic & Pastoral Review, November 1984 under the title "The Acceptable Holocaust?"*

Crisis in Medical Ethics

"storm troopers of the medical profession"

In the periodical *California Medicine* for September 1970, there appeared an article presenting the official views of the California Medical Association on the relationship between modern medicine and the worlds of science, religion and morality. The article is an "eye-opening," "mind-blasting" philosophic bomb in the field of ethics. If patients are not already totally defenseless against a medical profession that has lost all sense of the sacredness of human life and persons, they soon will find themselves so. The article states that modern science and medicine have destroyed traditional morality.

For science and medicine have successfully changed public opinion, the Church and the Law on what is ethically good or evil. The time has come, it claims, to place a relative value on human life. Now, since medicine alone has the true knowledge of human life and behavior, the community of medicine alone, using the scientific method, has the right to formulate the new ethic to which all men would be called to submit.

Perhaps a brief look at the thought of some famous modern scientists will indicate how we have arrived so suddenly at the man-made ethics of the new "medicine-men." Acting on the scientific dogma-slogan that "man has come of age," that his infancy and adolescence, which were ruled by the "security blanket" of the existence of a superstitious God and a transcendent Heaven or Hell sanction, has now been superceded by his maturity and liberation in this golden age of science: Dr. Edmund R. Leach, prominent anthropologist, is refreshingly frank about man's present position and role as creator of his own code of morality. In an article modestly entitled: "We Scientists Have the Right to Play God," he writes: "The scientist can now play God in his role of wonder-worker. But can he — and should he — also play God as moral arbiter?... There can be no source for moral judgments except the scientist himself. In traditional religion, morality was held to derive from God, but God was only credited with the authority to establish and enforce moral laws because He also was credited with supernatural powers of creation and destruction. These powers now have been usurped by man, and he must take on the moral responsibility that goes with them."

In explaining why man has usurped these powers of creation and destruction and why man must accept the responsibility of making and enforcing his own moral rules, Dr. Leach relies on the famous Feuerbachian thesis which states that God, after all, was only a projection into the beyond of fearful ignorant man's best qualities. Dr. Leach cleverly exposes the human functions falsely attributed to that mythical Deity thus: God as

Creator sets the cosmological clock ticking; as lawgiver, He promulgates the moral code; as judge, He imposes sanctions on criminals; as "trickster," He arbitrarily interferes in human affairs, testing and gathering His own clique of the righteous as He segregates them from the wicked; as mediator, He judges and saves sinners.

Dr. Leach concludes: "These attributes of God are by definition 'superhuman,' but they are nevertheless qualities of an essentially human kind. The God of Judaeo-Christianity is, in all His aspects, whether creator, judge, trickster or mediator, quite explicitly anthropomorphic, and the converse is equally true. There is necessarily something godlike about every human being.... But unless we teach those of the next generation that they can afford to be atheists only if they assume the moral responsibilities of God, the prospects for the human race are decidedly bleak."

Konrad Lorenz, the Viennese zoologist, in his book *Concerning the Natural History of Aggression,* has made precisely the same demand that the scientists alone can formulate a human ethic. And he calls on all men, in disciplines other than his own, to follow the ethics of the scientists with a new and becoming humility. More recently, Jacques Monod, a biologist and Nobel prize winner from France, made much the same claim. In his book, *Chance and Necessity,* which became an instant best-seller in Europe, he called upon Jew, Greek, Christian and Marxist, in short, on all those who stood in the millenia, to come to terms with the moral fact that science, and science alone, has the right to determine man's future. The old Western-tradition animists are out of date with their theories about man's nature, theories which are fairy tales. Discounting all of the contributions made by the sages of history concerning man's nature, origin and destiny, Monod comes as close as any scholar to embracing a doctrine of absolute biological determinism as the explanation of all that man is and all man does.

Among the immoral practices escalating in the medical profession, perhaps, to date, the worst is the direct interruption of the generative process already begun, and above all, the directly willed and procured abortion of a living fetus. Encouraged by a Supreme Court decision, justified by the flimsiest of sophistical arguments, the medical profession is engaged in a booming abortion business. The Supreme Court argued that the woman has the right to terminate a pregnancy she does not want, thus giving her quasi-absolute dominion over her own body and over the body and life of the child in her womb. When reminded of the clear meaning of the Fourteenth Amendment of the Constitution which proves that "No State shall deprive any person of life, liberty or property without due process of law; nor deny to any person within its jurisdiction the equal protection of the laws," the Supreme Court got bogged down in a game of antics in semantics saying: "The Constitution does not define 'person' in so many words. The use of the word is such that it has application only postnatally." The fact is, however, that the indubitable understanding among men is that wherever there is human life, a human person is an accepted, self-evident *datum*, more immediately understood by all men than any definition of a person could be. The Constitution never defines the nature of liberty, justice and a host of other immediately known philosophical and spiritual realities. It seems never to have occurred to the Supreme Court that the Constitution never was formulated to enter the business of defining philosophically self-evident realities, realities known immediately in the hourly, engulfing ocean of experience, realities which are yet paradoxically inexhaustible and never known completely because of their infinite dimension of mystery.

In his strong dissenting opinion Justice Byron R. White condemned the decision in favor of abortion "as an exercise of raw judicial power," and continued his reasoning thus: "I cannot accept the Court's exercise of its clear power of choice by interposing a constitutional barrier to State efforts to protect human life and by investing mothers and doctors with the constitutionally protected right to exterminate it." This dissent is reasonable and just, for humanness, or a human person, is inherent in any human, living being. Humanness, or the reality of being a human person, is not an accidental quality or right conferred on living human fetuses by the process of growth in time, nor by society, nor by the State. Moreover, the court hedged in its explanation by saying that abortion must be considered by medical judgment necessary for the preservation of the life or health of the mother. Thus today doctors legally perform abortions on five grounds: incest, rape, potential deformity of the fetus, threat to mental health and threat to physical health of the mother.

Now incest and rape were introduced as motives for allowing abortion because of their emotional value, a value calculated to open the legal door in the end to abortion on demand. For, consider for a moment, which of the two parties to an incestuous relationship would ever seek an abortion on the grounds of incest at the risk of degrading themselves in the attendant publicity? And why would not a woman who was raped not seek immediate medical care rather than wait a month or two to have an abortion on the grounds of rape? No, the human embarrassment of opposing legal abortion on these two emotional grounds was the wedge used to extend this imaginary legal right to abortion to other far less sensitive areas of human conduct, indeed to areas of merely potential deformity, possible threat to mental and physical health. In a word this ruse made abortion on demand legal at any stage of the pregnancy, even up to the moment of normal delivery.

For such is the elastic character of the understanding of the mother's health as a criterion for abortion that the Court's decision is a practical *carte-blanche* permission to abort at any time. It is a curious irony that the

Supreme Court, founded to preserve the right to life which is the foundation of any free society, has instead legally blessed the unnatural license of a mother to murder her fetal child for the sake of her own private whims and conveniences. And the Medical Profession, in exploiting this legal weapon against innocent, defenseless human life, has perverted its Hippocratic Oath from the promise to save human life to the ploy of exploiting human death via abortion. Dr. Sean O'Reilly of the Department of Neurology of the George Washington University Medical Center, addressing the Catholic Physicians Guild and the Appollonia Guild of Buffalo, asked his medical colleagues this most serious question: "Has the decline and fall of the Medical Profession changed the meaning of the M.D. from that of Medical Doctor to that of Merchant of Death?"

Now that the Medical Profession has succumbed to a morally sick society and works with its principle that murder is the best therapy for the solution of its social problems, we are reminded of one of the ugliest chapters in German medical history. For in order to upgrade the German race, the Third Reich ordered its psychiatrists to get rid of the nation's mental patients. The horrendous result was that 240,000 of 300,000 German patients were liquidated in specially constructed carbon monoxide chambers during the years of World War II. At that time actual deformity justified murder. But today, here in America, potential deformity justifies and legally permits murder. Where there is no ethic, there is no law, no rights, no obligations; nothing is sacred, nothing transcendent; justice, love and humaneness are nonexistent. Where there is no ethic, there is rather only one law, that of the jungle, of power — naked, brutal, ruthless, merciless power. Where there is no transcendent ethic, no eternal law to protect the defenseless, innocent prenatal life, there will be none either to protect the lives of postnatal citizens. In a world where each woman's privacy is absolute, man has created a monster society where, in the words of Kafka, each person lives as "a sect unto himself," or each family is under siege and lives on the defensive against the aggressions of the State. For in such a society every human relationship is dissolved into fear and trembling where *homo homini lupus,* "Man is a wolf to his fellowman," becomes the order of the day.

What next?

Gordon Rattray Taylor, a scientific journalist, in his book *The Biological Time Bomb,* wrote of the prospects of genetic engineering, the possibility of test tube babies and the likelihood of defective embryos appearing in the first stages of experimentation. Then he declared: "The necessity of destroying the defective embryo which constitutes abortion under present laws in many countries, will no doubt arouse resistence. Those countries who do not consider the destruction of the embryo to be abortion until after the fifth month of pregnancy, or some other stated period, will therefore be at an advantage.'' Now in a world in which man is made for science instead of science for man, those who supply abortion on demand had better ask themselves if abortion on demand of the State and euthanasia on demand of the State and sterilization on demand of the State can be far behind.

One of the great philosophical errors of the day is the seemingly enlightened view — though it is only an unproved assumption — that the worth, the humanness, the personhood of a man lies exclusively in his social utility. One immediately gets into a sticky moral dilemma as Robert Goney did who proposed to assess the relative social worth of mentally defective people on the basis of their mother instincts, or of dwarfs on the basis of their ''court jestering.'' Do not persons have value in themselves and in their own families? The Christian moralist finds the person's intrinsic worth in his metaphysical creaturehood, in that intrinsic relationship he has to the Supreme Being who creates him from nothingness because He loves him and guides this Image of Himself through the trials of time back to Himself as the matured, freely achieved likeness of Himself (*Similitudo Dei*) in glory.

On the false principle that the worth and dignity of a person lies exclusively in his social utility, the conduct followed by parents and doctors in the famous ''Baltimore Case'' seemed justified. In that case, you remember, a Mongoloid was born to a couple and needed simple surgery for relief of an internal blockage. The couple instructed the surgeons not to operate, but to allow the child to die. No food was administered to the child who took fifteen days to die. On this false principle as to the intrinsic worth of any person, society has lessened drastically its tolerance for the weak, imperfect, unlovely, unacceptable, old and sick. It has pressed the medical profession into what it euphemistically regards as a service to man — the murderous eradication of useless people. And such people are considered no longer to be persons precisely because they are socially useless and an economic burden. Thus in a world in which men and women are being manipulated by the fears of population explosion and a genetic apocalypse, there is overconcern for spaceship Earth, but a scientific, murderous contempt for its human crew.

Dr. Garrett Hardin, professor of biology at the University of California at Santa Barbara, wrote an article in the periodical *Science* for 31 July 1970 entitled ''Parenthood: Right or Privilege?'' In this he makes it unmistakably clear that he considers parenthood a privilege granted by society rather than a natural, inalienable right bestowed on human persons by their Creator. Moreover, he calls for mandatory State control over man's reproductive activity. Indeed in a symposium held in New York City in

1970 Professor Hardin posed the problem of man today in a mathematical equation. "Population times Prosperity equals Pollution." Then he added: "To reduce pollution one must reduce either prosperity or population, and it is better to reduce population rather than prosperity."

On 15 February 1972, in the periodical *Internal Medicine News,* Professor Hardin goes even further. He takes not only the view that voluntary population control is self-defeating, but he contends that "the desire and/or ability to use contraception effectively as a trait . . . will be perpetuated in the offspring of those who do so": and he sees "the lack of this desire and/or ability perpetuating itself in the offspring of those who do not." "Surely," writes Rev. Charles Carroll, of Collegeville, Minnesota, in commentary, "it would be difficult to find a more unequivocal statement of absolute biological determinism and/or a doctrine of man which represents a more radical reduction of man to a molecular system. Implying that the individual is genetically programmed to contracept or not to contracept by his forebears, he (Hardin) believes that it is 'poorer people,' those who come from a long line of poor ancestors, and are apparently unable to better themselves who are least motivated to use contraception." Rev. Carroll continues: "One of the rationales for mandatory controls, apparently, would be the presence of genes within certain groups in the population that were adapted to the 'culture of poverty'."

Now abortions for incest or rape are clearly situations where two crimes do not make a morally good situation. Then, too, medical reasons for abortion today are very rare. Dr. Roy Heffernan of Tufts University has written: "Anyone who performs a therapeutic abortion is either ignorant of modern medical methods of treating the complications of pregnancy or is unwilling to take the time to use them." Even Dr. Alan Guttmacher — of Planned Parenthood Fame — stated in an article in *McCalls's:* "With the rapid strides of modern medicine, few women require abortion to preserve life." There were 115,000 deliveries at the Margaret Hague Hospital in New Jersey from 1947 to 1961 during which time not one abortion was done.

Moreover, there is no direct relationship between pregnancy and mental illness. Dr. Gino G. Papola, in an article in *L'Osservatore Romano,* English edition, entitled "Abortion Today: A Doctor Looks at a Modern Problem," writes: "In the past several decades, abortion for psychiatric reasons has progressed from being a rarity to the most common reason given for abortions. Some psychiatrists, including Dr. Myre Sim of England, feel there are no psychiatric grounds for the termination of a pregnancy. Most authorities agree there is only a slight risk of suicide in a woman with an unwanted pregnancy. Actually, psychiatric patients are the most unsatisfactory patients to abort because they are as likely to suffer postabortal guilt complexes and depressions as they are to benefit from being rid of the pregnancy." When it comes to the aborting of a fetus because of the possibility of deformity, let us think ahead and see if we are willing to be logical enough to kill a child already living in a deformed body. In this connection a certain Kathleen Collins wrote the following letter to *The Daily News* of New York for 13 August 1974: "I was born without any arms and legs, and was shocked by the statement of a priest that seriously deformed infants should be allowed to die. I know for a fact that I can do almost everything anyone else can do, if people will give me a chance. I'm now working at a summer job. Next fall I'll be a senior at St. Francis Prep high school, and I intend to go to college. I and many other handicapped children don't want pity, tears or 'mercy' killing. All we ask is a chance."

As for abortions for social reasons or economic reasons, all that is got rid of is the child. The social and economic problems remain. As if the killing of all the poor would solve the problem of poverty! Nor does liberalizing the abortion laws reduce the criminal abortion rate. A report from Sweden pointed out that, after twenty-five years of legalized abortion, the number of criminal abortions has not changed. The reason given in the report is as follows: "The legalizing of abortion alters the climate of opinion among the public and even the courts of law. The result is that criminal abortion becomes less abhorrent. The public becomes abortion-minded." Then too abortion on demand fits in nicely with the sexual revolution, its increase in promiscuity and with its concomitant escalation in venereal disease.

In the temper of the times in which the legal is identified with the morally good, and the physical-social handicap with the morally bad, a course of action is being followed which is as morally unacceptable today as the bringing of newborns to the Lesch for sorting and disposal was in ancient Sparta. Sir Arnold Lunn, in his book *The New Morality* calls doctors who bow to the mood of the moment and fulfill demands for abortions, "storm troopers of the medical profession," predators of the most innocent and defenseless life who, in immaculate white, invade the sanctuary of the womb and slaughter the innocent.

There is good reason to fear for the future of medicine in this country. It is one thing to pronounce the demise of the Judaeo-Christian ethic, as the California Medical Association has done. It is quite another to set up the ethic of absolute freedom, which is in reality a license to create ethical, political and cultural chaos. And as Order without Freedom is the tyranny of dictatorship, just so Freedom without Order is the tyranny of chaos. In the words of Rev. Charles Carroll, Episcopalian priest of California, in his article "Medicine Without an Ethic," published in the *Louisiana State*

Medical Society's Journal: "When we succumb to the fear of a genetic apocalypse; when we decry the pollution of the gene pool; when we claim that specimens from the amniotic fluid give us infallible diagnoses of coming defective or normal babies; when we demand prenatal examination of the unborn, what is there to prevent abortion of the woman whether she wishes to be aborted or not? Can we not admit, if only to ourselves, that when we talk of such things and contemplate the ways and means by which we might improve the 'gene pool', we are talking about denying some the right to participate in the reproductive process and, if only by implication, we are talking about 'the drafting' of others? When the physician, for example, agrees to sterilize every patient at his or her insistence, what is there to protect the physician or patient when it is the State that insists?" Certainly there are doctors who would disapprove of liquidating all diabetics, but would have no qualms of conscience in sterilizing all diabetics in the interest of improving the genetic pool for reproduction. Such is the confusion in the medical profession today concerning morality.

But as if the confusion were not enough, there are those who want to eliminate even the possibility of natural motherhood. In the periodical *Atlantic* for May 1971, Edward Grossman, a student of George Wald at Harvard, wrote an article entitled: "The Obsolescent Mother." It treats of the reproduction of human life *in vitro,* that is in the test tube. Grossman suggests and supports the development of the "efficient artificial womb" in the hope that, if it catches on culturally, "it will mean that the awefulness associated with pregnancy and childbirth will have nothing to feed on, and motherhood, if it continues to excite any awe at all, will not do so more than fatherhood." Furthermore, he insists that the mother "will find that society does not expect her to have a special relation to her offspring" and that "a society that can grow fetuses in a laboratory will be more disposed to have meaningful day and night care centers and communal nurseries on a large scale, for the State, being now a third parent, will wish to provide for the maintenance and upbringing of its children." Then "natural pregnancy may become an anachronism...the uterus will become appendix-like." This thinly disguised contempt for woman and her sublime vocation of motherhood reveals that technocratic mentality in medicine today that would tinker with human beings and their bodies as if they were no better than man-made machines.

How then are we to determine the ethically good or evil in medical practices? What criterion are we to use? Must we be guided by custom, popular opinion, utility, sentiment or scientific ideals? Or do we have a surer, more objective and transcendent standard? Mere sentiment and selfish advantage of the individual or group or even of society must be rejected as being standards that are too fickle and lend themselves to visionary tyranny over the individual person. Custom, popular opinion, if they are ever safe guides to true morality, are so only when they conform to some higher, unchangeable, eternal norm. Thus, the nearest objective criterion of ethical goodness is man's rational nature as such, considered completely in itself and its relationships.

Inner consciousness tells man that he is capable of arriving at truth and that he is free and responsible for his human acts. Reason makes known to him that he is a created being made for a purpose, and that all his fellow-men were created with the same rights and duties which he has. Toward the Supreme Being, his Origin, he has an obligation of worship, obedience and service. Toward his fellowmen he has an obligation of justice and charity. Thus man's human acts are ethically good if they befit and perfect his rational nature, considered in itself and in its relationships.

The medical doctor should beware of the false idea — so prevalent today — that he is a physician to society rather than to the individual patient. Moreover, the medical doctor must have medical competence and surgical skill. He must practice a code of ethics that corresponds to right reason. For, as a professional man, he must be guided by reason, not by sentiment, nor expediency, nor scientific ideology, nor filthy lucre. He must attend his patients with the sole intention of curing them, not killing them. He must use the remedies normally most adaptable to curing each disease. He must guard professional secrets carefully. He must protect his patients from a State turned aggressor. The physician must remember that medicine without a valid ethic will leave himself, his patients and society as a whole without an adequate moral and legal defense against the despotism of Dachau. This is particularly true in a world in which so many are willing to sacrifice others for themselves rather than sacrifice themselves for others.

The true physician, loyal to his Hippocratic Oath, adheres to the 1948 Declaration of Geneva, the United Nations Declaration of the Rights of the Child, and supports the Declaration of the Doctors of North America which hold that: "Physicians should have respect for human life, regardless of age, illness, disability, or degree of dependence" and further that: "The deliberate killing of human beings, born or unborn, to solve psychologic, social, economic or eugenic problems is directly contrary to the role of the doctor." Thus the true physician will oppose any man-made laws which pervert his profession into being a profession that preys on people and puts to death, for a fee, innocent humans.

For the physician must never forget that bad morals cannot make good medicine, nor can good morals make bad medicine. We hear the authentic voice of good medicine in the words of Dr. L. Hemingway who writes: "A sudden, cataclysmic change in direction of 'being' occurs only once in each person's existence, and this is at the moment of conception. Prior to gametic fusion, there is no person, but only a sperm and an ovum. Both of these are destined to die (unless they fuse, that is). The unfertilized ovum has a life-span of a few hours, and the sperm lives only for two or three days. Their fusion produces a dramatic change. The two gametes, instead of dying, become a zygote which is destined to live. Development thereafter is continuous, uninterrupted, and without any semblance of a dramatic change even remotely resembling that which occurs at fertilization. . . . The natural life of the human person begins at the moment of conception and ends at the moment of death. The aim of medical practice is to keep these two events as far apart as possible, and ensure that, as far as is practicable, the period in between is spent in happiness and health. Abortion, which terminates a human life almost as soon as it begins, obviously violates this principle as far as the infant is concerned. Abortion is therefore directly contrary to the aims of the medical profession.''

Doctors, therefore, should keep certain truths unyieldingly in their consciences and adhere firmly to the resolution of defending them. They are: 1) Human life begins at conception. This fact is known to biologists and geneticists. It is conceded even by the pro-abortion lobby for the most part. 2) The human being in question is innocent, defenseless and has sacred, inalienable rights, especially the right to life. 3) There are never any medically good reasons for abortion. Anyone maintaining the contrary may be evil or ignorant of modern advances in medicine. 4) Even if there is thought to be a threat to the life or health of the mother, her innocent offspring, at whatever age, has a fundamental right to life. This is not, nor can it be, abrogated by any ''due process'' or other legal proceedings. 5) Sterilization of healthy organs to avoid reproduction is directly contrary to the aims of the medical profession and hence always immoral mutilation.

Finally, the true physician must always be mindful of the warning in *Proverbs:* ''There are six things the Lord hates, yes, seven are an abomination to Him: haughty eyes, a lying tongue, *hands that shed innocent blood,* a heart that plots wicked schemes, feet that run swiftly to evil, the false witness who utters lies and he who sows discord among brothers.''

And of the physician who stands firm in the face of trials and follows the law of God in his practice, Holy Scripture writes: ''Hold the physician in honor, for he is essential to you, and God it was who established his profession. From God the doctor has his wisdom. . . and he beseeches God that his diagnosis may be correct and his treatment bring about a cure.'' The physician who works in harmony with the law of God will gain the esteem of his fellowmen now and the crown of life from the Author of life hereafter.

Reprinted from *Friar,* September 1975.

Jonestown: New Moloch State

Jonestown, the Marxist caricature of a Christian Church, conferred on its faithful only one sacrament — the sacrament of death.

Contemporary diabolism cannot be dismissed by sophisticated atheistic intellectuals or updated theologians as a "lot of harmless fun-and-sex games." Well-organized satanic groups are mushrooming all over the Western world. Satan is starring in almost as many movie and TV shows as the most beauteous damsels or the most famous Godfather chieftains. Today's world is saturated with witchraft and occultism, a world which is continuing to demolish the temples and altars of God and is setting up altars to demons in Houses of Harlotry and Idolatry. There is evidence which proves that sadomasochistic rites have led all too often to serious injury and sacrificial deaths among California cultists. These brutalities reflect the undeniable morbid aspect of the occult revolution. Voodoo is becoming increasingly noticeable in many Southern and Southwestern states, as well as in New York City, Los Angeles, Chicago and New Orleans.

It took the Tate-La Bianca murder court proceedings, which lasted for more than a year in 1970 and 1971, to shock and frighten the world into a realization of the extent of the diabolical influences characteristic of a modern society that produced the Manson family. The grim combination of sex, violence, drugs, witchcraft and Satanism that led to the horrible slaughter of seven persons in a ritual sacrifice indicate clearly that a wave of wickedness is engulfing modern society. The mood of revulsion and terror following the Manson slayings was heightened even more when Dr. Victor Ohta and his family were murdered less than a year later by a young occultist with ecological paranoia. Then followed the tragic ritual slaying of a teenage Vineland, N.J. satanist. Believing that he would return at the head of a legion of devils, Patrick Newell was pushed to his death by two friends after performing a satanic ritual. The cult of Satan had already spread to as many as seventy young Vinelanders before the killing took place. A month later an elderly man was stabbed to death in Miami by a twenty-two year old satanist who believed that she had seen the devil in person. Daily the grim episodes of violent diabolism can be found in increasing numbers in newspapers and magazines. This massive publicity may be a possible factor in the faddish popularity of pathological occultism. In May 1972 the suburban community of Waukegan, six miles north of Chicago, was shaken by lurid accounts of diabolical rites performed by groups of drug-drenched teenagers and adults. Night-time revels in local cemeteries with satanic invocations, animal torture and even human sacrifice rounded out these bloody and bizarre liturgies.

The growing corps of devil's advocates are preparing a world that will be ready and eager to accept the ideals and rule of the Antichrist when he comes. For the world is fast becoming one vast supermarket peddling porn, objects of magic, idolatrous statues, trinkets of superstititon. In an atmosphere of violence, rebellions, wars, international intrigues and the creeping advancement of politically and militarily organized atheism, contemporary man already fearfully feels that Armageddon is in the very air he breathes, in the chemicals and foods that sustain his body. Despite the myths establishing the twentieth century as the most enlightened, the herald of eternal progress, the Dark Ages and the Renaissance were not as black as our present era. Medieval ideals were far superior to those of the present age. For in those times man was inspired by faith and tried to live coherently with truth and virtue, despite his many faults. Today, however, man is oppressed and wearied by the loss of faith, the autocracy of technology and the collapse of his institutions, especially of organized religions. As a result, he lives in a world that has become a witches' cauldron, a weird brew of sex, flowers, drugs, incense, tear gas, acid rock, rhetoric, bombs and blood. Enter the Antichrist, ruler of the Moloch World?

Pagans demand sacrifice

We have seen so far that when the true God is banished from man's society, new gods rush in to replace him. But perhaps what has not been clearly seen today is that when man accepts new gods in his practice of the occult, he also necessarily brings about a revival of the politics of ancient paganism. A normal development of the worship of pagan gods was the creation of a divine state that rested on a theology of continuity, that is, on the denial of the Creator-creature distinction. The pagan theocratic state could take the lives of its children, or any members, as a sacrifice to the god of the state. The worshippers of Moloch ordered their sons and daughters to pass through fire as a form of sacrifice and testing. Thus God's prohibitions to the Chosen People against occult worship were not only a means of protecting people's lives morally from perverse practices, but also a means of restricting the power of the omnipotent political rulers who were theoretically unbounded by the restraint of limited, reasonable men and could take human life indiscriminately in the name of the god Moloch. Rousas Rushdoony gives a description of what he calls the "Moloch state:"

> While relatively little is known of Moloch, much more is known of the concept of divine kingship, the king as god, and the god as king, as the divine-human link between heaven and earth. The god-king represented man on a higher scale, man ascended, and the worship of such a god, i.e., of such a *Baal*, was the assertion of the *continuity* of heaven and earth. It was the belief that all being was one being, and the god therefore was an ascended man on

that scale of being. The power manifested in the political order was thus a manifestation or apprehension and seizure of divine power. It represented the triumph of a man and of his people. Moloch worship was thus a political religion. . . Moloch worship was thus state worship. The state was the true and ultimate order, and religion was a department of the state. The state claimed *total jurisdiction* over man; it was therefore entitled to *total sacrifice.*[1]

Now a religious, pagan state that claims total jurisdiction over man is a state directed by demons through the actions of rulers who justify their tyranny by having recourse to their Moloch god. Such a state provides its subjects not with law and justice, but with order — a man-centered, oppressive, demonic order. It begets the totalitarian state. The modern world everywhere is succumbing to the power of such a Moloch state. For secular, rational and occult humanism denies that there is any really transcendent, higher-than-human voice or authority that cares for man. Secular and occult humanists are at one in denying the true God. They are at one in divinizing man, the secularist through science, the occultist through demonic powers. Both seek power. The secularist seeks political power in the name of humanity; the occultist seeks the power of the underworld in the name of humanity. But both seek power for their own benefit. And both eventually come together to create the super-instrument of power, the modern omnicompetent state which claims absolute authority over the life and death of each citizen.[2] Rushdoony expertly unmasks the nature of the state:

> The Moloch state simply represents the supreme effort of man to command the future, to predestine the world, and to be as God. Lesser efforts, divination, spirit-questing, magic and witchcraft are equally anathema to God. All represent efforts to have the future on other than God's terms, to have a future apart from and in defiance of God. They are assertions that the world is not of God but of brute factuality, and that man can somehow master the world and the future by going directly to the raw materials thereof.[3]

Somewhere George Santayana emphasizes man's "brute necessity of believing something as long as life lasts." But a disembodied creed cannot inflame hearts. A revelation must pour forth from the soul of a Messiah if it is to win men's adherence. We read that "God draws men through the cords of Adam." Not to be outdone, Satan seduces men through the wiles of pseudo-saviors. And in our day liberation is in the air. Thus the many Moloch states of our age have their redeemers, prophets, emancipators. Ronald Knox tells us that "when strong currents of spiritual emotion, aroused by some religious crisis, sweep through a multitude of human hearts, physical (and spiritual) reactions of an abnormal kind are liable to occur as their by-product."[4] Now just such a frenzied phenomenon caused the rise and sudden, blood-curdling fall of Jonestown and the Peoples' Temple in Guyana. For Jonestown, Guyana, is a classic case of the modern revival of the Moloch state. Let us analyze briefly its rise and fall.

Look out for number one

The Peoples' Temple arose in an era when magnetic preachers and prophets are sweeping huge audiences out of their minds by the whirlwind of their utopian oratory and projecting them into an apocalyptic golden or ghastly age, depending on the mood of the prophet. What were the spiritual influences that unleashed the floodgates and fostered the mass suicides and murders in Jonestown? By way of preparing the social milieu for the creation of the Peoples' Temple, one of the most basic causes must be the massive apostasy by Christians in the West from faith in the Judaeo-Christian God of revelation. Because of this apostasy the relentless advance of the ice-cap of secularism in America has produced a heartless, affectless society in which nobody tends to care for anyone but himself, for anything but instant self-gratification. In a society that seeks sex without love, violence for the thrill of it, drugs for the get-away-from-it-all trip, the sensibilities of citizens are blunted. An Auschwitz is attained in which the slaughter mills of abortion and euthanasia are legalized. The Center for Disease Control in Atlanta, Georgia, gives us a statistic which proves incontrovertibly that the United States has become a Moloch state. It states that for the two years 1976–1977 in the United States 3.1 million babies were born and 1.2 million were legally aborted. Newsweek for August 1978 gives even higher figures. Indeed the figures given must be rather conservative, for there is no penalty imposed for not reporting abortions. Here is a nation that has usurped the power of God over life and death. In the name of its new secular gods, Progress and Liberty, titles that are false fronts for Rebellion and Licentiousness, many formerly Christian nations are driving their sons and daughters through the demonic fires of sacrificial murder. Thus France, England, Italy and other so-called Christian nations, having legalized abortion and while preparing to legalize euthanasia, have become Moloch states. Such brutalized states, with their corrupted institutions, abandon citizens to the scourges of drugs, street terrors, broken homes, schools of scandals and, in general, to a coarse, venal, profligate quality of life, a life of fear and loneliness.

Religions are in crisis

Now today many false christs on the prowl for lost sheep — and the Rev. Jim Jones was one of these *par excellence* — fully realize that the established religions are in deep crisis. They see Churches genuflecting before the world, substituting the city of Progress for the City of God. They hear churchmen trafficking for souls by offering them security and riches instead of challenging them to attain sanctity through a life of loving self-sacrifice and service. In place of the virtues of faith, hope and charity, the updated preacher urges souls to practice the art of self-awareness, self-assertion, self-fulfillment. Self-watchers are engaged in the most boring, futile activity imaginable. They become mental and moral midgets. Perhaps this explains in part the mass exodus of clerics, religious, teachers and youth among the disenchanted faithful.

The prophet Jim Jones and his wandering flock first sought to better the heartless society at home by filling the spiritual vacuum they encountered with humanitarian activities. Under the facade of effusive affection, understanding and a flood of welfare services they recruited hundreds of neglected souls. But their sect was doomed to failure for it was founded on the lie that religious socialism can save men. Jones himself was always a liberal, or rather a zealous Communist posing as a liberal; to keep up appearances he preached the gospel of social salvation, camouflaging it with a thin veneer of Christianity. His faith was a false and cruel caricature of Christianity.

On the verge of being revealed as an evil, false prophet, Jones led his flock into the promised land of the lush Guyana jungle. There he founded his charismatic community, the Peoples' Temple. There, free from the prying eyes, ears and mass media of a hostile world, Messiah Jones, by now permanently exalted and sick with paranoid utopian fantasies, ascended the throne of God. Formerly, while doling out liberally social goodies, he claimed to be the reincarnation of Jesus. Now he demanded the service of adoration from his faithful. For in the wake of his tremenduous political, social and monetary successes in collusion with liberal, humanistic politicians, the savior Jones enthroned himself as the sole idol of his kingdom. The Moloch Jones began to devour his subjects. His megalomania having soared to infinite proportions, Jones now claimed to be the very God who made the heavens and earth. His picture became a necessary relic for subjects to ward off evil. He ruled his slaves with the use of physical and psychological torture; he imposed on the community regular mass-suicide drills. He was the peoples' political, social, religious and even phallic god, compelling his subjects to serve his most unnatural egotistical, monetary and sexual lusts. Having totally controlled their lives, he brainwashed and drilled them to deliver, sheep-like, into his hands the power to decide the time and the manner in which he would deal out to them their deaths.

Established religion has failed

Jonestown, the Marxist-liberal-socialist caricature of a Christian Church, conferred on its faithful only one sacrament — the sacrament of death, of suicide. Of old Moloch asked his sons and daughters to pass through fire as a holocaust to himself. Modern Moloch in the Peoples' Temple — in a liturgy reminiscent of stoical heroics — asked his children to gather in community and drink the cup of cyanide together. Thus a church of naive, hoodwinked, simple folk was led astray by an evil, militant communist, posing as a God-man liberal do-gooder. For the devil and the emperor Jones sacrificed himself and his followers on the altar of the inflated ego of the revived, modern Moloch state. When they had all drained the chalice of cyanide, the Peoples' Temple became a Church of the dead. The modern Moloch state was left a city of suicides and murders, a city of rotting corpses.

There is a warning and somber lesson to be learned from the carnage exacted by the modern Moloch state, whether that takes place in the jungle of Jonestown or in the abortion mills of Western cities. The warning is that established forms of Christian religions have lost their hold on and power to attract most people — especially the educated middle class and even the masses of the poor. Why is this so? Because such religions have secularized the Christian message. They teach in favor of the Christ of Karl Marx instead of the Christ of the Gospels. Even so-called Christian universities no longer teach a love of truth nor the skill in attaining, defending and sharing it. They are teaching the American, Molochian gospel of power and wealth. In the consequent metaphysical and spiritual darkness these universities have so diluted revealed truth that their graduates enter the professional world either as bemused agnostics, enraged atheists or "chicken Catholics." These mal-formed Catholics, when they are not attacking and misrepresenting the faith, are unable and unwilling to speak up in its defense, much less suffer and die for it. So too have the churches adjusted and distorted the original deposit of the faith, the process being rationalized, of course, by the desire to clarify and update the Christian message. But the end product is always the same, a teaching conformed to the spirit of the world which prefers Jesus to be a revolutionary leader, a social reformer; a world too which wants God's Church to be a kingdom of this earth, tailoring everlasting truths to the exigencies of man's temporal convenience.

Jonestown: a Communist front

The millions who turn away from such utopian Christianity are preyed upon by pseudo-saviors and captured as lost sheep by the many prophets like Jones who hunt in the savage wilderness that lies at the fringes of the cult desert. We have now further evidence that the Christian facade of the

Peoples' Temple was a phony front for a so-called Communist utopia. Letters have been found testifying that the cult leaders were planning to bequeath more than $7 million to the Communist Party that rules the Moloch state known as the Soviet Union. One letter, read at the coroner's jury in Matthews Ridge, Guyana, December 17, explained that the Peoples' Temple was turning over "all our assets" to the Soviet Union "because we, as Communists, want our money to be of benefit for help to all oppressed peoples all over the world, or in any way that your decision-making body sees fit." This letter and four others were addressed to Fyodor Timofeyev, the consul for the Soviet Union in Georgetown, the Guyanese capital.

The somber lesson to be learned is that a religion that promises progress in liberty, science, education, economic and social welfare, without belief in a transcendent God, cannot produce a secular utopia in which all will be content to live in peace. The starry-eyed men of the Enlightenment produced a Moloch state that ruled with a Reign of Terror and plunged Europe into nationalist wars that led to the apotheosis of the emperor-god, Napoleon. The incurable optimist-rationalists of the nineteenth century produced the secular gods and architects of totalitarian Molochs — Marx, Lenin, Stalin, Mao — the imperialist tyrannies of Communist Russia and China. The Moloch states of race and blood were engendered by the Nazi-Facist tyrants Hitler and Mussolini. The tragic truth is that the gods of modern Moloch states have been the architects of such worlds of depravity as Auschwitz, the Kremlin, Cuba, Viet Nam, China, Jonestown and others. But the Moloch states of the West are no better than those of the East. Besides devouring its children on the one hand supposedly for humanistic reasons, Western Moloch states on the other hand have gone in for creating babies "by mechanizing the generative act." In legalizing the production of test-tube babies, they are playing God according to secular standards. For laboratory fertilization severs the inherently, God-given intelligible relationship between the unitive and procreative meaning of sexual union. The Moloch states of the West have replaced the God of love who creates and resides in the heavens, with the god of technocracy who experiments and flaunts the law of love in the laboratory. Nor will the facade of religious adornments hide for long the atheistic steel and concrete that enslaves, tortures and murders millions in these Moloch states. If there is any lesson for men in the massacres of Jonestown and all modern Moloch states, it is this: "It is a terrifying experience to attempt to escape from the Divine Lover. Every flight from him leads down the road to serfdom and violent self-destruction"

The inspired Psalmist gave mankind this lesson long ago in terse, clear, dogmatic language. "Unless the Lord builds the house, they labor in vain who build it." This truth holds for the building of families, societies, nations, international communities and, above all, of Churches. Jonestown and all Moloch states tragically specify the meaning of the vanity of building without the Lord. For they demonstrate that building without the Lord is equivalent to building with the aid of Satan. And any city that rises from Satan's blueprints can only end up a City of Hatred and Violent Death. Moreover, in testifying that Satan is not dead, Jonestown and every Moloch state also witness to the truth that neither is God. If the world is not to be destroyed by that final pseudo-savior, the Antichrist whom the present world seems bent on welcoming and who at his coming will orchestrate all evil revolutionary sects so expertly that the very framework of society will shatter into pieces under his wicked wand, it will have to come to terms humbly and lovingly with the Word and Law of the Living God.

Notes

[1] R.J. Rushdoony, *The Institutes of Biblical Law,* Nutley, N.J., Craig Press, 1973, p. 32.
[2] Gary North, *None Dare Call It Witchcraft,* New Rochelle, N.Y., Arlington House Publishers, 1976, p. 33.
[3] R.J. Rushdoony, *op. cit.,* p. 35.
[4] Ronald Knox, *Enthusiasm,* New York, Oxford Press, 1950, p. 110.

Reprinted from *Homiletic & Pastoral Review,* December 1979.

Trojan Horse in the City of God

Whenever a creed, culture or civilization is under assault, it has the option of capitulating to or conquering its enemy.

Rejuvenation will be its reward for courageous counter-attack; extinction its penalty for cowardly surrender. The history of every creed testifies to this ancient, universal lesson.

Today it is universally agreed that Christianity — as creed, culture and civilization — is under siege from the forces of secularism, which embodies a system of doctrines and practices that rejects any form of religious faith or worship and sets up autonomous man, "standing on his own feet," emancipated completely from any need for what is beyond himself, "come of age," totally self-sufficient.

I contend that Christian civilization in the West is dying from the poison of secularism and that the West's intellectual, moral and even religious leaders are wittingly and unwittingly injecting this poison into the dying organism.

For in the secularist forces we come face to face with a metaphysical revolt against reason and a theological uprising against God, especially against the God of Christianity.

This double-pronged revolution not only pits believer against non-believer, but Christian against Christian, layman against clergyman, theologian against theologian and even believer and non-believer against lawful authority everywhere — in the Church, the state, the family.

About a hundred years ago the worldly philosophers shocked the philosophical world by rejoicing over Nietzsche's raging cry of despair: "God is dead!"

Hegel paganized Christianity in a fifth gospel. Feuerbach replaced theology with anthropology, establishing man as his own god. The historian David Strauss explained away the Gospels as myths expressing Jewish aspiration. Comte replaced theology with sociology, creating a Church and priesthood of scientists. Marx divinized economic man. Sartre divinized himself, calling God Silence...Absence...the Void.

Today a few modern *theologians,* too, are proclaiming the death of God, a Christianity without God, a new gospel of atheism.

Summarizing this "new" theology we can say: it is a spiritual drug, derived from a substance known as self-sufficient humanism which grows and feeds on man fallen from grace, and is prepared from the following ingredients:

God is irrevocably dead as a person. At best the word "god" can only mean a depersonalized "ground of one's being," or "ultimate concern" of man, or man's "suffering for and in his fellowman."

Faith in God is but a hope for the future; it dissolves each moment into love of man.

The Christian is no longer a forgiven, redeemed, divinized sinner, but merely a man at the side of his neighbor, of his enemy, of the needy.

The task of the Christian is, in the words of Altizer, "to affirm and even will the death of God."

Jesus is merely a Nietzschean superman, torn from the bosom of the Trinity, freed from History as man's greatest social worker, whose authentic existence calls each man to face up to his own approaching death by existing for others.

The Scriptures, Old and New, are demythologized, washed, thoroughly rinsed of any transcendent, supernatural, miraculous, divine beings or meanings.

We have thus a distorted hallucinatory theology, expurgated of God, the God-Man, a real Resurrection, Ascension, of the supernatural and divine in any degree. We have a religionless Christianity, a Godless theology, a blind faith grounded on an existentialist philosophy of revolt and aimed exclusively at humanitarian projects. Salvation is of man in this world.

Is it any wonder that modern society has, under the influence of this poisonous drug, developed panic reactions and become psychotic?

As might be expected, the revolt against orthodox theology has led to a revolt against Christian morals. For the public morality is but the prolongation and projection into practical human activity of the inner philosophical and theological convictions of a people.

The new morality reflects the "permissive" mentality of the times: any crime is now justified, *depending solely on the circumstances.* Its major emphases are license in sexual practice and its major good works are militant enterprises in the causes of minority pressure groups and civil rights.

But these and similar crusades — in behalf of pacificism, free filthy speech movement, obscenity literature, rejection of prayer in schools, etc. — are conducted from purely secular, humanitarian motives.

A morality without sin (for sin obviously is sin before God), without, in the words of these solons of secularization, "crippling guilt," without "rigid, archaic rules and codes," far from freeing man *from* conformity and *for* maturity, actually ushers man into an age of anarchy. For once God, the Supreme lawgiver, is banished from reality, then anything is allowed in human conduct.

Nor can law and order be preserved through the idol that is substituted for God. Guiltless man, say the progressive humanists, is always responsible for his actions, no longer, of course, to God, but before the Future, before History. But History and the Future are mere relative, depersonalized abstractions, while moral responsibility exists only among persons, towards each other and God.

According to the Rev. Harold O.J. Brown, Congregationalist minister

of Harvard College and Harvard Divinity School, the major mistake of
the heralds of God's death is this: they have abandoned the Bible as their
unique source of light and authority, which for 400 years kept the Christian
churches close to the Word of God, and gave their theology its vigorous
vitality and character; they have substituted for divine authority whatever
human authority is at the moment in fashion.

They banish God, yet still fond of the Christian vocabulary, they
continue to use it, perverting it in an effort to find comfort in a sentimental
optimistic religiosity which is a blasphemous caricature of Christianity.

For all their bravado, says Rev. Brown, the high priests of this neo-
paganism are already "conducting the funeral services" for secularized
Christianity. "This is inevitable and probably desirable once the principle
of authority has been lost. *A secular church will not long survive.*"

The very words of Holy Scripture testify against this possibility. "Unless the Lord builds the house, he labors in vain who builds it." And the
Son of God warned man of his total impotency when left solely to his own
resources. "Without Me you can do nothing."

Truth, far from being divisive, is the source of agreement and unity
among men. But if the funereal prophets in the West are impotent to
discover and share the truth about God and authentic morality, if they
are helpless to defend the valid, permanent rights of the individual and
society, then the decline and fall of Christian civilization will accelerate
downward from the eclipse of God to the eclipse of man, from the eclipse
of man to the obliteration of his Christian heritage.

What attitude, then, should a believer take in the face of those for
whom God is dead and Christian morality a myth?

Only the uncompromising, whole-hearted faith and love of the believer
can melt the uncompromising, whole-hearted rebellious hardness of the
atheist. Faith begets faith and love, love. Perfect faith dissolves perfect
skepticism. To be able to lead men and save ourselves and others, then,
believers must be the deepest witnesses of God they can become.

The free society of the West is desperately in need of leaders, of men
in love with the truth; for only by sharing divine truth and transcendence
will man escape the shackles of matter, motion, measurement, and time.

"It is possible," writes Christopher Dawson, "that the more science
a culture has, the more religion it needs."

We will not be saved by escalated wars on poverty, disease or lack
of water supply. Nor will we be saved by bigger and grander social welfare
programs, fine as these may sound and seem. Rome possessed a magnificent, full-bodied system of law which is still with us today. Yet that law
could not save a Roman way of life which preferred bread and circuses
to its moral commitments.

Oliver Goldsmith, 18th-century British poet, novelist and playwright, wrote, "Ill fares the land; to hastening ills a prey where wealth accumulates and men decay."

If the West is to cure its spreading addition to crime, she will have to heed the wisdom expressed by Abraham Lincoln in a speech delivered in Springfield, Ill., in 1837;

"Let reverence for the laws be breathed by every American mother to the lisping babe that prattles on her lap; let it be taught in schools, seminaries and in college; let it be preached from the pulpit, proclaimed in legislative halls and enforced in the courts of justice. And, in short, let it become the political religion of the nation, and let the old and the young, the rich and the poor, the grave and the gay of all sexes and tongues and colors and conditions sacrifice unceasingly upon its altars. Let every American, every lover of liberty, every well-wisher to his posterity, swear by the blood of the Revolution never to violate in the least particular the laws of the country, and never to tolerate their violation by others."

If we embrace this salutary course of action, the West will, under God, enjoy a new birth of freedom, a fellowship founded on these rock-like truths — the love of God and of Christian morality.

Reprinted from *Men of the South,* February 1967.

Detroit: A Call to Revolution in the Church

About 1,340 delegates from 152 dioceses and 1,100 observers from around the nation met in Detroit from October 21 through 23 in a conference sponsored by the U.S. Conference of Catholic Bishops as a culmination of the Church's Bicentennial celebration. The theme of the conference was "A Call to Action." The purpose of the action was "Liberty and Justice for All." But the theme actually developed by the conference was "A Call to Revolution." And the purpose of the revolution was "A Classless Church for All." The following are the observations of this delegate who participated and represented the Confraternity of Catholic Clergy, a group counting close to 1,000 priests and 15 bishops, founded two years ago.

Now in every rigged convention there is a selected slogan patented by the planners and calculated to justify to the world their pre-arranged victory. I notice that *The N.Y. Times* was quick to catch, and zealous in scattering to the journalistic winds, the clever myth concocted by the directors of this conference. Giordano Bruno would have cheered the astuteness that produced this tool of deception. *Se non è vero è ben trovato:* "If it is not true it is very well invented."

On October 22 *The N.Y. Times* tells us: "Although a broad array of church members are in Detroit, the character of the delegation is clearly reformist...."On the 24th we read in those august pages: "Roman Catholics from a broad spectrum of the church today neared the end of a three day conference...A remarkable cross section has now spoken... Like the (Eucharistic) Congress, the conference is largely a lay affair." On the 25th the same theme swells in intensity: "It (the conference) was the most representative meeting of the Roman Catholic church in its history in this country...." And, as if unable to cease singing the same song, the *Times* was on stage again October 27 four days after the conference closed: "A diversified group of delegates took full advantage of a chance to recommend changes" is the subtitle to a glowing wrap-up story on a meeting that sent *The N.Y. Times* into great expectations for the coming of a democratic Catholic Church founded on the revelations of progress and humanism. Within the body of the last article we read: "Delegates could hardly be described as belonging to fringe groups. They were chosen by bishops. They represented a wide assortment of people."

Who chose delegates?

The N.Y. Times' correspondent, Kenneth A. Briggs, author of all the articles quoted, parroted perfectly the slogan of the ruling radicals at the conference. But what were the facts? First, it is not true to say the delegates were chosen by the bishops. Most of the bishops had neither the time nor energy to choose delegates, nor did they know the majority of delegates from their own dioceses. For example, no bishop chose me. And the same was true of dozens of other delegates I met. The delegates were chosen by middle-management committees made up of new breed priests, liberated nuns and dissident intellectuals. Moreover, these bureaucrats chose delegates for the most part with mind-sets practically identical with their own on revolutionary solutions for religious, social and political problems. It was carefully estimated that forty percent of the delegates were clergy. Women made up another forty percent; the majority of these latter were nuns, a few in religious garb, the overwhelming rest in secular attire, frequently in pants suits. Just how representative of the 49 million Catholics in the U.S. are such specialized types? Then too, there were the other special interest groups of delegates — ex-priests, ex-nuns, homosexuals, minority caucuses for Christian Marxism, Socialism and pacifism. At the bottom of the totem pole were the few Catholics who wanted to keep the historical Church, despite some questionable changes called reforms. If there was one glaring fact about the ''Call to Action'' conference, it was that the delegates by far did not represent the vast majority of American Catholics — neither bishops, priests nor laity. They did represent a miniscule core of intellectual insurgents, disaffected clergy, religious, ex-seminarians — all enthusiasts for the creation of an American democratic Catholic Church.

A few observations should be made on the general and particular meetings that formed documents and passed resolutions on religious and social questions. *The N.Y. Times* (October 27) tells us that these meetings ''were a taste of the democratic process on the widest national scale...'' Nothing could be further from the truth. It was a common experience to see honest opposition cut-off crudely and silenced. Opponents of ruling radicals were often told ''to stop making debating points, to cease referring to encyclicals, council documents and traditional teachings.'' They were warned ''to lay aside philosophical definitions and disciplined, coherent thinking.'' Especially did the female chairladies insist that ''they wanted input that emphasized religious experience and social concern.'' Only thus could the documents on Church, personhood, family, ethnicity, work, humankind, neighborhood and nationhood become relevant to our times. Often when resolutions embarrassing to the ruling strategists were presented, the chairperson, with mind teeming with schemes, would slowly repeat the resolution meanwhile motioning some ideologically kindred spirit to man a microphone quickly — such spirits hovered close to microphones everywhere. The carefully selected messenger would then move to end debate on the resolution. Another companion would quickly second the motion and the resolution was shouted down by a vote that ended a discussion that never got started. This process went on *ad nauseam;* the meetings were in the hands of the haters of open discussion; they feared nothing more than intelligent dialectics. And they steam-rollered the opposition through an abuse of parliamentary tactics that was in fact academic intolerance. For the manipulators were hell-bent on obtaining certain predetermined goals and they came prepared to brook no opposition.

Rebels took over

This became so clear from the very outset that John Cardinal Krol could not keep silent about it. In an interview with *The Detroit Free Press,* which printed his remarks in the Saturday October 23 issue, the Archbishop of Philadelphia made this complaint: "Rebels have taken over the conference." He then specified thus: "The conference was being manipulated by a few people who had received the support of a naive group of little ladies." Now the few people manipulating the meeting were agitator-priests, Saul Alinsky types. Indeed one of these Monsignori boasts continually that he is a spiritual child of agitator Alinsky.

Now Saul Alinsky, who died in 1972, is still very much with us as a charismatic leader. He is the author of two very influential books *Reveille for Radicals* and *Rules for Radicals.* A Marxist humanist and atheist, some brief thoughts and methods of the man will help us understand what went on at the Detroit conference. Alinsky teaches: "Truth is relative and changing: *everything* is relative and changing." And it is on this relativism that the organizer of a movement must thrive. For Alinsky the enemy is within and the war for change is to be waged within the community to be changed. He writes; "The first step in community organization is community disorganization...The organizer dedicated to changing the life of a particular community must first rub raw the resentments of the people of the community; fan the latent hostilities of many of the people to the point of overt expression. He must search out controversy and issues, rather than avoid them, for unless there is controversy people are not concerned enough to act...Any revolutionary change must be preceded by a passive, affirmative, non-challenging attitude toward change among the mass of our people. They must feel so frustrated, so defeated, so lost, so futureless in the prevailing system that they are willing to let go of the past and chance the future...The job of the organizer is to maneuver and bait the establishment so that it will publicly attack him as a dangerous enemy. Such a counterattack then puts the organizer on the side of the people...A revolutionary organizer must shake up the prevailing patterns of the people's lives — agitate, create disenchantment and discontent with the current values to produce a passion for change." In this system religion becomes politics and politics becomes religion. And this explains why so many priests, infected with the virus of Alinskyism, are enraptured at destroying the traditional Catholic Church.

'Western' society gets blamed

The priest manipulators of the conference lived up perfectly to the coarse, crude methods of their mentor. Their tactics produced from their audience — delegates and observers — distorted reactions against the Catholic Church, the United States, the First World of the West, business corporations, the white man; all these hysterical reactions led to accusations of criminality against these sectors of Western society and to a frenzied cry to bring these sectors to their knees. No injustice, no war, no poverty, no sickness, no difference or restraint, however reasonable, but was used to condemn these sectors as responsible for all the evils in the world. The whole conference was an activity-oriented frenzy and propaganda orgy. Now "the naive group of little ladies" were, though the Cardinal was too charitable to specify them, the not-so-naive liberated nuns who responded with emotionally charged outcries, clappings and vote-acclamations to the wand-waving of their exalted leaders.

The anti-intellectual, anti-rational tone of the proceedings was spiritually suffocating. With a shock it dawned on me that I was witnessing a new, alarming, growing phenomenon in the Catholic Church. A movement of Catholic "Know-Nothings" was making a play for power in the Catholic Church. And their first move was to discredit their Church before the world by mounting a witch hunt against her, supposedly to uncover her injustices, her subversive political activity and her disloyalty to the ideals of her Master. In reality this witch hunt was meant to harass and weaken the entire ecclesiastical structure. These agitated Catholics revealed themselves fully at the conference. They were ignorant of Catholic dogma, morals, canon law, philosophy, culture and history. But the most dismal aspect of their ignorance was that they did not give a tinker's damn about it. Indeed they gloried in their ignorance! Their contempt for truth was demonstrated every time they tittered against papal teachings and the age-old doctrines of their Church. Their contempt for justice and moral balance was demonstrated when they demanded that the Church change her doctrines on artificial contraception, abortion, the right to national defense, the right to private property, the right of reasonable profit. Their contempt for authority — divine and human — was demonstrated when they shouted against laws reasonably restraining the use of liberty, when they rejected the divine plan for salvation, when they resented such metaphysical and physical differences as God established in the diverse vocations, sexes and services for the salvation of man. Nor were these exalted souls really interested in "liberty and justice for all." They voted down a resolution presented by an Eastern European group condemning tyranny behind the iron curtain. I had to check with a friend to make sure I heard correctly. He assured me I had. The reason given for the rejection of this resolution was that it was decided that "no anti-Communist statements were to be placed in any of the final documents. This would be too negative." Once again, favorite treatment for the universal enemy, the pet of the rascal radicals. Of course, previously it had not been considered too negative to represent the Church, the West and especially the U.S. as the architects of tyranny.

A demonstration erupts

Some years ago Paul VI caused a world-wide commotion by speaking in his Wednesday allocution of the smoke of Satan seeping into the Church of God through the cracks in the walls of the faithful. On October 13, eight days before the opening of the Detroit conference, Paul VI told the world in his allocution that "the tail of the devil is functioning in the disintegration of the Catholic world." (Corriere della Sera, 14 ottobre, p. 7) The allusion is to the Apocalypse where the tail of the dragon is said "to be dragging along the third part of the the stars of heaven and dashing them to the earth." Without a doubt there was a demonic dimension at the meeting in Detroit. One need merely relate the dramatic event that occurred near the end. As resolution after resolution opposing the radicals was defeated and things were speeding-up to allow participants to catch homeward bound planes, a group of four or five young men (they seemed to belong to the frustrated Eastern Europeans) quietly walked into the hall carrying a banner before a suddenly silenced and astonished audience. The banner read: "When you leave this city, take our red cardinal with you." A few policemen then went into action. They reached for the banner and were on the point of roughly ushering the young men out of the hall when cries from the audience mollified their conduct. "Take your violent hands off those men. They have a right to express their opinion." The policemen then restricted themselves to persuading the men to leave quietly. Suddenly the young men shouted in unison: "Judas, Judas. Traitor priests!" They continued this for some minutes as they slowly left the hall. And their voices were heard gradually dying away with the one word returning weaker and weaker: "JUDAS, JUDAS, Judas, Judas, judas, judas!"

Bishops were culprits

One has merely to read the list of over one thousand arrogant demands this conference made upon the Church to realize that its own psychological violence provoked the violence of the young men. The conference sat in judgment, in the chair of Peter not of Moses, on the Church. It preached downward to the hierarchy, scolding them, demanding a reform of their lives, and listing privileges they must give up at once, or at least share with all the faithful. Russell Kirk in National Review, December 10, 1976, reports this incident. "You came here to listen, not to talk," said one militant priest to an unhappy bishop who had attempted to utter sense at one of the workshop sessions. Perhaps the most despised persons at the conference were bishops. Why? Because they enjoyed the fullness of orders; they exercised the power of ruling; they possessed the authority of teaching. And the radicals, moved by the spirit of violent envy — though they themselves would call it the spirit of the theology of hope — demanded all these gifts for themselves. These haters of hierarchy and order demanded a flattened down Chruch, a Church that functioned through theological egalitarianism. And they wanted such a Church today or tomorrow at the latest. One need just read the finalized documents to be appalled at the madness that prevailed at this conference.

As Russell Kirk wrote in *National Review:* "Call to Action was the monstrous baby of Cardinal Dearden of Detroit upon whom the Church had conferred responsibility for celebrating the Bicentennial." But when one reads Cardinal Dearden's report of the Detroit conference to the Bishops' meeting on November 9, 1976 in Washington D.C. one is surprised to find not a monstrosity but a darling child destined to bring great news to the Church of the future. How can one explain this wide divergance of opinion between two such distinguished persons? Let me attempt an explanation. It is within the setting of a fond father evaluating the bizarre anatomical diversity and behaviour of a loved, though flawed, child that the Cardinal's praise of the Call to Action conference must be understood. We need not look for conscious distortions in such passages as "We bishops were able to bring together what must surely rank as one of the more diversified assemblies in our history," even though many bishops explicitly disassociated themselves from the conference and many others lamented the fact that the conference was anything but deliberative. Rather, the explanation must be found in the fascination for exaggeration and the use of hyperbole in praising one's own creature. That fascination will suffice to explain this passage and others: "It could be said that the intelligence, enthusiasm and commitment of those who were chosen to attend the conference is a testimony to the discernment of the bishops who appointed them." This is the tactic of lulling the bishops to sleep on the disaster that was the Detroit conference by lathering them in flattery. Or take this passage: "people do expect us to continue the process by responding with decisive action where it is called for, and with honest disagreement where that seems necessary. The key to our action in the future is to continue the process, to build on the hopes that have been awakened, to act upon our clear responsibility for the unity, fidelity and vision of the Catholic community." All this is but high-flown nonsense. The people do not wish the shouting and the tumult of Detroit to continue; they were scandalized at it; fears not hopes were awakened in them; they saw in the Detroit meeting not the responsible building up of unity, fidelity and vision, but rather the destruction of unity, fidelity and supernatural vision by a revolt against reason, revelation and the sacred authority of the Church. As an architect of the Call to Action, the Cardinal is open to an accusation of special pleading in attempting to whitewash his own creation. *Cicero pro domo sua* has been for centuries, indeed since the fall of Adam, the whitewash syndrome used to explain away failures. But it will not wash.

Even when he reluctantly admits "hasty, untidy, careless, even extreme" defects in the conference's proceedings, the Cardinal cannot leave the brush alone. "Yet even these flaws can be exaggerated," he writes. It is my contention as well as Russell Kirk's and many other delegates and observers at the meeting that the flaws were often so blasphemous that they could hardly be exaggerated. Indeed, because the Cardinal attempts to minimize these flaws one is scandalized at his carelessness over the serious-ness of the situation. Here was a frenzied meeting in which disgruntled Catholics irrationally attacked the Catholic Church; Mystical Body of Christ.

In viewing the hysteria of the delegates, this writer was reminded of the truth of Dryden's poetic lines: "Great wits are sure to madness near allied... There is a pleasure, sure, in being mad, which none but madmen know."

Demands were made

The following are some of the conference's mad demands which the Catholic Church simply cannot grant without ceasing immediately to be the true Church of Christ. If she granted them, she would become a Church of the world, a snake pit of radicals. She would become a center of doctrinal, moral, chaotic disorder and psychoneurotic distress. The radicals demanded: 1) Divorced, remarried couples to receive Holy Communion while still living in adulterous unions. 2) Ordained women priests and bishops. 3) Women given the power to preach the Gospel with authority. 4) A reversal on the doctrine of artificial birth control. 5) A mitigation of the doctrine on abortion. 6) A teaching approving Marxism, Socialism and pacifism as doctrinally true and morally good practice. 7) A denial of the right to property and to reasonable profit. 8) The creation of a new Church, democratic, non-hierarchical in structure, a classless church.

The following are some of the demands the Church simply cannot fulfill for that is not her mission: 1) Wipe out poverty, ignorance, prejudice and war. 2) Democratize the whole world. 3) Stop the sale of arms every-where. 4) Back the E.R.A. as a constitutional amendment. Like her Saviour, the Church will not turn stones into bread, thereby becoming the

Mother of Socialism or a millenium of this world. Finally, here are a few demands the Church will most probably not grant in the interest of her supernatural mission to make converts of all nations: 1) Allow married men to be ordained. 2) Allow priests to marry. 3) Revoke the vow of celibacy of priests and religious. 4) Lift the excommunication from divorced, remarried Catholics still living in adultery.

A final word of advice to Cardinal Dearden, Archbishop Peter Gerety and Msgr. John Eagan, prime movers at Detroit in the drive to create a democratic church of the future in a five year program. Such a democratic church will not be accepted by American Catholics, for such a church would be a man-made utopia, incapable of saving anyone. The Holy Spirit and the Vicar of Christ will preserve Catholics from such a sterile kingdom of this world. Bereft of Christ, such a church could only become an instrument of the Sons of Satan in their war against the flock of Christ. To loyal, perceptive bishops, priests and laity who still love their traditional, apostolic Church, it is of no small significance that the world is rejoicing over the debacle at Detroit. Such faithful souls know that when *The New York Times* rapturously reports the wild doings of a conference of Catholic enthusiasts and projects their redimensioned model of the Church as the inevitable Church of the future, then proper Church authorities better grab the holy water sprinkler, the prayer manual of exorcisms and, if need be, the legal instrument of excommunication before it is too late. Only by at once applying these remedies vigorously (Alinsky would insist on the *vigorously*) will the temple of God be cleansed effectively of its iconoclasts and the true Catholic Church rescued from the savagery of latter-day malcontents posing as concerned Catholics. Superstition? Hardly. Rather security measures against outside agitators and inside traitors.

Reprinted from *Homiletic & Pastoral Review,* March 1977.

Detente All Round: Prelude to Antichrist?

La detente, in its original meaning, signified the trigger of a gun. *Lacher la detente* means "to pull the trigger." Through wider application *la detente* came to mean a catch that starts or stops a movement, a gadget for releasing the striking of a clock, a control piece. Thus the pulled trigger fired the cocked gun; the released catch set-off the wound-up alarm.

In the spiritual world, therefore, it would be the aim of a tactic of detente to dissipate dangerous tensions, to set-off alarms for protective actions. Unfortunately, however, today detente indicates merely slow maneuvering for sly surrender to tyrants. It is a policy instrument that degrades the art of home and foreign politics by dragging both into the dust and dreariness of defeatism. Vainly hoping to relax international tensions and avoid nuclear war, the free West regularly succumbs to the demands of the monolithic East. This policy of detente is one of tragic self-delusion; it dissipates no dangerous tensions. Hence it is bound to be a failure on the political, economic and military level because it was, and is, a continuing betrayal on the moral and religious level of human relations. It is a superficial, simplistic policy, lacking vision and depth. For this tactic of detente is doing nothing to reinforce the foundations below that are crumbling away and threatening a sudden collapse of the Western world. Attempting with detente to treat merely the symptoms of the sick society, the leaders of the West do not yet realize that detente itself is the essential virus in its own malignant sickness. Let me explain.

Religious detente: apostasy from God

The root evil of the tactic of political detente is to be found deep in man's metaphysical, religious rejection of God. For man's social attitudes on the fundamental relations of community life, his just claims and moral obligations are determined by his care or carelessness about his relationship to God. Even Socialist Proudhon had to marvel at how political problems were assumed into theology. In his *Confessions of a Revolutionary* we read: "It is a cause of wonderment to see how in all our political problems we invariably stumble up against theology." But Donoso Cortes in his "Essay on Catholicism, Liberalism and Socialism," commenting on Proudhon's wonderment at God's presence everywhere in politics, writes: "There is nothing here that should cause surprise except the surprise of Proudhon. For theology, by the very fact that it is the science of God, is the Ocean that contains and embraces all the sciences, just as God is the Ocean that contains and embraces all things." And it was the great St. Augustine who said that in its roots every serious political problem has a causal nexus with faith or lack of faith in God. The Psalmist long ago had written: "Unless the Lord builds the house, they labor in vain who build it."[2] This is a truth that applies to Nations as well as to families and the Church.

Thus the fundamental evil of detente is that man has abandoned faith in and love for God. Man has sued first for separation then divorce from God and followed this rupture with a new engagement and remarriage to his new idol, technological humanism. Mankind is living in an age in which the West denies God through an addiction to technological scientism while the East escalates a messianic war against God through its addiction to dialectical materialism. The West has divinized Security and Technocracy; the East, Science and Revolution. But in both camps atheistic humanism has become the State religion. And both of these systems of secular humanism eclipse the person, eliminate his freedom, deny his human-divine value and subject him to the tyranny of technological impersonalism. The alarming signs of the times testify to a fierce spirit of evil advancing everywhere. It is the spirit of rebellion against God and man. Hitherto the powers of government in each country, as yet relying on God and reason, were firm and vigorous enough to restrain this rebellion. But today many agnostic countries can barely contain that lawless spirit, while many others have actually legalized the principle of lawlessness itself, the principle of license masquerading as liberty.

We are reminded of St. Paul's warning to the Thessalonians. In the last days there will be an aweful, unparalleled outbreak of evil everywhere. This will be called the Great Apostasy. In the midst of this general falling away a certain Man of Sin, having the image of Satan and breathing hatred toward God and man, will appear. He will exercise frightening preternatural powers of destruction against the just. This Child of Perdition will be so special and singular an enemy of Christ that he will be called Antichrist.[3] For just as types of Christ went before Jesus, heralding his coming, so shadows of Antichrist have already preceded him. St. John the Evangelist warned Christians of his day thus: "Little Children, it is the last time. . . even now there are many Antichrists whereby we know it is the last time."[4] But compared to the final Antichrist all forerunners of him were so many mini-Antichrists. This Arch-Antichrist will orchestrate revolutions so expertly that the very framework of society will shatter into pieces under his wicked wand. In a stunningly evil way, he will knit together his total-itarian rule of heresy, sedition, revolution, schism, war — indeed of every evil movement — and hurl them effectively against the Church. Preceded by apostasy, conceived in apostasy, gestated in apostasy, born in apostasy, the Man of Sin will come to total power through a General Apostasy. In other words, Antichrist could never have existed except for the decision of the majority of persons in East and West to apostatize from God and to join the forces of atheism.

Am I foolishly playing the prophet of gloom and doom in saying we are entering the Age of Apostasy? Are there no evidences to convince us that some such apostasy is being formed, gathering forces, gaining ground on us every day? Everywhere in the world, but quite visibly and formidably in the most powerful, civilized nations, we are witnessing a supreme effort to govern men and dominate the world without Religion. It is already an accepted and spreading dogma that Nations should have nothing to do with Religion, that Religion is merely a private matter, an affair of one's own conscience. In effect it is widely accepted that Truth is neither a personal nor social need and, therefore, society ought to allow Truth to fade from the face of the earth. It is considered futile social action to continue to advance a system of Truth and absurd to attempt to hand it on, further developed, to our posterity. Again in almost every country there is a united, powerful movement to crush the Church, to strip her of power and place. Everywhere we discover a feverish, litigious endeavor to get rid of Religion in public activities — in schools, in mass media, in social transactions, in political affairs. Societies are said to be built on the principle of *Utility*, not on the principle of *Truth*. Again *Experience* not *Truth* or *Justice* is accepted as the end or rule of State activities, enactments of Law included. Numbers, not Truth, is the final ground for maintaining this or that creed, morality or law, it being practically believed that the many are always in the right, the few in the wrong.[5] Even the Bible is given so many meanings over and against its obvious one that it is reduced to having no meaning at all, to being at best a pleasant myth, at worse a dead letter. In the end Religion is denied any objective, historical reality such as is displayed in written dogmas, ordinances and sacraments. Rather religion is confined to each person's inner feelings, experiences and psychological reactions. Thus cast into the dark world of variable, evanescent, volatile feelings, Religion is discredited in the minds of many when, in fact, it is not already destroyed there.

It must be admitted that in the West the conflict between the children of the New Humanism and the faithful is escalating in ferociousness. The spirit ruling in the great cities is avaricious, luxurious, self-dependent, irreligious, arrogant, ungodly, falsely liberal and sacrilegious. The offspring of the New Humanism are agnostics, atheists, apostates, lovers of this world with tastes, opinions, habits immersed in materialism, with hearts riveted to the vagaries of this time, minds moulded by vanities of passing pleasure, with thoughts rising no higher than personal comforts and gains, with a haughty contempt for the Church, her ministers, her sacraments, her devotions, her lowly faithful, with a lust for rank and station, an ambition for the splendor and fashions of the world, an affectation for refinement, a dependence upon their own powers of reason, an habitual self-esteem and finally with an utter insensibility to the heinous sins they are committing against God and man.

Dogmatic detente: flight from revelation

Such rebels bear the characteristic mark of Antichrist. That brand is their open denial that Our Lord Jesus Christ is the Son of God and that he came to redeem men. St. John the Evangelist states that the denial of Christ is aptly called the spirit of Antichrist. Thus these modern enemies of Christ radiate the spirit of Antichrist, are disciples of Antichrist, can be called Antichrists.[6]

It is hardly surpising that the City of Satan, in its attack on the Catholic Church, would concentrate its big guns on two major doctrines that constitute the heart of the Catholic faith: 1) the Eucharist as the real substantial presence and true eternal sacrifice of Jesus Christ in the consecrated host; 2) the Virgin Mary as Mother of God. Both these mysteries are reduced to being Christian developments of old pagan myths, fables which attempted to explain the origin of the universe through monistic and cosmological forces. Daily within the Church one is saddened at the waning reverence for the Eucharist and shocked at the growing blasphemies against the Eucharist and the Mass. The Mystery of Iniquity has opened an offensive against the Mystery of Faith. In the opinion of the ex-Canon M. Roca, found in his book *Glorieux Centennaire,* the mystery of the Incarnation was not an assumption of a human nature by Jesus Christ, the Second Person of the Trinity. It was merely "an inoculation of the divine into the human." It is thus that the masses, all unknown to themselves, receive the divine influence in their moral ways and secret acts. It is also thus that in the rites of the Church, this divine innoculation is admirably symbolized in the ceremonies of baptism, the Eucharist and the other sacraments. Thus the Eucharist considered as a rite is merely a symbol, but considered as the cosmological reality that it expresses it is the presence of the Cosmic-Christ, of the Christo-humanity in everything. Therefore, in reality transubstantiation is only the presence of Christ in the human. Civilization, whether advancing or regressing the flow of history and human communications will become "communion" for everyone through an osmosis of cosmic dimensions. This is a species of Christo-genesis rooted in evolution.[7]

This mythical "Eucharistization" from the theories of Teilhard de Chardin is supposed to be the phenomenon through which Christ assimilates to himself humanity and, through humanity, the universe itself. Thus transubstantiation, by divinizing the universe, enlarges and prolongs Christ's incarnation. The Word inserts itself through this inoculation into the cosmic elements. It is true Teilhard attributes a secondary character to these phenomena which for him flow out of the consecration at Mass. But it must be noted that if this procedure of "Eucharistization" is dialectically turned as an antithesis to the inoculation posited by Roca, the result is such a convergence that what the Council of Trent defined as "the immediate and individual presence of Christ in the consecrated host "through the admirable and singular conversion of transubstantiation can no longer be clearly distinguished as being distinct from the original, creative, universal presence of God in all things. From such an explanation one gets the impression that "cosmic holy Communion" is a real possibility and that sacramental transubstantiation is merely its symbol. Thus the Sacrament of the Holy Eucharist is counterbalanced, and the idea of the communion of all men among themselves is considered the real holy communion in the "Christo-Social-Spirit." We read Roca again: "This holy communion for all men takes the place of sacramental communion and it can happen that transubstantiation operates in all men more rapidly than in so-called Christians who accept the empty formula and dead letter of the Sacrament of the Eucharist. . . Here is what I call transcendental and rational theology. The theologians of the future will accept this explanation and type of theology."[8]

Such variations on gnosticism, symbolism and modernism attack the authentic teaching of the Magisterium on the Holy Eucharist. They are to be rejected with zealous contempt. We now emphasize three errors concerning the Blessed Virgin. Just as Christ is not the Son of God, but the inoculation of the divine into the human, so Mary is not the Mother of God. Rather she is the key of all cosmogonies, i.e., the fulfillment of all goddesses created by the pagans to explain the origin of the universe, the fulfillment of Gaia, Demetra and Iside. Mary thus represents the living, Feminine Principle or Immaculate Wisdom incarnated and united with the Masculine Principle the Celestial Divine Spirit, from whose sposal union a new divine race of men comes forth. Mary thus received a priesthood, which however has remained hidden up to our times. Today, as knowledge of women has developed, women, in consequence of Mary's priesthood, may become priestesses themselves and even Papal consorts in the Church of the future. Roca concludes as follows: "Thus under two parallel tiaras and in a cloud of incense men will behold the Pope and his Consort pontificating together as spouses, symbols of the sacred, divine Duality — the Power of Masculinity and Femininity, the Spirit and the Anima, the two universal principles of the celestial Diade and of the androgynous (hermaphroditic) priesthood."[9] These fables are nothing but a marvelous mixture of the theories of updated Gnosticism, Catharism and Cabalism, all occult religious philosophies condemned as heresies by the Church.

Newman on the coming of Antichrist

More than a century ago when times were rather peaceful, even Christian, compared to the general apostasy and religious confusion of our day, John Henry Cardinal Newman, with the vision of a prophet, predicted the desolation of our day: "Surely there is at this day a confederacy of evil, marshalling its hosts from all parts of the world, organizing itself, taking its measures, enclosing the Church of Christ in a net, and preparing the way for a general apostasy from it. Whether this very apostasy is to give birth to Antichrist or whether he is still to be delayed we cannot know; but at any rate this evil apostasy and all its tokens and instruments are of the Evil One and savour of death."[10]

It is certainly profitable for Christians to reflect on the First and Second Coming of Christ, to keep their hearts prayerfully alert, awake to the hope and longing of His Second Coming. Christ Himself exhorted us to look out for, recognize and study the signs of his coming as Judge of the living and the dead. We are also encouraged by the Fathers of the Church to think often and much of this final judgment, to dwell on the particular accounting each of us must make. Such religious reflection will nurture a profound and saving faith; it will increase an intelligent, far-seeing wisdom in the faithful follower of Christ. For in the light of His Second Coming the face of the wicked world is unmasked. In this prayerful reflection the veil will fall from our eyes and we will clearly see how the world is secularizing, corrupting and desacralizing the whole superstructure of society — politics, economics, law, education — indeed, the whole strata of personal and social activities. We will understand how this process of cosmic perversion is preparing the stage of history for the Coming of the Man of Sin who will quickly seize total power and set himself up as God in his own right.

Detente as liturgical disorder

Once again we find that Cardinal Newman foresaw another serious attack upon our faith. This time he warned Christians against innovators who would relax Christian forms and usher into the Church liturgical frenzy. Such devotees of change question every Christian form of prayer, every posture of devotion, every devotion itself and the very personal or traditional symbols of the faith. Their lust for innovation is used as a battering ram against the stability of long-established sacred rites, which have been witnesses and types of precious Gospel truths for Christian communities. Hurriedly, even violently, they replace divine forms with new diluted Masses, new prayers, new sacraments, new churches — all of which confuse the faithful. Newman writes: "No one can really respect religion and insult its forms. Granted that forms are not immediately from God, still long use has made them divine *to us;* for the spirit of religion has so penetrated and quickened them, that to destroy them is, in respect to the multitude of men, to unsettle and dislodge the religious principle itself. In most minds usage has so identified them with the notion of religion, that one cannot be extirpated without the other. Their faith will not bear transplanting. . . Precious doctrines are strung like jewels upon slender threads.''[11]

Moreover, the new forms are without splendor, flattened, undifferentiated. Why was kneeling replaced by standing? Jesus Himself fell on his knees and on his face as he prayed to his heavenly Father. Satan too knows the meaning of worship and man's need for it. He tried to get Jesus to fall down and worship him. Why has the liturgical year and the Mass been so unfortunately mutilated that the faithful are now confused about the Mass, the saints, the holy seasons? Why was the Gloria, that prayer of total concentration on God's Majesty and Goodness, restricted practically to Sundays alone? Is the faith really renewed and vivified by obscuring our sense of community with the Christians of apostolic and ancient times? The new liturgy no longer draws us into the true experience of reliving the Life of Christ. We are deprived of this experience through the elimination of the hierarchy of feasts.[12] Then too the new forms are the result of experimentation. But one experiments with things, with objects that one wants to analyze. Experimentation is the method of science. But a liturgy is full of mysteries, of realities in which one must participate. Experimentation only desecrates mysteries. The wretched idolatry of tinkering with sacred realities has, unfortunately penetrated the Church and produced a mediocrity-ridden liturgy, a show for spectators that distracts from the holy, frustrates intimate communion with God and vulgarizes, where it does not suppress, sacred actions, symbols, music and words. In reality such diminished liturgies have renewed nothing. Rather these innovations have emptied churches, dried up vocations to the priesthood and sisterhood, driven off converts and opened the doors wide to a flood of renegades. Even though valid in its essence, such a new liturgy cannot inspire for it is colorless, artificial, banal, without the odor and flavor of sanctity. A humanized, popularized liturgy will never produce saints; only a divinized liturgy can accomplish that miracle.

In our times it is no secret that the enemies of the Church want to destroy belief in the divinity of Christ. Once the liturgy is humanized, Christ the Center and Object of it becomes the humanist *par excellence,* the liberator, the revolutionary, the Marxist ushering in the millennium; he ceases to be the Divine Redeemer. We must be alerted to those who plan, by convincing us to abandon our sacred forms, at length to seduce us into denying our Christian faith altogether. The Church is attacked by these Sons of Satan, in and outside her fold, because she is a living form, ''the sacrament — sign and instrument — of communion with God and of unity among all men; because she is the visible body of Religion. Hence these shrewd masters of sedition know that when her sacred forms go, religion will also go. Violate the *lex orandi* and you must inevitably destroy the *lex credendi.* That is why they rail against so many devotions as superstitions; why they propose so many alterations and changes, a tactic cleverly calculated to shake the foundations of faith. We must never forget, then, that forms apparently indifferent in themselves become most important to us when we are used to using them to nurture our lives in holiness.

Places consecrated to God's honor, clergy carefully set apart for his service, the Lord's Day piously observed, the public forms of prayer, the decencies of worship, these things, viewed as a whole, are sacred relatively to the whole body of the faithful and they are divinely sanctioned. Rites sanctified by the Church through ages of holy experience, cannot be disused without harm to souls. Moreover, in the words of Newman, "Liturgical reformists must ever be aware of the following truth: Even in the least binding of sacred forms, it continually happens that a speculative improvement becomes a practical folly, and the wise are tripped up by their own illusions."[13]

Bishops would be wise to follow Newman's conclusions in this war on the sacred liturgy. "Therefore, when profane persons scoff at our forms, let us argue with ourselves thus — and it is an argument which all men, learned and unlearned, can enter into: 'These forms, even were they of mere human origin (which learned men say is *not* the case, but even if they were), are at least of a spiritual and edifying character as the rites of Judaism. And yet Christ and his Apostles did not even suffer these latter to be irreverently treated or suddenly discarded. Much less may we suffer it in the case of our own; lest stripping off from us the badges of our profession, we forget that there is a faith for us to maintain and a world of sinners to be eschewed.' "[14]

The Fathers of the Church emphasize the corruption of the liturgy that will prevail at the last days. As the end draws near, the Church will be subjected to a fiercer, more diabolical persecution than any previously suffered. There will be a cessation of all religious worship. "They shall take away the daily sacrifice." Some Fathers interpret these words to mean that Antichrist will suppress for three and a half years all religious worship. Others remind us that Antichrist will set up his throne within the temple of God and demand worship of himself from his depraved followers. St. Augustine wondered whether Baptism would be administered to infants. We are living in times so wicked that many nations will not allow innocent human beings natural birth much less the grace of supernatural rebirth. The reign of Antichrist will be supported with a galaxy of miracles, such as the Magicians of Egypt effected before Moses and Simon the Sorcerer displayed before Peter and John. St. Cyril writes: "I fear the wars of the nations; I fear divisions among Christians; I fear hatred among brethren. But enough! God forbid that it should be fulfilled in our day! However, let us be prepared.''[15] Thus we see that over and above the persecution of blood and death, there will be a persecution of craftiness and subversion. The Man of Sin will be effective in splitting-up and dividing Christians. He will be successful in dislodging many from the rock of salvation, in driving many into heresy and schism, depriving them of their Christian liberty and strength.

In the presence of this terrifying prospect, what Christian can look for salvation from politics? Hope for peace from a political detente that strives for a balance of powers, a nuclear stand-off, an appeasement through economic favoritism and a piece-meal surrender to the enemy's plan for global conquest is nothing but a form of foolish whistling-in-the-dark. For such political tactics of defection are the inevitable evil fruits of religious forms of disruption that have previously dethroned God, the Church and the world of sacred values. Peace will never be the result of policies that promote commerce, cultural exchange and many varieties of communication. Such policies are like cheap cosmetics beautifying a dying body in preparation for its burial. But in the realm of the spirit fighting for the victory of Truth and Justice is a necessary condition for victory; faith and courage pave the path to peace; fortitude in trials of strength is the guarantee of life and liberty. In the realm of the spirit it is futile to attempt to quarterback a tie, especially against an enemy who will settle for nothing less than one's total destruction. A strategic stalemate between Satan and society, man and Mammon, atheism and Christianity is an impossibility. We either conquer the forces of evil or they conquer us; we either join the forces of God or the forces of evil; compromise is unacceptable by both sides. Our actions and loyalties in this struggle, though performed in time, are determining our eternal as well as temporal destiny. There is a radical, most important nexus between spiritual health, with its will to win, and the material forces at hand for victory. Without spiritual health, the overwhelming material resources for victory will be dissipated in the feeble hands of a sick nation that draws back because its heart is cowardly, its head confused, its vision blurred, its hearing dulled, its attention flagging and its feet slipping. Such a nation may rattle its armaments in comic bravado, but it frightens no tyrant. Such a nation plays the international clown, for, though it arms, it is not prepared to draw and, though it draws, it is powerless to shoot.

As the will of the West is inflated by its rebellion against God, that same will is simultaneously vitiated before the technological terror of its own weapons and those it helped create for the world of organized, militant atheism. For the West has lost its transcendent motive for "fighting the good fight," for finishing an honourable course. Not having kept the faith, it is now morally paralyzed, incapable of projecting a cogent politics of peace with dignity. Its politics falter; events are out of control; things fall apart. With the escalation of violence, crime, confusion, wars and rumors of wars emanating from religious apostasy and political disengagement, the stage is being set for the Coming of Antichrist. Is he waiting in the wings? Will he soon receive his cue from Divine Providence to make his entrance? Will he play out in our time of history the tragedy of the abomination of desolation and the consummation of the universe? True, his name and his time are known only to God. But the portents of his nearness are evident everywhere in the general desertion of the faith.

No doubt agnostic and atheist sophisticates will smile patronizingly at the prophecy of Antichrist's coming in a pestilence of heresies, preternatural heroics and wars. Progressist Christians will join the intellectual scoffers. It was thus in the days of Noah who was laughed to scorn as he built his ark of salvation. It was thus in the days of Abraham as he pleaded fruitlessly with Sodom and Gomorrah. It was thus in the days of Christ as he wept over the city of Jerusalem. All these skeptics were wiped out violently for their incredulity. It will be thus at the end of time. For the wicked are too proud to accept and understand the ways of God. In those last perilous days men shall be lovers of themselves, covetous, boasters, proud, blasphemers, disobedient to parents, unthankful, unholy, without natural affection, trucebreakers, false-accusers, incontinent, fierce, despisers of those who are good, traitors, heady, high-minded, lovers of pleasure instead of lovers of God, scoffers walking after their own lusts and jeering: Where is the promise of His Second Coming? Men will be despisers of government, presumptuous, self-willed, calumniators of civil and religious authorities, promising everyone liberty while subjecting themselves and their fellowmen to the corruption of run-away licentiousness.

Conclusion

The basic issue of detente, then, is not how does the West domesticate Soviet totalitarian despotism? But rather how does the West reverse its own conduct of moral perversity? When will the West return to its life of sanctifying tensions through a faith that loves and serves God? When will the West renew its dangerous war of tensions against the world, the flesh and the devil? When will it cease being unfaithful? When will it reject half-measures that temporize in the face of its moral obligations? When will it finally accept God's grace and justification as the only cure for its spiritual exhaustion? Saintly Christians alone can give the example and inspiration for a universal reconciliation with God. Such Christians never forget they are pilgrims without a lasting city here below, but striving forward to the eternal city which is to come. They reject the temptation to live in ease and comfort; their first priority is a life of prayer and self-restraint; they reject the pursuit of money, prestige and power as the primary activity of man. Such faithful Christians form "little islands of holiness" everywhere, but especially in their homes which will surely but slowly re-Christianize a neo-pagan society, even as the little band of original disciples Christianized the pagan Roman Empire. "Will I find faith when I come?" asked Christ concerning those last days. We Christians must be his eager heralds, watching for the morning, the light, the signs of His Second glorious Coming. For despite the general Apostasy that will be prevalent at that time, the Lord will be welcomed in His Final Coming in power by the remnant of His Faithful Christians. These will rejoice exceedingly, knowing that this Parousia will put an end forever to the despicable detente of sin, will gather in His elect and establish eternally that *entente cordiale*, that eternally loving communion with God known as the Beatific Vision.

Notes

[1] Donoso Cortes, *Ensayo Sobre el Catolicismo, el Liberalismo y el Socialismo* (Buenos Aires: Editorial Americales, 1943), p. 23. "Mr. Proudhon ha escrito, en sus *Confesiones de un revolucionario,* estas notables palabras: 'Es cosa que admira el ver de que manera en todas nuestras cuestiones politicas tropezamos siempre con la teologia.' Nada hay aqui que pueda causar sorpresa, sino la sorpresa de Mr. Proudhon. La teologia por lo mismo que es la ciencia de Dios, es el Océano que contiene y abarca todas las ciencias, asi como Dios es el Oceano que contiene y abarca todas las cosas."

[2] Psalm 126.

[3] 2 Thess. 2:1-11.

[4] 1 John 2:8-25.

[5] John Henry Cardinal Newman, *Discussions and Arguments on Various Subjects,* London, Longmans, Green and Co., 1888, pp. 59, 60.

[6] 1 John 2:22.

[7] M. Roca, an ex-canon, *Glorieux Centenaire,* p. 537. Quoted by *Si, Si, No, No,* a monthly periodical published in Rome, Italy, Marzo 1976, Anno II, Numero 3.

[8] Ibid. p. 537.

[9] Ibid. pp. 497, 506, 507.

[10] Newman, Ibid. p. 60.

[11] John Henry Cardinal Newman, *Parochial and Plain Sermons,* Vol. II, Christian Classics Inc., Westminister, Md., 1966, pp. 75, 76.

[12] Dietrich von Hildebrand, *The Devastated Vineyard,* Franciscan Herald Press, Chicago, 1973, pp. 70, 71.

[13] Newman, Ibid. p. 78.

[14] Newman, Ibid. p. 78, 79.

[15] John Henry Cardinal Newman, *Discussions and Arguments on Various Subjects,* p. 102, Newman quotes St. Cyril's *Cateche. xv, 16, 17.*

Reprinted from *Faith and Reason.*

Häring Erupts

Morality Is For Persons, the final draft of a series of lectures given by Fr. Bernard Häring in a workshop seminar at Catholic University in the summer of 1967, is put forth as a "soul searching" re-examination of ethics and moral principles. "Morality," he writes, "has to be justified by the good of persons in community and by the community of persons." What emerges is a drastic metamorphosis in the moral teaching of Fr. Häring. The giant of Catholic moral teaching who wrote *The Law of Christ* a decade ago has, in his pursuit of new moral truths and standards, fallen into the Hegelian net of historical relativism.

According to historial relativism, what is true for one age is not necessarily true for another. Ideas are dialectically and historically dynamic; there is a time for their appearance, development and acceptance. When they are "in the air," when they give form and tone to a generation, when they create the spiritual climate of a civilization, then they are true and good for that epoch. One is reminded of William James' crude criterion for truth, "the cash value of an idea." In effect, if there exists a large market that will accept a certain moral judgment, then that judgment is true and good, for "morality has to be justified by the community of persons." Socio-historical popularity has displaced objective evidence, reason and revelation as the criterion of truth and moral goodness.

The absolutely important categories of the true and the false, the good and the evil have been substituted in the treatment of ethical problems by the following picayune criteria: Is the moral judgment modern or ancient, in step with the times or a throw-back to tradition, dynamic and alive or static and dead? Fr. Häring is more intent on approving human action that is dynamic, modern and relevant, than conduct which is founded on truth and performed according to God's will. The substitution of such volatile, irrelevant guidelines for the eternal commandments of God is both an intellectual inversion and a spiritual perversion.

Having developed a new set of moral standards, it is not surprising that Fr. Häring establishes a new goal for moral life. Whereas Christian moral theology calls Christians to imitate the holiness of God by living in the Faith of Christ ("Be ye perfect as your heavenly Father is perfect"), the new moral theology calls Christians to the attainment of "maturity" in this world with their fellowmen. Man's response to the standards of a changing world becomes far more important than man's response to the commandments of God, "the Father of lights with whom there is no change, nor shadow of alteration." Fr. Häring calls this bringing Christians "from the ethics of the yardstick to an ethics of responsibility."

In an effort to attain prestige and acceptance for the tenets of his new morality, Fr. Häring systematically ridicules throughout the book the

traditional Catholic morality, urging at every opportunity the secularized
Christianity and morality found in Heidegger, Nietzsche, Teilhard, Sartre
and Bultmann. The vocabulary strives to remain Christian, but the thought
is pagan. In the eyes of Fr. Häring the good Christian is "authentic, mature,
existential, dynamic, open, free, restless for reform, an enemy of the *status
quo.*" None of these terms is specifically Catholic or even Christian. Nor
are the ideals that may be represented as their content Christ-like or divine.
Nietzsche and his pupil Heidegger found all these ideals in the "godless
self-gods" of this world. For the truth and moral ideas advocated in this
new terminology are at best a goal of goodness restricted to this world.
Häring's so-called new ethics is thus nothing new: it is a stoical sanctity
in and for the *saeculum;* in effect, an anti-Christian morality.

Because he has founded the good moral life on false standards, Fr.
Häring's statements about the nature of good and evil are mostly erroneous.
For example, the implication that every moral status quo is evil because
it is a status quo fails to take into account that the desire to preserve the
status quo is in itself morally neutral. What makes the desire to keep a
moral status quo evil is the actual evilness of the status quo, for example,
the sexual perversion prevalent in Sodom and Gomorrah. This situation,
accepted by the "popular morality" in those cities, was an abomination
of evil in the sight of God and anyone defending it or preserving it was
an evil person. Another example: Fr. Häring accepts the Nietzschean and
Heideggerean idea of evil: "a desire for security." What a trivial notion
compared with the metaphysically tragic reality of the mystery of evil! St.
Augustine writes that evil is *amor sui usque ad contemptum Dei,* that is, "Evil
is the love of self even to the extreme of hating God." Not so for Fr. Häring,
for whom only the "existentialist person" is the true Christian: "The existentialist person has no desire for a monotonous life, a static secure routine
that desires to make no response to the wonders of God's living, changing
world. Especially at this time the true Christian desires a venturesome life
that answers God's call for this time and place...."

For Fr. Häring, the Catholic who lives by the providence of God, a
life perhaps not so venturesome, is a "sick" person: "If, instead of this,
we offer youth only a 'holy rule' that remains forever 'as it was in the
beginning,' having no pertinence here and now, then our appeal will be
only to sick people suffering from a security complex."

What lesson can the reader learn from the decomposition of the moral
thought of Fr. Häring? Above all, this lesson: in the breezy aftermath of
Vatican II, theologians like Fr. Häring have promulgated a new ethical
program for salvation which abrogates in effect the program of the Saviour
himself. "If you wish to enter eternal life," Christ warns men, "keep the
commandments." And He responds to the woman who beatified His

mother: "Nay, rather blessed are they who hear the word of God and keep it." For their part these men counter with this doctrine: "If you wish to enter eternal life, observe solely the dictates of your conscience."

At first sight there seems to be no conflict between these two moral projects for a holy life. Nor, so it seems, is there in the latter commandment a question of creating new moral doctrine. Christian moralists have always taught that the proximate norm that enlightens and guides the individual in his human conduct must be his practical reason, his private conscience. Every man must follow his personal conscience in whatever it commands or prohibits.

The falsity in these theologians' moral teaching is to be found in their strange conception of the nature and functions of the conscience. To use a metaphor, the conscience is an interior, intelligent loudspeaker that transmits God's law to man and at the same time appeals to him to live up to that law in order to become a reasonable, free, responsibly holy person. Catholic moral theology, therefore, insists that it is always essential that private conscience be *instructed* in the laws and Holy Will of God.

An ignorant or misinformed conscience is like a receiver set that has lost connection with divine communication headquarters. Conscience is always a created capacity in man; it is always totally dependent on its Divine Creator and on the sources of truth the Creator has put at its service: experience, the exercise of the valid reasoning process, the light of revelation, the infallible guidance of the Magisterium of the Catholic Church. Each individual conscience starts life in total darkness with respect to what is morally good or bad. The private conscience must, therefore, humbly, nay eagerly, allow itself to be informed and formed by the many sources of truth God has provided for it. In this true vision of the nature and function of private conscience, it becomes clear that the first duty of conscience, the first duty of the moral person is *not* to discover within itself its own contents and hold this up to itself as God's law. For fallen man, darkened in intellect and weakened in will, that procedure can only lead to total deception and spiritual disaster in the slough of self-serving subjectivism. Instead, the first task of the private conscience is to discover its moral imperatives in the commandments of God and the teachings of His Church. The first obligation of private conscience is to scrutinize the divine laws of both natural and supernatural revelations and to live up to those laws. Private conscience can never become a law unto itself, can never become its own absolute legislator.

Yet according to the teaching of men like Fr. Häring, conscience need not go out of itself for its moral norms. All it has to do is pay attention to its own desires, enthusiasms, discoveries, weaknesses and tragedies. It must look at these, of course, from both a personal and historico-social dimension; it must acknowledge its debt to science and accommodate itself to the historical currents dominant in the present age. What a travesty of the sublime nature and noble function of the god-like gift of private conscience! What was created to bring human persons to know God and to live in the communion of holy love with God and one's fellowman is now degraded to being an instrument for avoiding the hard sayings of reason and revelation and for fleeing the noble, even heroic, sacrifices demanded by God's loving law for the achievement of God's holiness and glory in man.

But when private conscience becomes absolute in moral matters, then God's law and God's sanctity are abolished and substituted for by worldly standards and secularized sanctity. The result is the approval of all manner of foolish doctrines and conduct: against nature, against Christ, against His Church. In this very book Fr. Häring continues to oppose the clear moral teaching of *Humanae Vitae,* and approves immoral methods of artificial birth control (against nature). In public lectures he has suggested that people who have gotten divorces from valid but incompatible marriages should be allowed to remarry (against Christ). He allows masturbation as a means of obtaining male seed for medical examination (opposing the clear prohibition of this means as immoral by Pope Pius XII).

This book is full of irrational, strident criticisms of the Church and Catholics. Instead of presenting cases that illustrate moral principles, Fr. Häring tells gossipy stories that systematically disparage the pre-Vatican II Church, its doctrines, institutions and teachings. This is scarcely an improvement over the casuistic method of studying morality. Whatever the limitations of that method, it never stooped to uncharitableness in order to drive home petty, personal prepossessions. Much of the pettiness in the book, which might have been tolerated in off-the-record lectures in a workshop, cannot be accepted as serious scholarship in a tome published for general study. In fact the book is an irrational explosion against the traditional moral teaching of the Catholic Church. Everything erupts from the Häring soul like hot lava, but it cannot stand up under the scrutiny of reason and revelation. If the positive, noble and sublime aspects of the traditional moral teaching of the Church are simply ignored, the many dangers inherent in the thrilling morality of self-decisional salvation are also overlooked. Morality in Fr. Häring's "system," founded as it is on the doctrine of historical relativism, is trendy, fickle, contradictory, indeed, trivial. If taken to its logical conclusion, the Häring ethic, like that of Nietzsche and Heidegger, would arrive at a position beyond good and evil. For once the private subjective conscience is made the sole source of morality, all moral responsibility ceases. A responsibility to one's self alone is no responsibility at all, since the self can always change its moral standards to suit its historically evolving needs. A system of morality so devoid of objective norms, yet using Christian terminology, can only lead to a post-Christian terror.

Reprinted from *Triumph*, November 1971.

Nixon in China — A Political Pilgrim

Some incurable optimists would have us see Mr. Nixon in Peking as an American Moses confronting Mao, the Chinese Pharaoh, with a divine mandate to convert at once and return to the "family of nations." Needless to say, this religious analogy, projected and enhanced with moralistic rhetoric, is an impious fraud. There has been no missionary mandate from God, Church or Country to "Go Down Nixon." Neither has there been any appeal from godless self-god Mao to "Come, let us reason together." The plain truth is that the President of the United States is a mendicant pilgrim to Peking. And perhaps the most depressing aspect of this truth is that he is a mere political pilgrim.

We get the uneasy feeling that we have been down this road before. History is an implacable witness, teaching us, in the wise saying of Santayana, that "those who cannot remember the past are condemned to repeat it." In the era of Nazism, Neville Chamberlain visited Munich for the purpose of inviting Hitler's Germany back into the "family of nations." In order to satisfy Hitler's voracious appetite, Mr. Chamberlain, with the connivance of the Western world, fed Austria and other small European nations to the Nazi beast. Umbrella in hand and smile on his face he returned to London proclaiming to the world "peace in our time."

While Nazism was digesting its new victims and London's ambassador to peace was celebrating his taming of the German monster, Mr. Churchill shrewdly applied the following analogy to the reality of the situation: Mr. Chamberlain thinks that if he feeds the crocodile often enough, this beast will eventually be satisfied; in reality the crocodile's appetite will become so voracious from these frequent feedings that it will never be sated short of devouring Mr. Chamberlain and the whole of Europe.

It might be well for Mr. Nixon to recall the tragic fate of Mr. Chamberlain and the Europe, not to mention the world, of the nineteen-forties as he begins to feed the Dragon of China with small nations of Asia.

Now the bargaining with Red China over the destiny of Free China and the Far East contradicts the professed policy of the United States for the last 25 years. America has sacrificed thousands of American lives and vast treasure in Korea and Vietnam to guarantee the freedom of the Far East. It helped create SEATO for that specific purpose. Communist China remains today as great an aggressor as she was when branded such by the United Nations on the occasions of her invasions of Tibet and India and her perpetration of genocide in the conquered territories.

What new evidence has presented itself to explain the President's sudden respect for the Chinese Communist State? It is evident to the whole world that Red China has undergone no perceptible moral conversion. Indeed, a recent Senate subcommittee document reports that Mao's regime murdered between 34 and 64 million persons, primarily political dissidents and minority ethnic groups. The mere passage of time cannot make a hardened aggressor-nation fit to enter the community of nations as a trustworthy member. Is it possible America no longer has any stomach for the ugly truth that Mao's China remains a criminal state dedicated to the conquest of its free and peaceful neighbors?

We are driven to seek the explanation for the President's pilgrimage to Peking in the mind of the President himself. Some cynics explain that Mr. Nixon, realizing he is in political trouble, is visiting Peking for the sole purpose of guaranteeing his re-election. If he can monopolize the peace issue by this visit, his enemies will be left naked before the electorate on the matters of both war and peace.

As a moral philosopher I would propose a deeper motive for the President's new China policy. It flatters the pride of all men, but especially of men in high position and power, to think that they are above the radical metaphysical conflict raging eternally between the forces of good and evil. Instead of aligning themselves with the good against the evil, they fall into the magnificent delusion of thinking themselves capable of harmonizing these irreconcilable enemies. Vain and presumptuous enterprise! The moral philosopher knows that God himself cannot stand above the conflict between good and evil. Indeed, being the essence of moral goodness, God is necessarily the eternal punisher of men and societies addicted to criminal activity. Thus, what God himself necessarily keeps asunder, Mr. Nixon is trying to join together — a world dedicated to criminal aggression and a world dedicated to civil liberty. Consequently, the President's new China policy is foredoomed to failure as a peace move, though it may succeed in getting him re-elected as a political ploy. But the transcendent moral reality that must be confronted by all Americans is this truth: When politicians become gods, citizens and nations become pawns in the ruthless struggle for power.

Reprinted from *New York Times*, February 19, 1972, the date of Nixon's arrival in Peking. Op. Ed. page.

Aldo Moro: Another Victim of Detente

A statement issued by the bereaved family of Aldo Moro, president of the Christian Democratic party in Italy assassinated by the Communist Red Brigade, said in part: "The family wraps itself in silence and asks silence. History will pass judgment on the death of Aldo Moro."

But the sobered mind of the religious and political philosopher simply cannot keep silence. It profoundly taxes itself to discover and explain the causes for the unparalleled crescendo of all forms of savage assaults on innocent persons and institutions. For the escalation of terrorism represents a spiritual monstrosity similar to a hydra-headed serpent; it is a persistent, militantly advancing evil with many causes. Indeed, the apostles of the new barbarism are not demonically sick individuals. To have recourse to such an explanation is to fall into an abyss of nonsense.

To paraphrase a shrewd statement of Dr. Johnson: "Why is it that we hear the loudest yelps for liberty among the drivers of slaves?" We ask: "Why is it that we hear the loudest uproars for justice among the assassins of innocents?" The fact is that terrorists belong to intelligent, well-trained expertly organized cadres who have raised nihilistic anarchism to the altars of religion.

In the name of the religion of humanitarianism they perform their terrible massacres, stalking society beneath the mark and curse of Cain. Their fundamental dogma seems to be, "I kill, therefore I am." At the root of this dogma lies the satanic spirit of the great refusal, "I will not serve; I will rise above the throne of God!"

Inspired and sustained by a metaphysic of murder, centers of professional terrorism have mushroomed all over the world. They seem bent on demonstrating the truth of Oscar Wilde's aphorism: "Moderation is a fatal thing. Nothing succeeds like excess." Moreover, they zealously strive to attain both the subject and object of Shakespeare's truism: "Violent delights have violent ends."

The issue of terrorism clearly involves religious, philosophical, ethical, legal, economic and, *inter alia,* political considerations of a most radical nature, touching the very roots of the Judaeo-Christian tradition.

Here we would consider but one of the causes for the organization and escalation of international terrorism. Authority has failed to confront courageously the agencies of violence and shrunk from the responsibility of applying quickly the penalties of the law to convicted assassins. Why?

One reason is that religious and political leaders are still in a paralytic trauma from the horrible experiences of Nazism and Fascism. Their weak rationalizations claim that today there is need for a more humane, less authoritarian policy towards all criminals and especially towards the architects of international anarchy. Whence arose this cult of softness?

The sign of connivance

Back in the days of "the great thaw" between Communist Russia and the West, the incurably optimistic oracles among the ruling classes began chanting the song of peace. A spirit of buoyant euphoria swept through the West. Good Pope John XXIII was embracing Communist journalists; Red Russia released to the West some political and religious prisoners to demonstrate its good will. The golden glow of detente rose with every sunburst from the East.

> Hope about uniting our broken world gave birth to a theory of convergence between the free nations of the West and the Soviet Union with its satellites. It was a tranquilizing, drowsy theory which induced in the West loss of contact with and moral insensibility to the harsh truths of reality.

Even the Catholic Church, gathered in a mighty General Council at the Vatican, caught this spirit of universal convergence. When 450 of its fathers from 86 countries petitioned to have the Council produce a special document in which, for the benefit of the whole world, "the Catholic social doctrine would be set forth with great clarity, and the errors of Marxism, socialism and communism would be refuted on philosophical, sociological and economic grounds," the petition was rejected as being too divisive. And the tactic used to defeat the petition was the device of the lie.

What happened to the 450 signed interventions to have "a solemn reaffirmation" by the Council on the long standing doctrine of the Church on this matter?

Fr. Ralph M. Wiltgen, S.V.D., in his book *The Rhine Flows into the Tiber*, writes: "From four different sources I learned that the person who withheld the interventions from members of the joint commission was the commission's secretary, Msgr. Achille Glorieux of Lille, France...the French prelate had acted as a 'red light' for the interventions on communism....

Archbishop Garrone of Toulouse was obliged by the Council to make a public admission of negligence....He stated that the interventions on communism had reached the office of the commission within the proper time, but were not examined when they should have been, because unintentionally they had not been transmitted to the commission members."

Thus clerical intrigue, motivated no doubt by the desire to achieve convergence with the Communist world, thwarted the opportunity of the Church in General Council to break an embarrassing silence on the intrinsic evil of communism.

The policy of dialogue

With the defeat of a conciliar try for a special schema on communism, Pope Paul VI called for a policy of dialogue with atheistic communism. This posture of concession was further developed into a policy of *la mano tesa*, the extended hand of friendship, known politically as *ost-politik*, that eagerly tolerant permissiveness and trust in Communist humanism which has led to political compromises between the Church and the Communist states. What have been the results of this difficult dialogue?

1. The dialogue has succeeded in seducing many Catholic leaders away from the sole purpose of the Catholic Church's existence — its mission to bring all men to salvation in Christ. It has cleverly maneuvered them into substituting a utopian Christianity whose purpose is to bring all men to natural happiness.

2. The dialogue has produced thousands of Catholic adherents — bishops and priests included — to Christian Marxism, Christian Socialism and an army of Catholic dissidents from their Church's teaching on many essential dogmatic and moral matters.

3. The policy of Catholic detente is succeeding in secularizing Christian nations, e.g., France, Italy, Spain, etc., and has so strengthened their Communist parties that candidates of the Red party have won regional governing power and are on the threshold of winning national power.

4. The daily surrenders to the myth of peaceful coexistence with the Communist hegemony have demonstrated to the enemy that the West has lost its faith in the truths and ideals of Christianity. For a decline in Christian courage is always a certain sign of a prior abandonment of Christian convictions. Aleksandr I. Solzhenitsyn, in his commencement address at Harvard University on June 8, 1978, analyzed accurately the spiritual malaise from which the West is dying.

"A decline in courage may be the most striking feature an outside observer notices in the West in our days. The Western world has lost its civil courage, both as a whole and separately, in each country, each government, each political party and, of course, in the United Nations. Such a decline in courage is particularly noticeable among the ruling classes and the intellectual elite, causing an impression of loss of courage by the entire society.

"Of course, there are many courageous individuals but they have no determining influence on public life. Political and intellectual bureaucrats show depression, passivity and perplexity in their actions and their statements, and even more so in theoretical reflections to explain how realistic, reasonable as well as intellectually and even morally warranted it is to base State policy on weakness and cowardice.

"A decline in courage is ironically emphasized by occasional explosions of anger and inflexibility on the part of the same bureaucrats when dealing with weak governments and weak countries not supported by anyone, or with currents which cannot offer any resistance. But they get tongue-tied and paralyzed when they deal with powerful governments and threatening forces, with aggressors and international terrorists.''

5. The folly of attempting an ''historical compromise'' with communism has led to a Western self-deception, the belief that a type of ''European communism'' is compatible with a system of Christian democracy. But only massive, continued violence can transform one of these systems into the other.

6. Despite all the friendly endeavors to domesticate communism, international intrigue and violence have escalated in frequency and ferociousness; national wars of liberation have increased the number of countries that have disappeared into the Communist hell. Africa has been allowed to become an uncontested Communist continent of conquest, while all the time the West is being reduced to naked feebleness.

The naivete of the policy

Why is it that Catholic leaders express an artless belief in the good intentions of Communist tyrants? Even great minds have fallen for this rose-tinted fantasy. Jean Cardinal Danielou had written: ''She [the Church] shares with all men without exception, hence even with Communists, a concern for the material advancement of civilization.'' But are the Communist leaders really concerned with the material, spiritual, or even cultural advancement of mankind?

The testimony of Eugene Lyons, once a youthful enthusiast for the Communist cause and a sympathetic American journalist for many years in Moscow, dissolves the roseate myths of a humane communism and cuts to the cruel core of Marxist barbarity. In his *Workers' Paradise Lost* we read:

''By 1934 when I departed from Russia, nothing was left of the high mood of dedication, traces of which I had still found among Communists six years earlier. The very vocabulary of idealism had been outlawed. 'Equality' was lampooned as bourgeois romanticism. Excessive concern for the needs and sensibilities of ordinary people was punished as 'rotten liberalism.' Terror was no longer explained away as a sad necessity. It was used starkly and glorified as 'human engineering.' Means had blotted out ends and have held this priority every since. The Marxist theory of permanent class struggle rules out compromise, reform, truce, common humanity, mutual respect, family loyalties.''

But long before Eugene Lyons wrote his testimony in 1967, two great Popes had already warned the world against yielding to made-in-the-Kremlin myths of Communist mellowization. In 1937 Pope Pius XI wrote in his encyclical *Atheistic Communism:*

"See to it, Venerable Brethren, that the Faithful do not allow themselves to be deceived! Communism is intrinsically evil, and no one who would save Christian civilization may collaborate with it in any undertaking whatsoever. Those who permit themselves to be deceived into lending their aid towards the triumph of communism in their own country, will be the first to fall victims of its error. And the greater the antiquity and grandeur of the Christian civilization in the regions where communism successfully penetrates, so much more devastating will be the hatred displayed by the godless."

In a Christmas message, "The Contradiction of Our Age," to the whole world in 1956, the year of the shocking slaughter of the Hungarian people by Russian Communists, Pope Pius XII had to warn Catholics again not to go into orgies of optimism over the supposed evolvement of Khrushchev's communism into an open society welcoming political dissent:

"We must with deepest sadness mourn the help given by some Catholics, both ecclesiastical and lay, to the tactics of obfuscation, calculated to bring about a result that they themselves did not intend. How can they fail to see that such is the aim of all that insincere activity which hides under the name of 'talks' and 'meetings'? Why enter a discussion, for that matter, without a common language, or how is it possible to meet if the paths are divergent, that is, if one party rejects or denies the common absolute values, thereby making all 'coexistence in truth' unattainable?

"Out of respect for the very name of Christian, compliance with such tactics should cease, for as the Apostle warns, 'It is inconsistent to wish to sit at the table of God and at that of his enemies.'

"And if there be still any vacillating spirits, notwithstanding the black testimony of 10 years of cruelty, the blood just shed and the immolation of many lives sacrificed by a martyred people should finally convince them."

Moro: architect of collaboration with communists

Aldo Moro was a model family man, an excellent Catholic, a man of great dedication. Professor of Law, intimate friend of Pope Paul VI, Moro was an expert politician of compromise. Indeed, he was perhaps the perfect incarnation of Vatican II's policy of accommodation with the Communists. Shortly before his death he stated that Communist participation in the Christian Democratic government was "inevitable." He thus engineered the recent convergency of a special nature between the Christian Democrats and the Communists. This parliamentary coalition tied Italy's power to rule itself to Communist approval and control, in effect handing political power over to the enemy of the free Italian State.

Moro justified his policy of compromise by calculatingly creating ambiguous slogans. He called cooperation between Christian Democrats and all radical left-wing parties "parallel convergencies," an impossible policy demanding such mental, political and moral gymnastics that catastrophic failure was inevitable.

Under the slogan "creative flexibility," he disarmed the nation and lulled it to sleep over the enormity of escalating violence and intrigue. He refused to see any enemy to the left; for him the only national threat came from right-wing, neo-Fascist violence. His antics in semantics indicate that he never seemed to realize the depth of the spiritual agony through which Italy and the whole of Europe was passing. For when one plays with baffling figures of speech, with fuzzy formulas calculated to obfuscate real dangers, one, in effect, dethrones truth which alone can make and keep nations free, one fosters an ambiguity that psychologically prepares citizens for slavery.

Moro seems never to have realized that ideas have consequences and that the violent ideas of the Communists would beget an army of terrorists. Lawyer and not a metaphysician, he viewed the art of governing solely from the legal aspect.

As long as legal rapport between parties was contracted for and on paper, he acted as if the nation's freedom was assured. The agreement of minds and hearts on essential truths and moral responsibilities seemed naively presumed. But to base the structure of political life primarily on legalistic relationships not founded on mutual spiritual ideals is to build a nation on the sands of metaphysical and moral contradictions. Such a nation must necessarily crumble before the onslaughts of criminal terrorists.

Yet Moro was too well informed not to have realized that the Communist party was the major cause of violence. For over 30 years it vilified the state, advocated class warfare, radicalized the labor unions, polarized church and state on education, divorce, abortion, the Lateran Treaty, etc.

As far back as 1970, the prefect of Milan, who represents the Ministry of Interior (responsible for law and order) in the Milan province, forwarded a classified report to his superiors in Rome indicating that there were 20,000 potential terrorists in his area. But, once again political considerations caused the prefect's warning to go unheeded. Moreover, *L'Unità*, the official daily of the Communist party termed the prefect's report "provocatory" and called for his resignation.

Moro also cooperated with the Communist party in dismantling the Italian Secret Service so that police could no longer track down spy groups and terrorists. Ironically, they were unable to track down Moro's assassins in Rome itself.

Yet a recent British study affirmed that "The *carabinieri* [Italy's military police vested with both military and civil jurisdiction] could clean up terrorism in Italy in weeks" if only the government's instability, which is due to its total dependence on Communist votes for survival, could be eliminated.

Moro knew that the Red Brigades and comrades were the ideological offspring of the party whose saints are Lenin, Stalin, Castro, Che Guevara. Yet he constantly compromised with this Synagogue of Satan. Did he not realize that the roots of Communist terrorism are nourished in the soil of man's metaphysical rejection of God, his own creaturehood, of Being itself?

It seems never to have dawned upon him that the See of Moscow took him as an archenemy for attempting to seduce Italian communism into a schismatic branch, cut off, going its own heretical way, chasing ideals opposed to those of its Pope and Church in Moscow. For his attempt to corrupt Italian communism by wedding it to the rottenness of a dying bourgeois society, Moro was ruthlessly tortured and assassinated by Moscow's trained zealots for Marxist orthodoxy.

And as a warning to Communist leader Enrico Berlinguer, lest he stray too far in the direction of the bourgeois paradise, the bullet-ridden body of Moro was delivered close to Italian Communist headquarters, close enough too to Christian Democratic headquarters to cause any leader there, thinking of mellowing Italian communism into a run-away Tito-type, to reflect seriously on the grisly consequences that are the wages of sins against the Red party.

There remained one final irony in Moro's tragic end. President of the Christian Democratic party, in line to be almost surely Italy's next president, as a reward for his parliamentary compromise with the Communists, Moro, the *maestro* of convergencies, while still a hostage of the Red fanatics, attempted to persuade his own party to enter another compromise — to free 13 Brigade terrorist leaders on trial in Turin in exchange for his own liberation.

Undoubtedly, Moro must have been less than himself in making this proposal, depressed, frightened, tortured, even drugged. But this compromise was morally and politically unthinkable; it would have released upon 55 million Italians, the whole of Europe and the world, ideological criminals vowed to overturn society and this in order to save one politico's life. Such a surrender would have destroyed the Christian Democrats as a party and ushered the Communists to the seat of power.

By a sort of Grecian tragic fate, Moro, the great compromiser, was assassinated because his own party was forced to realize finally that collaboration with the Communists eventually becomes the crime of the cowardly abandonment of the State.

As Solzhenitsyn put it in his Harvard speech: "To defend oneself one must also be ready to die; there is little such readiness in a society raised in the cult of material well-being. Nothing is left then, but concessions, attempts to gain time and betrayal."

In the specious ceremony of detente Communists will always devour Christians. For the children of this world, being of ill will and eager to deceive, are wiser than the children of light who are of good will yet peculiarly eager to be deceived.

Reprinted from *Human Events,* September 30, 1978.

The Need for Fortitude

"In our time more than ever before," said St. Pius X at the Beautification of Joan of Arc (Dec. 13, 1908), "the greatest asset of the evilly disposed is the cowardice and weakness of good men, and all the vigor of Satan's reign is due to the easygoing weakness of Catholics. Oh! If I might ask the divine Redeemer, as the prophet Zachary did in spirit: 'What are those wounds in the midst of your hands?' the answer would not be doubtful. 'With these I was wounded in the house of those who loved me. I was wounded by my friends who did nothing to defend me and who, on every occasion, made themselves the accomplices of my adversaries.' And this reproach can be levelled at the weak and timid Catholics of all countries."

St. Pius X depicted the true condition of a society that was abandoning God everywhere. Today Christendom is hopelessly divided by heresy and schism. The majority of men are satisfied to live in religious indifference, when not expressing animosity and hatred of Christ and his Church. The love for truth is an endangered virtue among intellectuals. Men resent any attempt to enlighten them about God and reject outright the very idea of conversion to Christ. To talk of converting anyone to Christ is to introduce a divisive impertinence into social life. Yet the same persons listen eagerly to heretical tales; they cannot drink in enough slanders against the Church. We are living in an age of religious modulation, an age of compromise with doctrinal error, an age of accommodation with neo-pagan immorality.

Everywhere in the world, but quite visibly and formidably in the most powerful and civilized nations, there is a supreme effort to govern men and dominate the world without Religion. It is already an accepted and spreading dogma that nations should have nothing to do with Religion, that Religion is merely a private matter, an affair of one's own conscience. In effect it is widely accepted that Truth is neither a personal nor a social need and therefore, society ought to allow Truth to fade from the face of the earth. It is also considered futile social action to continue to advance a system of revealed truths and morals and absurd to attempt to hand these on, further developed organically, to our posterity. We are living in an anti-intellectual, anti-spiritual age where all reality is reduced to sense and psychological experience.

Again in almost every country there is a united, powerful movement to crush the Church, to strip her of power and place. Everywhere we discover a feverish, litigious endeavor to get rid of Religion in public activities — in schools, mass media, social transactions, political affairs. Societies are said to be built on the principle of Utility not on the principle of Truth. Again, Experience, not Truth or Justice, is accepted as the end or rule of State activities, enactments of law included. Numbers, as computerized from opinion polls, is the final ground for maintaining this or that creed, morality or law, it being practically believed that the many are always right, the few always wrong. Even the Bible is given so many meanings over and against its obvious one that it is reduced to having no meaning at all, being at best a pleasant myth, at worst a dead letter. In the end Religion is denied objective, historical reality such as is displayed in written dogmas, ordinances and sacraments. Rather Religion is confined to each person's inner feelings, experiences and psychological reactions. Thus, cast into the dark world of variable, evanescent, volatile feelings, Religion is discredited in the minds of many when, in fact, it is not already destroyed.

It must be admitted that in the West the conflict between the children of the New Humanism and the Faithful is escalating in ferociousness. The offspring of the New Humanism are agnostics, atheists, apostates and lovers of this world, immersed in materialism, with hearts riveted to the vagaries of this time and with minds moulded by the vanities of passing pleasure. They exhibit a haughty contempt for the Church, her ministers, her sacraments, her devotions, and her lowly faithful. They display a lust for rank and station, an ambition for the splendor and fashions of the world, an affectation for refinement, a dependence upon their own powers of reason, an habitual self-esteem and finally an utter insensibility to the heinous sins they are committing against God and man. Such rebels bear the characteristic mark of Antichrist identified by St. John the Evangelist — an open denial of Our Lord Jesus Christ as the Son of God who came to redeem men.

In the Apocalypse, chapter 9, after the fifth angel sounds his trumpet, we read: ''And I saw a star which had fallen from heaven to the earth, and there was given to him the key of the bottomless pit, and there went up from the pit a smoke like that of a great furnace; and the sun was darkened and the air, by reason of the smoke of the pit. And out of the smoke locusts went forth upon the earth and they were told — to harm only such men as have not the seal of God upon their forehead.''

Now in prophetic symbolism falling stars almost always refer to tepid, weak, wicked or apostate bishops and priests who are harbingers of grief and disaster to the Church. The key to the shaft of the abyss is an emblem of their apostasy. These traitorous clerics ally themselves with the rebellious angels. Instead of using the keys of the kingdom of God, which they have received from the Church through their priesthood, to suppress and defeat satanic forces while advancing the holiness of the faithful, they rather misuse their priestly powers to foster and propagate error and evil, to open the abyss and let loose upon the earth the plagues of darkness and wickedness. Today too many fallen stars are misusing their sacerdotal powers to seduce, enslave and precipitate into damnation vast numbers. Out of the darkness of the pit they have loosed the forces of error, evil and scandal. The smoke streaming from the pit darkens the sun of Christ's truth and infects the air with decadent immoral odors. Everything is cast into confusion; darkness infests the world of religion and reason; grace, the life-giving air of the soul and body, is strangled out of the supernatural organisms of the children of God. Moreover the darkening of the sun and sky betokens the eclipsing of the teaching authority of the Church, the lowering of men's respect and love for her, their loss of reverence for her Master and the demeaning of both Christ and his Church to the level of mere natural beings.

The answer to stars falling from heaven onto the earth through the pristine betrayal of Lucifer is stars that stand fixed in the heaven of fidelity to God with the courage and fortitude of Michael. The remedy for the tepid is the zealous, for the weak the strong, for the timid the brave, for the wicked the holy, for the apostate the apostle. The Church is sorely in need today of priests who are men of God imbued with the virtue of fortitude, of bishops who are "valiant in battle."

Fortitude is that virtue which enduringly resists difficulties of mind and body while persistently seeking, defending and spreading the truth and holiness of the Gospel. St. Thomas reminds us that fortitude is especially concerned with overcoming the fear of performing difficult deeds for the glory of God. This virtue prevents a soldier of Christ, and above all officers in Christ's army such as bishops and priests, from fleeing the field of battle, from betraying the brethren when real or imaginary obstacles present themselves. The great fault of the pusillanimous is that they succumb easily to irrational fears and leave the field of battle to enemy forces. This moral deformity reveals a lack of faith in the cause of Christ and a distrust of the assurance he gave his followers when he said to his Apostles: "Have confidence. I have overcome the world." The defect of irrational fear weakens virtue and renders Christians cowards. All the Apostles except Judas overcame this fear when they received the gift of Fortitude from the Holy Spirit on Pentecost Sunday. And priests should pray daily for this gift which the Holy Spirit will never deny them.

But fortitude is not merely a passive virtue, a patient suffering of assaults of the enemy. Again St. Thomas states that "it is not outside the genus of fortitude to go on the offensive for the sovereign good of man and the glory of God." St. Joan of Arc, a mere girl of nineteen unprepared by nature or training to do battle against hardened veteran soldiers, nevertheless, fearlessly followed the will of God and drove foreign infidels out of Catholic France. In the beginning Joan resisted and protested to her heavenly voices: "I am a poor girl; I do not know how to ride or fight." In vain, for the voices only reiterated: "It is God who commands it." Such was her fortitude that she courageously faced all manner of trials, repugnances, humiliations and finally the ignominious death of being burned at the stake as a witch-heretic in order to remain faithful to the will of God and to fulfill the heroic mission God entrusted to her. At the words: "It is God who commands it," Joan rode forward to certain victory under her banner bearing the words *Jesus, Maria,* with a picture of God the Father, and kneeling angels presenting a *fleur-de-lis.*

It is time for priests and bishops to mount a campaign to defend the faith with fortitude. "It is God who wills it!" Theirs is the honor and duty to defend the realities of revelation, the honor of Christian virtues by waging an inexorable war on error and vice. "Woe to me," said St. Paul, "if I do not preach the Gospel of Jesus Christ." Bishops and priests, like the Apostles, must be undeterred by human respect, by the world's contempt, by humiliations, by false brethren, by the allurement of pleasures, by the threats of political powers, by the desire of honors and the credit of a great name on earth. Like the Apostles, they ought to rejoice to be able to suffer something for the name of Jesus Christ. Fortitude will lead them to behave magnanimously, with manliness, stability, constancy, forebearance, firmness and perseverance. For in the words of St. Augustine: "Fortitude is a form of deep love which moves a man of God to be willing to bear all trials for the glory of God." Bishops and priests must heed the advice given by St. Paul to St. Timothy:

"I admonish you to stir up the grace of God which is in you by the laying on of my hands. For God has not given us the *spirit of fear,* but of power and of love and prudence. Do not be ashamed of testimony for Our Lord..." "O Timothy, guard the trust and keep free from profane novelties in speech and the contradictions of so-called knowledge which some have professed and have fallen from the faith...But do thou be watchful in all things, bear with tribulation patiently, work as a preacher of the gospel, fulfill thy ministry."

A priest endowed with the gift of fortitude is not deterred even by the threat of death from remaining faithful in the service of God, of man and of the Church.

Reprinted from *Confraternity of Catholic Clergy,* September–October, 1977.

Part III

Philosophy

Atheistic Humanism in the U.S.A.

There are many forms of atheism. Basically, all atheism can be classified as an objective system of thought or a subjective stand against God. Each form of subjective atheism is rooted in a person's dynamic experiences and the historical forces that influence him in making his decision against God. The mystery of a person's atheism is as inexpressible as the mystery of a person's faith. For both lie in the depths of the Yes or No will act to grace and in the motives, culpability, euphoria, failures and successes of the individual. To attempt to plumb these influences would be indiscreet, hazardous, indeed an exercise in futility. After all, each person is responsible for making the analysis that will justify in a reasonable manner his own beliefs or lack of them.

On the other hand, there are atheisms that are constructed and defended by philosophical reasoning. These atheistic philosophies are proposed as objective truth free from prejudice. Indeed they are expounded with a zeal that seeks to make converts to a community of atheists. Herein lies the importance of such atheistic formulations. They create a world-wide, dynamic climate of convictions that also produce a world-wide active consensus on moral conduct.

Among current atheistic formulations claiming to be founded on reasons are the following: *historicist atheism, scientistic atheism, metaphysical atheism,* and *humanistic atheism.* All types of modern atheism have one basic dogma in common, namely the human, even religious experience and conviction that depicts God as useless, indeed, as an obstacle to man's intellectual and social growth. To put it more radically, God is of no importance to modern man. We will touch briefly on the first three types of atheism and then concentrate on *humanistic atheism,* the type predominant in the United States. As we shall see, the roots of humanistic atheism are to be found in the three above-mentioned forms of atheism.

Historicist atheism holds that atheism is not merely a simple accidental choice; is is rather the result of a historical process. Modern atheism is aware of its antecedents; it sees itself as the outcome of a long historical process that reveals man's coming of age in scientific disbelief. This is not merely a "psychological" development; it is rather a rational justification.[1] Thus current atheism is a post-Christian phenomenon, a reaction against decadent Christianity.

Theology becomes politics

Christianity concentrated on the value and dignity of man. It did this, according to Marx, "by a detour...by a Mediator." Yet the detour of the Incarnation is merely, for Marx, a mythical, imaginative expression of the discovery of Man by a man.[2] This theme of the incarnation is emphatically expressed by F. Jeanson thus: "Did God become man one day in order to cease to be a man thirty-three years later?" No, for "Jesus particularizes the universal according to everyone's intention."³ Christianity also proclaimed the diffusion of the Spirit; so man must also demythologize Pentecost, making it now signify the animation of human society by itself, the revelation that man governs the universe by his own vital impulses. Naturally when one speaks of "Man," it is a question of social man, humanity as a whole. It follows that laicization of the Incarnation and of Pentecost must be accompanied also by laicization of the Church. For the Christian, certitude and faith are found in union with the Church and in solidarity with all other Christians. Similarly, in a world that is historically entering the epoch of "planetization," the whole of humanity struggles in the process of realizing itself as the god of Humanity. Here also solidarity with the mass of men plays a role analogous to the role that the Christian attributes to his union with the Church. In this sense it is now possible to say that atheism and the problem of God have become "political problems."⁴ This explains why Marx's critique of theology is transformed into a critique of politics, while anthopology becomes a primary discipline.

Bultmann used the process of demythologizing, demystification, the reduction of sacred symbols with such success that historicist atheism is reigning in a significant part of the Eastern world. Indeed such atheism is spreading so rapidly in the Western world as well that it is not beyond the realm of possibility that soon we may have to recognize in humanity as a whole a majority of officially declared atheists. Then will have arrived that age of apostasy which St. Paul prophesied must be the necessary prelude to the arrival of "the lawless one," "the man of sin,"⁵ or in the words of St. John the Evangelist, "the Antichrist."⁶

Nature is now the panacea

Thus the history of man, not merely the history of philosophical and theological thought, is most important for understanding contemporary atheism. And that history comprises three fundamental aspects: a) the advance in the knowledge of nature, b) the explosion in technology, c) the reassessment of the world of human values. The advance in the conquest of nature's laws has interposed nature between God and man; nature not God now solves man's problems. God has disappeared as unnecessary. In a similar fashion technology's amazing achievements have so divinized man's Ego that man's early attitude toward and dependence on God is now regarded to have been an ignorant, superstitious, magico-religious reaction to the wonderful, the unknown — a response normal enough for mankind in its infancy and puberty stage of social-scientific development.

Science is king

Metaphysical atheism, on the other hand, rejects a study of nature, the causes and the totality of things. It reacts against a rational philosophy that attempts to give the ultimate explanation which relates to the origin of things. Thus it will not accept the metaphysical arguments for the existence of God; it accuses them of being static truths, mere abstractions devoid of all effective or affective proof. This form of atheism, also known as atheistic existentialism, teaches that all reality is absurd, contingent, superfluous. There is nothing to be understood in beings-out-there, for they have no meaning. Each existential man gives things their meaning according to the way he wills to conduct his life. Hence the meaning given things has value merely for the person who confers this meaning. It follows that, in this type of atheism, being and absurdity, being and cipher, being and non-sense are the only interchangeable absolutes. Jeanson confesses that "there is no way in which a human consciousness (an intra-mundane being) can grasp the world as a totality."[7]

Marxist atheism is dressed in scientific garb, yet Marx was anything but a scientist. As a hybrid system of atheistic philosophy, Marxist atheism consists of a union of the dialectical method of Hegel with the evolutionary materialism of Feuerbach. Marx accepted Hegel's postulate that, at the heart of all reality works the principle of contradiction. But, unlike Hegel, Marx claimed that the sole reality working itself out into full self-consciousness is matter, not idea. According to this method of mutual antagonism, contradiction and the dialectic of the drawn dagger, there is only one reality — matter — the blind forces of which evolve into plant, animal, man, society. Through a perpetual conflict of forces and by a law of inexorable necessity, matter achieves its final synthesis in the classless, atheistic society.

This atheism conveys an air of naive oversimplification. But the prestige of the exact sciences engenders among non-professionals such a naivete which enters into the constitution of "scientism." Economics, work, societies, politics even ethics are subjected to a scientific study. All knowledge is seen as "human sciences"; all realities must be subjected to an operational research, a science of decision, "the scientization" of religion, morality, philosophy all in the matrix of dynamic atheism. Contemporary atheism seeks to appropriate these scientific procedures, and this constitutes one of its essential notes.

Man is god

Perhaps the most exhilarating form of atheism is atheistic humanism. The feat of Prometheus challenging and defying the old gods in snatching fiery power and bringing down to man on earth the arts and freedom is still a thrilling and popular scene. This titan represents "man come of age," man emancipated from childish beliefs, liberated from sexual taboos, able to create for himself a world of plenty, a society of peace.

Atheistic humanism is America's brand of atheism. It teaches that the human race has reached a leap of advancement, a progressive mutation, not in the organic or bodily sense, but psychologically, a mutation of such high caliber that it can no longer count on any outside forces to solve its problems. Man must only count on himself if he is to achieve the challenge of creating a cosmos of plenty and a utopia of temporal glory. He may no longer flee for refuge "under the umbrella" of divine authority. The state of the world is no longer compatible with "the idea of an omnipotent, omniscient and all-benevolent God." There are no dogmas, no "static," permanent truths, no objective principles or fixed concepts that can help explain the mystery of existence in general or the mystery of spirit in particular. "Objective truth is rather a function of developing mind and is always marked by historicity."[8] "All we can do," says Sir Julian Huxley, "is to truly accept facts."[9] After all, the old philosophy which held that truth is so objective that it can exist apart from anyone's possession of it, with "ideas always up there in heaven," was nothing more than a disguised theology. And for this reason in such a superstition there was no place for a historical dimension of truth, no space for development, no life for growth. Harvey Cox could write in his *Secular City*: "Religion is in a sense the neurosis of culture; secularization corresponds to maturation, for it signifies the emancipation of man first from religion and then from metaphysical control."[10] All that we have and all that we need is given to us in technopolis, even if technopolis is not an easy cup to drink.[11] Today we realize that "truth is an affair of history, of the human subject, of experience and hence is affected by all the relativity of history. We must cease worshiping certainties. For when certainty enters a question, authority also enters as the implacable enforcer of certainties."[12] And authority is the enemy of free intellectual research, of scientific advancement, of social development, or moral maturity.

We have a doctrine of thought here typically American, a humanistic, pragmatic philsophy, a positivistic, empirical, humane, progressist atheism. Let us examine some of its major tenets.

In 1933 there appeared in *The New Humanist* magazine the "Humanist Manifesto I." In this document a group of thirty-four prominent persons, calling themselves "liberal humanists" defined and enunciated the philosophical and religious principles that seemed fundamental for all mankind. The word "religious" as used by the humanists should not deceive the reader. It has no connection with a religious faith in God or membership in a Church; it is used merely for its attractive power and is reduced to a feeling of humanitarian concern for humanity. Fifteen theses are clearly affirmed. They are the historical result of the fact that science and economic change have disrupted old beliefs. Without numbering these theses, we epitomize them in a paragraph thus.

Utopia — next stop

Humanitarian humanists regard the universe as self-existent, not created. Man is a part of nature who emerged as the result of a continuous process. Traditional dualism of mind and body must be rejected. Man's religious culture has nothing transcendent as its origin but is a product of the gradual development of his interaction with his natural environment and social heritage. Thus his religious civilization and culture are imposed by the circumstances of his birth, growth and station in life. Science has so conquered nature that it has proven that there is no supernatural, cosmic guarantee of transcendent, permanent human values. Religion must establish its hopes and plans on the scientific spirit. The complete realization of human potentiality in time is the purpose of man's life. Replacing the old attitudes of worship and prayer, the atheistic humanist experiences his religious emotions in a heightened sense of personal life, in cooperative efforts to promote social well-being. Only humanists face up to crises because they recognize their naturalness, apply the principles of an enlightened education, follow the path of mental and social hygiene and eschew the wishful, sentimental hopes of religious dreaming. All associations exist for human fulfillment. All religious institutions, therefore, must be reconstituted rapidly so that their rituals, ecclesiastical methods, communal activities may function effectively in a secular world according to the needs of the modern world. A socialistic system of economics must be instituted to replace the cruel, profit-ridden, consumeristic free enterprise system. Humanism affirms life rather than denies it. It seeks satisfactory conditions of life and the greatest happiness for all men.[13]

Incurable optimism shattered

Forty years later in 1973 *The Humanist* magazine published "Humanist Manifesto II." Why was there need for another manifesto? First because the incurable optimism of the humanists about the goodness of natural man was shattered by the nighmare brutality of World War II in which some fifty-four million soldiers and civilians were slaughtered. Then too the humanist utopian dream that a sane and sanitized society would inevitably arise from the theses of Manifesto I was rudely dissolved by the savage politico-social systems of Nazism, Fascism, Communism and other totalitarian regimes. But did the humanists learn from the harsh realities of history that their philosophy of man, naturally good and atheistic, was a fantasy, a mythical monster, a politico-moral Leviathan and crooked serpent that

would always devour its devotees? George Santayana's wise saying was
realized in their case: "Those who will not learn from history are condemned
to repeat it."

Nothing was learned from the historical tragedies of the last fifty years.
Repeating doggedly the theses of Manifesto I, the humanists added some
more alluring principles to their atheistic philosophy. They state that
morality is *autonomous* and *situational* (their emphasis), needing no theological
nor rational sanction. No deity can save man, man must save himself.
Promises of immortal salvation or fear of eternal damnation are both illusory
and harmful. They distract man from his present concerns, from self--
actualization and from rectifying injustices. Modern science discredits such
historic concepts as the "ghost in the machine" and the "separable soul."
The human species emerged from natural evolutionary forces.

In the matter of abolishing war and attaining world peace, Manifesto
II states: "We deplore the division of humankind on nationalistic grounds."
History states it is time *"to transcend the limits of national sovereignty"* (emphasis
in the original). What is needed is a World Community, composed of
cultural pluralism and diversity that renounces violence and force as a
method of solving international disputes. War is obsolete. So is the use
of nuclear, biological and chemical weapons. A planetary imperative calls
for regulation of the ecosystem, for control of excessive population, "for
the use of technology as a *vital key*" (emphasis in the document) to human
progress and scientific advancement.

Manifesto II concludes, in part, thus:

> We urge recognition of the common humanity of all people. We
> further urge the use of reason and compassion to produce the
> kind of world we want — a world in which peace, prosperity,
> freedom, and happiness are widely shared. . .We are responsible
> for what we are or will be. . .At the present juncture in history,
> commitment to all humankind is the highest commitment of which
> we are capable; it transcends the narrow allegiances of church,
> state, party, class or race in moving toward a wider vision of
> human potentiality. What more daring goal for humankind than
> for each person to become, in ideal as well as in practice, a citizen
> of a world community. It is a classical vision; we can now give
> it new vitality. Humanism thus interpreted is a moral force that
> has time on its side. We believe that humankind has the potential
> intelligence, good will, and cooperative skill to implement this
> commitment in the decades ahead.[14]

Whereas only thirty-four publicly known persons signed "Humanist
Manifesto I," two hundred and sixty-two prominent persons signed

"Humanist Manifesto II." This demonstrates how widespread atheistic humanism has become in America and how many persons of prestige publicly, proudly, even evangelistically proclaim their allegiance to this form of cultural atheism. For this is the most positive and most dynamic form of contemporary atheistic humanism; it is also the most social and, consequently, the most realistic. For it is, in effect, the love of humankind, against God. It reveals without disguise the atheistic persuasion that God is useless.

Five characteristics stand out

In 1980 the humanists, alarmed at the growing threat to their ideology posed by the emergence of fundamentalist Christian groups as a force in the 1980 elections, timed an election-eve Secular Humanist Declaration to counteract the influence of these groups. Worried that the American public was finally seeing through their humanitarian hypocrisy in fastening their atheistic ideology on the whole nation, the humanists in this Declaration reacted irrationally, branding all their opponents as members of vigilante groups out to destroy civil rights. They called upon all fellow-humanists to join a crusade against these "right-wing" groups. Fortunately, the American voters were not fooled by humanist propaganda. They defeated five out of six lawmakers on the national level, and others on the local level, who were disciples of the humanist ideology.

The Humanist Manifestoes are as dogmatic and unequivocal as the Apostles Creed. They give no rational proofs for their dogmas; they present them simply as an expression of a naive, growing faith in humankind. Not a single thesis in their documents is presented with dialectical, rational expertise. They use a rhetorical device calculated to enlist the good-willed, unwary reader's acceptance of their statements. But against this alluring device they make use of ridicule to debunk the absurdity of the views of their opponents. Very cleverly they wrap their atheistic ideology in the verbal cap and gown of "scientific" and "modern." They use these incantations much as a witch doctor uses a magic talisman, to confer a fraudulent prestige on their mythology and they hope that simple people will fail to discern this hypocritical ploy.

Despite their declarations of compassionate love for humankind, atheistic humanists approve abortion, suicide, and all varieties of "sexual exploration" and immoral "life styles." Not only do their manifestoes destroy basic human rights, they also have political and social implications which severely degrade mankind. The Manifestoes, while sounding a high moral tone, supply no practical advice, nor do they concern themselves at all with the personal moral growth of the individual. They also aim to legalize, and thus institutionalize, immoral crimes that lead even to infanticide.

Atheistic humanism has become an idolatrous religion in North America. There are five characteristics of this idolatrous ideology. Its *anthropocentrism* raises humankind to the highest throne of all being. In the face, functions, fortunes and future of mankind is to be found the only god worthy of man. God is loved and served only in humanity. The primacy of humanity is identified with the primacy of God. Then there is the doctrine of man's *immanence in this world*. The salvation of mankind is to be found in a kingdom here, not hereafter. Salvation means liberation from social sin — ignorance, hunger, underdevelopment, political oppression, economic exploitation, sexual repression, over-population. Personal sin is no longer relevant in today's historical context. Humanists, enlisting under the banner of democratic Socialism, must achieve the utopian kingdom by destroying the consumeristic, profit-obsessed society. Thirdly, *the Good News* of atheistic humanism is cultural not spiritual, happiness not holiness. It is to be found in the greatest pleasure for the greatest number. Fourthly, *the church* of atheistic humanism has its idols too, those of the French Revolution — Reason, Equality, Fraternity, Liberty. In its official litany of saints are also to be found Nature, Humankind, World Community, Democracy and a host of other bloodless abstractions. Fifthly, *the New Passion* of atheistic humanism is humankind not human persons. For it sees no contradiction between the religion of humanity and the slaughter of defenseless innocents in the womb. Each year atheistic humanists approve an increase, in terrifying proportions, of the number of human persons killed legally in the womb. To be sure, they do not accept these murders in a spirit of wanton cruelty but with the cold benevolence of ideologues determined to control over-population and improve the quality of life, thus forcing mankind and men to conform to their enlightened master plan for them whether they like it or not.

Replying to the above mentioned errors briefly, we make the following observations. Atheistic humanism as a religion of man which hates God produces a decapitated love for man who is lovable only because God loves him, made him in his own image and likeness, sent his Son to redeem him and his Holy Spirit to sanctify and glorify him. Without love of God, love of man has no meaning and no chance of maintaining itself in permanent fidelity. Atheistic *anthropocentrism* eradicates the spring and fountain of love of man, as well as the motive of service to man, when it eradicates God from the human conscience.

They are agents of discord

The straitjacket of *immanence* divinizes the World and History, prevents salvation from entering history from above, denies the transcendent, eschatological kingdom and reduces the religion of humanity to being a mere political ideology. The true destiny of man is not achieved in this world which is passing away like a scenario, but in eternal life in the next world where justice and love will triumph because then God will be all in all. Social sin is destroyed only when the heart of individual man is changed from personal sin to personal sanctification.

As regards *the Good News of atheistic humanism,* it is a grave and arrogant attempt to substitute the gospel of progress for the Gospel of Revelation. Man is not made for happiness here but for holiness here and eternal holiness and happiness hereafter. History has shown that the ideal of temporal happiness promised by atheistic humanism is a cruel hoax. Marxist Russian, Cuban, Chinese atheistic humanisms have produced Gulags of torture and degradation. On the human level, humanism cannot subsist without the assistance and stimulus of God and religion. The fallen animal in us is too strong if there is no divine authority of fear and love. And in the soul, the higher part of man, the self ends up at best in enlightened selfishness, at worse in brutal lust for power, position, the credit of a great name on earth, if the intimations of another world are ignored.[15] American humanism is presently producing a chaotic, terror-ridden nation; the American dream is fast becoming a national nightmare.

The Church of atheistic humanism is in reality The Secular City of Harvey Cox, a man-made society subject to the whims of fickle mankind. In America it is fast becoming the Sacrilegious City, bereft of all sense of the sacred as it is buffeted by the gales of revolution. Progress as a god is fading fast with economic recessions. Its sentimentalized forms of materialism and pantheism are unavoidable by-products of a faith that has sickened, grown feeble and died. It can never guarantee humankind temporal happiness or peace. There is too little divine folly in atheistic humanism; its altogether this-world kind of wisdom accepts Christ only on its own terms and makes God a confederate supporting a disinfected, smoothly run, rich-in-food, circus-enjoyable material paradise.[16]

As for *the New Passion of atheistic humanism for humankind,* this is the sterile love of a non-entity, of an abstraction. For mankind is a non-historical fiction, tailored to push propaganda for progressist ideology. Only individual persons exist and, since atheistic humanism destroys basic individual human rights and values, it is truly a will-o'-the-wisp ideology that would create a political and social community of nations which would severely degrade men.

What lifts atheistic humanism out of the class of being an obscure cult is the list of big names who have signed its Manifestoes and Declaration. The list includes some of the most influential persons in education and philosophy in the last half century. These men have forced the schools to eliminate prayer, academic standards, moral training, the virtue of patriotism. They object to the teaching of philosophy as truth, of theology as the revealed word of God. They have tremendously influenced the courts to legalize abortion, obscenity, pornography and other evils. In so secularizing America, they have replaced its Christian tradition and culture with a post-Christian paganism, establishing atheistic humanism as the *de facto* religion of the United States.

In a profound assessment of atheistic humanism, Fr. Martin C. D'Arcy, author and famous English Jesuit, wrote:

> Atheistic humanism has established one ugly fact beyond dispute. It is that whereas in ancient and more simple days concupiscence and lust for power were the conspicuous vices, today our modern atheistic humanist-optimists have brought about the corruption of the mind — they are philosophers fiddling like Nero while Rome is burning; they are the new moralists making a virtue of revolution, disobedience, hatred of authority; they are the new theologians denying the truths of revelation, attacking the faithful, putting God in a casket and cremating his ashes.[17]

But in ravaging the holy and hierarchic Mystical Body created by God in Christ, they are agents of discord, with the result that they work, in the words of Shakespeare, "to make a sop of all this solid globe."[18]

Notes

[1] Jean-Marie Le Blond, "The Contemporary Status of Atheism" in *International Philosophical Quarterly,* February 1965, pp. 37–55.
[2] *Ibid.*
[3] Francis Jeanson, *La foi d'un incroyant* (Paris: Ed. du Seuil, 1963) pp. 114, 123.
[4] Jean Lacroix, "Le sens de l'atheisme actuel," *Esprit,* 22 (1954) pp. 167–191.
[5] Paul, 2 Thess. 2:3.
[6] 1 John 4:3.
[7] Jean Lacroix, *op. cit.*
[8] Charles Davis, *Clergy Review,* August 1966.
[9] Sir Julian Huxley, *The Humanist Frame* (London: Allen & Unwin, 1961).
[10] Harvey Cox, *The Secular City* (New York: Macmillan, 1965).
[11] Martin C. D'Arcy, *Humanism and Christianity* (Constable, London 1969).
[12] *Ibid.,* pp. 90, 91.
[13] Paul Kurtz, *Humanist Manifestoes I and II,* (Prometheus Books, Buffalo, N.Y., 1973).
[14] *Ibid.*
[15] Martin C. D'Arcy, *op. cit.,* p. 190.
[16] *Ibid.,* p. 104.
[17] *Ibid.,* p. 199, 200.
[18] William Shakespeare, *Troilus and Cressida.*

Reprinted from *Homiletic & Pastoral Review,* March 1982.

St. Thomas, Justice and Marxism

For the last fifteen or twenty years there has developed in Christendom a new religious mentality. Something called "Marxism," in reality Communism, has produced a strong fascination, even irresistible attraction in the souls of many Christians. This magic spell tends to lead Christians to see the Kingdom of God being attained in the realization of social progress and to view Christ as the precursor of today's socialist struggles. Marxism is now presented as the only effective technique for bringing about the over-throw of oppressive systems and for replacing them with a universal socialist philosophy of life founded on the principle of justice for all. Christians bewitched by this interpretation of the Gospel assume that the message of Christ can be identified with the call to revolution. They thus consider it an apostolic activity to cooperate with explicitly Marxist groups dedicated to violent, revolutionary actions for the liberation of man and society from all forms of exploitation.

Some questions must be asked and answered. "Did Christ come to call mankind to political and social revolution? Is the Gospel message a blueprint for intellectual, sociological and economic liberation? Was Christ in his teachings concerned primarily about "justice in this world?"

All four Evangelists answer these questions with eloquent clarity. Jesus is announced by John the Baptist whose preaching is of a high moral order. John urges the high and the low to return to God in the silence of prayer, in the practice of justice, in the baptism of repentance for the remission of sins. When he baptizes Christ the Spirit descends upon Jesus in the form of a dove and the voice of the Father proclaims Jesus as his beloved Son. Jesus begins his public life, not by fasting in the squares of Jersualem in order to gain publicity against the social injustices of the day. His is not an ideological hunger strike. But Jesus prepares for his public mission by, as it were, undergoing the spiritual exercises, by making a closed retreat in the desert before his Father away from the prying eyes of the masses. These were forty days and nights of silence, prayer and fasting. It is quite obvious that Jesus is not preparing to announce either a social or political plan of reform through the instrument of revolution.[1]

The gift is grace

Rather Christ is driven by the Spirit into the desert "in order to be tempted by the devil." Thus his battle is not immediately with the tyrants of this world. He is at war with the kingdom of Satan. It is a spiritual war against the powers and principalities of hell whose domination over mankind he prepares to destroy forever. Prayer and fasting in a sustained spiritual struggle will alone cast out these demons and free men to become children of God.

Thus Jesus by his life and teachings calls mankind to a spiritual liberation, to a life of freedom with God in grace; it is a call not to public manifestations, violence, propaganda, but to interiority, recollection, repentance. The Gospel calls man not to mere "justice in this world," whether economic or political, but to that justice and justification which signifies a life of holiness with Christ in God. In the teachings of Christ man is called to a higher than natural, to a divine, supernatural justice through a life of faith and fidelity with Christ himself as the God-Man and Saviour of mankind. It follows that the evangelical freedom won for man by Christ consists primarily, not in the liberation of man from other men, but in the liberation of man from Satan, his own sins and eventually from death.

In short, the justice Christ came to establish for men is the interior justification of men which makes them children of God in grace. The kingdom Christ came to establish is a spiritual kingdom of interior holiness, of the liberty of the sons of God, of the peace of the communion of saints. It goes without saying that growth in this supernatural justice will necessarily be accompanied by and coincide with growth in temporal justice and in the achievement of great benefits for man in his exterior social, economic and political life. Nevertheless, the divine type of justice and justification preached and brought by Christ does not coincide with temporal justice; it is infinitely superior to temporal justice and perfects human nature, with all its natural virtues, in the order of grace. It is temporal justice which is often called today "liberation" or "development" but strictly speaking this justice is not the essential message of the Gospel and has nothing to do directly with God's economy of salvation as revealed in the life and teachings of Jesus. Christ himself stressed this truth when he urged his listeners to act as follows concerning their natural needs: "Therefore I say to you, do not be anxious for your life...for your Father knows that you need all these things. But seek first the Kingdom of God and his justice, and all these things shall be given you besides."[2] Christ came to give man the Father's justice, a pure gift of grace beyond our natural powers. Temporal justice is well within man's achievement. Great men like Socrates and Plato and others actually attained a high degree of natural justice.

The spiritual is swept away

Morality is the prolongation of a metaphysical philosophy of man into the exterior actions that man performs with knowledge and freedom. For a man's convictions strongly influence his conduct. Hence a false metaphysics about man will inevitably lead to a false moral code for man in his private and social actions. Now the Marxist philosophy of man is a hybrid system of ideology. Marx combined the dialectical method of Hegel with the evolutionary materialism of Feuerbach in what he called the scientific explanation of reality. Marx accepted Hegel's postulate that at the heart of reality works the principle of contradiction. But, unlike Hegel, he claimed that the sole reality working itself into full self-consciousness is matter, not idea. According to this scientific method there is only one reality — matter — evolving in a dialectic of metaphysical hostility, the blind forces of which develop into plant, animal and man. Through a perpetual conflict of these forces and by a law of inexorable necessity man himself evolves from economic, political exploitative communities into the masses, the dictatorship of the proletariat, the Marxist state and achieves his final synthesis in the classless society.

In maintaining that matter is blind and exists alone with evolutionary forces, that society is merely a higher, more complicated form of matter, formed ineluctably by the necessary laws of nature, Marxism degrades the intrinsic sociality of man. It reduces man to being a mere external accretion added to matter by the determinism of the historical process. Thus atheistic, anticreationistic, Marxism denies God as a transcendent, eternal body and soul. It rejects the survival of the soul after death and the hope of eternal life. Thus the whole world of spirits is swept away by its radical materialism. On the liberating effect of this Marxist humanism Engels has written:

> ...The old metaphysics...accepted things as finished objects ...this dialectical philosophy dissolves all conceptions of final, absolute truth and of absolute states of humanity corresponding to it. For it (dialectical philosophy) nothing is final, absolute, sacred. It reveals the transitory character of everything and in everything: nothing can endure before it except the uninterrupted process of becoming and of passing away, of endless ascendency from the lower to the higher. And dialectical philosophy is nothing more than the mere reflection of this process in the thinking brain.[3]

Thus Marxist ethics is a moral relativism; nothing is final, absolute, sacred in it. On the contrary, St. Thomas writes that "justice is the virtuous habit whereby man renders to his fellowmen their due by a constant, perpetual will. Justice is that supreme, fundamental virtue which directs all other virtues to the good of the other and to the common good." Quoting Cicero, St. Thomas writes: "The object of justice is to keep men together in society and mutual intercourse." Thus justice is a virtue of the will which, following the light of reason and the natural law, freely gives each man his due, seeking the personal good of the individual and the common good of the community.[4]

But Marxism rejects transcendent truths and hence transcendent values and an immutable moral code. Since man himself is in constant flux, ethical values must also be in constant flux. For there exist only values immersed in evolving historical reality. Thus good and evil are in constant flux. But Marx, and the Party leaders, take it upon themselves to decide from moment to moment what is good and evil. Here is what Lenin writes on the flux of morality:

> In what sense do we repudiate ethics or morality? In the sense that they were preached by the bourgeoisie, who declared that ethics were God's commandments. We, of course, say that we do not believe in God. . . We repudiate all morality that is taken outside of human, class concepts. . . We say that our morality is entirely subordinated to the interests of the class struggle of the proletariat.[5]

Now let us listen to Marx's imperious demand that his ethics be followed because of his passion and scientific justification for it. David Caute comments on this Marxist imperiousness:

> When writing of actual revolutions, Marx discarded all pretensions to scientific impartiality. There was no inconsistency in this: according to Marx, subjective revolutionary passion is at every stage an agent of the historical process. But one is entitled to ask whether in the mind of a single man — Marx's — subjective passion and scientific analysis can at any point be separated entirely.[6]

Pope Pius XI wrote of Marxist justice the following critique: "A pseudo-ideal of justice, of equality and fraternity in labor impregnates all its (Communism's) doctrine and activity with a deceptive mysticism, which communicates a zealous and contagious enthusiasm to the multitudes entrapped by delusive promises.'"[7] We thus see that Marxism strips man of his divine dignity in his origin and his destiny; it cancels his liberty, robs him of his uniqueness and removes all restraints that check the eruptions of blind impulse. Marxism recognizes no rights of the individual before the collectivity; it rejects all hierarchy in being and in divinely constituted authority whether in the family, state or church. Moreover, the individual is denied any property rights over material goods or the means of production; private property is eradicated; human life is stripped of any sacred or spiritual character and marriage with family life is reduced to a purely artificial, civil institution totally subordinated to the plans of the collectivity. The morality of the workers has no transcendent standard, but whatever fosters the class struggle is good, whatever hinders it is evil. Now any counterfeit virtue is in reality a vice that gains credence because it is posing as a virtue. What is the vice that hides behind the facade of Marxist justice? *That vice is envy.*

St. Thomas defines envy as "sorrow at another's good fortune." Another's material and spiritual prosperity is apprehended by the envious person as an evil, a threat, an occasion of calamity. Hence, initially envy strikes out against another's good fortune and good name. But as it grows in intensity of hatred, the envious seek to destroy the very ontological, hierarchical goodness of being. Envy of another because of his material affluence is evil enough, but envy of another because of his spiritual blessings is the most perverse form of hatred. St. Thomas calls such envy a capital sin.[8]

Marxism is a disease

Now the philosophy and practice of Marxism is characterized by symptoms that reveal its specific disease to be the capital sin of envy. There is the hatred for being, for the hierarchical order of being, for transcendent values, for the other-worldly, eternal destiny of being. This envy explains Marxism's hatred of the Judaeo-Christian God because he is a God of goodness. It aims at replacing God with the proletarian masses, under the direction of Party supergods, even as Lucifer sought to seize God's throne with the aid of his legions of self-divinized demons. Marxism's envy is revealed in its enraged hatred of man as the special object of God's love. This ineffable love drives Lucifer and his demons into such envious madness that their whole activity is concentrated on seducing man to cooperate in a worldwide human uprising against God. Having imitated the Luciferian legions in their revolt against God, Marxists also imitate hell's angels in their efforts to destroy man as God's lover. They scheme to make mankind into a society of militant atheists, demoting them from their high post in the hierarchy of being into an egalitarian "herd collectivity" and "termite colony." For Marxist man the meaning of world history is not the salvation of mankind through the deeds of the God-Man, but rather it is the re-creation and salvation of man through his own work.

Indeed, man as his own creator, will finally be liberated when he conquers or escapes utterly from his own creature-hood and dependence on *time*. Herbert Marcuse, a contemporary Marxist, writes that "the fatal enemy of man's lasting gratification is *time*, the inner finiteness."[9] Claude Lanzman, another current Marxist, affirms the same thought, not in terms of internal finitude, but in terms of man's final end. "In transcending the limits the world imposes upon us, man conquers both the world and himself ...Man's will has become the very reason for his existence. There is no end for man higher than man himself. Man is his own beginning and end, his own Alpha and Omega."[10] Thus Marxist man escapes into eternity, into timeless freedom from all dependence, pressure, subordination. This is man's final cult, his only religion — the idolatry of man's adoration of himself.

And yet despite this divinization of man, Marxist envy simply cannot be placated. It has even raised envy to the level of a virtue, a virtue whose mission is to create ideal man and society. But in order to achieve this ideal Marxism has developed a huge bureaucracy wielding frightening centralized power and zealously working to wipe out all differentiations, whether of being or wealth. Marxism has welded together a far-flung political hegemony, a terrifying, colossal, technically advanced military apparatus, an omnipresent internal army of secret police, a world-wide system of spying, a vast network of concentration camps — all instruments of institutionalized envy in a messianic campaign to conquer the earth for the establishment of a global, atheistic classless society. Today there is not an iota of moral idealism or humaneness in the Marxist system. Indeed, it is an act of the greatest naive self-deception to believe that Marxism ever seriously sought to establish a just society. The testimony of Eugene Lyons, once a Communist enthusiast, dissolves the roseate myths of a humane Marxism. He writes:

> By 1934 when I departed from Russia, nothing was left of the high mood of dedication, traces of which I still found among Communists six years earlier. The very vocabulary of idealism had been outlawed. 'Equality' was lampooned as bourgeois romanticism. Excessive concern for the needs and sensibilities of ordinary people was punished as 'rotten liberalism.' Terror was no longer explained away as a sad necessity. It was used starkly and glorified as 'human engineering.' Means had blotted out ends and have held this priority ever since. The Marxist theory of permanent class struggle rules out compromise, reform, truce, common humanity, mutual respect, family loyalties.[11]

St. Thomas quotes St. Gregory the Great on other vices that flow from envy: "From envy arises hatred, talebearing, detraction, joy at the neighbor's misfortunes, grief at his prosperity." Thomas calls these ugly vices "envy's daughters."[12] They are rampant in Marxist countries. The machinery for spying and repression is so vast that it strikes terror into the hearts of each of the billion slaves. No regime in all history ever spawned such appalling systems for surveillance, denunication, punishment, intimidation. Marxist countries have legalized an enormous number of "crimes against the state" for which the death penalty is extensively applied. Citizens' mail is read by state authorities; phones are tapped, state spies, like vermin, infiltrate offices, factories, mines, farms, universities, libraries, hotels, railroad stations and churches. Even children are trained to report on their parents. Millions of youth are enrolled in Party vigilante brigades to inform on their neighbors' ideas and practices. One segment of society is constantly informing on another, like rats preying on rats.[13] Almost every family in the vast empire of Marxism has lost at least one member to this insatiable beast. Moreover, the ugly practice of committing religious and political dissidents to mental institutions has increased, thus perverting professions and institutions established to cure the sick into prisons and procedures for breaking the minds and spirits of the brave and the healthy. Then there is the cruelty in the concentration camps. Elinor Lipper, a German prisoner, conveys this horror to us in her book *Eleven Years in Soviet Prison Camps:*

The first murder in history was perpetrated from the motive of a grotesquely secular greed and spiteful envy. Cain killed his brother Abel, not for land or cattle, but because Abel gained a position of preferential love in the eternal memory of God. Just such a secular spiritual envy motivates Marxism. It is a thousand times more heinous and terrible than material voracity. The Spanish poet and philosopher, Miguel de Unamuno, writes on this subject: "If the so-called problem of life, the basic problem of food, were ever solved, the earth would be turned into a hell, as the struggle for (spiritual) survival would become even more intense."[15]

Marxism's greatest crime is that, after presenting itself as a messianic liberator it then changes into a flaming dragon. It dethrones man's most civilizing activities — the pursuit of truth and practice of love. In their place Marxism substitutes man's most primitive, monstrous deeds — the practices of lying and hating, thus also fostering the eruption of social volcanoes of violence that such sins beget. Philip Spratt, former British-Indian communist leader openly stated: "The communist movement runs on hate — the leading theorists are quite frank about it — and hate is a potent fuel."[16] Marx founded his ethics on the pseudo-science of historical materialism. Lenin added an emotional fanaticism to this morality by following the radical immoralism of Nechayev. Lenin associated with Sergei Nechayev before he ever met Marx. In 1868 Nechayev wrote his celebrated CATECHISM OF A REVOLUTIONIST, in which he renounced all norms of civilized behaviour and prescribed every imaginable depravity in the pursuit of the *ideal*. It is as fanatic, hate-packed a document as the human brain has ever produced. The revolutionist, he wrote, "knows only one science, the science of destruction, which does not stop at lying, robbery, betrayal and torture of friends, or murder of his own family.''[17] His central dictum that ''everything that contributes to the triumph of the revolution is morally good,'' has been accepted by Marx, Lenin and their disciples to this day, indeed this doctrine figures in every Marxist pronouncement on morality. Max Eastman writes that ''the confluence of these two streams of thought (Nechayev and Marx) is one of the greatest disasters that ever befell mankind.''[18]

The work of justice is peace

Nor has Marxist so-called justice attained for man an economic paradise. Rather, Marxism has a dreadful history of economic incompetence in the Soviet Union, China, the Iron Curtain countries, Yugoslavia, Albania, Cuba, Cambodia, North Korea, Vietnam. Far from achieving economic justice and human liberation, Marxism establishes universal economic destitution and slavery for the masses. For wherever it reigns, the Marxist regime, in which a new class of undemocratic elite dominates, is ruthlessly engaged in the violation of human rights in order to bolster its continuance in power and its ideological, inefficient, inhuman, indeed, impossible pursuit of an unnatural industrial development, founded on an enraged, envious hatred.

St. Thomas, in his *Summa,* coherently demonstrates, where he treats of justice, a truth proclaimed throughout Holy Scripture: *Opus justitiae pax.* ''The work of justice is peace,'' peace between God and man, peace among men. On the other hand, the system of thought and conduct elaborated by Karl Marx and his disciples — the system of Marxism which has dominated Russia now for 67 years and presently dominates about a third of the world's population — demonstrates with mountains of blood-curdling evidence, the terrifying truth proclaimed throughout history: *Opus invidiae bellum.* ''The work of envy is war,'' war between God and man, war among men.

Now Christ warned mankind to judge a tree by its fruit, not by its foliage. Marxism's ''pseudo ideal of justice, of equality and fraternity in labor'' presents a pleasant foliage to the unwary who expect good fruit from its tree. But the tree of Marxism is fertilized with a false metaphysics and thrives on the sap of satanic envy. It can only produce the bitter fruits of hatred, violence and war, never the good fruit of justice and peace.

Notes

[1] Marcel Clement, *Christ and Revolution,* Arlington House Publishers, New Rochelle, N.Y., 1974.
[2] Matt: 6:25, 32–33.
[3] Friedrich Engels, "Ludwig Feuerbach and the End of Classical German Philosophy," (1886) in *Marx and Engels: Selected Works,* Moscow, Foreign Languages Publishing House, Vol. II, 1955.
[4] St. Thomas Aquinas, *Summa Theologica,* Part II, Q. 58, a. 2.
[5] V.I. Lenin, "The Tasks of the Youth League," A Speech delivered at the Third All-Russian Congress of the Russian Youth Communist League, Oct. 2, 1920, in *Selected Works,* Vol. IX, New York International Publishers, 1943.
[6] Essential *Writings of Karl Marx,* Introduction and notes by David Caute, A London Panther book, 1967.
[7] Pope Pius XI, Encyclical *Atheistic Communism,* March 19, 1937.
[8] St. Thomas Aquinas, *Summa Theologica,* Part II (Second Part), Q. 36, a. 4.
[9] Herbert Marcuse, *Eros and Civilization,* Beacon Press, Boston, 1955.
[10] Claude Lanzman, *Les Temps Modernes,* No. 112–113, May, 1955.
[11] Eugene Lyons, *Workers' Paradise Lost,* Paper Back Library, N.Y., 1967.
[12] St. Thomas Aquinas, *Summa Theologica,* Part II (Second Part), Q. 36, a. 4.
[13] Eugene Lyons, op. cit.
[14] Elinor Lipper, *Eleven Years in Soviet Prison Camps,* Regenery, Chicago, 1951.
[15] Miguel de Unamuno, *The Tragic Sense of Life in Men and Nations,* Princeton University Press, N.J., 1972.
[16] Eugene Lyons, op. cit.
[17] Eugene Lyons, op. cit.
[18] Eugene Lyons, op. cit.

Reprinted from *Homiletic & Pastoral Review,* July 1980.

St. Thomas, Human Liberty and Academic Freedom

Christians are living in an age when the fight for truth is in the twilight, when false teachers without have found allies opposed to the truths of reason and revelation among the members of the Christian household. Man is witnessing today a world-wide secularization of philosophic, transcendent, Catholic doctrines, values and institutions. A generation that is contesting the God of reason and revelation is simultaneously presenting man with a new, technocratic, apocalyptic human adventure in a rivalry calculated to rob God and Christ forever of the allegiance of men's minds and hearts.

From the center of Christendom the popes of modern times have tirelessly provided the light and courage needed to call back the nations to their divine destiny of walking in truth and righteousness. From Leo XIII in his encyclical *Aeterni Patris,* through Pius XI in *Divini Illius Magistri,* through Vatican II's *Declaration on Christian Education* and including John Paul II's *Sapientia Christiana,* the great concern of the Magisterium has been to concentrate on the mission of leading the embattled Church and a vagrant academic world back from a fascination with doctrinal-moral novelties to a renewed love for the truth and an inflamed zeal to share that truth with all men.

Quite naturally the Magisterium and the faithful have looked to Catholic intellectuals for supporting leadership and guidance in this crisis. Indeed, they have entrusted into their care the all-important, scientific and spiritual formation of their children in the hope of restoring, through the future leadership of these youths, all men and all things in Christ. For, in our revolutionary age when, thanks to the marvelous means of communication, the control of the many by the few is a realistic, effective technique, it becomes quite easy to conquer a people through the conquest of their intellectuals, through an undermining and subverting, that is, of their religious, political and educational institutions.

Events are happening in Catholic universities which are making the Catholic community, and the larger Judaeo-Christian community as well, anxious about the intellectual, social, moral and political activities of these institutions. It seems profitable, then, to recall here the essence and purpose of a university in general and of a Catholic university in particular. This inquiry will help us understand why universities have degenerated from their noble natures and abandoned their loftiest ideals.[1]

The nature and purpose of a university

According to Cardinal Newman, "the university is a place of *teaching* universal knowledge...Such is a university in *essence,* and independently of its relation to the Catholic Church."[2] Now it has always been a rational civil and Catholic understanding that the university administrator, professor or student, like every other citizen, is bound to patriotic duty and, in harmony with that, to a dedication to academic truth with a loyalty to the arts and sciences that transcends merely political duties. After all, the university is a community of scholars and students associated by the common objectives of the intellectual-moral pursuit of truth and integrity. This academic community is united by common agreement on method-ology, demonstrations and experiments suitable to each discipline of learning. Moreover, this society of scholar-students has always been con-vinced that, since it was created and sustained by the vision and needs of the larger religious and civic communities, its vocation is to be at the service of these larger communities which continue to inspire and sustain the academy as a necessary instrument for the attainment of the common good.[3]

The nature and goals of the Catholic university

The Catholic university functions on the highest level of Catholic Education; it is but one means to achieve the goals of all Catholic education. For all Catholic schools on every level exist and function in order to direct the formation of human persons to their final, eternal goal, to the temporal good of society in which they live, and to the maturity in personhood that is achieved by growing up in Christ. Thus, the Catholic university owes its origin to and receives its mission from the Catholic Church and the Catholic community. It may never truthfully claim to be independent of either. For it is a matter of the bond of faith and fidelity that a Catholic university include within its definition and its responsibilities the obligation to form its students in the authentic Christian message as that is promulgated by the Magisterium in union with the Vicar of Christ. For only when teaching in harmony with the Magisterium does the Catholic university provide its faculty and students with that unique Catholic education which is alone capable of inspiring their lives with the spirit of Christ.[4]

The Catholic university, then, is a community of minds associated to teach and research the natural sciences, social sciences, history, literature, philosophy, theology and the liberal arts. But what distinguishes the Catholic university is that it provides explicitly for a Faculty of Theology that teaches its own religious creed as a science, that is, as a body of organized, researched dogmas and precepts, known as its religious philosophy of life. "The Catholic college or university seeks to give the authentic Christian message an institutional presence in the academic world. Several things follow from this. Christian commitment will characterize this academic community. While fully maintaining the autonomy of its being a college or university, the institution will manifest fidelity to the teaching of Jesus Christ as transmitted by his Church. The advancement of Christian thought will be the object of institutional commitment. The human sciences will be examined in the light of the Christian faith. The best of the Christian intellectual and spiritual tradition will be blended with the special dynamism of contemporary higher education in a way that enriches both."[5]

Moreover, the Catholic university would also provide a chapel on the grounds, a place of worship for the administration of the sacraments and the religious service of spiritual counselors. In the Catholic university there is no compromise between natural goals or academic excellence and the higher goals of the Catholic Church, namely the transformation of all natural truth in the new light of its relationship to the truth of revelation. Nor is there any compromise between the natural goals of moral excellence and the higher goal of the Church, holiness, that is, the elevation of all natural moral goodness to the transcendent level of sanctity through man's acceptance of the grace of salvation in Christ. For here is an excellent milieu to demonstrate that grace does not destroy but builds on and elevates nature.

The Catholic university as prodigal son

Unfortunately, today the Catholic university has become restless in its natural home. Everywhere it is loosening its filial bonds with the Teaching Church and, often enough, deliberately cancelling out its Catholic connection and tradition. Already, like the Prodigal Son, some Catholic universities have gathered up immense wealth from their Father's house — religious communities, Catholic students, the properties and monies that have generously flowed in astronomical figures from the hearts of Catholic parents who gave their children to Catholic universities believing in the ideal of a Catholic education that prepares and leads souls to the beatific vision — and these former Catholic universities have journeyed into the far country of the secular magisterium. There they are squandering their Catholic patrimony in false teaching and loose living. When asked why they cut their religious roots and erased their Catholic character, they display an incoherent inability to define themselves, their policies, their goals or even their continued existence. What happened to such fallen-away institutions?

The loss of the Catholic perspective

Conduct flows from convictions and when conduct changes into consistent depravity it is because convictions have been corrupted. Cardinal Newman always contended that the university was an incomplete and stunted world if it tried to function in isolation from the assistance of the Catholic Church. As for the Catholic university, Newman stressed that "it is ancillary to the Catholic Church, first because truth of any kind can but minister to truth; and next, still more, because nature will ever pay homage to grace; and thirdly, because the Church has a sovereign authority, and when she speaks *ex cathedra,* must be obeyed."[6] Despite this clear teaching, some Catholic universities refuse to submit to the Magisterium.

They have removed themselves from the total context of all Catholic education and its proper goals. They identify themselves as entities with their own natures and purposes totally independent of the Catholic Church. The Church is regarded by them as an outsider, a threat to their autonomous existence and unlimited academic freedom. Denying their origins from the Church and the Catholic community, they necessarily also deny any institutional commitments to both.

In the 1967 Land O'Lakes statement on "The Nature of the Contemporary University," endorsed by many prominent officials of leading Catholic universities, a declaration of independence from the Magisterium was promulgated by many Catholic universities; it reads thus:

> The Catholic university today must be a university in the full modern sense of the word, with a strong commitment to and concern for academic excellence. To perform its teaching and research functions effectively, the Catholic university must have a true autonomous and academic freedom in the face of authority of whatever kind, lay or clerical, external to the academic community itself. To say this is simply to assert that institutional autonomy and academic freedom are essential conditions of life and growth and, indeed, of survival for Catholic universities as for all universities.[7]

Later in 1971 the revolution of some Catholic universities became even more focused and articulate in a statement put out by the North American Region of the International Federation of Catholic Universities (IFCU): "The Catholic university is not simply a pastoral arm of the Church. It is an independent organization serving Christian purposes but not subject to ecclesiastical-juridical control, censorship or supervision."[8] Just such a free-wheeling status of revolution did the delegates of Catholic universities from all over the world, led by a large militant North American faction, fight for at the Second International Congress of Catholic Universities held in the Vatican under the auspices of the Congregation of Catholic Education from November 20 to 22, 1972. After much heated and frank discussion, the delegates rejected the following amendment to the document being prepared on the role of the Catholic university in the modern world, an amendment which was proposed so as to harmonize the liberty of the Catholic university with the universal mission of the Catholic Church to spread the Gospel and bring all men to salvation in Jesus.

> The truth which the Catholic university has to research and transmit has a double source: science and revelation. Therefore, the Catholic university, in its statutes and regulations has to provide adequate means to guarantee in an autonomous and efficacious

manner, fidelity in research and in teaching not only to science but also to Catholic doctrine, in conformity with its essential note of 'fidelity to the Christian message as it comes to us from the Church.'[9]

In effect, then, the attending universities voted to reject any institutional, statutory, academic allegiance to the teachings of Jesus Christ as transmitted by his Church through the Magisterium. Unfortunately, in rejecting this amendment, such Catholic universities rejected what Cardinal Newman called their "necessary ancillary and ministrative role in the Church."

The reasons for the revolution

Why have certain universities broken their historical institutional relationship with the Magisterium of the Church? Some say that money is the root of their rejection of their Catholic commitment. Their strategy is to don secular clothes and to slip into the worldly surroundings of the governmental and foundational empires of wealth and thereby to gain eligibility for the vast educational monies made available by these worldly powers to self-proclaimed aconfessional schools. But to the person of deeper spiritual vision money is seen as merely the superficial explanation for the college-university drop-out from the Catholic Church. The unhealthy fever for money is merely a symptom of a more profound spiritual malady. The mysterious explanation is that the Catholic university, in the persons of its leadership, prior to its surrender to secularism, had already so devaluated the faith that Catholicism had finally become negotiable for material gains.

Various means have been used to project and rationalize the Catholic university's challenge to Church authority. There is the attack by the intellectuals on the Roman Curia which today has been unmasked as having been all along a veiled attack on the papacy itself. There is the deceptive explanation of collegiality which down-grades the head of the Church in his hierarchical collegiality and exaggerates a sort of horizontal, consultative collegiality of the faithful. There is the politicizing of the principle of subsidiarity which creates a revolutionary uproar for imaginary supernatural rights for special groups, rights never existent within the Church. There is the attempt to democratize the Church, to create a "one-man, one-vote" policy whereby the truth of dogmas and the integrity of morals are decided by majority vote instead of by the Magisterium. There is the attempt to so acculturalize the Catholic Church to specific nations that national churches such as the American, French, Dutch, African Churches tend to weaken and even break their bonds with the Holy Roman Catholic Church, causing division and confusion everywhere. There is the false ecumenism founded on egalitarian irenicism which disregards serious differences in dogmatic truth and ignores the authentic teaching office of the Church thereby fostering the doctrinal and moral chaos known as indifferentism and relativism. Finally, there is the arrogant attempt by internationally influential theologians to identify themselves as part of the Magisterium and *sources* of revealed truth.[10]

Gradually, over the years the essential purpose of the Catholic university has been radically changed. Lusting after secular academic excellence, huge student bodies, expensive science complexes, political prestige and financial power, Catholic university leaders somehow lost sight of the unearthly purpose and spirit of the Catholic mission in time and began to work merely for worldly goals fueled by material motives. Thus, in many of today's Catholic universities intellectualism is preferred to Catholicism; relativism to truth; situationism to moral integrity; scientism to faith; subjectivism to reality; immanentism to the transcendent and anarchism to authority. The essential purpose of these so-called Catholic universities has *de facto* been changed, despite the continued lip service still paid to the original Catholic ideal. The light and love of this world have made tragic advances against the light and love of Christ.

St. Thomas and freedom

What makes the human person the image and likeness of God is the spirituality of his soul. As a person, each human being is an ontological, dynamic, unique, intelligent, self-conscious, non-transferrable, free subject who holds his final destiny in his own hands. Each person enters the great dialogue with his Creator through the activities of intellect and will. There can be no neutrality in the presence of the Supreme Being. Each person is capable of accepting God and his creation as truth and of adhering to them freely in love as goodness. Hence, St. Thomas calls freedom in man the spiritual appetitive power of the soul that derives from his intelligent nature, whereby a human person is able to choose or reject God, his eternal law, his revelation, providence for all creation and especially for mankind generally and for each person in particular. Freedom is that spiritual power which either chooses to love or hate God with a preferential act of acceptance or rejection. This power of election is given to man so that he may imitate God in choosing truth and goodness in their plenitude.[11]

But, of course, man does not go to God in a Robinson Crusoe fashion. He is called to attain truth and holiness for himself, but also to share them with his fellowmen. St. Thomas writes:

> Since man is a social animal, one man naturally owes another whatever is necessary for the preservation of human society. Now it would be impossible for men to live together, unless they believed one another, as declaring the truth to one another. Hence the virtue of truth does, in a manner, regard something as due

(the neighbor)...Therefore truth is a part of justice, being annexed thereto as a secondary virtue to its principal.[12]

The true nature of academic freedom

Now since it is an endowment of a creature, man's freedom is necessarily metaphysically and morally limited. Unlimited human freedom is a contradictory illusion, a slogan hiding an impossible reality, the cruel hoax of a non-entity. Man freely takes positions; he says yes or no to invitations to act or not act, to act or not act in a certain way. But this freedom is also the basis of his responsibility, a responsibility necessarily presupposed in him as a person capable of bearing metaphysical and moral values as well as disvalues. Thus academic freedom is rooted in the intellectual activity of man whereby he alone, as a person, is called to a dominion and stewardship of the universe through a conquest of truth. *Positively,* then, academic freedom is a generous guarantee to the unimpeded access to the evidence of the truth in any science. Academic freedom is thus bounded by the canons and axiomatic truths of each discipline of learning. Thus, again *positively,* academic freedom is both purposive and responsible. It is never an end in itself; no exercise of freedom ever is, but it is always a means to an end — to the attainment of truth and goodness. Hence it must never be absolutized, for it then degenerates into its antithesis — academic license. As limited, academic freedom has its own built-in rules. Its requirements are conditioned by predefined directions towards the truth of each particular science. Man's moral right to academic freedom arises from his indestructible natural activity which is necessary for the scientific achievement of truth. This right is founded on man's connatural inner dynamism of the human intellect's hunger for the plenitude of truth.

Negatively, academic freedom, at the very least, means immunity from unreasonable restrictions, both from within and from outside the academic community, of the right to communicate the results of one's researches through lectures and publications, and the right to be immune from unreasonable restriction in the pursuit of the teaching profession.[13]

Now freedom of expression and teaching may require regulation under certain circumstances, especially when what is false is purposely taught as truth and what is immoral is presented as good. For true knowledge is intolerant of error, of falsehood, of quackery. No one in his right mind will entrust his body to a surgeon who is a quack doctor. Nor will any one order his prescriptions from an incompetent pharmacist. Man must be intolerant of error, of incompetence, of quackery; his very life, health and, indeed, the common good depend on this healthy intolerance. Man's proper response to falsehood is to reject and denounce it; his proper response to truth is to seek and speak it. No professions will tolerate quacks. Why should the university? Why should the Catholic Church? What we are emphasizing here is that academic freedom is inherently a restricted endowment, a product of reason. It has responsibilities as well as rights. It must meet these responsibilities and exercise these rights in a reasonable manner for its own preservation and vigorous advancement. For academic freedom needs protection. Hence it must normally regulate itself from within the university, even as it realizes that it is subordinate to the higher authorities whose communities it serves — the State and the Church of which it is itself a beneficiary. But if it will not regulate itself from within, it will have to be regulated from without for the sake of the common good.

Academic freedom, therefore, should not be entrusted to those who would work for its destruction by subverting the free State or Church societies within which a free university exists and flourishes. For such subverters would be the first to suppress academic freedom if they came to power. Thus no professor can claim the right to teach against the right of others to hear the truth. Civil or Church societies are not obliged to tolerate those who would not tolerate them if they had the power. The Bill of Rights was never meant to become a suicide pact. Authorities are not obliged to tolerate those who would subvert the civil or ecclesiastical order under the cloak of freedom of study and teaching. A free university, no more than a free nation or Church, can afford to tolerate a nest of ideologues whose total intellectual project is to subvert the truths and morals of the societies in which they function.[14] For example, in a free State a communist is unfit to teach; in a Catholic university a heretic is unfit to teach. The reason is because neither of them is a truly free person. The mental servitude to Party dictation in the former and to rebellion against the deposit of the faith in the latter has led them both to reject the metaphysical, moral and revelational values of Christian civilization. For, in the words of Christ, "The truth shall make you free." Indeed the truth alone can keep you free. Whereas the communist works for the triumph of the Party over the Patria, the heretic works for the dethronement of Christian truth and the enthronement of falsehood. And both exploit the privileges of academic freedom because by training, purpose and dedication, they intend not to share but to twist and torture the truth. Both are useless and dangerous as teachers. As a matter of justice to the civil and ecclesiastical communities, who pay their salaries and bestow other privileges for a service they have prostituted, both should be removed from teaching and prevented from attaining other sensitive public positions in which the common good is at stake for as long as they remain addicted to their false and wicked ideologies.

Conclusion

The university that has fled from the bosom of the Catholic Magisterium into the arms of the secular magisterium has made the grave mistake of setting itself up as a separate entity, with its own nature and purpose defined in terms of the "unconditional pursuit of truth free from all constraints." Having mistakenly absolutized its nature, it also foolishly absolutizes its exercise of freedom. St. Thomas tells us that the virtue of justice is that good by which reason puts order into the operations of man, so regulating his will that he freely gives to all what is their due. And commutative justice moves men to give others, as persons or as groups, what is due to them.[15] Now the totally independent Catholic university willfully violates the rights of the Catholic Church from which it receives its existence, sustenance and mission and to which it owes a faithful academic service. Instead, such a university mistreats the Church as an extern, an alien, a threat to its existence because the Church demands a responsible accountability on how this university is fulfilling its academic mission. The so-called Catholic university does this under the false rubric that it has a right to unlimited academic freedom. Then, too, such a university also violates the rights of the Catholic parents and students who have contracted with the institution, at great financial sacrifice, for a deeper, scientific orthodox training in the Catholic faith and morality. By allowing all sorts of dogmatic and moral errors to be taught by false teachers as if they were genuine Catholic doctrine, such a university breaks its contract and defrauds its students and their parents of a service to which they have a right in natural and contractual commutative justice. Money taken under these conditions should, by right, be restored to the offended parties.

Now moral, civil and canon law protect the sanctity of contracts, each in its own sphere, but the moral law which demands rectitude in the use of responsible freedom, is the guardian of all justice. That the Church must be ostracized from her own academic institutions and her faithful defrauded of their money under the rubric of a pseudo-academic freedom is a scandalous act of academic and contractual injustice, calling for reform and restitution. This injustice was repudiated by the Vatican Congregation of Catholic Education in plenary session in October 1969:

> To fulfill its mission, a Catholic university must be seen as existing not only in the world, but also in the Catholic community and therefore it is related to those who preside over the Catholic community: the Catholic hierarchy. Obviously, the specific purpose of the Catholic university cannot be realized if those whose proper function it is to be the authentic guardians of the deposit of the faith are relegated to a marginal place in its life and activity.[16]

Order, as St. Thomas excellently explains, is the unity created by the harmonious functioning of many beings. Thus, true and genuine social order demands that the various members of a society be joined together in some firm bond which guarantees that the society in which they work will attain the principal purpose for which it was founded. The power of this coherent union will then fructify in the goods produced and the services rendered to its members and the community at large. Thus, both employers and employees of this unified vocational group will cooperate in friendly harmony to attain the common good, each functioning in its own sphere. But such a union will become powerful and efficacious only in proportion to the fidelity with which each person and the whole group strives to attain its principal goal by discharging its professional duties and excelling in them.[17]

Applying this clear and profound reasoning of St. Thomas to the Catholic academic community, it is easy to conclude that in all Catholic schools at every level, but especially in the Catholic university, the common interests of the Church must predominate. And among those interests the most important is to promote to its utmost ability, fidelity in teaching and research to Catholic doctrine and morals as they come to men through the Magisterium, so that every student, every professor, every person, every human institution, indeed all things, may be restored in Christ. That is the purpose of academic freedom in institutions of Catholic learning.

Notes

[1]Rev. Joseph F. Costanzo, S.J., "The Academy and the City," a pamphlet, Cork University Press, Ireland, 1961.

[2]John Henry Cardinal Newman, *The Idea of a University,* Image Books, N.Y., 1959, p. 7.

[3]Fr. Costanzo, S.J., op. cit.

[4]S. Thomas Greenburg, Director of the Institute of Catholic Higher Education, 4 pamphlets on "The Problem of Identity in Catholic Higher Education," #2, 1973, St. John's University, N.Y.

[5]U.S. National Conference of Bishops' Letter on Education, "To Teach as Jesus Did," *L'Osservatore Romano,* Eng. Ed., November 15, 1972.

[6]Newman, op. cit. pp. 414–415.

[7]Quoted by Fr. Charles E. Curran in his article in The Catholic Mind for February 1980, "Academic Freedom: The Catholic University and Catholic Theology."

[8]Ibid.

[9]From the working documents of this Congress at which I was an invited observer. The documents are in my file.

[10]Greenburg, op. cit. Pamphlet on *The Challenge to the Church's Authority,* December 31, 1976, Published by the Institute of Catholic Higher Education, San Antonio, Texas.

[11]St. Thomas, *Summa Theologica,* Part I, Q. 83, aa. 1, 2, 3.

[12]St. Thomas, op. cit. Part II of Part II, q. 109, a. 3.

[13]Fr. Costanzo, S.J., "Academic Freedom and the Intellectual," a pamphlet, Cork University Press, Ireland, 1960.

[14]Fr. Costanzo, S.J., "The Academy and the City," as above.

[15]St. Thomas, *Summa Theologica,* Part II, 1a, q. 61, aa. 2 and 3.

[16]Quoted by Charles Rice in his book *Authority and Rebellion,* Doubleday & Co., N.Y., 1971, p. 178.

[17]St. Thomas, *Contra Gentiles,* III, 71; *Summa Theologica,* Part I, Q. 65, a. 2 etc.

Reprinted from *Studi Tomistici* VI — Thomistic Studies, Vol. VI, Acts of the VIII International Thomistic Congress, Rome 1982.

Christian Marxism: Sacrilegious Demagoguery

The immortal Shakespeare, seeking the source of dreams, penned these well-known lines: "We are such stuff as dreams are made of." Then plunging deeper into man so as to precision the exact power which produces our reveries, the Bard asks: "Tell me where is fancy bred, or in the heart or in the head?"

We hope to answer Shakespeare's question at the end of this essay. But only after we have examined the anatomy of perhaps the most fatal fantasy threatening the faith of Christians today — the dream of Christian Marxism.

Today the long march of certain Catholic groups towards the acceptance of Marxism, begun some years ago, has achieved its terminal stage.[1] Physically, psychologically and ideologically Christians are embracing Marxists and vice versa. For it is not a mystery to anyone that certain Catholic groups have accepted Marxism not only in its method of analyzing capitalistic society and adhering to it as a political instrument for the revolutionary change of the existing order, but likewise, accepting Marxism as historical materialism, they adhere to this as the philosophic instrument for the interpretation of all history, above all, the history of the Church. Thus for these groups Marxism has become the only exegetical key in which one may read and interpret historical facts, especially "the fact of Jesus." Hence they have recently proposed a materialistic reading of Holy Scripture as well as of the Gospels. All the texts of Christianity, as well as the whole history of the Church ought to be analyzed on the assumption that historical materialism is true, as a science which expresses the exigencies, the needs of the struggle of the proletariat to create a Socialist society. Recently there was held an international theological convention promoted by the Ecumenical Center called "Agape," from July 20 to 28, 1975. Its theme was: "The Interpretation of the Bible and Historical Materialism." This convention was held as a continuation and profounder study of the work begun by an earlier Congress held from April 4 to 6, 1975, Senegal, by Christians For Socialism from the region of the Marches in Italy. That congress too treated the theme: "Towards a Materialistic Reading of the Bible."

The journey seems fatalistic

It is interesting to recall briefly the steps of this long march of Christians towards acceptance of Marxism and, above all, to follow the iron logic which unites each phase of the journey to the next. This unstoppable, almost fatalistic journey, from one stage to the next right to its logical conclusion — which is adherence to Marxism even as a philosophy — ought to place on their guard those who think they can pick and choose Marxist principles at random and yet remain safe in the faith. For example, some select the Marxist analysis of society and yet reject its philosophic vision, i.e., historical materialism. Others choose historical materialism but reject Marxist atheism which, however, is necessarily connected with its materialism. For, in reality, Marxism is a unified ideology; all its elements hold together and sustain each other reciprocally. It is impossible to separate them, unless one wants to pay the price of torturing himself with intellectual acrobatics and coming up with contradictory theories and chaotic practices.

Can Marxism be baptized?

As is generally known, during the Sixties the posture of the Catholic world in the face of Marxism, and in particular of Communism, changed radically. It went from eye-ball to eye-ball confrontation to that of dialogue and "fraternization." Both sides, Catholic and all shades of Atheistic Socialism, interested themselves in learning more profoundly the positions of the other. Not only were ideological meetings on high cultural levels held between them, for example, the meeting between Christians and Marxists promoted by Paulus-Gesellschaft in 1966 at Monaco in Bavaria and in 1967 at Marainske Lazne in Czechoslovakia — but there was at base a rich flowering of initiatives that multiplied meetings between Catholics and Marxists. Much more ardently did the Communists show themselves in favor of this dialogue, for they were acting more from political than from cultural interests.

Unfortunately, some Catholic groups did not content themselves solely with dialogue; they seemed more interested in baptizing Marxism. Thus, making a distinction between the Marxist analysis of society and historical materialism as it evolves in the dialectic, they taught that a Christian, without accepting historical materialism, could, nevertheless, make his own the Marxist analysis of society, both as a conceptual means for understanding the mechanisms of capitalistic society and as a practical instrument in the political fight for the revolutionary change of that society into a socialistic society. But acceptance in theory and in practice of the Marxist analysis of society must lead logically to the acceptance also of historical materialism.

In fact, in order to make his analysis of capitalistic society stand up, Marx made use of the means given him by the science of economics in his day as well as of the observations he made of the conditions of the workers. But he principally made use of an ideological vision of historical reality, that is, of Hegelian idealism turned upside down into a historical materialism. Thus, at the foundation of the Marxist analysis of capitalistic society are to be found some iron-clad ideological presuppositions, theories never proven by the tests of experience, experiments or excogitations. The first and most important of these presuppositions is that society is fundamentally formed and moulded by its economic forces, so much so that the superstructure (political and juridical institutions, philosophical and moral ideologies, religion, art, etc.) is determined in the final instance by the economic infrastructure. From this presupposition, which constitutes the nucleus of historical materialism, Marx brought forth other novel prinicples. First, the historical evolution of society takes place according to the Hegelian laws of the dialectic (affirmation — negation — negation of the negation), and this dialectic takes place with the iron law of necessity. Another gratuitous theory stated that Capitalism contains in itself the very contradiction that will bring it down in ruin so that Socialism will necessarily follow it. Then there is the presupposition that the history of every society right up to our own has been the history of the struggle between the classes. That is why class struggle is the motor, the driving force of history. There is this final theory, namely that the protagonists of the class struggle in capitalistic society are the class of the bourgeois and the class of the proletariats.

Really, the Marxist analysis of society, for all that it is called "scientific," (it really is not scientific, for even history has proven it to be false; not even Marx's scientific predictions have come true!) cannot be neutral in the face of philosophy, but depends essentially on its own school of thought. Therefore, consistency demands that anyone who accepts Marxism and makes his own its analysis of society cannot fail to make his own also its doctrine of historical materialism which is its foundation and forms the very warp and woof of this ideological system. This explains why many Catholics, having at first accepted solely the Marxist analysis of society, eventually find themselves, without realizing why, accepting also its historical materialism.

Without faith nothing is left

But once having accepted historical materialism, "Christian Marxists" cannot escape a grave enigma. How will they be able to reconcile historical materialism with the Christian faith? There are two possible ways of resolving this problem. The first abandons the Christian faith because it is irreconcilable with Marxism; the second reinterprets Christianity according to the principles of historical materialism in such a way as to save (so it hopes) its valid core, while jettisoning only Christianity's "anti-revolutionary aspects."

Some Christians followed the first procedure. Diverse reasons have moved them to take this course; for many of them it has proved to be a way of sorrows. In the first place, they claim they were depressed with the inefficaciousness of the Christian faith to achieve reform. They add, moreover, that they were impressed with the vitality of Marxism, finding in it such a fullness of meaning and such a powerful stimulus for political reforms that their faith was rendered superfluous. Unfortunately, little by little these illusions faded in their hearts. Then followed their conviction of the radical opposition between the Christian faith and Marxism. They now not only saw the Church as the natural ally of Capitalism, but they discovered more profoundly in the Christian faith an ideology that sustained and justified capitalistic exploitation. Progressing from this "anti-capitalistic choice," they concluded that it was impossible to adhere simultaneously to the Church which, in their eyes, sustains Capitalism and to Socialism which fights to destroy Capitalism. It became impossible for them to adhere to a reactionary ideology like the Christian faith and to a revolutionary, progressist program like Marxism.

We are thus witnessing the conscious abandonment of the Christian faith, in this group, even of the very name of Christian. And the tragedy is that this betrayal of the faith is motivated by a sincere desire to save mankind from the "sin of the world," namely economic exploitation. These Christians have — some wittingly, others unwittingly — insisted on baptizing Socialism and Communism, accepting even their methods of class struggle and revolution in the quest for man's liberation from economic injustice. Influenced by the rhetoric of these salvation systems, such well-intentioned Catholics have made it their misssion to plunge the Church into the class struggle; they aim at reducing the Church's apostolate of redeeming men from sin and Satan to an apostolate of liberating men first from poverty and eventually from all forms of domination. Their entrapment in this sterile adventure has been cleverly achieved by their atheistic friends. In the dialectics of friendly detente with the forces of atheistic Socialism, many Christians have surrendered to the spirit of the world. They have succumbed to the seductions of non-believers and followed false, double-minded prophets. Theirs has been a fatal concession, the whole of the deposit of the faith and even the treasury of Christian morality. They have been persuaded to interpret Christianity according to Socialist-Marxist principles. These so-called "Christian Socialists" or "Marxist Christians" are now teaching a new understanding of the faith, of the Gospels, of the Church — a new way of living in harmony with the Marxist vision of history. And so they proclaim insistently that they are liberating the Gospels and the Church from the ideological superstructures of a decadent, capitalistic society. They emphasize that they are returning both the Gospel message and the Church's mission to their true, original, revolutionary inspiration and vigor.

Unfortunately, ideas have consequences and violent ideas have violent consequences. Thus these Marxist Christians have been infected with more than just the ideology of their atheistic friends. For in a hostile dialectics of confrontation with their fellow-Christians, they do not shun open warfare against the Church and "Christian ideology." They attack the Church with the animus of a prosecutor accusing a man in the dock of criminal activity. Only thus can we explain the fact — incredible at first brush — that certain groups of the extreme Catholic left, on the one hand, parade their strict fidelity to Marxism, while on the other, they exhibit ruthless harshness towards the Church and the Christian faith. Moreover, these groups are for the most part made up of youths who are Catholic in origin and formation. Infected also with the activist dialectics of the class struggle and violent revolution, they go beyond dialogue to distortion and anathema against the faith, the Magisterium, the whole Church. Such is their furor against the Church that, in opposing her teaching, they eviscerate the authentic Gospel revelation, demote Christ to the level of a mere man, the Church to the level of a mere natural institution and render Christianity meaningless.

Now the majority of Christian Marxists attempt to follow a second path, that is, they seek a new understanding of the faith and a new way of living it within the Marxist vision of history and within the evolution of the class struggle. They attempt a reinterpretation of Christianity beginning with the principle of historical materialism. Having done that, they claim it is necessary to liberate the Gospel from the ideological super-structures which, though mouthing a message of liberation of the poor from exploitation, nevertheless sustain Capitalism the oppressor in the seat of power. They must restore in a Marxist manner alone the revolutionary vigor of the Christian message with its original destructive force. For these reasons, they are convinced they must achieve a dialectical unity between Marxism and Christianity; they actually believe they can be fully faithful to the Gospel and the Christian faith.

The Church is their legacy

But, to what Gospel and to what Christian faith? Not certainly to the Gospel handed down by Christian tradition, nor to the faith transmitted and still taught by the Catholic Church. In fact, in applying the Marxist analysis to the faith and history of the Church, the Marxist Christians are led to conclude that the institutional Church has developed in history and is still developing today the objective function — they prescind from the subjective good will of the Church — of sustaining and defending the ideology of the dominating class as found in Capitalism. Thus they arrive at identifying the institutional Church with the enemy of the masses. And again, they come to the conclusion that the Church has read, and is still reading, Sacred Scripture, especially the Gospel, from the viewpoint and interests of the dominating classes. The faith she is propagating, therefore, is in substance an ideology supporting Capitalism; it is, after all, a real "opium of the people," and "force of alienation."

If the faith is ever to be liberated from the ideological superstructures of capitalism and prevented from becoming an instrument for the justification of Capitalism, the Church will have to reread the Gospel from the viewpoint and interests of the proletariat. The poor and the oppressed must reappropriate to themselves the Gospel stolen from them and made to serve against them. This means that the Gospel must be read with an orientation toward socio-political problems, from a platform favorable to the poor and the exploited, from the project to construct an alternative society to that of the bourgeois model. And in thus reading the Gospel, one must make use of the principle of historical materialism, that is, one must make a "materialistic" reading of the Bible. For the Church's reading of Scripture cannot be neutral. If it is not a "materialistic" reading, then it must be a "bourgeois" and "idealistic" one.

Now a "materialistic" reading of the Bible is opposed to the "bourgeois" interpretation which is the one the Church has actually been rendering in the interests of the dominating classes. Moreover, the "materialistic" is also opposed to the "idealistic" reading, that is, the interpretation which begins from the ideal values of the dominating class, and gives special privilege to a "spiritual" sense of the gospels. For according to the Marxist Christians, first the Fathers of the Church, then the medieval exegets, finally the modern exegetes and even the progressists, in their reading of the Gospel, have all fallen into the trap of idealism and spiritualism. Rather, one must read the Gospel and, therefore, interpret the person of Jesus and his evangelical message from an analysis of the social relationships of production and from the influence these exercised on the religious and political life of Israel in the Palestine of the first century.

Is the Gospel subversive?

Only thus will one become aware of the subversive and revolutionary character of the political and religious actions of Jesus, at war, as he was, with the social and economic organization, with the political power and religious ideology of his times. Jesus, in fact, broke decisively with the ideology of the dominating classes — the high priests, the Sadducees, the Pharisees — and even with the Zelots who wished to better economic and political relationships, but without changing them radically. And even if Jesus did not succeed in transforming the society of his times, he at least opened new vistas of liberty. Thus, today the Gospel must be a subversive narrative or, after the example of Jesus, it should once again aim at sustaining in believers the drive to break with the ideology of the dominating classes and to construct a classless society. But it can do this on one condition only, namely, if man succeeds in discovering the true nature of the political, social and religious actions of Jesus which were revolutionary. He will do this only by violently removing the "spiritual," "idealistic" encrustations imposed on the Gospels by the institutional Church, acting as an ally of the powers of Capitalism.

The fruit of such a "materialistic" reading of the Gospel will finally be a new conception of the Christian faith which, the more it recedes from the interpretation presented by the institutional Church, the more will it lose every mark of alienation, thereby becoming efficacious in the construction of a classless society. Then, and only then, will Christianity cease to be the "opium of the people."

Logic demands leaving

The problems arising from the acceptance of historical materialism and a "materialistic" reading of the Bible are many and serious; nor could we pretend to treat them adequately here. In this article, however, we will place three questions to our Marxist Christians. Convinced of their seriousness and good will, we know these questions will not leave these Christians indifferent, not if they wish to remain with the faith and continue as members of the Catholic Church.

The first question arises from the fact that Christian Marxists accept as valid Marxism's analysis of society. Now, this analysis is an unjustified simplification of reality which is infinitely more variegated, complex and unpredictable than the Marxist theory supposes it to be. But to accept the Marxist analysis of society leads these Christians to see in the institutional Church and its hierarchy the guarantor of Capitalism. Indeed, if it is impossible to be neutral in the class struggle, then, even when the Church is pretending to remain above the battle, she necessarily ends up on the side of Capitalism. Well, then, if what the Marxist Christians say is true, we ask: How is it possible for you to stay within the Church when you see her as the enemy you must fight with every available means, since, as you hold, you cannot make peace with her?

Is it in or out?

To solve this problem some Marxist Christians have created small Christian communities, in more or less open rupture with the institutional Church. But in acting this way they fail to solve anything; they only complicate the problem. For either the community they enter is convinced it is living as part of the universal Church and then the problem of contestation continues to fester within it. Or the new community is convinced it is outside the Catholic Church, since it broke its bonds with the essential structures of the Church. But then such Marxist Christians must realize in their consciences they no longer belong to the Church and cannot coherently pretend they remain within her bosom. Thus, in our judgment, the Marxist analysis of society is an inadequate, misleading means not only for the authentic understanding of society as it actually exists, but also as an inadequate evaluation of the actually existing Church.

Now our second question is: How do you Marxist Christians preserve the transcendent, metahistorical, supernatural origin and destiny of Christianity? Marxist Christians cannot honestly avoid putting this question to themselves for, since they seriously and coherently accept historical materialism, they must also accept that the economic structure determines the superstructure in which religion plays an important part. Thus, for historical materialism Christianity is a product of the natural and economic and material structure. On the one hand, then, Christianity becomes a *necessary* product because all that is historical for Marxism evolves with iron-clad determinism from the dialectic. Yet, on the other hand, Christianity is a *historical* product, which suggests that it is subject to changes just as all human events and institutions are. And in particular it is to be expected to change with the changes of its economic relationships. Thus, we cannot see how Marxist Christians preserve the supernatural, transcendent, meta-temporal character of Christianity. They cannot at the same time accept historical materialism and claim that Christianity is a reality that transcends history because of its divine origin and destiny. That is to say, they cannot without falling into a contradiction, be true Marxists adhering to historical materialism, and true Christians believing in a Church founded on divine origins. We must conclude then that whoever accepts historical materialism renounces by that very act Christianity, as it is revealed in Holy Scripture and handed down by the living Church.

Now when one works out a reinterpretation of Christianity, that is, when one liberates it from all theological, transcendent and spiritual encrustations, and makes of it a human, historical message of revolution favoring the exploited, and when one even introduces into Christianity the new distinction between "faith" and "religion," rejecting religion as alienating ("religion is the opium of the people") and accepting faith as a revolutionary, subversive force, how can this hybrid reality be still called Christianity? Has not Christianity been thus diluted into being an ideology in the service of proletarian revolution? Do not the Marxist Christians fall into the same — though opposite — fault for which they attack the institutional Church? Their fault is that they too have made of Christianity an ideology, a sign of opposition to capitalistic society. Formerly they accused the institutional Church of making Christianity an ideology, a sign set up for the conservation of the dominating classes.

They make Jesus only man

The third question we put to the Marxist Christians concerns their "materialistic" reading of the Bible and the Gospel. When they apply historical materialism to the person, actions and message of Jesus, are they not forced to deny his divinity? Have they not reduced Jesus to being a mere, simple man and nothing more? Certainly, when reading the Gospel, one must keep before one's mind the socio-economic and political conditions in which Jesus worked and preached. These help us understand many things about the life and death of Jesus. Nor ought this truth be astonishing, for the Word incarnate is truly man, inserted in real, human history. Thus, one can also make a valid historical reading of the Gospel. But it is a tactic of deception to pretend to establish as *the* exegetical key for the reading of the Gospel the principle of historical materialism. For this tactic aims at seriously eviscerating the whole of Christianity. It necessarily reduces Jesus to being no more than a simple man who, living merely as a prophet and performing solely messianic, royal duties, instigated the class struggle against the possessors of power — the priests, scribes and ancients — who were using religion as an ideological cover for their socio-economic super-structure of tyranny and domination.

Jesus tried, but failed

In other words, the "materialistic" reading of the Gospel makes of Jesus a mere political subversive and his death becomes nothing more than a political assassination. But then, of course, Jesus is no longer the Son of God who dies for the redemption of the multitude. His opposition to the possessors of power is no longer situated on the religious realm of the divine, but rather in a purer, natural, more interior orientation. Yet, just such a similar theological reading of the Gospel by the institutional Church is held by the Marxist Christians to be ideological and bourgeois. It seems they want it both ways; their new interpretation of the faith must be pure, interior, even theological in their own sense and then it is the true faith. But when the Church teaches a spiritual, interior, pure, theological faith, then she teaches an exploiting ideology. For the Marxist Christians the death of Jesus is only the consequence, the conclusion of the class struggle he instigated — a failure, to be sure, but a noble blow against tyranny.

At this point what is left of Jesus? Nothing, except the tragic image of a courageous man who fought for the liberation of the poor and was defeated. We have in Jesus merely the record of a subversive man to whom we can go for inspiration in the existing class struggle. And, as a matter of fact, from the "materialistic" reading of the Gospel — so states the con-clusion of the document of Senegal — this valid hypothesis favoring labor emerges, namely, the indication that Christ was a subversive. "We think," the document says, "that such an indication about Jesus can create a new richness for the basic communities and groups within the proletarian militia." This indication that Jesus was a subversive "can also enrich the historical camp of Marxism," states the same document. And finally, it can enlarge "that utopian horizon for personal and collective liberation towards which we are advancing." In other words, faith has become a secondary, strengthening force for Marxism, and Jesus Christ becomes a subversive just like so many others in history.

But if such is the case, if, that is, Marxism is sufficient to plot an efficacious strategy for the class struggle, capable of creating a new society; if Jesus is only one among so many men who fought for revolution and liberation — then the Christian faith becomes a useless, superfluous luxury and the reading of Holy Scripture time wasted.

Marxist Christians, despite their desire to give everything to their poorer brothers, become really seducers of the spirit. For they hold out as a utopian reality or possibility what is simply not realizable — the arrangement of a marriage between Christianity and all forms of Socialism, even Communism. But pope after pope has condemned this attempt, demonstrating how Christianity and Socialism are hopelessly incompatible, not only psychologically but, above all, ontologically. And no matter how often or expertly Socialism has its features lifted through the slick art of "new Christianity" surgery, it will never acquire the beauty of a human, much less Christian face. For Marxist Socialism and its milder breeds deny man the dignity arising from his divine origin and destiny; they strip man of the exercise of his liberty, initiative, creative intelligence in his wonderful worlds of religion, thought and work. Moreover, Marxist Socialism's appeal to the masses to revolt against established institutions under a supposed trumpet call from a Christ burlesqued as the Great Liberator and Grand Subverter, is sheer sacrilege and religious demagoguery.

The dream of "Christian Marxism" is now seen to be bred in the heads of Christian rebels, though sired by their own godless hearts. For, whereas Saints are such stuff as divine visions are made of, atheists are products of their own demonic nightmares.

Notes

[1]This article is inspired by an editorial in *La Civiltà Cattolica,* Italian Jesuit bi-monthly review for July 19, 1975. The editors there put "Tre Domande Ai 'Christiani Marxisti,' " that is, "Three Questions for 'Christian Marxists.' " I have developed their material in my own way.

Reprinted from *Homiletic & Pastoral Review,* March 1976.

Heidegger and Bultmann:
Keepers of the Cosmic Cage

Normally an able theologian is one who has already explored profoundly the presuppositional truths of theology, thereby becoming also a competent philosopher. One thinks immediately of such famous philosopher-theologian relationships as Plato and Augustine, and Aristotle and Thomas. For a scholar's intellectual forebearers mold his thought, and theologians, concerned as they are with ultimate realities, cannot escape the questions of Being any more than philosophers. Now the philosopher-theologian relationship we propose to study briefly here is the Heidegger-Bultmann intellectual alignment. Indeed, so integral is Heidegger's analysis of Being to Bultmann's theological system that it can be said no scholastic divinity scholar ever threw himself into the arms of St. Thomas with the fervor with which Bultmann embraces Heidegger. Bultmann states his conviction for the special relationship of Heideggerian existentialist philosophy to his work as a theologian thus:

> The 'right' philosophy — and that, we take it, means the philo-sophical outlook proper to theological study — is quite simply that philosophical work which endeavors to develop in suitable concepts the understanding of existence that is given with existence.[1]

Heidegger, in his analysis of existence, describes first everyday or inauthentic existence and then explains what is authentic existence for man. Using Heidegger's analytic method, Bultmann interprets the New Testament message as a theology of the true existential possibilities for man. His doctrine falls into two parts paralleling the Heideggerian dichotomy of authentic and inauthentic man. For Bultmann the life of man without Christ is inauthentic, the life of man in the Christian faith authentic. We hope to discover how far into the transcendent life of God both of these existential interpretations lead man.

Now Bultmann's thought is seen to be really a theological anthropology. His point of departure is how to interpret the New Testament in such a way that its teachings may become understandable and acceptable to scientific, secularized man. Bultmann wrote and taught during and after the Second World War. His scriptural analyses were radically influenced by that tragic event. His great pastoral concern was to bring modern Hitlerized youth to hear the Gospel message as an appeal from God and to respond to that summons in loving faith. In order to win the allegiance of these dechristianized youth to God, Bultmann thought he had to make the New Testament palatable to their secularized taste. The method used to accomplish this purpose was twofold: 1) The use of Heideggerian existential-ist ontology and 2) the cleansing of the Gospels of all their beclouding elements — mysteries, miracles and supernatural fables.

Now Heidegger too was deeply concerned with the tragic problems of that era. Troisfontaines relates that the traumatic experience of being thrown into the world destined to death seized the whole being of Heidegger when he was serving in the trenches during the First World War. Heidegger admits too that he was profoundly influenced by the New Testament, Paul, Augustine and, most of all, by Luther. Thus strongly motivated by theology in his researches into the meaning of Being, Heidegger developed a new point of departure. Central to his study is the actualization of real life. For him Being is actualized only in temporality. Consequently, essences or the inner capacities of things, since they are timeless creations of subjective thinking, are not, as Plato and the Scholastics taught, the primary object of óntology. The meaning of Being can be accurately discovered only by a descriptive analysis of the historically agitated human being, *Dasein*. This means that man is the tragic presence and locus (The Da) of Being (Sein). Yet Being is not to be understood as the ultimate reality, the transcendent God. For Heidegger, Being seems necessarily finite and temporal. And man is thrown into existence in this hostile world and challenged by his conscience to give meaning to its meaninglessness, to face up to his radical anxiety, to accept his own destination to death. This calls for a courageous exercise of freedom that gives man and his world meaning, projects man into the future and creates his own truth. For, *"the essence of truth is freedom,"* writes Heidegger, recalling a doctrine of his master Nietzsche and emphasizing it with his own italics.

Reflective introspection on actual human existence reveals that men live in two opposing styles. Some men live an *authentic* human existence, accepting the dereliction of being thrown into existence from an original Nothingness and a destiny through death into a final Nothingness. They admit human existence is trapped in temporality from its superfluous birth to its absurd death. Despite this radical absurdity, such men live courageously giving meaning to their lives through reflective, responsible use of their freedom. On the other hand, those who live *inauthentic* existences flee the anxiety and insecurity of reality; their beliefs, rules, ends, cares, ambitions are harmonized with those of the amorphous crowd in which they gladly lose themselves. They choose to be part of the *one, many, they* — preferring the peace of anonymity to the fight for subjecthood.

In a lecture entitled "Introduction to the Phenomenology of Religion," Heidegger presents St. Paul arousing the first Christians from their in-authentic lives of idleness while waiting for the Second Coming of Christ. They are not to expect that Coming on any fixed date; they are to get to work, to plunge into living their lives before the open and threatening, non-objectifiable clouds of the future. Moreover, Paul exhorts Christians not to flee to myths, fables, apocryphal or apocalyptic reports, but to stay put, stand up, face and accept the tragedies of actual life. In a lecture entitled "Augustine and Neo-Platonism," Heidegger warned modern man of the danger in Augustine of falsifying man's actual life — threatened by restlessness, suffering, the cross and death — through a Neo-Platonism that would change factually tragic life into a timeless, non-historical *fruitio Dei*.[2] In the violent turbulance of Luther's career Heidegger recognized the original character of Being's ambiguity and anxiety.[3]

Utilizing such Heideggerian concepts and terms, Bultmann went on to reveal the true meaning of the Gospels for modern man. His message is never theoretic; it is personalist, existentialist. The Heideggerian *Dasein* is just what the New Testament means by man. Therefore, most elements in the Gospels which seem to be objective representations of historical or doctrinal matters must be discarded. Why? Because the early Christian Church made too many concessions to metaphysics when it arbitrarily applied the whole mental kit of Hellenic myths and wonders to the true message of the Gospels. Greek metaphysics, Catholic and Protestant orthodoxies, idealist metaphysics and Protestant liberalism have wrought havoc with the pure message of the Gospels for twenty centuries.[4] This "criminal streak" in philosphy can only be removed from the Gospels by the process of demythologization. When this is completed, the true reality of the Gospels' kerygma proclaims that the only significance of Jesus is that he summons man to make a free decision to face up to his authentic self, to find himself in acceptance of his dire destiny to death. In Jesus man receives a mature understanding of his precarious existence and comes to terms with it. Thus the Crucifixion and the Resurrection of Jesus, as salvation events, are recalled not as history but as personal commitments. The decision to encounter God in these events is really the decision to achieve authentic manhood. Faith is achieved in man's interior, affirmative encounter with God; faith leads to the acceptance of Heidegger's particular understanding of human existence. Indeed, the preacher of the Word of God, in Bultmann's estimation, should stress this particular understanding of the Gospels, even using Heidegger's terms to expound the roles of God, Jesus and men in the adventure of salvation.

Now in order to justify his use of Heideggerian hermeneutics in his explanation of the Gospel message, Bultmann has to explain away the message of the New Testament writers. He insists that the Evangelists and Apostles did not write history. Rather they produced Jewish apocalyptic mythology of salvation in combination with Hellenic and Gnostic myths of redemptions and resurrection. But scientific thought has exploded these anthropocentric mythologies of transcendence. Nor will the modern mind accept them any longer. Thus, all images of direct divine intervention into human history must be discarded for they reduce God to a reality of this world and man to an automaton. Actually God is totally hidden, entirely absent from science, history and the cosmic universe, while man is totally immersed in this world. It follows, then, that Jesus is not God, nor does the Son of God become incarnate as the Son of Man. There was no Virgin Birth; there were no miracles; there was no physical Resurrection from the dead nor Ascension into heaven. These are sheer, rationalistic, Graeco-Judean myths. All that Jesus is is the "event of God's deed." Neither belief nor unbelief, therefore, are to be founded on exterior signs — miracles, divine interventions, historical events, ceremonies, sacraments. Moreover, sin is not an inherited or personal offense against God; it is merely cowardly flight from authentic existence. The faith that saves man is his response to God who, in the interior of man's conscience, challenges man to accept the Cross and the Resurrection not as actual, historical events which save men in themselves because they are deeds of the true Son of God, but as mere signs of God's calling. Then too, the Holy Spirit is not another Divine Person, but he merely signifies the individual's achievement of his decision to live selfishly no longer, but to live for others in a service of love.

In reflecting on Heidegger's existentialist ontology we find some valid truth in so far as it advances an analysis of man's existential condition. But we have to object to his analysis for not going far enough into the mystery of man. His ontology is truncated, pauperized by its refusal to transcend into the divine dimension of man's existence. For example, Heidegger justly reveals that man's fundamental experience of fear, dread and anxiety is bound up with his freedom and thrownness into the world destined to death. He correctly asserts that these experiences reveal that man is not at home in a hostile world.[5] We have here the New Testament description that "men are strangers and pilgrims on earth." Thus those who seek to be at home, content and secure in this world, live inauthentic lives. Yet even these cannot escape the anxiety that will eventually shatter their illusionary contentment. It is while he is standing on this precipice of ontological anxiety that Heidegger is also on the threshold of God and religion. For only a transcendent divine Other can give adequate meaning to the ontological malaise that disturbs the very metaphysical core of man's being. True, ontological anxiety does not explicitly reveal God, but it does lead directly to him if pursued with open mind and good will. Augustine profoundly analyzed the reality behind the *cor inquietum* of man. "Thou hast made us for thyself, O Lord, and our hearts are restless, until they rest in thee." Why did Heidegger not have the courage and faith to go beyond his philosophy of neutrality toward God? Why did he choose to remain in a state of atheistic ambiguity? And why too does Bultmann found his theology of the New Testament on this atheism of ambiguity? Neither scholar explains their one-sided interpretation of man's existence. We shall see that this reduced view of man's existence leads logically to pessimism and nihilism.[6]

When we look at Bultmann's existential theology of salvation we find a similar hesitancy to advance to the fullness of truth in God's revelation. Bultmann insists that man is pressed to a radical decision; he must choose God or the world, i.e., choose finding his true self in obedience to God or losing himself in serving the world. But is this the whole content of what Jesus taught? Does salvation consist only in man's radical decision to be an authentic person? Is not this also a terribly attenuated explanation of the Gospel message? Jesus claimed to be true God; he died on the cross and rose from the dead by his own and his Father's power to prove his divine origin and Person. Jesus performed works of wonder, controlling the forces of the visible and invisible worlds at will. These miracles called men to faith in his divinity, his message, his Church. Now Bultmann takes none of these historical events, nor the eyewitnesses of them, seriously, dismissing both dogmatically, the events as mere myths, the witnesses as well-intentioned but deluded creators of these myths. Like his philosopher-master, Bultmann refuses to enter the numinous world of the Divine Jesus.[7] We find that Bultmann's existentialist prepossessions make him skillful in fitting his facts into the framework of his theory, but he never demonstrates how his theories follow from the New Testament facts.

The modern biblical studies of Riesenfeld and Gerhardsson[8] demolish Bultmann's contention that the majority of Gospel narrations are community creations, etiological legends fabricated by the early Christians who ascribed to Jesus the origins of certain myths and practices. These scholars demonstrate that Jesus was a Jewish Rabbi, that his teaching was given in stock rabbinic fashion. This meant it was learnt by heart and handed down by word of mouth. In this context, one of the chief functions of the Apostles was to watch over this tradition, which was regularly taught and passed on in the Church's gatherings for worship. The Evangelists, therefore, regarded their function as that of bearing witness to Christ, not of composing edifying fiction. Ordered instruction and not imaginary *mythopoeia* was the genesis for the transmission of the Gospels in the oral period of the Church's teaching. This "holy tradition" of careful oral memorization gradually came to be written down, first in notebooks or codices or scrolls in order to aid the memory. By the middle of the second century these notebooks had percolated throughout the Church in the form of Gospels and Epistles. Then began the process of *mishnah*, i.e., the teaching of these Gospels and Epistles as Holy Scripture, as the new sacred Torah of the Christian Churches. Thus, creative interpretation was well nigh impossible, for the Apostles and Evangelists were bearers not only of the tradition concerning Christ but also of the correct interpretation of the New Testament Scriptures. It is important to realize that the sayings of Jesus were repeated and used by the apostolic witnesses in a manner which is similar to the rabbinical use of the Old Testament. Consequently, Bultmann's famous radical distinction between the historical Jesus who walked the roads of Palestine (*der historische Jesus*) and the Christ who gives meaning to the course of history (*der geschichtliche Christus*) is proven to be arbitrarily artificial and untenable. And his insistence that Christians can only know the latter through an act of faith independent of any divine deeds performed by him in Palestine is also seen to be a sterile exercise in selective exegesis. For Bultmann the Christ of Palestine remains dead and buried, whereas the Christ present in the consciences of men is a romantically visionary figure, a sort of masculine equivalent of Don Quixote's Dulcinea, in whose goodness men are to warm themselves with unsubstantial hopes for salvation. It is understandable, then, that Bultmann dismisses the studies of Riesenfeld and Gerhardsson with characteristic contempt: ''To me this construction seems to be untenable.'' It is significant too that he never explains why it is untenable. Actually, this post-Bultmann exegesis demolishes the Bultmannian postulates because it offers an explanation about the genesis of the Gospels based on New Testament data and then-contemporary Jewish methods of teaching, both of which demonstrate the Gospel narrations are more the result of a scrupulously preservative process than of a creative, mythological one.

As a result of their reductionist philosophies and theologies, Heidegger and Bultmann have become, as it were, keepers of the Cosmic Cage. In refusing to allow man and his world to find in God, their Creator and Saviour, the only reasonable and possible solution to their anxiety and alienation from each other and their Creator, Heidegger has abandoned man to a destiny of heroic despair or fatalistic heroism. Both Bultmann and Heidegger refuse to allow God to come in the flesh to save mankind and renew his universe; they seal off the cosmos against the possibility of miracles, mystical transformations, a salvation accomplished by a Crucified and Risen Divine Saviour. They seal the grave of Christ, indeed of every man, against resurrection to new life and against transcendence from the tribulations of time. Their existentialist philosophies and theologies beget doom and despair; their individualistic, self-decisional faiths beget stoically isolated heroes, not saints.

In contrast, faith in Christ as the true Son of God begets the family of God in the bosom of humanity. The New Testament Cross is an altar

of saving sacrifice; Bultmann's cross is a mere signpost. The resurrection
of the Gospels is "the first fruits" of Christ's and man's victory over the
forces of sin and death; Bultmann's resurrection is a verbal, empty symbol
of a fictitious conquest of death. Moreover, Bultmann's theology is strangely
silent about the intimate life of the Trinity; it has nothing of the splendour
or love of the trinitarian ministrations to man in creation, salvation, sanctification and glorification. Eschatological marvels disappear in Bultmann's
compressed hermeneutics. Within them the Christian is isolated, suffering
spiritual cramps as an ecclesiastical orphan. For the Church as a community
and the People of God is totally neglected by both Heidegger and Bultmann.
For Bultmann, the Church as a building is simply another place where
individuals, juxtaposed in crowds, privately choose or refuse God on hearing
the preaching of the Word. Church institutions, liturgy and sacraments
do not constitute for Bultmann a sacred social service in which the people
of God worship and work together. Church affiliation, in fact all ecclesiology
in his system of thought, is myth and magic. Rejecting holy bonds among
men, Bultmann repeats Luther's protestation that "the entire world is
merely profane territory." On quiet reflection, then, the existential
philosophy of Heidegger and the anthropological theology of Bultmann
founded on that philosophy turn out to be starkly cruel pauperizations of
the sublime revelations in the Gospels. Such great popes as St. Pius X and
Pius XII exposed the modern attempts to dilute the faith. They pointed
out that the movement known as Modernism is an attempt to make the
true faith palatable to the thought of the day by repudiating its objective,
supernatural character and reducing it to a matter of individual religious
psychology. It would be wise to remind ourselves that philospher —
Heidegger and theologian — Bultmann, wittingly or unwittingly it matters
not, have teamed up to launch upon the world the scourge of Neo-
Modernism. Perhaps, in order to understand the spirit of this movement,
no better advice could be given students of Heidegger, Bultmann and the
New Testament than that found in C.S. Lewis's pertinent book, *Miracles*:

> When you turn from the New Testament to modern scholars,
> remember you go among them as sheep among wolves. Natural-
> istic assumptions...will meet you on every side — even from
> the pens of clergymen. This does not mean (as I was often tempted
> to suspect) that these clergymen are disguised apostates who
> deliberately exploit the position and livelihood given them by the
> Christian Church to undermine Christianity. It comes partly from
> what we may call a 'hangover.' We all have Naturalism in our
> bones and even conversion does not at once work the infection
> out of our system. Its assumptions rush back upon the mind the
> moment vigilance is relaxed. And in part the procedure of these

scholars arises from the feeling which is greatly to their credit — which indeed is honorable to the point of being Quixotic. They are anxious to allow the enemy every advantage he can with any show of fairness claim. They thus make it part of their method to eliminate the supernatural wherever it is even remotely possible to do so, to strain explanation even to the breaking point before they admit the least suggestion of a miracle. . . In using the books of such people you must therefore be continually on your guard. You must develop a nose like a bloodhound for those steps in the argument which depend not on historical and linguistic knowledge but on the concealed assumption that miracles are impossible, improbable or improper.[9]

Notes

[1]Rudolf Bultmann, *Kerygma und Mythos,* Hamburg, Vol. II, p. 192.

[2]W.J. Richardson, *Heidegger: Through Phenomenology to Thought,* The Hague, 1963, pp. 663-671.

[3]Thomas F. O'Meara, O.P. and Donald M. Weisser, O.P., Editors, *Rudolf Bultmann in Catholic Thought;* essay by Helmut Peukert, "Bultmann and Heidegger," New York, Herder and Herder, 1968, p. 204.

[4]André Malet, *The Thought of Rudolf Bultmann,* translated by Richard Strachan, Doubleday & Company, New York, 1971, p. 331.

[5]Martin Heidegger, *Being and Time,* translated by John Macquarrie and Edward Robinson, Blackwell, Oxford, England, 1967, pp. 228-235.

[6]John Macquarrie, *An Existentialist Theology,* Harper Torchbooks, New York, 1965, pp. 84, 85.

[7]Ibid., pp. 22, 23.

[8]Harold Riesenfeld, "The Gospel Traditions and Its Beginnings." B. Gerhardsson, *Memory and Manuscript.* Both of these works are treated in an article by Joseph A. Fitzmayer, S.J., "Memory and Manuscript: The Origins and the Transmission of the Gospel Tradition." *Theological Studies,* Sept. 1962, pp. 442-457.

[9]C.S. Lewis, *Miracles,* pp. 197 ff. Quoted also by E.L. Mascall in his book, *The Secularization of Christianity,* Holt, Rinehart and Winston, New York, 1965, pp. 235, 236.

Reprinted from *Rehabilitierung der Philosophie (Rehabilitation of Philosophy)* Bookfest in honor of Dr. Balduin Schwarz, international philosopher, 1974.

Sartre's Rage Against God

Sartre relates his final break with God in an incident which drew from him anger and blasphemy.

> For several years longer, I kept up public relations with the Almighty; in private, I stopped associating with Him. Once only I had the feeling that he existed. I had been playing with matches and had burnt a mat; I was busy covering up my crime when suddenly, God saw me. I felt His gaze inside my head and on my hands; I turned round and round in the bathroom, horribly visible, a living target. I was saved by indignation: I grew angry at such a crude lack of tact, and blasphemed, muttering like my grandfather: 'Sacré nom de Dieu, de nom de Dieu, de nom de Dieu.' He never looked at me again.[1]

Whatever life and strength it has, all atheism, negative or positive, has its power from its awareness of God. It is a parasite that feeds on God. Comte and Marx substituted Humanity — the scientific priesthood and the proletarian masses — as the God of positivism and socialism who would explain, justify and fulfill the course of world history for the temporal happiness of society. Sartre, on the other hand, divinizes the individual. Each individual, in his absolute denial and rejection of God establishes himself as the ultimate creator of meaning, missions and morals in a world of endless discord and contradiction. The only authentic enterprise capable of achieving human greatness is the life totally committed to the revolt against God, religion of any kind, but especially against Christianity. It is hardly surprising, then, that throughout his literary works Sartre challenges man to act alone, boldly, without any other justification for his deeds than to defy and destroy God. In The Flies, Orestes has just killed his mother in an act of rebellion against the whole moral order of God. He flings this defiance into the face of the offended God: "You will have no power over me except the power which I myself acknowledge. You created me but you did not have to create me free. You are God and I am free. We are both equally alone."[2]

In the drama, The Devil and the Good Lord, Sartre sets out to prove that God does not exist and that, even if he did, he would be a cruel useless tyrant. His hero is a German cavalry officer of the sixteenth century, named Goetz. Goetz performs evil for the sake of evil, but above all because evil provokes God. He rejects doing good because "what is good has already been done...by God the Father. As for me, I invent."[3] He kills his brother and rejoices over the deed because by it he made "God's heart bleed." "God is the only adversary worthy of me. I shall crucify God tonight," he boasts, as he plans to massacre twenty-thousand inhabitants of the city of Worms. The reasoning behind this prospective massacre is quite perverse. "God's suffering is infinite and that makes the one who makes Him suffer likewise infinite." When the prophet Nasti attempts to persuade him to abandon his nefarious plan, Goetz objects vigorously:

But what do I care for mankind? God hears me; it is God I am deafening and that is enough for me, for he is the only enemy worthy of my talents...It is God I shall crucify this night, through you, and through twenty-thousand men, because His suffering is infinite and renders infinite those whom he causes to suffer. This city will go up in flames. God knows that. At this moment He is afraid; I can feel it, I can feel His eyes on my hand, His breath on my hair, His angels shed tears. He is saying to Himself: 'Perhaps Goetz will not dare...' exactly as if He were a man. Weep, angels; I shall dare. In a few moments I will march in His fear and His anger. The city shall blaze; the soul of the Lord is a hall of mirrors, the fire will be reflected in a thousand mirrors. Then I shall know that I am an unalloyed monster.[4]

When it is desperately pointed out to Goetz that to do good is far more difficult than to do evil and infinitely more God-like, he is fascinated with this reasoning, abandons his plan against the city and agrees, on a bet, to live for a year and a day as a hermit-saint. Goetz enters upon a strange Sartrean life of penance. He fasts and vows perfect chastity. Yet, despite this vow, this remarkable monk continues to keep his mistress. But, of course, the arrangement becomes perfectly reasonable when it is realized that his mistress's presence is essential to his penitential life, since Goetz also employs her to whip him in a traditionally masochistic ritual. The conversion is never more than a spiritual perversion, despite Sartre's efforts to convince us of its authenticity. The peasants themselves can smell its hypocrisy. In the end, a year and a day later, when the city of Love he worked to establish is destroyed by war, Goetz, in bitter disillusionment, turns on the silent God who abandons even those who serve Him.

I alone, I supplicated, I demanded a sign, I sent messages to Heaven. No reply. Heaven ignored my very name. Each minute I wondered what I could BE in the eyes of God. Now I know the answer: nothing. God does not see me, God does not hear me, God does not know me. You see this emptiness above our heads? That is God. You see this gap in the door? It is God. You see that hole in the ground? That is God again. Silence is God. Absence is God. God is the loneliness of man. There was no one but myself; I alone decided on Evil; I alone invented Good...I, man. If God exists, man is nothing; if man exists...Heinrich,

> I am going to tell you a colossal joke: God does not exist. . . He
> does not exist. . . Joy, tears of joy. Alleluia! I have liberated us.
> No more Heaven, no more Hell; nothing but earth. . . Farewell
> to monsters, farewell to saints. Only men exist[5].

Back to the life of crime goes Goetz with a vengeance. He brings his comedy
of good to an end with a murder. In a struggle to the death with the possessed
priest, Heinrich, Goetz stabs his opponent mortally. His new cause is to
be a man among men, to fight for mankind's betterment. He assumes
command of the peasant armies and plans a war against their exploiters.
But to do this successfully, he tells the prophet Nasti, that he must begin
again at the beginning. When Nasti asks what that beginning is, Goetz
explains:

> Crime. Men of the present day are born criminals. I must demand
> my share of their crimes if I want to have my share of their love
> and virtue. I wanted pure love: ridiculous nonsense. To love
> anyone is to hate the same enemy; therefore, I will adopt your
> hates. I wanted to do Good: foolishness. On this earth at present
> Good and Evil are inseparable. I agree to be bad in order to
> become good. . . I killed God because He divided me from man-
> kind, and now I see that His death has isolated me even more
> surely. I shall not allow this huge carcass to poison my human
> friendships. . .[6]

Sartre is fond of attacking Christianity. His animus against the
Christian God seems to be a classic case of the souring of a disappointed
lover. As his estrangement from the Christian God became more and more
embittered, Sartre, after the manner of a modern Voltaire, caricatured the
image, dogmas and history of the Christian religion. He loved to use its
theological language for the joy he experienced at always perverting it. He
held it against God that man was trapped in an absurd rat-race of existence
in a cruel world. He deeply resented the frustration and gloom of being
superfluous. "I had been told over and over again that I was a gift from
heaven, much longed for, indispensable. . . I no longer believed this, I still
felt that you were born superfluous."[7]

Unfortunately, the relatives and friends of his family milieu were incapable of introducing Sartre to the majesty of the true God of revelation,
the divine mission of Christ and the sublime destiny of each man through
his call to membership in His Church. Sartre himself has spoken of a public
dechristianization which deplores the style and manner of the faith. He
describes in piquant terms the family performance at Sunday services. "On
Sundays the ladies sometimes went to Mass, to hear some good music or
a well-known organist: neither of them was a practising Catholic, but the

faith of others helped them to ecstatic enjoyment of the music. They believed in God just long enough to enjoy a toccata.''[8]

Moreover, Sartre can never quite rid himself of the obsession that God is looking at him. He fights against this vague menace all his life, in his own experiences and those of his main literary characters who are really his alter egos. Just as the look of God had frightened and angered him when he had set fire to a mat, so too, on a memorable occasion when he was going to school, he again encountered God and again had to dismiss Him.

> One morning, in 1917, at la Rochelle, I was waiting for some companions who were supposed to accompany me to the *lycée;* they were late. Soon I could think of nothing more to distract myself, and I decided to think about the Almighty. He at once tumbled down into the blue sky and vanished without explanation: He does not exist, I said to myself, in polite astonishment, and I thought the matter was settled. In one sense it was, because I have never since had the least temptation to revive Him.[9]

Sartre has not given the temptation to revive God the slightest opportunity to present itself. The reason is that he has been so busy mocking and deriding the mythical God of the Christians. He has traveled a long road of estrangement from God between the age of thirteen, the end of his life-period covered by *The Words,* and his present exalted arrogance toward the deity. As a boy, his parting with God vibrates with tremulous regret and nostaglia. "I needed God...He was given to me...Unable to take root in my heart, he vegetated in me for a while and then died...there might have been something between us." Forty years later, regret and nostaglia have degenerated into scornful derision. In perhaps the most blasphemous scene he has created throughout his many dramas and novels, Sartre, incarnated in Goetz, wallows madly in a Luciferian assault against the crucified Christ. Goetz's mistress, Catherine, in a dying, delirious condition and pleading for a priest to hear her confession, is brought to the Church in the presence of Goetz and laid at the feet of the life-sized crucifix. The priests flee the church, refusing her any last sacraments. The faithful remain to mock and consign her soul to hell. In a rage, Goetz clears the church and, alone with the dying sinner, addresses the crucified Christ, begging a sign of Catherine's salvation:

> Lord, these sins are mine. Thou knowest it. Render to me what rightfully belongs to me. Thou hast no right to condemn this woman since I alone am guilty. Give me a sign! My arms are ready; my face and breast are prepared. Blast my cheeks; let her sins become puss oozing from my eyes and ears; let them

burn like acid into my back, my thighs and my genitals. Strike me with leprosy, cholera, the plague, but redeem her!

Didst Thou die for mankind, yes or no? Look down on us: mankind is suffering. Thou must begin to die again! Give! Give me Thy wounds! Give me the wound in Thy right side, the two holes in Thy hands. If God could suffer for their sins, why cannot a man? Art Thou jealous of me? Give me Thy stigmata! Give me Thy wounds! Give me Thy wounds! Art Thou deaf? Good heavens, how stupid I am! God helps those who help themselves! (*He draws a dagger from his belt, stabs the palm of his left hand, then the palm of his right hand and then finally his side. Then he throws the dagger behind the altar and leaning forward, marks the breast of the Christ with blood.*)

Come back, all of you! The Christ has bled. See, in His infinite mercy, he has allowed me to bear His stigmata. The blood of Christ, my brothers, the blood of Christ is flowing from my hands. Fear no more, my love. I touch your forehead, your eyes and lips with the blood of our Lord Jesus Christ. . .Die in peace. . .The blood of Christ, Catherine.

Catherine dies in the presence of her new saviour with these words: "Your blood, Goetz your blood. You have shed it for me."[10]

Irrational assumptions of Sartrean atheism

It is now time to evaluate the symmetrical appearance of the Sartrean synthesis of reality. His first exceedingly gratuitous assumption is a metaphysical assertion. Rejecting previous forms of dualism, Sartre apodictically presents, in the first chapters of his *Being and Nothingness,* his own radical dualism. It states that all being is divded into *l'en-soi,* being as it is itself, and *le pour-soi,* human consciousness. There is no being beyond these. Now the world of objects, that is, non-human reality, is so strong, so dense as to be completely meaningless. By contrast, human reality is so weak, so contingent that it is confounded with nothingness. Radically, then all being is absurd, superfluous. No proof is attempted to establish the truth of this dualism. These are, in reality, a matter of choice; no proof is needed for what one chooses to postulate. Here is Sartre's basic act of faith. The following six hundred pages elaborate and defend this metaphysical dogma.

Whereas other thinkers explained consciousness in terms of a spiritual dimension and high fruition of the superior being man, Sartre holds the opposite. Other philosophers have demonstrated that the world's many characteristics of unity, beauty, intelligibility, order and diversity, already present ontologically, become humanly actualized in the awakened and appreciative mind. But for Sartre, the conscious mind is a hole, a tear, a secreter of ''nothing'' in the otherwise solid wall of being. This perverse, unproven axiom sets up the specious proof for the non-existence of God. For it establishes, by pronouncement alone, the absence of order, meaning, direction in the world. Discord, contradiction, nothingness, chaos reign at the heart of each thing and within the ensemble of all things. The two types of being metaphysically oppose each other; they render God, not only non-existent, but impossible. For God, in order to exist, would have to be the self-identification of Infinite consciousness with the world of objects. But on Sartre's initial assumption, consciousness and the world of objects are mutually exclusive. Moreover, since there is no consciousness apart from the world — for consciousness is always consciousness of something — God not only does not exist, but *creatio ex nihilo* is also impossible. For creation would presuppose God already existing as a conscious subject before there were objects to be conscious of. Now this situation would deny the very nature of consciousness. Of course, Sartre assumes here that God is conscious of beings other than Himself in a way that is identical to man's consciousness. But if we admit that God's consciousness is supposed to be like man's in a univocal sense, then certainly we cannot conceive God creating the world. Thus, by an initially optional division of all being, by an imposition of inherently contradictory definitions on these modes of being, by the arbitrary announcement that God could only be the unity of these contradictions, were they raised to the infinite and personalized degree, Sartre has conveniently pre-arranged that God not only does not exist, but cannot exist. For God would have to be the identification of the ideal with the real, something consciousness reveals to be utterly impossible. The Sartrean atheism, therefore, is founded on the metaphysical misinformation that all being is inherently: contradictory, meaningless, absurd and superfluous.

Of course, the Christian thinker sees the basic error in Sartre's ontology. Consciousness is not a lack, a minus of being; it is rather a fuller achievement, a plus of being. If man's consciousness appears for no reason at all, if it has no relationship to an absolute consciousness, then all thinking is impossible. For thinking is a pursuit that presupposes a pursued. And truth is the reality so avidly pursued. Now if the thinking process ''secretes nothing'' as its inevitable product, instead of grasping fuller truth, then truth is non-existent and Sartre's own philosophizing is undermined. Moreover, the Christian mind sees no contradiction in the unification of infinite, dynamic self-consciousness and immutable, infinitely perfect being. For the Christian this is exactly what God is insofar as the human mind can grasp Him darkly. God it utter, total Self-consciousness, sheer Dynamism while simultaneously being pure, immutable, permanent Being. For the

Christian, God is a mystery not a logical problem; God is an infinite Paradox, not an unintelligible contradiction. The Christian does not know how these paradoxical characteristics cohere in the Absolute Being; he cannot explain their presence in a positive manner. Yet he knows that there is no contradiction, that these characteristics are not mutually exclusive. And he knows this truth in a negative way, from the very analysis of the concepts involved. Sartre, in placing a contradiction between these aspects of being, is concluding beyond the evidence that is available. Moreover, what the Christian mind knows through the deductions of native reason in a negative manner, it also knows more amply and positively through the revelation of faith. The one God is infinitely self-conscious because He is three Divine Persons. This God knows himself perfectly in the Person of the Absolute, Substantial Word. He loves Himself in the Person of the Substantial Spirit. The Christian at least has the intrinsic, metaphysical consistency of the concepts garnered from philosophical reflection and the external, revelationary testimony received from the God-Man to assert and defend his adherence to God. Sartre has neither the one nor the other of these sources of truth to corroborate his atheistic ontology. As a matter of fact, Sartre never claims that his ontology can *demonstrate* the truth of his atheism. It is with him more a matter of choice. In the final analysis, God does not and cannot exist for Sartre because Sartre wants it and prearranged it that way.

We pass now to the moral assumption for the non-existence of God. It states that: God is irreconcilable with human freedom. For, if God as Absolute Liberty existed, then man would be caught in the inescapable strait-jacket of determinism. If God the creator determines what it means to be human, then freedom has vanished into man's total dependence upon God. But to be free means to be a subject, which is what man is. And far from being produced as an essence according to a pre-conceived plan of God, the "Superior Artisan," man rather falls into existence through the exercise of his power of choosing. Thus, being totally independent of a non-existent God, man is absolutely free to create his own values, whatever he will become in himself and whatever the world will mean to him. Sartre falls into the metaphysical trap of presupposing that the definition of essence excludes freedom. Moreover, he merely assumes that the definition of existence demands that it always precede essence. Once again, as in the case of being, the origin of liberty is utterly absurd; it has no metaphysical or reasonable foundation.

On the contrary, the Christian sees that capacities come with every new being, every new nature. Freedom is present as a potentiality even before the child beings to exercise it. Where does it come from? Sartre holds that freedom, like all being, is superfluous, absurd; it comes from nowhere. He calls freedom a "sickness" of human existence. The Christian, on the other hand, sees liberty as an essential qualification of the human individual, a gift given freely by God with the gift of human nature itself. True, liberty is an ambiguous power capable of destroying its possessor according to his responsible or irresponsible exercise of it. Once again Sartre makes God and man free in an univocal sense; once again he fails to understand the paradoxical nature of the freedom in God and the freedom in man. If God's absolute freedom were identical to man's freedom, then, of course, we could not conceive how man could be free. He would be a mere automoton or puppet directed wholly by the divine decisions. But, of course, this is not the case; man is conscious of directing himself by his own decisions. God is absolutely free, yet He does not suffocate the freedom of man. How are the two freedoms possible, if man is totally dependent on God as a creature? We are again in the presence of a mystery, a truth above and beyond, but not against, reason. But Sartre superficially concludes that this relationship must produce determinism. Sartre rejects all mysteries, except the mystery of the absurdity of all reality. For the Christian, freedom is a mysterious gift from the Absolute Freedom, God. For Sartre, freedom is a mysterious curse from the absolute Absurdity of the World of reality.

Yet Sartre is right and does man a great service when he analyzes the relationship between anxiety and freedom. Each person alone must decide whether he will seek the divine or the demonic. Despite the aweful responsibility involved, man must not allow the feeling of dread to paralyze him. He must choose or suffer the degradation of "bad faith" and immoral existence. Sartre is unhappy about having to face life and its decisions alone. It is most distressing to him that God's support is unavailable. For man, isolated and unsupported, is condemned to invent himself every moment. In this nostalgic analysis Sartre unwittingly witnesses to the truth that God is real, that He stirs the soul of man by arousing his metaphysical hunger, conscience and liberty for the Absolute Other. Man cannot remain unmoved when he contemplates the abyss between God and himself, between reason and revelation, between the message from God and the message from himself. Sartre again serves man well by insisting that his misgivings over these sacred decisions cannot be surmounted merely by dispassionate proofs, norms and principles. Witnessing to truth and moral causes must also be made through decisive action. Truth and meaning are not only attained in thinking but also in action.

But Sartre's conclusion is all wrong. Man does not have "to go it alone" in an absurd world with the desperate exercise of his unlimited freedom. God and religion are not merely human projections, as all intellectual atheists from Hegel to the present teach. The reality of God is quite compatible with each man's reason and freedom, since Absolute Intelligence and Liberty is essentially diffusive of itself and is the very source of man's endowment with these spiritual powers. Thus the presence of God in reality is not a projection, but a call to communion. And religion is the dialectic of that communion, a dialectic of truth and love, of sacrifice and self-donation. True, this communion does not of itself remove anxiety from the human condition, for during the temporary testing period of the dialectic there is always the possibility of man's fall into infidelity. Thus, Sartre's error consists in making man's freedom the whole meaning and story of life. The unrestricted exercise of each man's freedom cannot begin to give an adequate account of the world, human beings, truth, morality and man's destiny. To say that it can is to identify all values — true or false, wicked or noble — with the capricous choices of all men. From that erroneous principle there can only emerge a project for social suicide. We now wish to evaluate that project.

What can be said of Sartre's social assumption that intersubjective love is impossible? First, this teaching is built upon the fundamental doctrines of atheism and the absolute freedom of man. In that sense it is both an assumption and a conclusion. It is an assumption insofar as it is not at all demonstrated to be a universal truth. It is a conclusion in so far as it is a logical result of Sartre's break with the Absolute Other and his seizure of unlimited liberty for each man. The Christian thinker rejects Sartre's narrow explanation of the role of the other in interpersonal relations. It is not true that the only role of the other is to achieve the destruction of my subjectivity. Nor is that my goal in relationship to the subjectivity of my fellowmen. The other is not always a hostile, conniving, seducing starer, plotting how he can dominate me. The purpose of intersubjective relations is not to dominate or be dominated. It is simply not true that no other intersubjective relationship is possible than sado-masochistic interaction. It is a travesty on love to reduce it to being merely one form of domination along with seduction, hate, desire and cruelty. Christian thinkers reject this sick analysis of man's social relationships.

Christians see in the initial relationship of man with God a communication of gifts and a communion of destinies in mutual love. The Transcendent Lover bestows being, dignity, mission, destiny on man as the other whom He has loved and called into His presence. The Transcendent Lover gives Himself freely without any hint of trying to dominate the freedom of man, but rather honoring him with an invitation to collaborate with His Benefactor in the venture toward human sanctity and happiness. Neither is the No of conflict the only answer men give to the call of their fellowmen. Indeed, millions of martyrs, confessors, virgins, saints from all walks of life have answered Yes to the invitation of God to live with Him. And in answering Yes to God, they have also said Yes to their fellowmen. Nor is the essence of man's relationships incarnated in the look of hate. For Sartre, every look is of hate, every embrace a "kiss of death." Granted that the kiss of Judas is always a possibility, the fact is that it is not the only possibility; it is not the only predetermined eventuality in man's social life. If it were, where would be that vaunted, unlimited freedom Sartre claims for man?

There is also the look of love, genuine, concerned with the happiness of the other. This look expresses a will to communion, to service, not to domination. The look of God creates human persons: "I have loved thee with an everlasting love, therefore, have I drawn thee, taking pity on thee." The Gospels record that the look of Christ raises up, restores, saves man. The look of Christ melted Peter into repentence; the look of Christ transformed Magdalene from sinner into saint; the look of Christ raised in an instant with Himself into paradise a blaspheming thief on the verge of hell. The person of every child is created by the loving looks of its parents and relatives. The truth is that man thrives as a person under the light of the approval of others. In the end, the look of love conquers the look of hate. It is never Christ who flees the gaze of Satan; it is Satan who flees the look of Chirst and begs for asylum in swine. But the look of love creates subjectivity in both lover and beloved because in its expansive climate of mutual self-donation the lovers achieve the plenitude of their beings as persons. In every intersubjective relation, in every society the last word on its social vigor is not with the mind but with whether one loves. Sartre does not love; he does not even love himself, for according to the abstractions of his mind, love is an impossible ideal. Society is a jungle of scheming tyrants seeking to dominate one another. Such a social philosophy can only beget a society of murderers or a society of suicides, depending on whether men decide to seize power or despair over attaining the grace of communion.

In the spirit of ethical adventuresomeness, Sartre attacks what he calls "the spirit of seriousness" and equates it with "bad faith." When men appeal to a universal moral law in the hope of dodging hard decisions, they are acting false roles. When men immerse themselves in God, prayer, religious services or transcendent activities of any kind, they are fleeing the tasks of freedom for this life. Thus Freudians with thier libidos, communists with their classless society, Christians with their heaven, anyone who deceives himself about the present duty by concentrating his faith on the future, all these are hiding behind "the spirit of seriousness" but living in "bad faith." What then is good faith in Sartre's social philosophy?

Good faith is practiced by the man who works to liberate himself from his own egotism and to collaborate for the freedom of others. Thus, when Sartre, in the day of the underground Resistance, schemed and worked for the freedom of France and French prisoners, he was living in "good faith", for he was living for others. This was certainly morally good activity. No Christian would quarrel with this self-commitment. But the question arises: How is such commitment to the good of others possible under the Sartrean social theories? For under his theory of universal conflict in interpersonal relations, such commitment to the welfare of others is well-nigh impossible. According to Sartre, men do not know what is good for other men since they have no nature, no values, no liberty, no destiny in common. Moreover, each man's exercise of liberty is always aimed at enslaving others. Sartre's theory denies the possibility of common sociality among men; in practice he now demands self-commitment to others. Moreover, his phenomenological descriptions of intepersonal activities stress egotism and conflict, frustration rather than social fruition. It is this inconsistency between doctrine and deed that has led the Marxists to dismiss Sartre's thinking as "the last, convulsive effort of the alienated individual in a dying bourgeois world."

For all its vaunted phenomenological method, Sartre's philosophy is in its main themes a product of pure subjectivism, a creation of a mind divorced from concrete reality. Sartre is, in a word, the worst kind of rationalist, the kind that expresses contempt and irreverence for concrete reality and favors a towering love for the disembodied mind. He himself testifies in *The Words* on how he became that way:

> A Platonist by condition, I moved from knowledge to its objects; I found ideas more real than things, because they were the first to give themselves to me and because they gave themselves like things. I met the universe in books: assimilated, classified, labelled and studied, but still impressive; and I confused the chaos of my experience through books with the hazardous course of real events. Hence my idealism which it took me thirty years to undo[11].

The truth is that Sartre always confused "the chaos of his experience through books...with the course of real events." The truth is that he has failed to undo his idealism or rationalism. Who, but a man hopelessly divorced from and hostile to the sacred, concrete mystery of parenthood, could have written this unrealistic nonsense against human love: "The rule is that there are no good fathers; it is not the men who are at fault but the paternal bond which is rotten. There is nothing better than to produce children but what a sin to *have* some!"[12]

It is tragic to watch Sartre move from idol to idol in a vain effort to replace his banished God. The sign of the sacred has shifted from Catholicism to Belles-Lettres, to fame as a writer, to revolution on behalf of social causes under the banner of socialism and Marxism. Today Sartre admits his complete disillusionment over his chosen idols: "... I know quite well that no one is waiting for me. I have renounced my vocation but I have not unfrocked myself. I still write. What else can I do?"[13]

Sartre has analyzed sin with deep penetration. It is the bitter estrangement from God and from our fellowman. It is the great divine-human schism. He has exploded the secularized myths that guarantee man happiness in and through temporal achievements. No present, no future earthly conditions of man will ever make life worth living. He has stressed once again, in a stark manner, man's personal responsibility for making his own being and world. He has focused the mind and heart of man on his great power of freedom with all its dangerous possibilities. He has ruthlessly unmasked the poses men take to escape hard decisions. He has re-created the confrontation between freedom and grace. He has forced the collectivized atheism of Positivism and Marxism to come out from behind their protective wall of science and politics in order to prove to the individual that absurd existence is worth living. He has put their panaceas to a severe test.

But in the last analysis Sartre's philosophy leads logically and directly to despair and suicide. His doctrine of salvation leads men to the abyss of atomism. His first and final word on life, liberty and love is that they just happen and are always absurd, contradictory and doomed to frustration. His world of atheism is a kingdom of nothingness plunged into intellectual darkness, convulsed with spiritual hate and peopled by inhabitants who curse God and destroy each other in their vain attempt to seize His vacant throne.

Notes

[1] Jean-Paul Sartre, *The Words*, A Penguin Book, London, Translated by Irene Clephane, 1967, p. 65.
[2] Jean-Paul-Sartre, *No exit and three other plays*, Vintage Books, New York, translated by Stuart Gilbert, 1963.
[3] Jean-Paul-Sartre, *The Devil and the Good Lord and two other plays*, Vintage books, translated by Kitty Black, New York, 1962, p. 46.
[4] Ibid., p. 55.
[5] Ibid., pp. 141-142.
[6] Ibid., pp. 145, 147.
[7] Jean-Paul-Sartre, *The Words*, Penguin, London, Translated by Irene Clephane, 1967, pp. 104-105.
[8] Ibid., p. 19.
[9] Ibid., pp. 155-156.
[10] Jean-Paul-Sartre, *The Devil and the Good Lord and two other Plays*, Vintage Books, translated by Kitty Black, New York, 1962, pp. 101-102.
[11] Jean-Paul-Sartre, *The Words*, Penguin, London, Translated by Irene Clephane, 1967, p. 34.
[12] Ibid., p. 14.
[13] Ibid., p. 157.

Reprinted from *Warheit, Wert Und Sein (Truth, Value and Being)*, a Bookfest honoring Dr. Dietrich von Hildebrand, famous international philosopher and author on his eightieth birthday, 1970.

Dietrich von Hildebrand:
Philosopher and Prophet of Truth

Dietrich von Hildebrand, son of the famous sculptor Adolf von Hildebrand, was born October 12, 1889 in Florence, Italy where his father was working at his art. He passed his first eight years in Florence, a city he ardently loved all his life. Italian was the first language he spoke, being as proficient in it as the scholarly natives. From age eight to sixteen he spent six months in Florence and six months in Munich where his father was creating three magnificent sculpted fountains, today the marvel of all who view them. Because of constant travel, Dietrich was taught by special tutors and completed his studies in rhetoric at age sixteen. Then he went off to the University of Munich.

There he met Max Scheler whose genius and personality were a deep inspiration to him. Already at nineteen years of age von Hildebrand was critical of some of Scheler's philosophical positions. From Munich he went to Goettingen and studied under Edmund Husserl and Adolf Reinach. He attained his doctorate in 1912. That same year he married Margaret Denck and they had one son, Franz. In 1914 he and his wife converted to Catholicism. He obtained a teaching position at the University of Munich where he lectured from 1919 to 1933. During these years he had already undertaken a prophetic crusade against totalitarian ideologies. For in the fall of 1923, when the Nazis attempted their *Putsch* in Munich, he had to flee for his life. The Nazis sought to kill him for his public opposition to their grotesque philosophy of racism.

God had given von Hildebrand an all-consuming love for truth. Throughout his long life of 87 years he never compromised on truth. God also endowed him with a remarkable vision of mind that discerned at once the nature and morality of the metaphysical, moral, religious and political movements of his day. In advance of almost everyone else, he grasped and exposed the errors and evils of Nazism and Communism. Even when vast numbers of his fellow Christians — bishops, priests, intellectuals and men of good will — hailed the coming to power of Hitler, von Hildebrand raised his voice and plied his pen against this tyrant and all he stood for. Von Hildebrand revealed to his countrymen how man is never content with merely forsaking the fountains of living water in Christianity, but moves on to hew broken cisterns as substitutes. Nazism and Communism were the broken cisterns hewn by the enemies of God and man; these cisterns could neither hold water nor sustain life. They would produce a deluge of death and destruction. Unfortunately, too many Christians, like the Israelites of old, were casting off God and his revelations in Christ. They refused to listen to God's prophets and fell down before the idols of racism, totalitarianism and militarism. Von Hildebrand had come too soon with his message of warning; he was too far ahead of his time. The people were living in the delirium of national exaltation and could foresee nothing but victory and prosperity on the horizon. This prophet of doom was a nuisance and a traitor to Pan-Germanism. Not only was he not listened to, he was opposed. Von Hildebrand decided to flee Germany and to fight for his country as an exile. Then began his perilous Odyssey, a flight that kept him one step ahead of the agents of tyranny who sought to kill him.

Von Hildebrand abandoned the magnificent home of his father and his teaching position at the University of Munich. He went to Florence and lived at the home of his sister, his total possessions being 100 D. Mark. This was in 1933 when the Nazis succeeded in coming to power. Again von Hildebrand escaped just in time, for the Nazis had already condemned him to death for his public opposition to their racist Weltanschauung. At the end of 1933 von Hildebrand offered his services to chancellor Dollfuss of Austria. He founded, under the patronage of the Chancellor, a weekly review, *Christliche Staendestaat,* an anti-nazi publication dedicated to unmasking the falsities and cruelties of Nazism and Communism. Von Hildebrand wrote 80 articles for this weekly. He exposed Nazism and Communism as twin devils, the former a totalitarianism of the crooked cross dressed in brown, the latter a totalitarianism of the hammer and sicle dressed in red; the former a national, the latter an international Fascism.

Escape from the Nazis

In 1935 von Hildebrand became professor of philosophy at the University of Vienna. The Nazis attempted to prevent him from giving his courses. But the Minister of Education sent 48 police agents to protect him in his work. It was known that Chancellor Dollfuss was pleased with the work and writings of von Hildebrand. Chancellor Dollfuss was assassinated in July 1934. On February 12, 1938 Hitler held a meeting with Austrian Chancellor Schuschnigg at which he insisted that von Hildebrand's activity should be curbed. Four weeks after this meeting, the *Anschluss* took place; Austria was violently invaded and annexed by Nazi Germany. Nazi agents swiftly seized the apartment in which von Hildebrand lived. They knew the place and apartment perfectly. They went directly to a secret hiding place in the chimney to get their victim. But von Hildebrand had miraculously escaped on March 11, 1938, thanks to his Swiss passport, possessed as an inheritance from his grandfather Bruno who had become an honorary citizen of Switzerland. As a refugee in Switzerland he lived off the charity of his friends and the kindness of Swiss Catholics. In 1939 he was invited by Msgr. Bruno de Solages to become professor at the University of Toulouse. But in 1940 the Gestapo was again on his heels. In Vienna the Prefect of Police, learning that the Nazi underground was planning to assassinate von Hildebrand, called and warned him to take precautions for his life. He was saved thanks to the devoted heroism of Edmond Michelet who furnished him with false papers, enabling him to flee France, pass through Spain and arrive in Portugal. Once in Portugal, he learned that the Rockefeller Foundation had been looking for him for several weeks. Jacques Maritain, his friend, had persuaded the Foundation to place von Hildebrand's name on a list of 100 persons they would work to rescue from the Nazis. Von Hildebrand had so successfully covered his tracks out of France that no one knew where he was. He remained some time in Portugal and then left for the United States by way of Brazil. In New York he became professor of philosophy at Fordham University where he taught until 1960, the year of his retirement. He lost his first wife in 1957 and in 1959 he married Alice Jourdain, his pupil and then his collaborator.

The work of von Hildebrand

Von Hildebrand is an original, world-famous Christian thinker. His work is characterized by three major features: reverence for the human person, joy in the affirmation of the world of values and zeal in the exposition of the fecundity of the intimate inter-relationship between a living Christian faith and philosophical thought. He has produced a most impressive body of work since he started writing over sixty-five years ago. Never a mere scientific spectator, von Hildebrand is not interested in making philosophy an idea, or word or problem game. He never overwhelms his reader with *tour de force* formulas or obscure, pedantic expressions. He is an ardent seeker and joyful herald of truth wherever it can be discovered, in the freshness of things, the mystery of persons, the flash of divine revelation. Herald though he is, he is, nevertheless, rigorously insistent on precision and objectivity. Yet for all his objectivity, he never wraps himself in the mantle of neutralism. His work leaves no doubt that truth and holiness are meant to be mankind's common treasure and that this philosopher works to make both come alive in his fellowmen. But though he presents truth in a direct and enthusiastic manner, von Hildebrand knows that the human person is so sacred that truth can never be forced upon him. In all his works von Hildebrand allows truth to speak for itself. He hopes his reader will freely work to achieve what he has presented.

Perhaps von Hildebrand's greatest, most original contributions to philosophy have been made in the field of values, natural and supernatural. He clearly explains that values can never be neutral. Indeed their non-neutrality is an essential characteristic of values. For it belongs to the essence of values that they demand an appropriate response from persons. The necessity of adequate value-response is a truth brought forth by von Hildebrand which sheds completely new light on the profound relationship between human persons and the whole hierarchy of values, from God in whom all values are founded to the lowliest of creatures which radiates value in some degree. Von Hildebrand has explored in an inspiring way the truth that what makes man fully human, what makes him more than human, indeed divine, is his capacity to understand, to be influenced by and to respond in adequate ways to both naturally good and supernaturally holy values. No Catholic writer, as far as I know, has ever treated the sanctifying power of purity, marriage and consecrated virginity with the *prise de conscience* that von Hildebrand had displayed. He went beyond most in revealing the religious significance of natural values. And his friend Jacques Maritain marveled at von Hildebrand's rare ability to unveil the unearthly beauty of the supernatural values of the Catholic faith. The influence of his work on purity, marriage and consecrated virginity can be discerned in the allocutions of Pope Pius XII (who had been his friend in Munich) as well as in the documents of Vatican II wherever they treat of these holy subjects. Though his ethical writings have been most influential, though his philosophical writings have pitilessly revealed the bankruptcy of that subjectivism and relativism dominant in modern philosophy, yet his sublimest work is surely his *Transformation in Christ:* On the Fundamental Attitude of the Christian. This book has been an inspiration to thousands of Christians and a door opening out on Christ and His Church for thousands of others.

Division of his works

As we have stated von Hildebrand has left posterity an astonishing harvest of inspiring works, some 30 books, hundreds of articles, 2800 pages of memoires and thousands of pages of other documents just about ready for publication. His writings can be divided into three groups. First, his religious writings, such highly acclaimed books as: *Transformation in Christ; Liturgy and Personality; Marriage; Purity and Virginity* are known and read in many languages. Second, 6 volumes on Ethics, among which his classic *Christian Ethics,* 1 on Epistemology, 2 on Aesthetics, 1 on the Metaphysics of Community, 1 large volume on the Essence of Love to which he devoted 13 years of thought and research. Third, his works in defense of the Church and of orthodoxy. Among them we find: *The Trojan Horse; Humanae Vitae: A Sign of Contradiction; Celibacy and the Crisis of Faith; The Devastated Vineyard,* and many others. His complete works have been published in part by Kohlhammer (Stuttgart) and Habbel in Germany. In 1970 Pope Paul VI bestowed upon him the Order of St. Sylvester in recognition of his work for and witness to truth.

Even after he retired from teaching in the classroom, von Hildebrand was in great demand as a lecturer. He continued to work enthusiastically in America and Europe. From the podium he lectured against the rise of neo-modernism, the desacralization of the liturgy, the revolt against sacred authority, the advance of militant atheism in the whole world. All these lectures appeared as articles or in published books. Every summer he traveled back and forth from America to Europe keeping his lines of communication humming with the wisdom of the best minds of both continents.

Yet during the last few years of such activity von Hildebrand was gravely ill with a weak heart. But his love for the Church and truth would not allow him to take a much needed and well earned rest. He was ever the *miles Christi*. Such was the charm of his person that he had friends everywhere, among peasants, among the high and the mighty. And yet he was as unaffectedly at home with peasants as with popes, all of the latter he had met from Benedict XV to Paul VI. In his last years he received the Sacrament of Extreme Unction five times. Even while in the Intensive Care Ward with other patients in serious condition, he managed to bring joy to his fellow sufferers. On hearing that one of the patients was Italian, he cheered the person by speaking his native tongue and filled the patient with joy by singing the *canzone, Dolce Napoli*. Von Hildebrand exuded joy as his predominant attitude. I remember driving with him and his wife to the airport, after they completed a lecture tour at Loyola University in New Orleans in 1965. Songs were sung by the von Hildebrands for the duration of the 13 miles. Both polyglots, they sang in many languages. His joy was infectious; it arose from his deep faith and boundless hope in Christ; it enlarged the souls of his listeners. For him to serve God was to reign and rejoice.

On January 8, after having lost consciousness due to low blood pressure, he recovered and intoned the *Te Deum*. When he came to the words *non confundar in aeternum* von Hildebrand tried to sing the *Te Deum* of Bruckner, but his voice failed him. From September on he spent 41 days in a clinic. During this time Holy Mass was celebrated in his room and he answered the prayers with great fervor, as well as received Holy Communion with intense recollection. He recovered enough to return home on January 24, but on the 26th, conscious to the end, as he accepted a glass of water, God called him to himself.

Von Hildebrand loved a special saying of Our Lord that resounded strongly in his soul. He felt these words were a call from Christ to him. "I have come to cast fire upon the earth, and what is my will, but that it be enkindled." To all who knew him well, von Hildebrand was Christ's kindling on earth. He fulfilled so well the salutary functions of divine fire. He enlightened, leading men to Christ by his teachings and writings. He purified, unmasking errors and evils that obscured truth and holiness. He glorified, revealing the beauty and holiness of Christ and His Church. His supreme goal was that men might achieve transformation in Christ. At the graveside it was said of him: "Dietrich, Christ's kindling, has now flared up into eternity."

Reprinted from *Christian Order.*

Gabriel Marcel: Philosopher of Communion

On September 20, 1964, at Frankfurt am Main, the Börsenverein des Deutschen Buchandels presented Gabriel Marcel — dramatist, philosopher, composer, author and literary critic — with its annual Peace Prize.[1] Some seventeen months later this *"philosopher of peace"*, visited Loyola University in New Orleans on March 25, 1965, and spent three days with the students and faculty. His presence was the academic climax of the year. Some 3,250 academicians and citizens poured into the Field House to be held spellbound by his lecture on *"Man Before the Death of God"*.

The whole audience was moved deeply by the magnetic charm of his person, the brilliance of his analysis of contemporary atheism and the fierce yet sympathetic ardor with which he outlines the intersubjective encounter that Christians must create between persons before their death-of-God brethren will discover and accept the presence of God that shines through in every existence.

The man

Perhaps this era's outstanding philosopher, who worked hard for more than fifty years unmasking the hidden prevarications that have produced our *"broken world"*[2] and revealed the transcendent values that can yet save it from utter ruin, was Gabriel Marcel, a truly remarkable man. Wherever he went — and he traveled the whole world, except those regions walled against freedom which feared his presence — his delight was to be known as a neo-Socratic, not as an existentialist, a label he detested for its vulgar connotations. Just as Socrates in Fifth Century Athens played the gadfly to his fellow Athenians, stinging them into an awareness of their ignorance and into an alertness to their sacredness, so Marcel has been raising difficulties these many years for the easy conscience of an age which is secure in the possession of its material progress and smug in the splendor of its intellectual learning. Marcel's excavations into lived experience represents in modern philosophy a break with the myopic dogmatism of natural science which affirms that the transcendent can never be encountered within the confines of experience. Moreover, these same probings run counter to the empty sophistries of the abstractionist philosophers who drain reality of its mysteries and desecrate it with techniques of degradation. Marcel's kind of philosophy probes the mystery and meaning of existence, of the human person; he refers to this kind of thought as a *"concrete philosophy, a philosophy of existence"*.[3]

The main elements of this concrete philosophy may be summed up under three headings:

  1) The main truth in philosophy is: the doctrine of participation.

  2) The main question for philosophers should be: how to think participation.

*3) The main answer to that question is: participation is thought through
a secondary reflection that is creative and free. The ascent to the plentitude
of being, i.e., to communion is achieved mainly through the activities of
fidelity, hope, love.*[4]

The doctrine of participation

Basic to the thought of Gabriel Marcel is the need to break out of
the barriers of monadic immanence. Trained in German-constructed
philosophic systems, Marcel as a youth experienced the bitter loneliness
of a man who is stranded and cut off in a desert universe, furrowed with
moral imperatives and darkened with clouds of invincible despair. On the
brink of a complete breakdown, he rejected idealism irrevocably, throwing
off its mental strait jacket and plunging deeply into that current of personal
and passionate research known as lived or concrete experience. There, in
exhilarating wonderment, he discovered the physical tensions among cosmic
creatures, the gravitational sociality of truth between human intelligences
and the magnetic attractions of presences towards each other and beyond
to the plenitude of the Absolute Presence.

Marcel's principal insight was uttered superbly long before by St.
Augustine: *"To know the truth we must be in the truth"*. Another shorthand
expression of this intuition might be: to philosophize is to invoke the being
which is present unsummoned, to love the being which is present unloved.
The last word in the philosophic quest is not expressed with the detached
mind but with the whole person freely committed to a love for truth. Man
must freely attest the indubitable presence of being. The knower to whom
being is present must become the lover by whom being is embraced,
otherwise the knower maintains the sterile position of being an isolated,
insularized ego. The fact is that the experience of being arises in participation; even more strictly, it is an experience of communion: *esse est co-esse,*
to be is to-be-with. There can be no I, no knower except in so far as there
is communion. A self segregated, sealed off from other selves, quite simply
is not. The self surges into being within communion.[5] To be a creature
is to be related, to be co-present to others. The continuing existence of
the self is a gift from a transcendent generosity. Nay more, the most intimate
and refined treasures of the self are created within the reciprocal generosity
of other selves.

Being in a situation

Philosophical pronouncements, therefore, on ultimate reality cannot
be made by detached observers. A universalized thinker, withdrawn from
the inexhaustible immediacy of being, is a nonentity. Truth is won only
within our situation. Philosophy starts within the situation; what exists is

what is present in my incarnate consciousness. My body sets me down, with an exclamatory awareness of my standing out as manifest and immersed, in a world of dynamic beings. And my I — body-soul unity as subject — is so bound up, interrelated and consubstantial with a universe which enlarges and multiplies my powers that Marcel can say that *"I exist"* tends to merge with *"the universe exists"*.[6] Sensation, as a higher activity of participation, entails my immediate submersion into the sensible world and the encompassing, sensible world's invasion of my being; sensation is a fuller experience of the sociality of all being. Presence transcends the spatial and temporal limits of sensation; it is an influx of new being, a meeting of I and Thou beyond the frontiers of the visible, in a genuine co-esse and intimacy between spirits. Thus, for Marcel, a steady retreat from one's situation tends to erase the subjecthood, the being of the one fleeing. For thereby the existential bonds that ground and found a subject as this unique, dynamic person are broken, and the displaced person degenerates into the tragically diminished, deracinated person. The wholeness of sanctity is the fruit of communing with God in creatures; the wholeness of sanity is the fruit of communing with creatures in God.

Reflection and communion

When he considers the thinking life of man, Marcel discovers therein a dual highway to the life of communion. Primary reflection tends to dismember the unity of lived experience; it analyzes, investigates. Under its penetrating rays objects are violated, subjects insularized from the immediacy of their milieu. Their lifeless, skeletal structures are revealed. Such dissolvent thinking obstructs the path to participation; it is actually a retreat from communion. Yet it need not irrevocably obstruct participation. Primary reflection's function and role in the elaboration of science and technology can never be underestimated. It solves problems, answers inquiries into objects, manipulates and reforms the world external to subjects. If engaged in only as a preparation for a higher form of communion, primary reflection need not effect the social tragedy of divisiveness. But if it becomes the dominant reflective activity of man, it leads man to handle all reality as one vast, intricate problem, reducing the world of subjects to a segment of the world of objects; men, thereby, become machines; communities collectivized communes.

But not all reality can be grasped by the merely problematic inquiry. Mystery is much more than a problem; it is an encounter with being which necessarily includes the questioner among the data being appealed to for a greater degree of philosophic truth. Curiosity is the characteristic mood coloring the approach to problems, hence of primary reflection. Wonderment is the characteristic mood coloring the approach to mysteries, hence as we shall see, of secondary reflection. What is freedom? What is being? What is love? These are mysteries, not problems. The real metaphysical question is not *"What is being?"* but *"Who is there?"* Philosophic thought will never exhaust the infinite profundity of these natural mysteries; they have no solutions. For the researcher of freedom, being, love is always anxiously encompassed within freedom, being, love. Hence, man never solves philosophic mysteries; he either grows in them or withers in his flight from them. And he freely decides which he shall do.

Secondary reflection recognizes the inadequacy of scientific thought and the solutions attained by primary reflection. Secondary reflection, therefore, moves to fill out the limited viewpoint of analytic reflection. It does this by recovering the original experience — the *actual* world, the *actual* self, the *actual* God met in my *actual* situation.[7] Secondary reflection comes to grips with mysteries, never fully fathoming them, but re-establishing their vital immediacies to the experiencing subjects. Secondary reflection directs thought back to participation, to communion by plunging the thinker from the conceptual world back into the oceanic complexity of the real world. Secondary reflection prevents man from keeping dismembered what he ought only keep distinguished — ideas and realities, putting the former in the service of the latter. Secondary reflection turns thought towards participation, towards communion, away from the disruptive forces of abstractive prescinding.

Reflection, then, is essential for the plenitude of communion; it functions, however, on different levels of mental activity. Primary, analytic reflection problematizes all being, dissolves the concrete, dismisses mystery. This process reaps a great harvest of scientific gains. Secondary reflection synthesizes disrupted reality, reconquers the unity of lived experience, restores the immediacy between subject and object and subject and subject and completes the vast harvest of things with the infinitely richer harvest of persons living in the plentitude of communion. Things are excellent, but inadequate; communion is absolutely essential for human existence. But the return to participated being is a free adventure; nothing compels man to return. Men may refuse to exercise this creative philosophic reflection; they may insist on treating mystery as though it were a problem. Nevertheless, only the voluntary passage back to the realm of mystery can liberate men from the tyranny of things, from the mere, monotonous mental contact with a neutral, anonymous universe. Secondary reflection is really a metaphysics of liberty;[8] it makes men come fully alive in a living, free personal encounter with created beings and the Personal Absolute Being.

Achievement of communion

Marcel's whole philosophical advancement has been dominated by two fundamental obsessions about being. First, *"what I shall call the exigence for being''.* Second, *"the obsession with beings grasped in their singularity and at the same time caught up in the mysterious relationships which bind them together''.*[9]

Every being has in some degree, as evidenced by its dynamic, conscious and unconscious activities, a metaphysical hunger for more being, for higher degrees of being, for getting beyond and higher than itself, for adhering to another and superior being. In man the need for more being, for transcendence, is fulfilled through communication, communion and community. The acts which give man access to being found him as a subject-in-communion. In his quest for the achievement of communion and community among men, Marcel presents a practical and militant philosophy of intersubjective, social activity, an activity that takes a stand for *engagement* in the lives of one's fellowmen and against the spectator-attitude of philosophic relativism and moral neutralism. The *witness, the man of encounter* are living examples of men who take concrete approaches toward the plenitude of communion. Such men are men of fidelity, hope, love. In such concrete activities as fidelity, hope, love, man must affirm and embrace being in the very teeth of the temptation to deny and despair over the possibility of achieving communion.

Fidelity

Fidelity is a spontaneous, self-donating presence of an I to a Thou; it is *"presence actively perpetuated''*,[10] especially toward one in need of comfort and strength in time of trial. Fidelity defies absence; it triumphs over visible separation, especially over the apparently absolute separation called death.[11] Fidelity is a victory over time, vicissitudes, tragedy. Moreover, fidelity is creative; the self fidelity donates is the self fidelity creates. And fidelity creates the person who responds affirmatively to the invocation of being. Hence fidelity achieves the ideal self in freedom; there is nothing automatic about the process. A faithful friend is one who never fails me, who stands up under all manner of circumstances, who never slips away, who is always *with me.*[12] *A being who is faithful chooses to be loyal, but by the same act he chooses never to betray. Here, then, is the paradox of fidelity: the more man descends into intersubjective fidelity, the more he simultaneously ascends into transcendence. Fidelity to being is really fidelity to God.*

Hope

Hope, too, is essentially a trans-subjective appeal to a Thou; it is founded on the humble and patient openness of one who is available, eager to participate in the experience of communion. The person who hopes is a person in need of others. According to Marcel, authentic hope is expressed in this intimate formula: *"I hope in you for us''.*[13] Hope appears defenseless against the tragedies of time. Yet its whole force lies in its appeal to the

Thou, in its invincible assurance that the Absolute Thou is always present, anxious, willing and able to grant ultimate salvation. Thus, hope expands beyond time; it pierces eternity; it is another name for the hunger for being, another advance in the participation of the intimacy of communion. Hope extends limitless credit to the Thou, trusting the Thou will never fail. Hope is borne up by a communion whose atmosphere is eternal. Not a cumulation of evidence, but a presence, appealed to against mountains of contrary evidence, evokes hope. Hope has its finest hour when it refuses to despair, when it challenges the very evidence that would doom men to despair, when it hopes even against and beyond all hope, if that were possible. Thus, hope is a free, generous self-donation and participation in the goodness of the Thou. Hope is never experienced as a gamble; it transcends the vagaries of doubt; it embraces the Absolute Presence Who cannot fail. *"Even though he should destroy me, I shall not doubt."*

Love

Love is the climax of creative, interpersonal activity; it conquers the infinite chasm between being and nothingness. Love creates the world it loves *ex nihilo;* love leaps the divide between subject and object to achieve union. As for the physical and spiritual space between subjects, love razes the temporal barriers of things that would obstruct their communion and the moral decay that would obliterate their presences. Marcel asserts that *"love only addresses itself to what is eternal; it immobilizes the beloved above the world of genesis and vicissitude".*[14] To love a person is to say to him: *"Thou at least shalt not die".*[15] Marcel's insight here is precisely this: within time fate destroys things, but it cannot, within or beyond time, ever prey on that by which Thou art a Thou. For I and Thou are eternal participants in indefectible Being. The lover experiences himself and his beloved as assumed into the Absolute Lover. Love creates both the I and the Thou, for loving creates lovers. But it creates them in the climate of eternity. Marcel affirms that every opening of an I to a Thou is an act of love that grounds the lovers simultaneously in communion and transcendence. *Love* is communion; love creates a permanent community of communion. For love assures the lovers that their experience of intersubjective presence would be a monstrous hoax if it did not arise from the assurance of the encompassing absolutely loving Presence who founds and guarantees the being and the community of the lovers.

Conclusion

Marcel has used many literary forms to probe reality: journals, diaries, essays, critiques, lectures and dramas. His career as a dramatist has been long, productive and crowned with awards for excellence in France — the

Great Award for Literature from the French Academy and the Great National Award for Letters. Concerning Marcel's drama I have written elsewhere:

> The student of Marcel's drama is struck by the author's extreme sensibility to the anxieties and trials of his times. The climate of impending doom — political, social, economic, scientific, artistic and, above all, moral — permeates his drama. His early dramas, before World War I, reveal his apprehension over the coming destruction of Europe. Between the major wars, his theatre demonstrates that Marcel was never taken in by the postwar illusion that the millenium of perpetual peace and plenty had arrived. He tested the deceptive euphoria of the Western leaders in the fire of their alienated masses whose primary attitude was one of hateful indignation and whose favorite activity was violent destruction. His later dramas are rooted in the human anxieties that have become ever more acute since the liberation of Western Europe. Some of the burning controversies his dramas portray are resistance or collaboration with the enemy (L'Emissaire); racism (Le signe de la croix); socialism (Le Dard); procreation (Croissez et multipliez); voluntary exile from one's fatherland (Rome n'est plus dans Rome); the twilight of a common meaning (La dimension Florestan); the laceration of the modern conscience (Mon temps n'est pas le votre).[16]

Thus we see that the whole of Gabriel Marcel's thought seeks to answer some very perplexing questions. How can man be persuaded to return from the mental derangement which is the fruit of excessive *"technocratic thinking"?* How can the wide-awake philosopher stem the tide of history that is running strongly in our age toward the fragmentation of the person and simultaneously, paradoxical as it may seem, toward the collectivization of the masses? How can the *watchman* philosopher liberate men from the mercilessness of their own techniques? How can the philosopher of *engagement* persuade an uprooted society of its essential need for rejuvenation within metaphysical and theological roots? How can the philosopher *physician* cure modern society of its fascination for its own moral disintegration? How can the philosopher of peace call man back from his race to military suicide?

The concrete thought of Marcel certainly affords the remedies for man's estrangement from himself, his fellowman and his God. Such a philosophy of communion, if freely engaged in, is capable of restoring a sense of the sacredness of life; it can neutralize the dangers of pernicious abstractions; it can reactivate respect, reverence and humaneness in the whole of the human condition. For a philosophy rooted in a profound sense of mystery cannot fail to foster the spirit of expansive wonderment and humble gratefulness. Only a philosophy of communion can level the barriers to transcendence and open the world to accept freely the grace of conversion — a grace that turns man away from the pride and narrowness of self-sufficiency and towards the humble self-donating intimacy, inwardness and presence that can be enjoyed solely within the communion of both human and divine communities.

Notes

[1] G. Marcel, *Philosophical Fragments,* The University of Notre Dame Press, Notre Dame, Indiana, 1965. Included in this volume is Marcel's acceptance speech: "The Philosopher and Peace".

[2] G. Marcel, *Le Monde Cassé,* Desclée de Brouwer, 1933. A play which presents the tragedy of the broken world.

[3] G. Marcel, *Metaphysical Journal,* Regnery, Chicago, 1952, p. VIII.

[4] Kenneth T. Gallagher, *The Philosophy of Gabriel Marcel,* Fordham University Press, New York, 1962, p. 116.

[5] G. Marcel, *Being and Having,* Dacre Press, Westminster, England, 1959, p. 237.

[6] G. Marcel, *Metaphysical Journal,* Regnery, Chicago, 1962, p. 323.

[7] Kenneth T. Gallagher, *The Philosophy of Gabriel Marcel,* Fordham University Press, New York, 1962, p. 42.

[8] G. Marcel, *Creative Fidelity,* Farrar, Straus, New York, 1964, p. 26.

[9] *Ibid.,* p. 147.

[10] G. Marcel, *The Philosophy of Existence,* Philosophical Library, New York, 1949, p. 22.

[11] G. Marcel, *Creative Fidelity,* Farrar, Straus, New York, 1964, p. 152.

[12] *Ibid.,* p. 154.

[13] G. Marcel, *Homo Viator,* Regnery, Chicago, 1951, p. 60.

[14] G. Marcel, *Metaphysical Journal,* Regnery, Chicago, 1952, p. 63.

[15] G. Marcel, *The Mystery of Being,* Vol. II, Regnery, Chicago, Gateway Edition, 1960, p. 171.

[16] V. Miceli, S.J., "Marcel: The Drama of Transcendence", *THOUGHT,* Fordham University, New York, Summer 1965, Vol. XL, No. 157, pp. 195–224.

Reprinted from *Social Digest,* September–October 1966.

Marcel: The Ascent to Being

Every era is called upon to collaborate in the perfection of the human being and the human condition. This call is often concretized as a dramatic challenge to surmount a present crisis and to emerge with transfigured vigor to a more exalted state of personal and communal living. There is no doubt that mankind is at present in a particularly grave state of turmoil. A struggle is raging between false utopias and authentic incarnations of humane and human community-institutions. The issue as to which type of community — the ideologically abstract or the concrete and authentically valid — will possess and rule mankind has not yet been resolved. That social upheaval, a widespread phenomenon, is testified to by the forces of revolution that are in the field and acting as catalysts toward community chaos in many nations throughout the world. Anxiety and fear are a very common and prolonged experience in our times.

The philosopher of depth sees that certain realities are involved in these physical and psychological experiences — realities that have ontological priority over the experiences themselves and must be discovered, through reflection, as authentic, if the experiences are to be meaningful and useful at all.

Perhaps the era's outstanding philosopher of depth, hard at work for over thirty-five years unmasking the hidden prevarications that have produced this ''broken world'' and revealing the transcendent values that can yet save it from utter ruin, is Gabriel Marcel. Marcel has unerringly identified and exposed the modern cultivation of that age-old metaphysical malignancy that is always disruptive of organic society:

> The history of modern philosophy, as I said before, seems to supply abundant illustrations of the progressive replacement of *atheism*, in the grammatically privative sense of the word, by an *anti-theism* whose mainspring is the will that God should not be.[1]

This cultured atheism works for the destruction of the felt and recognized presence of God; it produces the ''Lucifer-man'' who questions everything with a will for the radical rejection of being. A world dominated by Lucifer-men endorses the optimism of the Age of Enlightenment, whose logical heir Marx still is. It blindly accepts the arbitrary postulate that history is inevitably moving toward a progressive sort of self-fulfillment. A world such as this justifies murder on an unimaginable scale by its claim that only through such sacrifice will the completely happy society be ensured.

Marcel sets himself the task of unmasking this ''ghastly lie.'' He vividly delineates the major contestants that are engaged in a struggle to the death over the family of mankind:

But recently I have quite often had occasion to say that there we have what does seem to me a real possibility of choice for man: *between the termite colony and the Mystical Body:* and the gravest danger anybody could commit would be to confuse one with the other.[2]

How does Marcel explore this struggle and upon what metaphysical foundations does he base his own analyses and solutions to it? He indicates the direction of his researches to us when he says that "what matters today is that man should rediscover the sense of the eternal, and withstand those who would make his life subservient to an alleged sense of history."[3] Since Marcel's whole life has been his own rediscovery of the sense of the eternal, we will first look at Marcel the man before we go into his philosophical solutions for the turmoil of our times. For if anyone's philosophy has been and still is identified with his living, that person is Gabriel Marcel.

Revolt against idealism

Marcel is an original and prophetic thinker. He was not always this but developed into an outstanding Christian philosopher of creative insight and fresh inspiration *per viam duram* — in the crucible of long years of patient suffering. An only child, puny, possessed of extreme sensibility, he endured the bitterness of loneliness in an a-religious, but culturally advanced, family milieu. To break through the barrier of isolation, to fulfill his desire to communicate with others in a world beyond his own, Marcel developed a great love for the theater, communicating with imaginary companions of his own creation in the absence of live age-mates.

While yet a young student, Marcel was subjected to the rigors and tensions of the fiercely competitive learning process on the Continent. This took its toll of his health and caused much bodily suffering. Jourdain writes of this situation:

> At an early age still, Marcel knew another type of suffering: the *insolubilia* of human existence, the difficulties in ourselves and in others which impeded the bilateral movement toward our communion, desired as it may be. Like many a gifted child, he suffered in school: the pedantic, the scholarly approach of his teachers barred his way to the beauty and depth of the classics. He was put under constant pressure, through an atmosphere of competition and even rivalry which is so widespread in many European schools.

This partly accounts for the poor health which has been Marcel's affliction, and which has no doubt quickened his sense for suffering in others: the thoughts he has left on this topic bear the unmistakable seal of one who knows sorrow. Marcel, therefore, will never offer shallow consolation to the sufferer, for experience has taught him that *"compartir"* implies one's loving identification with him who suffers.[4]

At first an enthusiastic Hegelian, Marcel in 1909 at the Sorbonne held that "the most truly real could not by any means be what is most immediate, but on the contrary, the most truly real is the fruit of a dialectic, the crowning completion of an edifice of thought."[5] German-constructed philosophic systems exercised an extraordinary ascendancy over him and filled him with "the intrepidity of an idealist." But he soon became irritated with and incredulous of these systems because of the impossibility of passing in them from the Absolute I to the concrete, created I, the latter being regarded by Marcel as the only true I within his experience.

Thus the young philosopher found himself stranded and cut off in a desert universe, furrowed with moral imperatives and darkened with clouds of invincible despair. At this time Marcel lived in a state of hypertension that reached now and then the intensity of an unbearable paroxysm. Could the end of all philosophic endeavor be the immersion of reality and of all individual destinies into an Abolsute where all is absorbed and lost? Marcel resented and finally rejected this philosophic doctrine. He abandoned his attempt to write a systematic synthesis on the whole of philosophy à la the post-Kantians, stating that "he decidedly would not be conformed to the rules of the philosophic game such as these have been observed up to contemporary times."[6]

With that declaration of philosophic independence, Marcel was at last free of his idealistic strait jacket to plunge directly into that current of personal and passionate research — lived experience. Gilson writes of this fresh Marcellian approach:

> Through an initial procedure, which he has never since betrayed, this philosopher has written nothing which has not been reaped from the depths of his being or directly tested by his own experience. There is scarcely anyone, even among the greatest, to whom we can attribute that praise. And the most constant historical experience seems to assure works sprung from that source of a perpetual freshness, which so many philosophical systems, ambitiously erected by dint of artificial contrivances, have lacked from their birth. In philosophy as elsewhere, only the authentic endures, and that is why like Montaigne, like Pascal, like Maine de Biran, Gabriel Marcel is assured of always having readers. In his work man speaks directly to man; he will always have readers because he will never cease to make new friends.[7]

From the moment Marcel rejected Idealism in search of created presence, he saw things in wonderment, with precision, in their plentitude. Once he willed to encounter the created Thou, he was drawn as by a magnet, all unknowingly at first, to the tri-personal Presences of the Absolute Thou. Having opted to concentrate on concrete reality, Marcel ceased being a mere observer, a ratifier, and became a witness for transcendent, spiritual being. As witness, he contributed to the enrichment of the revelation of natural mysteries, to the renewed advent and the growth of the truth that is in need of being brought to articulate awareness under the circumstances of the contemporary crisis. Through the years he was to become fully conscious of the significance of his concrete philosophy:

> A concrete philosophy is drawn as by a magnet by the Christian data. For the Christian, there is an essential conformity between Christian revelation and human nature. Thus, the more one penetrates into man's nature, the more one places oneself within the axis of the great Christian truths.[8]

What are the actual, concrete circumstances of the human condition that Marcel has been encountering ever since he descended from his Hegelian empyrean? Marcel has worked in an era of catastrophic unrest, in a world shattered by two major wars and still plagued by cold ones. Fear, repression, insecurity are still characteristic of modern man. Marcel sees that even today, after so much suffering and disillusionment, modern man, in his effort to escape from subjective loneliness, is still desperately fleeing from and yet paradoxically clinging to heartless collectivities.

Marcel is quick to accept and utilize what underlies this mass flight of individuals to collectivized society, namely, that the peace, happiness and prosperity of man depend upon his life within community. It is not by insertion into the colony of the masses, but by a conversion to the communion of loving inter-subjective living that the displaced person of our era will attain his spiritual and social coherence.

In World War I Marcel worked with the Red Cross, devoting himself to its investigations concerning persons who had disappeared in the war. Each day the broken human spirit sought his services, as parents, relatives and friends groped to find, in and through him, their missing loved ones. Contact with so many sorrows revealed to Marcel the drama of human existence and of communion. He rebelled against the depersonalized questionnaires, the arbitrary simplifications, the superficial arrangements to which these suffering souls were submitted. In World War II the odious experience of the Nazi occupation frequently precipitated him into melancholy moods. Yet, all through these experiences, he continued to grasp the pulse of existence and, because of his spontaneous interest in others and his sympathy, he renounced ever more emphatically the facile intellectualism and the way of abstraction that contributed so much to the dehumanization of persons and of society. Few men have opened themselves with greater graciousness to so many aspects of the spiritual world and responded to them with more dedication. With such affective richness and depth, it is not surprising that he continued to advance along the great lines of his personalist philosophy.

How does Marcel understand the role of the Christian philosopher in this age of crisis? Despite the attack on Christianity, Marcel has developed no defense mechanism, no inferiority complex in the face of the enemy. Without diminution of Christian courage, nor any abdication of his spirit of liberty, nor of his frankness, Marcel stands forth as the philosopher of faithfulness. His popularity as a thinker and lecturer in the non-Catholic academic world has been remarkable. Jourdain testifies thus:

> Now we know it for a fact that non-Catholic thinkers are infinitely more attracted by a courageous and bold philosophy which organically incorporates given religious data (such as the datum of holiness), than by a stifled and abstract presentation of Christian truths, intimidated by the very thought of being suspected of crossing boundaries between philosophy and religion.
>
> Von Hildebrand and Marcel have been criticized for not hesitating to mention in their writings the phenomenon of sanctity. Some have even thought of excommunicating these philosophers from the stronghold of 'pure' philosophy. Few have, however, understood that the phenomenon of holiness is *given* independently of any theological acceptance of the conditions which must be fulfilled so that this mystery may be born: '. . .la sainteté. . .est une donnée.'[9]

The role of the Christian philosopher for Marcel, then, is, negatively, to defend against the withering effects of narrow and abstractive systems of thought that drain reality of all its mystery; positively, to extend the horizons of being, of presence, of participation by witnessing to the need and achievement of a world in communion.

To live with is for Marcel a need of nature that calls for fulfillment in a spirituality of communion within a fraternity of community. Because he is capable of receiving, because he chooses to give himself, Marcel makes the powers of his talents and temperament reach their highest perfection in his free choice for a philosophy of communion. The gift of self and of receptivity expand and fulfill themselves in the works of life only through mutual exchanges:

There can be no authentic depth where there can be no real communion; but there will never be any real communion between individuals centered on themselves, and in consequence morbidly hardened, nor in the heart of the mass, within the mass state. The very notion of intersubjectivity, on which all my own recent work has been based, presupposes a reciprocal openness between individuals without which no kind of spirituality is conceivable.[10]

"A reciprocal openness between individuals" is the clue to the foundation of Marcel's philosophy, a philosophy which, because it is founded on the datum of the exigence for intersubjective communion, is engaged in the discovery, the defense and the loving adherence to created I's and the Absolute Thou's.

It is when he is discovering new philosophic frontiers in the universe of communion that Marcel's genius is at its best. Marcel has explored and developed this region perhaps with greater insight and thoroughness than any other philosopher of our times. He has made innumerable reflective investigations into this sphere of the spiritual. His unexpected discoveries have been enlightening. He never tires of extending the frontiers of ontological communion, for the simple reason that he knows that this area of the mystery of being is inexhaustible and can never be fully mapped.

Thus, for the reasons already considered, Marcel eschews total systems of philosophy which claim to be able, if not today then sometime in the future, to explain the *totum* of truth. Such claims betray the arrogance of total systems. Marcel, who is impressed with the limitless plenitude of all being and truth holds the position expressed by Schwarz toward every authentic philosophy:

> There is a paradox inherent in the very undertaking of philosophy, and it results in a dilemma seemingly insurmountable. Philosophical truth cannot possibly be isolated truth. The *totum* of truth must in some way make its presence felt, but philosophy itself cannot give the total truth. The history of its systems bears empirical witness to this fact. As Kierkegaard puts it, "the world is a system but only God knows the system."[11]

Ever since he broke out of his social isolation, ever since he escaped from philosophic narrowness, Marcel has found his excursions into lived experience hopeful and fruitful undertakings. He has deeply realized the ontological hierarchy of being; he has hungered to arrive at the summit of this hierarchy. But he has appreciated also that there is no direct route to that summit open to man in his present position as pilgrim. So quite humbly and realistically he has employed a method which Marcel de Corte has called the "ascending spiral," a method which moves ceaselessly up the ladder of participation from spirit to spirit until it arrives at the peak of communion. The stages of that philosophic journey will be the concern of the rest of this essay, especially as they effect the growth of communion in community. These stages are called by Marcel himself incarnation, sensation, primary reflection, communication, intersubjective communion and finally the human and divine communities in communion. Naturally, it will only be possible to touch on the inexhaustible depths of each of these plateaus in the plenitude of being in this synthetic conspectus of Marcel's ascent to being.

The full and the empty

Marcel is of the conviction that there is something radically inadequate about the traditional approach to philosophizing on reality via the One-Many category. The approach badly dichotomizes, renders static and sterile and separates into inimical groups, through impersonal logic and ruthless planning, the whole of dynamic reality. Such a mental climate for philosophizing leads ultimately to an atomized or collectivized universe of being and men.

> We have to reject the atomic just as much as the collective conception of society. Both, as Gustave Thibon has so pregnantly remarked, are complementary aspects of the same process of decomposition — I would say of local mortification.[12]

Marcel's insight consists, negatively, in refusing to concentrate on the numerically accidental character of being — the One and the Many — and, positively, in exploring with patient intensity the metaphysical and spiritual ambivalence of being as the Full and the Empty. This view of reality, as infinitely essential, is profound and eminently fruitful.

> I have written on another occasion that, provided it is taken in its metaphysical and not in its physical sense, the distinction between the *full* and the *empty* seems to be more fundamental than that between the *one* and the *many.*[13]

Out of the depths of our emptiness we testify to our abiding needs, the greatest of which is the *besoin d'etre,* the metaphysical hunger for being and not merely for the idea of being. The Absolute we yearn and strive for is not a neat, systematic construct of our own minds, but a dynamic reality that resists our every effort at adequate characterization and comprehension. Thus, for Marcel, philosophy is a total act of vital concern; subjectivity is not divorced from reality but is a most important constituent of true philosophy; philosophy is the reciprocal clarification of two unknowns — the subject and the object. Thus metaphysics can only be carried on as a function of the exigence and the radical need for being. Nor must this openness to and fundamental need for being be thought of as a mere passive condition of emptiness; it is rather a dynamic principle within being which drives toward richer participation in Being Itself.

> Get rid of the interpretation which converts metaphysical need into a sort of transcendental curiosity. Metaphysical need is a kind of appetite — the appetite for being. Being, as I said before, is expectation fulfilled. . . . We have always with us the contrast of the full and the empty, and which, speaking generally, has so far only been considered in its physical aspects. Our activity needs to be exercised to the full in a world of fullness.[14]

Thus whoever affirms or denies being does so in relation to this dynamic need for fullness. There must be being, and I desire to participate in it; to experience a thing as being is to experience it as plenitude; being is fulfillment; it is a principle of inexhaustibility.

The need for fullness which is seated in the person, in me, implies more than something which is wanted; it signifies something which is demanded. When Marcel says that being is fulfillment, he is not considering fulfillment on its own as something in itself, but as what "is involved in the life of consciousness which finds fulfillment something to satisfy a profound requirement."[15] Moreover, the yearning for a fuller being is not experienced as a downward movement, nor merely as a horizontal surge; it is, above all, a soaring above and beyond — toward the Absolute Principle of Plenitude Itself. In other words, the exigence for being coincides with the demand for a vertically upward transcendence. To be is to participate in what is eternal. Marcel characterizes his notion of transendence as a "vertical 'going beyond' rather than as a mere horizontal going beyond."[16]

Although all reality has a certain characteristic aspect of transcendence, the idea of transcendence is fundamental to the general human condition. And paradoxical as it may seem, transcendence is grasped in and through intimately lived experience. Such experience is not an object, not something flung in my way, not something placed before me or in my path.

For I am *in* my experience and much of my experience testifies to my need for transcendence. Certain dissatisfactions, restlessness of heart, yearnings for sanctity and for truly creative work, callings to fulfill high vocations constantly proclaim that I am, by my very existence, "caught up within the poles of transcendence." Thus, Marcel insists that "the urgent inner needs for transcendence should never be interpreted as a need to pass beyond all experience whatsoever; for beyond all experience there is nothing."[17]

But the experience man has of other beings only mollifies and does not sate man's yearning for participation in the plenitude of being. The more man descends into intersubjective communion, the more he ascends into transcendence. By reading the transcendent aspects of lived experience and by plunging into the depths of all that is actual, Marcel succeeds in mining and refining something of the precious mystery of being that is hidden in the complexity of being. His philosophical refinements assure us of much that is meaningful in being and yet insist that, despite perennial excursions into its profundities, being will always remain full of mystery. The principle of transcendence reveals its inexhaustibility, but it also reveals the dynamic openness, the outward and upward surge, the intersubjective sociality of being.

The experience of transcendence signifies to Marcel that all created being is simultaneously both participation in being and appetitive drive toward deeper enrichment in ascending degrees of being. All being is dynamically oriented toward ontological communion. All being is insufficient and frustrated if isolated and self-enclosed from communion with other being. This is especially true of man, the self-conscious being, who eminently embodies within himself the ontological demand for fulfillment in communal plentitude. Yet man is free and thus dangerously capable of shutting himself off from intersubjective participation in transcendent being. He may decide, with Sartre, that others are predators and will to reject communion with the universe, with his fellow men and with God. He may choose despair and suicide.

For Marcel, however, nothing that exists exists in ontological isolation or solitude, but rather everything exists in a family of dynamic intersubjective relationships. No created being is totally autonomous; no created being is its own, but is always actively related to the plenitude of being. This is especially true of man of whom St. Paul says: "You are not your own."[18] And this same apostle, in his philosophy of salvation, his *philosophia Christi*, corroborates, with superior light from Revelation, the priority of participation in which all beings stand and hold together. His mystical and poetical vision reveals that the ontological communion in which the universe was founded and which was disrupted by the fall will be regained, nay more, will be assumed into a theological communion of divine glorification in the "new heaven and the new earth."

Thus the ontological theme at the heart of all lived experience is: To be means to participate. *Esse est co-esse.* To be "with" is an exalted dimension of being, inextricably bound up with the dynamic drive for transcendence. In the case of man, to be *with* involves the human person in a self-commitment to a dialogue with the animate and inanimate universe in the search for truth, and to a mutual self-donation with his fellow men for the attainment of the dialectic of love in a community of love.

Incarnation

The metaphysics of intersubjectivity provides Marcel with the category of incarnation. In the light of this aspect of lived experience, I am aware that the existential roots of my being are grounded in my experience of incarnation in my body which is a central given. Every man's subject-hood is fundamentally and not accidentally in his body. My first conscious discovery of myself is the awareness of my body, not as a disparate object or instrument known or possessed or used, but as that which is experienced as setting me down within existence and which makes of my first moment of existence the infallible exclamation: "Here I am! What luck!"[19]

But this I who am my body — not in a materialistic identity of spirit and matter, but as one existential subject that enjoys in its unity of self and body a direct linkage not only with objective reality, but, above all, with "being which is ulterior to any gap between subject and object"[20] — this I is nondetachable from the world of beings. To induce duality and disparateness between the self and its universe of lived experience is to isolate the self, to conceptualize the self, to introduce the rupture of discontinuity between the self and all other beings in the world. My experience and even my existence can then be considered as detached realities looking around for a subject in which to inhere. Whereas in reality, Marcel tells us that "existence and the thing that exists obviously cannot be dissociated."[21]

For there is an indissoluble bond between my existence and me, the existent subject. And my "I" — body-soul unity as subject — is so bound up and interelated with the whole of the universe that Marcel can say that "I exist" tends to merge with "the universe exists."[22] Although I enjoy the exclamatory awareness of my initial degree of participation in being in the pure immediacy that is my incarnation in my body, yet I must never be content with this gift-reception of my being and I must strive, in my drive for transcendence, to open myself, with all that I am and have, to the other, by the giving of hospitality to all other beings through creative acts of communion. Blackham interprets Marcel's thought thus:

> Life is achieved by resolving the tension in responsive feeling and creative activity, in which having is not eliminated but is assimilated to being, in which one and another become I and Thou; in which science is integrated with metaphysics; in which autonomy ("managing my own affairs") is transcended in liberty, which is participation; in which my body and the world with which it is consubstantial and which enlarges and multiplies its powers is the place in which I bear witness to Being; in which I work out my fidelity and my hope and keep myself open, fluid and ready to spend *(disponible)*. [23]

Sensation

Engaged in a context infinitely greater than itself, the I is by nature trans-subjective and proceeds, through incarnation in the body, to the inter-subjective activity of sensation. If things are in the world as in a field of care and concern, how much more so the subject man! Sensation, as a higher activity of communion, entails the immediate participation of the subject in the encompassing world; sensation is an early actualization and prolongation of the incarnation of the I in and with the sensible world; it is the second important way in which the I is made to be, for through sensation the presence of the I is consciously actualized in the world of concrete sensible beings. To be experiencing sensation is to be involved, engaged and communing or communicating with the dynamically relational structure that is the sociality of all being.

Marcel, speaking of "the presence of an underlying reality that is felt, of a community which is deeply rooted in ontology,"[24] admits that the very nature of this presence is mysterious and can only be glimpsed. In what he calls his "metaphysics of hospitality." He insists that in this world of dramatic tragedy there ought to grow up between the knower and the known, between the ill and the well, between the secure and the unprotected a bond of loving respect, that is meant to unite the precious and the precarious in a recognition of the sacredness that lies at the heart of all reality. This bond of love and respect touches something that is essential to all being, something that is of absolute not of relative importance.

What is the nature of this presence that man feels? A look at lived experience will help us capture something of its mystery. Now, we do not begin life by retreating from reality. The normal child is welcomed into a family that begot it in love and has been eagerly awaiting and preparing for its arrival. The child in turn reaches out almost frantically to embrace every member of the family and every object of the household. It is cause of constant wonderment to contemplate a child's wide-eyed openness and charming acceptance of the world of beings. Presence is seen as that mystery of personal immediacy that constitutes the main spiritual stem of society. Far from being akin to the inertia of static conformism, presence entails an energetic and prolonged assault on the love of the other. Thus, the I of a child, considered as a magnetic spiritual headquarters, cannot be reduced to any specified part of the child — not body, brain, soul. The I is rather a total, a world-wide presence which gains a growing degree of glory and self-confidence by putting forth itself, with all its charms and talents, to donate itself to the other, to the Thou. And in presence the Thou is called upon, appealed to as a qualified witness, to wonder and rejoice at the magnificent whole that is the act of self-donation in the child. The act which establishes the self of the child is the act by which the child attracts the attention of the others so that they may praise — perhaps even scold — but at all events, notice and enter into communion with the child.

Presence is not merely an idea, but rather, presence as presence is unconfined; it transcends the diminished limits of the logical order. As a matter of experience, it transcends the frontiers and even the vicissitudes of time and space; it exceeds its object on every side, like being itself; for true presence is involved in the mystery of being. True presence corresponds to a certain hold which being has upon us. A presence is a concrete, spiritual reality; it is a kind of influx of being. Presence is effective as soon as the I assumes responsibility both for the I itself and for the Thou. Presence is effective as soon as the I holds itself accountable for what the I does and for what the I says and thinks. Presence is the very essence of genuine *co-esse*, the heart of genuine intimacy. For there is a psychic as well as a physical distance, one not able to be measured in miles or meters. A loved one, physically afar at this moment, is actually much closer to me than the one now coldly addressing me in person.

Availability

Marcel warns us often enough that a steady retreat from one's situation tends to erase even the subject-hood of the one fleeing. For without an intersubjective commerce with one's existential surroundings, the subject, who is originally grounded and founded as this unique, recognizable, dynamic person in these particular circumstances, gradually breaks the existential ties that sharply delineate him as this unique person and, ceasing to exist as himself, inevitably evanesces into a rootless shadow of himself. The displaced person is too often a tragically diminished person. Surely, if sanctity is said to be attained by the person through his efforts *adhaerere Deo,* may not sanity be maintained by the person through his efforts *adhaerere rebus et hominibus?*

Availability is a more intense degree of presence and of communion. This total spiritual *disponibilité* overcomes the initial alienation of the creature from himself and from other persons that arises from his involvement in the sphere of his possession. To have means to be had, to be enclosed and enchained and oversolicitous concerning objects. Man's entire interests become centered on how to safeguard things even at the expense of his own inner growth and of a valid communion with others. Persons thus shut up within themselves become prisoners of their own feelings, covetous desires, dull anxieties that feed upon themselves. No longer awakened to the presence of being, they are ruled sometimes by desire, sometimes by terror. Pathetic blind men, such persons go through life as sleepwalkers.

The spiritual life that matures with the growth of availability, however, consists in a gradual conversion from having to being, from getting and spending in commerce to giving in communion, from getting poorer in the accretion of things to growing richer in a fuller participation in transcendent being. Availability is made clear when we say that the person who is at my disposal is the one who is able and willing to be with me with the whole of himself, especially when I am in need. While the one who is not at my disposal seems merely to lend himself to me with patent reservations. To the available person I am a presence; to the unavailable I am an object. Presence and availability involve warm reciprocity, something excluded from the depersonalized relationship of subject to object or subject to subject-object. Pessimism finds its metaphysical roots in the unavailability of the selfish. But hope and joy are founded on the uncluttered self-donation of the man who extends unlimited credit to the universe. A spiritually bankrupt mentality looks on men as so many needy cases open to organized help. But cases are objects that can become hopeless. The unavailable man faced with this hopelessness eventually slides into despair and suicide. *Sui vivere, suicidium.*

Suicide is the final act of unavailability and despair; martyrdom, of availability and hope. Man is free to choose either contradictory finale. The unavailable egoist breaks off communion with being. Pride, his self-centered source of power, destroys him as well as others. The man of availability, on the other hand, centers his strength in the Other; humility keeps him open to the Thou. The suicide renders himself utterly unavailable, slamming the door to life by his own hand. The martyr, however, stands fully available, donating his life as a witness for others. Death for Marcel is thus seen as either the "springboard of an absolute hope," or a perpetual incitement to treason.[25] The man of availability takes as his motto: "Not *sum* but *sursum.*" Not I am but I ascend. The man of availability consecrates his being to causes that transcend his own because they are participations of a Being greater than himself. Marcel sums up these causes in an excellent synthesis:

> Person — engagement — community — reality: there we have a sort of chain of notions which, to be exact, do not readily follow from each other by deduction . . . but of which the union can be grasped by an act of the mind. It would be better not to call this act by the much abused term of intuition, but by one which, on the contrary, is too little used — that of synopsis, the act by which a group is held together under the mind's comprehensive gaze.[26]

Problem and mystery

When we consider the mental life of man, the importance of Marcel's classic distinction between problem and mystery for his philosophy of communion must be stressed. A problem is an inquiry into an object, a thing external to me, out there, set over against me. I can solve a problem eventually with a perfectly correct answer, but the problem does not involve me in its solution. The analytical process of what is called primary reflection is an excellent instrument for the intellectual conquest of problems.

Primary reflection tends to dismember the unity of lived experience through its process of analytical investigation. Now this very activity is by nature trans-subjective and should be engaged in only as a preparation for a higher form of communal synthesis with the very objects of reality that pass under its rays of analysis. Yet we must never forget that its analytical procedures tend to violate objects and to insularize subjects. Thus primary reflection severs man from incarnation in the immediacy of his milieu. As purely analytical, its function and role in the elaboration of science and technology can never be underestimated. Yet, as a dissolvent, it does not further the relationship of participation; rather it emphasizes technical contact and commercial communication. It is actually a retreat from participation, from involvement in lived experience, hence its inability to explain or appreciate the totality, unity or quality of the unqualifiedly actual.

The higher form of mental synthesis is called by Marcel, secondary reflection. Secondary reflection is essentially recuperative of original experience; it reconquers the unity of lived experience; it identifies, exposes and fills out the partial aspects of reality that are categorized by primary reflection. Secondary reflection re-establishes the immediacy between subject and object and subject and subject that was necessarily ruptured by the objectifying process of primary analysis. Thus, secondary reflection is actually a new level of ontological participation and communion, superior to that of sensation in finality and intensity and making use of the very skills produced by analytical reflection as instruments toward higher transcendent communion. Secondary reflection prevents man from keeping dismembered what he ought only to keep distinguished — ideas and realities, putting the former in the service of the latter.

Thus mystery is much more than an analysis of an object, much more than a problem. Mystery is an encounter with being; it is an area of being that necessarily includes me, the researcher, among the data. When I philosophize on "What is being?" I am caught up, engaged with both the particular being that I am questioning and the being that I am. I cannot objectify my being, nor observe myself from outside, as if I were an object. Through primary reflection I enter into communication with objects, I interpret a way of having and I converse with an ideal or real interlocutor about a third party, about an it or him or they. But in secondary reflection I come to grips with mysteries and, above all, with the characteristically human mystery of the community which is instituted by the power of love. Here

I find persons in the plenitude of their being as Thou's to whom I am present
with a heightened self-donation of all that I am. Here I find myself as a
person in a higher degree of transcendence and self-possession the more
I open myself to the other Thou's in acts of fidelity, hope and love. "As
soon as there is presence, we have gone beyond the realm of problem."[27]
It is not the characteristic of being insoluble that identifies a mystery; a
reality that is nonobjectifiable, that is unverifiable lies in the land of mystery.

What is being? What is freedom? What is truth? These are not
questions that are colored by curiosity, the mood characteristic of the problematic. Thought will never fathom their inexhaustible profundity, never
discover nor express their solutions. All man can do is immerse himself
within these mysteries, content to grow in them in a spirit of reverent
astonishment and humble gratefulness.[28]

Reflection, then, is essential for the plenitude of human existence.
It is never meant to degrade the human condition, but to enrich life in
many ways. The danger lies in failing to see that reflection functions on
different levels of human activity. The work of primary reflection repays
man with a vast harvest of scientific and technocratic gains. These are
excellent but inadequate for human existence. For primary reflection, in
objectifying reality, represents a withdrawal from participation. The work
of secondary reflection fills out the inadequacy of the abstract, of the
scientific; this work restores and explores the mystery that is incarnated
in the actual world of beings in which I live and participate.

Techniques of degradation

Closely related to the above forms of reflection is the principal obstacle
to communion: the tendency to "objectify." Primary reflection introduces
a divisive force that tempts man to handle all reality as one vast and intricate
problem that challenges his wits for a full solution. The many objects in
that reality are approached as being exterior and unconcerned about man.
To problematize all being is to foster the spirit of abstraction which succeeds
in dissolving the concrete and in dismissing mystery from a world of wonderment. The practical prolongation of this spectator attitude is embodied in
a series of techniques that enables man to dominate matter and men by
subjecting everything to the mechanics of depersonalized planning.

Marcel warns us that social harmony does not exist in the modern
world because of the techniques man has developed for degrading his fellow
man. The pernicious habit of objectifying and reifying all being has effected
the tragedy of social divisiveness. Intellectually, the spirit of abstraction
harbors a contempt for the concrete conditions of existence. It reduces the
world of subjects, of I's and Thou's, to a part of the world of objects.
Practically, this will for the nondiscrimination and nonhierarchization of

being begets the harsh techniques that reduce men to machines and communities to collectivized communes.

The techniques of degradation consist in a spirit of self-depreciation that can be traced to a frustration and dislocation of that sense of being which is man's special claim to respect and reverence. The first technique of degradation is the habit of abstraction itself; it consists in the transformation of the attitude of imperialism to the mental plane. Secondly, this technocratic mentality atomizes and manipulates man as a chattel and assumes a complete mastery over him. Thirdly, a spirit of suspicion necessarily arises, once men feel themselves isolated and abandoned in an abstract universe. Fourthly, from this fracture of the organic harmony of society, there arises the attitude of radical detachment, a total lack of interest in the wholeness of man, and an excessive preoccupation with specialization in his parts as in the parts of a machine. Fifthly, the demolition of the social subject leads inevitably to the functionalized man, the ticket puncher or doorman who is merely an apparatus at the service of the herd community. And sixthly, in a stifling and overwhelmingly sad atmosphere, the pulverized man is subjected to the degrading outpourings of propaganda calculated to keep him submissive and inert under the hand of mediocrity, boredom and tyranny. Raw violence is essential as the climax of these techniques.[29]

Fidelity, hope, love

By way of contrast, the quest for communion is achieved by respect for mystery. Marcel presents a practical and militant philosophy of inter-subjective activity, one that takes a stand for *engagement*, in the lives of our fellow men and against the spectator attitude of ontological relativism and moral neutralism. The witness and the man of encounter are penetratingly discussed as living examples of the metaphysics of fidelity, hope, love. Such men are truly free because they belong to more than themselves. For freedom, at bottom, is an "ontological belonging," a "creative appurtenance,"[30] an acknowledgment and response to the invocation of being. The free act is not solely the subject's; it is simultaneously his and simultaneously a gift to him. The how of freedom lies in the mysterious land of being and communion. Yet the exercise of freedom, in its profoundest depths, is but the consent or refusal to render creative testimony to the appeal of being.

The man of creative testimony is also a man of values. In welcoming being he adheres to these "heralds of being."[31] Acceptance of the summons of truth, justice, loyalty is acceptance of one's growth in the plenitude of being. To refuse to be informed by values is to refuse to be, to reject growth in transcendence, for values have their principle in transcendent being. To refuse to be founded by values is to reject participation in an exalted,

"in an absolute self-possession, a calm in some way supernatural."[32] But
values are only incarnate in life in relation to perpetual struggle and sacrifice.
We do not die for ideas, for liberty in general, for truth in general. My
countrymen's call may possibly only be answered by my acceptance of
death. Yet the acceptance of this and all values testifies to the consciousness
of an immortal destiny. Were death the ultimate reality, values and being
would be annihilated.[33]

Fidelity, then, is "presence actively perpetuated,"[34] especially toward
one who is in need of my presence for comfort and strength in time of trial.
An historical example may help our understanding of fidelity. We have
in the situation of Peter, confronted by the servant girl over his tie to Christ,
an elucidation concerning the ontological role of fidelity. "Thou also wast
with Jesus the Galilean!" As a matter of fact, Peter was "with Jesus" in
the richest, most spiritual and intimate senses that Marcel has wrung from
this intersubjective expression of communion. Yet Peter denied the bonds
of knowledge, of co-presence, of collaboration, of natural and supernatural
communal living that had been mutually enjoyed by him in the company
of Christ. Formerly, these bonds had riveted the two to each other in a
communion of sublime love. Fidelity on Peter's part called for his public
avowal of his tie with Christ; it demanded his public prolongation of the
presence of his friend in himself; it urged the open defense of his friend
and the promulgation of his friend's many benefactions to himself and to
others. Had Peter performed — which he will do in an heroic degree in
the future — these acts of fidelity, had he been faithful in this trial, he
would have been acting in a spiritually creative way. His fidelity would
have creatively multiplied and deepened within himself, while testifying
before others to the unfathomable goodness of his friend, the presence and
goodness of the one who had chosen him the day he enlisted and eloped
with Christ. His communion with Christ, his ardent reassertion of his "we"
with Him, originally rested on the first instant he crossed over to Him.
It could only survive and wax strong on the instant-to-instant renewal of
his confessing of Christ before men under fair or foul circumstances. Fidelity
creates man's being never more fully than when it is triumphing over "the
absence known as death."[35] In our example, the presence of Christ is being
removed from Peter by arrest; soon death will attempt to obliterate the
very memory of Him. Now is the precise time for Peter to perpetuate their
co-presence by regathering his own being and rising to the unconditionality
of their mutual communion, by rallying and witnessing to the immortality
of their friendship.

Hope, too, is founded on the intimacy of communion. Its authentic
formula is: "I hope in you for us,"[36] where the thing hoped for is salvation
that comes from a Presence Who gives us invincible assurance that the

tragedies of time are not final answers to life, despite the seemingly overwhelming contrary evidence in history. Hope is borne up by communion in an atmosphere that is eternal; hope surges highest in the saint, for he is ever driving toward the transcendent, ever extending limitless credit to the Thou. To despair is to refuse — Judas-like — to live and collaborate in the vineyard of presence, of the Absolute Thou.

To hope, then, means essentially to be available, to participate — in the very teeth of the specters of trial, despair and death — in the experience of communion which, in this life, is the precarious adventure aimed at the exaltation of the community of Us. The hopeful man knows that no stable peace can be founded within himself nor among others unless men candidly and with serious conscience accept the fact that they are itinerants in time, called to establish here a community of fidelity, hope and love which hereafter will be taken up into the community of the Absolute Thou. Hope cheerfully comes to terms with this condition and *homo viator* rises above the trials of time, moves perseveringly beyond the criticisms that would destroy hope itself. For hope challenges the very evidence that would doom men to despair, the very evidence upon which men claim to challenge hope itself.[37] Hope is an expansion beyond the "closed time" of the here and now into the "open time" of the eternal hereafter. Hope is but another name for the exigence for being, for transcendence; it is the driving force within man the wayfarer.[38] For hope lives on the conviction that the Absolute Thou is always available, always exposable.

Love, again, is beyond the subject-object dichotomy. Love penetrates into the Infinite Presence. To love a person is to say to him: "Thou at least shalt not die."[39] Although fidelity, hope and love are essentially one, love may be considered as the climax of interpersonal communion achieved by lovers through the whole process of concrete approaches to being. Every opening-up of an I to a Thou is an act of love, is a degree of communion. Love is communion. Love grounds man simultaneously both in communion and in transcendence. Loving creates both the I and the Thou, for loving creates the lovers. Love addresses itself to what is eternal, above the entire order of genesis and vicissitude.[40] Marcel's point is precisely this: Within the participation of love this Thou is exempt from the penalties of things; fate may prey upon things; it can never overtake that by which Thou art a Thou. The more I love a Thou the more assuredly I grasp the Thou as an eternal participant in indefectible Being. At the height of communion, where total assurance is attained in love without any threat or fear or error or doubt, I experience the presence of the beloved as assumed into the Absolute Presence. It is then that I realize that I am able to love only in the climate of eternity.

Actually Marcel takes as his proof for the existence of God this "analogy of presentiality."[41] The loving presence that founds the created I-Thou relationship overflows and transcends in every direction into the loving presence of the Absolute Thou. The very prophetic affirmation of love: "Thou at least shalt not die," is already a faith and hope in the power, the goodness, the love of the Absolute Thou who is invoked as always present, always concerned, always willing, able and determined to sustain, in the communion of love, every created Thou. Of course, the assurance man gains through his faith, hope and love must always be renewed, intensified and strengthened against the betrayal of being to which he is forever being tempted.

The mystery of the family[42]

In the dialectic of communion that fructifies into community, the family, for Marcel, is the social cell of prime importance. This human solar system, of which the child is the center, exemplifies perhaps the most intimate form of "living with." The spiritual vitality of the family is crucial to the progress of communion within communities, for its tensions radiate into every other community. One of the reasons for the "broken world" is the atomization of the family. The spirit of abstraction, implemented with the tools of technology and the techniques of degradation, has uprooted the family, undermining its spiritual and ritual foundations. Displaced within congested cities, families have lost their religious rhythm and tend to become monotonously standardized. They have become victims of a variegated assortment of *divertissements* that identify life with escape from boredom.

The dilemma of our times is: to fulfill oneself or to escape into emptiness. Too much tragic evidence indicates that flight from reality has become extensive. Broken homes and divorces in mounting numbers testify to the flight from the fulfillment of marital responsibilities. Temporary contact and contract have replaced that mutually oblative union which was meant to endure as a presence that is eternally established. Families, bereft of cohesive spiritual communion, are unbearably self-conscious and aware of a gaping void in their lives. The rationalization of divorce and birth prevention is merely the violent transition from the extreme of abstract formalism to the extreme of abstract biologism. Both extremes are divisive of society for they ignore the essential unity of mankind and fail to appreciate its drive toward transcendent communities. Such metaphysical and moral techniques of degradation reduce progenitors to the status of begetters of broods who refuse to become founders of families. On the other hand, true parents first organize their own lives with the clear knowledge that they are not their own and then, through dedication to the creative vow — a prayer of marital communion forever — organize the lives of their children with the clear knowledge that their children no more belong to them than they do to themselves. This spirit of dedicatory service to the family community is instilled into children who grow up, in their turn, to become responsible builders and servants of communion within community.

Plenitude of communion — the mystical body

The quest for communion is achieved, then, by the plunge into mystery. Availability and personal permeability heighten the influx and overflow of presences among persons who are uncluttered with themselves. The nostalgia for communion in community in modern times has grown to a pathological pitch and men are adhering to two major forces that promise to assuage this homesickness. To confuse these forces or to identify them would lead to social suicide.

The "termite colony" certainly recognizes within the human condition and in the depths of human beings a restlessness and an anticipation for a better order. But opting to remain self-enclosed and to proclaim its self-sufficiency, the "termite colony" attacks the transcendental, asserting that all is here, with nothing beyond, offering men a utopia that will make them citizens of culture, progress, science, plenty, knowledge and leisure. These are noble goals for collectivized man, says Marcel, but not nearly noble enough for existential man — the *imago Dei* — who, despite all his weaknesses, is still suffering a secret attraction for membership in a divine as well as human family.

Marcel's philosophy is "open" in the sense that, while it moves upward toward its natural maturation in communion and community, it expects further completion from a dialectic of love from above, from a new and gratuitous influx of the Absolute Thou into the human milieu and into each human person. Marcel moves from the phenomenological and psychological thrusts toward fulfillment in communion and community to their metaphysical and theological plenitude. His philosophy stresses availability to whatever and whoever comes from above — new persons, new mysteries, a New Incarnation, new communions, a New Community. Preoccupied with the salvation of society from both atomization and collectivization, Marcel invites the modern philosopher to examine the implications of the Christian Communion in Community — the Mystical Body.

Notes

[1] Gabriel Marcel, *The Mystery of Being,* Vol. II (Chicago, Illinois: Gateway Edition, Henry Regnery and Company, 1960), p. 197.
[2] Gabriel Marcel, *Man Against Mass Society,* trans, G.S. Fraser (Chicago: Henry Regnery and Company, 1952), p. 140.
[3] Gabriel Marcel, *The Mystery of Being,* Vol. II (Chicago: Gateway Edition, Henry Regnery and Company, 1960), p. 185.

[4]Alice Jourdain, "Von Hildebrand and Marcel: A Parallel," in *The Human Person and the World of Values,* ed. Balduin V. Schwarz (New York: Fordham University Press, 1960), p. 13.

[5]R. Troisfontaines, S.J., *De l'existence à l'etre,* Vol. I (Paris: J. Vrin, 1953), p. 41.

[6]*Ibid.* p. 41.

[7]Etienne Gilson, "Un exemple," in *Existentialisme chrétien,* présentation de Gilson (Paris: Librairie Plon, 1947), p. 2.

[8]Gabriel Marcel, *Du refus à l'invocation* (Paris: Librarie Gallimard, 1940, p. 109. Translation by the author.

[9]Jourdain, *op. cit.,* p. 16.

[10]Gabriel Marcel, *Man Against Mass Society* (Chicago: Henry Regnery Co., 1952), trans. G.S. Fraser, p. 200.

[11]Balduin V. Schwarz, "Introduction," *The Human Person and the World of Values,* ed. Balduin V. Schwarz (New York: Fordham University Press, 1960), p. xiii.

[12]Gabriel Marcel, *Man Against Mass Society* (Chicago: Henry Regnery Co., 1952), trans. G.S. Fraser, p. 200.

[13]Gabriel Marcel, *The Philosophy of Existence* (New York: Philosophical Library, Inc., 1949), trans, Manya Harari, p. 3.

[14]Gabriel Marcel, *Metaphysical Journal* (Chicago: Henry Regnery Co., 1952), trans. Bernard Wall, p. 206.

[15]Gabriel Marcel, *The Mystery of Being,* Vol. II (Chicago: Henry Regnery Co., Gateway Edition, 1960), p. 51.

[16]*Ibid.,* p. 52.

[17]*Ibid.,* pp. 57, 59.

[18]I Cor. 6:19.

[19]Gabriel Marcel, *The Mystery of Being,* Vol. I (Chicago: Henry Regnery Co., Gateway Edition, 1960), p. 111.

[20]David E. Roberts, *Existentialism and Religious Belief* (New York: Oxford University Press, A Galaxy Book, 1959), p. 301.

[21]Gabriel Marcel, *Metaphysical Journal* (Chicago: Henry Regnery Co., 1952), trans, Bernard Wall, p. 321.

[22]*Ibid.,* p. 323.

[23]H.J. Blackham, *Six Existentialist Thinkers* (London: Routledge & Kegan Paul, Inc., 1961), p. 73.

[24]Gabriel Marcel, *The Mystery of Being,* Vol. II (Chicago: Henry Regnery Co., Gateway Edition, 1960), p. 19.

[25]James Collins, "Gabriel Marcel and the Mystery of Being," THOUGHT XVIII, No. 71 (Dec., 1943), 691.

[26]Gabriel Marcel, *Homo Viator* (Chicago: Henry Regnery Co., 1951), trans. Emma Craufurd, p. 22.

[27]Gabriel Marcel, *Being and Having* (Westminster, England: Dacre Press, 1949), trans. Katherine Farrer, p. 115.

[28]Kenneth T. Gallagher, *The Philosophy of Gabriel Marcel* (New York: Fordham University Press, 1962), p. 39.

[29]Gabriel Marcel, *Man Against Mass Society* (Chicago: Henry Regnery Co., 1952) trans. G.S. Fraser. The whole book treats these techniques, as does also *The Decline of Wisdom* (London: The Harvill Press, 1954), trans. Manya Harari.

[30]Gabriel Marcel, *Du refus à l'invocation* (Paris: Librairie Gallimard, 1940), p. 130.

[31]Kenneth T. Gallagher, *The Philosophy of Gabriel Marcel* (New York: Fordham University Press, 1962), p. 92.

[32]Gabriel Marcel, *Homo Viator* (Chicago: Henry Regnery Co., 1951), p. 143.

[33]*Ibid.*, p. 152.

[34]Gabriel Marcel, *The Philosophy of Existence* (New York: Philosophical Library, 1949), trans. Manya Harari, p. 22.

[35]Gabriel Marcel, *Du refus à l'invocation* (Paris: Librairie Gallimard, 1940), p. 199.

[36]Gabriel Marcel, *Homo Viator* (Chicago: Henry Regnery Co., 1951), p. 60.

[37]*Ibid.*, p. 67.

[38]Gabriel Marcel, *The Mystery of Being*, Vol. II (Chicago: Henry Regnery Co., Gateway Edition, 1960), pp. 181-182.

[39]Gabriel Marcel, *The Mystery of Being*, Vol. II (Chicago: Henry Regnery Co., Gateway Edition, 1960, p. 171.

[40]Gabriel Marcel, *Metaphysical Journal* (Chicago: Henry Regnery Co., 1952), trans. Bernard Wall, p. 63.

[41]Pietro Prini, *Gabriel Marcel et la méthodologie de l'invérifiable* (Paris: Desclée de Brouwer, 1953), p. 117.

[42]Gabriel Marcel, *Homo Viator* (Chicago: Henry Regnery Co., 1951.) Confer the chapters on "The Mystery of the Family," and "Creative Vow as Essence of Fatherhood," pp. 68-124.

Reprinted from *Thought* Magazine.

Marcel: The Drama of Transcendence

Theater fulfilled Gabriel Marcel's quest for communion even as music satisfied his hunger for recollection. "Very early in life," Marcel notes, "I experienced a kind of intoxication not only from calling forth persons distinct from myself but also from identifying myself rather completely with them so as to become their dragoman."[1] His vocation for the theater took root and thrived in the soil of his naturally sensitive dispositions and in the social isolation and discontent of the milieu in which he was raised. His father had an innate sense for the theater and was an inveterate reader of plays. Then too, the delicate, gifted Marcel was an only child and he tells us that "the theatrical persons with whom I was delighted to share dialogue held for me the place of the sisters and brothers whose absence I cruelly deplored."[2] Moreover, from infancy the precocious Marcel was involved in the diverse family strifes, sufferings and temperaments that obstructed communion and harmony among his relatives.

Music had already offered Marcel one type of supra-rational unity that allowed him to transcend the agony of his studies, the distressing trivia of daily life. Music restored him to himself as a consciously free person aware of a loftier reality that synthesized and fulfilled the fragmentary limitations of sensory experience. Perhaps play-writing could be another avenue to a mysterious, spiritual recuperation from the fragmentizing contradictions of incompatible humans? Marcel discovered it was. He relates that the plays in which he presented subjects as subjects, that is, in all their concrete reality without any philosophical premeditation, transcended objectivity and yet captured and conveyed to his audiences and readers the vibrant authenticity of full-blooded life.

Good drama is not likely to be written in the service of philosophical prepossessions, although Sartre's diabolical *No Exit, The Flies* and *The Devil and the Good Lord* are exceptions that prove this rule. Now Marcel's theater pieces are excellent drama, but they are never "thesis-dramas." Paralleling his outspoken contempt for closed systems of thought that arbitrarily contract and desecrate the plenitude of reality is Marcel's abhorrence of didactic dramas that artificially destroy the mysterious, complex, sublime and unpredictable freedom of human persons. His plays illustrate no preconceived doctrine that his characters must emit; nor is there any fatalistic destiny which they must undergo.

Not that there is no connection between Marcel's drama and his philosophical thought. There most assuredly is. "I have been a philosopher-dramatist," writes Marcel. "And I insist on their bond of union within me."[3] But his dramatic activity, begun as early as the age of five, was initially an autonomous creation. Long after his dramas are written, read and staged, his philosophic reflection — as another, maturer, independent response to his exigency for being — completes and elaborates the truths already seminally incarnated in his ambiguous characters and their complex conditions. Thus, drama holds a central position in Marcel's work. The exact reverse is true of Jean Paul Sartre, who is, above all, a philosopher first and whose drama is purposely derived from and subservient to his thought. Marcel insists on the priority of his dramatic vocation over his philosophic profession. He warns that "every attempt to expound my philosophic thought is condemned to serious failure if it does not include a study of my dramatic works."[4]

Gaston Fessard, writing of the bond between drama and metaphysics in Marcel's work, says: "Here the bond is substantial. And to such a degree that his dramas cannot surrender their deep meaning to one who fails to discern the metaphysical intuition residing at their core. Moreover, it is as if the reflections of the *Metaphysical Journal* realize their full and true meaning only when referred back to the dramatic personages from whose lips they first emerged fullblown."[5]

The reader, therefore, is not to see in the plays particular illustrations of themes previously expressed in abstract terms. The dramas present concrete situations more felt than conceived. Their deep significance is hidden behind the enigmatic faces of the persons embroiled. Even Marcel, their creator, may never capture the full significance of his own creatures. The way his protagonists respond to the trials in which they are intensely involved often enough surprises the author himself and Marcel admits that his heroes become clear and explicit to him only after years of philosophic reflection. And even then some of them remain obscure and hidden in mystery. Thus, if Marcel's philosophizing about existence is not always concrete, his dramatizing of it is always compact. His philosophy is complementary to his drama and in elucidating this bond between them Marcel can say: "It is in drama and through drama that philosophic thought grasps and defines itself *in concreto*."[6]

Alive, complex, inscrutably immersed in the realities of daily life, Marcel's characters never represent pure ideas or abstract schemes. Virtues and faults agonizingly coexist in his characters as they do in real people. Their dialogues do not lead the spectator to intellectual acceptance of proof-supported truths. "My theatre," says Marcel, "is the theatre of the soul in exile, the soul suffering from a miscarriage of communion with itself and with others."[7]

The characters are confronted with what is obstructing communion in themselves and others. They are at times lucid, disoriented, scattered, interiorly coherent or unreasonable; their lives are somber and tensely drawn-out; the tragedy of their interior alienation may eventually be illuminated by a sudden clairvoyance that pierces protagonists and spectators

alike, permitting both to perceive the barren state of their own souls. Such
"tragedies of thought" involve both actors and audiences in the mystery
of man and of his existence. "The tragedy of reflection quickly becomes
a tragedy of life, evolving from the conflict of man with his neighbor and
with himself."[8]

There is little of the lyrical or poetic in Marcel's plays; they are obsessed
with the seriousness of the human condition. Perhaps this is an excusable
excess. After all, Marcel is not writing *drames de divertissement*. By his own
admission, his theater is an art of communion and communion is its all-
pervading theme, but, more often than not, under a negative aspect. For
Marcel is a living witness, and has been for over sixty years, to the tragedy
of a violently desecrated and broken world in modern times. His theater,
therefore, trenchantly exposes contradictions rather than concords, sadness
rather than joy. Troisfontaines notes that "for the sensitive and sincere
Marcel, drama arises when lying, harshness, pride, daily banality, treason,
false fidelity thwart interpersonal communion and interior guilelessness.
Whence arises a frightful picture which is, nevertheless, so true! Thousands of forms of egoism, rejected love, saddening incomprehensions
which scarcely illumine some of the dramas with even a glimmer of resurrection."[9]

Yet, unlike Sartre, Marcel does not abandon his audiences to despair,
with "no exit" from the "sickness of being." In Sartre's existentialism,
"Hell is. . .other people"[10] in the sense that the other always threatens
his being, his freedom. Men are cursed with personal freedom and with
the predatory presence of other free men who are threats to each other's
integrity. Man's ideal is to be alone, completely self-sufficient, his own
creator. But man's dream and drive to become his own God is the primordial
idiocy, for the very idea of God is contradictory. "The first duty, then,
of the creature is to deny its creator." Thus, Sartre's plays turn out to
be propaganda pieces, attempts to popularize the philosophy that "man
is a useless passion"[11] whose fundamental, metaphysical experience is that
of nausea and whose noblest goal is the exaltation of his self-sufficiency
in antitheistic humanism. *The Devil and the Good Lord* dramatically rejects
a God who has already been metaphysically constructed as impossible. *No
Exit* demonstrates the predetermined fatuity of intersubjective communion.
The Flies proves *a priori* that antitheistic humanism is the only possible
authentic humanism.

Quite contrary to such dramatic ventures in ideology, Marcel's theater
is an experiment in metaphysics. It turns up a far more hopeful and sublime
reading of reality, despite the omnipresence of tragedy. If hell is man-made
— and there is a valid sense in which it is — it is created by man's willful
refusal to pass from the initial reception of the love-gift of existence to new

participations in being — in the world, in other men, in the Absolute. For Marcel, communion with others, not domination over others is at the heart of metaphysics. The unique, yet difficult, vocation of *homo viator* is to achieve his being in depth by gladly cooperating with other men, consciously making himself available both to them and to God. Such transcendence in Marcel's dramatic work consists in exalting interiorization and accepting the way of communion, no matter what obstacles must be hurdled to persevere on this way. Marcel ambitions in his plays to send the reader and the spectator back into his own soul, not isolated, but bound with compassionate love to the souls in exile depicted on stage, so that with a renewed glance at himself and his companions in real life, his taste for being may be revitalized and blessed with a mysteriously new degree of expansion. This sense of reality, this superior grasp of one's life and destiny is attained in the consciousness of communion.

Thus dramatic persons and tragic human situations embody Marcellian themes of communion years before Marcel ever gets around to understanding the persons themselves or developing the themes fully in his reflective, more mature philosophic distillations. With Marcel persons are always primary; he usually places them in situations which he himself has critically experienced; his living persons encounter and react toward each other in collisions of opposed instincts, minds and wills; the outcome of these encounters can never be accurately predicted. Troisfontaines, who has been privileged to peruse many of Marcel's unpublished works, relates that "there are a great number of unfinished plays in Marcel's files: for he has not been able to resolve the situation. On the other hand, sometimes he takes up and continues a play which he began years before, because now he finally sees the way in which the characters should develop."[12]

We have here an indication of the reciprocal development of Marcel's theater and his metaphysics. By a profound insight Marcel has come to realize that his feeling for tragedy is founded in the bosom of being. The tragedies that fill daily life constantly challenge men to transcend the temptation to restrict themselves solely to the possession, problematization and systemization of all being. Tragedy and dialects are engendered at the core of each personal life where the surge to be is confronted by the lust to have. This pulsating dialectic between being and having is the point of departure for every human drama. When having is victorious, the subject has surrendered to the temptation of self-alienation, self-objectivization, self-abandonment. Estranged from himself and others, such a "soul in exile" has lost authentic existence. Authentic existence consists in being-with others, not in having-against others. Even to attempt to possess oneself is to lose oneself. I can neither have myself nor my self-knowledge; I am both of these. To objectify myself or my knowledge of myself into the category of a possession is to problematize the essential mystery of my existence by freely abandoning my subjecthood.

The mode and milieu of man's existence is such that every man is tempted to flee himself through some form of objectivization. Some men identify themselves with their ideals; others accommodate themselves to the image demanded by the pressures of their circumstances; still others freeze themselves into postures they imagine are perfect for their professions. For Marcel, drama and philosophy, tragedy and dialectics are mutually created in this struggle to achieve authentic existence by conquering the temptation to flee into objectivization. It follows that Marcel's plays are a series of unmaskings of personages who have subtly, often even sincerely, succeeded in hiding themselves from themselves, and thus sealing themselves off from others. The dramatic roles lived by Marcel's characters, in their attempt to synthesize the metaphysical polarity between being and having into an inner peace of being, are as varied as real life itself. Here we shall restrict ourselves to four major categories of human activities that attempt to surmount this ambivalent dialectic: religion, art, morality and love. In our analysis of these activities, we will consider six of Marcel's dramas, taking two from each period of his creative activity in the theater. The three periods cover more than forty-two years of work with publication dates appearing from 1911 to 1953. The periods are divided into pre-World War I, between the major wars, and post-World War II.

Pre-World War I period

La Grace (1911, a play in five acts)

The time is 1910. Françoise Thouret is typical of the newly emancipated young women, endowed with a rigorously logical and uncompromising mind. A student of medicine, she is an ardent devotee of Dr. du Ryer, psychophysiologist and positivist par excellence. Under a pseudonym, she composes and stages a scandalous play which is a huge hit. Olivier, her brother, discovers her authorship and breaks down in *une crise de larmes*. Amused at his naiveté, Françoise is, nevertheless, deeply moved by his sense of decency. At twenty-three, characterized by a thirst for moral and intellectual clarity, Françoise is in revolt against pharisaism of any kind.

She is also passionately, physically in love with Gerard Launoy, dillettante and "mama's boy," who is endowed with an astonishingly tender temperament and also stricken with tuberculosis. Françoise rejects maternal advice against the marriage; she refuses Gerard's offer to break the engagement and rushes plans for the wedding. As to the warning that happiness can never ensue from this union with a sick man who has just severed a liaison with a paramour, Françoise retorts that she does not expect happiness, that silly, arid nothing; she will discover something better. Sick or not, her Gerard "is handsome because I love him, and I love him . . . because I am I."[13] So they marry and off they go to the mountains to regain Gerard's health.

But, to Françoise's horror, a spiritual abyss begins to yawn widely between them. Gerard's illness becomes the occasion for his conversion to Catholicism and his evolution in grace. For her part, Françoise is consumed by a double lie, the lie to herself — she has married to sate her violent passion — and the lie in her beloved — her marrriage to the dying Gerard is not an "act of supreme charity," as she allows him to think. And the lies are rendered more unendurable to her because Françoise can truly say of herself: " . . . Sincerity is perhaps the only duty I have understood, the only duty I want to fulfill."[14] Her friend, Antoinette, attempts to console Françoise, justifying her lie-life with rationalizations on an ever-recurring Marcellian theme: "At bottom what difference does it all make? Aren't people always impenetrable to each other anyway? What good is it to desire to be known as one is? Do you really know yourself and what you actually are?"[15]

Will love dissolve the life of double duplicity that ensnares Françoise? Grace is offered to heal the conflict. Gerard accepts this "unexpected gift from a spiritual and unfathomable power who has heard the appeals arising from my misery and defilement."[16] But Françoise, invited to participate, remains obdurate, becoming instead her husband's temptress. Olivier, repelled by positivism and envious of Gerard's conversion, confronts his sister's pride: "Even if such faith as Gerard's were an illusion, it is far more honorable than your truth."[17]

Their opposition on faith seems final. At this point, Père André is called in and attends Gerard. Françoise sums up the situation in a letter to her mother: "It is the last station; grace will soon accomplish its destructive work. Whatever I loved, whatever I desired . . . everything has been torn from me."[18] Gerard, for his part, realizes the emptiness of his past life, of his ventures in illicit love as a man of the world; he is haunted by the ruined rakes he has known. Some persons, it seems, must bound up to God from the springboard of iniquity; he sees in Père André the long-awaited sign of his salvation. The priest quiets his final worries: "Put no credence in a hell for the predestined." And Gerard exclaims: "My God! Save me from giddiness in the presence of the hereafter![19]

The impasse against communion locks into a spiritual rigidity. Gerard is almost over the threshold of the hereafter; Françoise is left behind and below. Daily, unavoidably they hurt each other. In desperation, Françoise admits her lie to Gerard: "No! I didn't foolishily throw myself into your arms for your sake, not for your sake. Nor was it to save you from despair that I refused to put off this mad marriage. It was for myself. . .I loved you. . .And now this sacrifice! My God, it is very simple: I desired you. . .Shall we end our sojourn in cloudland? Reality is not so noble. . .but it is much better, indeed, than idle myths which make men tipsy."[20]

The dream life between them is ended; grace can continue to grow. It begins to touch Françoise: "Do you believe that I have failed to follow the progress of your illumination, that I have not realized that its growth coincided with the growth of your sickness?" "Sickness is the instrument. . .," responds Gerard, "nature is always ignorant of its own capabilities; nature always acts as if it is everything, self-sufficient, forgetting that its source is outside, beyond itself, as is also its goal."[21]

But Françoise is still in revolt. Although she rejects faith, the struggle has shaken her loose from scientism. Bitter and in agony, she visits Professor du Ryer and denounces him for playing at positivism which is "an illusion of science, a diversion, a screen erected to seal off men from reality."[22] Yet isolated and lonely, deprived of love and certitude, she throws herself at the old professor, her illicit surrender seeming to fulfill her need for suicide.

Almost miraculously, Gerard recovers. What is more, he is taken with a physical passion for his wife. But his response is too late. Françoise confesses her infidelity; she has given her body to a man she does not love and cannot share herself simultaneously with others. And yet her old love is still aflame. "You do not see that you have reconquered me! The passion which rages within you consumes me also. Ah! Why was I destined to lose you at the moment I found you! I was bewildered, in despair. . .you spurned me. . .the first revenge life offered me. . . ." But Gerard, all forgiveness, sees divine providence in her betrayal which restores his moral composure. "Don't try to explain. . .your crime is not self-explanatory, but it can justify itself. . .Pick yourself up." But Françoise will not succumb to grace even now. "No! Not the insult of your pardon!" Gerard attempts to belittle his pardon and her crime. "I have not pardoned you. . .the cause of your deeds is beyond you." But Françoise continues to flee anywhere, away from forgiveness, even toward the grave. "No, not that!. . .rather death![23]

The shock of final separation brings Gerard to a serious relapse. On the threshold of death he regains his faltering faith. Olivier, unable to enjoy the religious certitude of his dying friend, exclaims: "The intensity of one's faith is surely the measure of one's being. . .Perhaps He (God) is only man's supreme longing." "God is free!" exclaims Gerard, raising himself with effort.[24] Then he dies. Françoise, in tears, hurls herself on the body of her dead husband, while Olivier, seeking the secret of the profound peace in that immobile countenance, murmurs reverently as the curtain falls: "Nothing remains but this look...and only on our faith in this look...."[25]

How did it all finally come out? Was Françoise converted? Did Olivier regain his lost faith? Is there a place beyond the barrier and mystery of death where love and faith can meet, where Françoise may accept the gift of faith and thereby attain communion with Gerard? Marcel, in a lecture years later on this play, admits of three possible answers. The objective answer is No! But this naturalistic response is utterly untenable; it misses the metaphysical, mysterious, miraculous dimensions of reality, hence it is superficial. The neutral answer is also inadequate; Olivier personifies that; he recognizes the reality of faith and grace, but refuses to become involved in either. Gerard's response is the only authentic answer, founded on the transcendent truth that man's aspirations for immortality are not the mere illusory flames of hearts on the verge of extinction, but divine dimensions of their mysterious existence.[26] Grace is far more than a dream, far more than a sublimated delirium for eternal existence; it is the experience of an abiding presence and communion with the loved one beyond the visible grave, beyond the invisible threshold of transcendence, within a living intercourse with the Absolute Thou.

Le Palais de Sable (1913, a play in four acts)

Roger Moirans, rightist politician, nationalist pro-clerical and champion of Catholic morality against Laicism's freethinkers, is receiving the plaudits of enthusiastic backers when the curtain rises on a French provincial town shortly before World War I. He has just routed the forces favoring secularistic public education in a meeting of the city council. High comedy and satire permeate the scene.

Quite understandably, Moirans is adamantly opposed to the divorce which his eldest daughter Thérèse, caught in an unhappy marriage, is contemplating. Besides the religious reasons for this opposition, there is its threat to his political career. Moirans' pride and joy is his baby Clarisse in which he sees the spiritual reflection of himself. But now Clarisse shocks her father by announcing her intention to become a Carmelite nun. The dramatic conflict revolves around Moirans' attempts to deflect Clarisse from the cloister.

Moirans is aghast at the possibility of witnessing the convent-burial of his spirited, intelligent, beautiful daughter. Clarisse, for her part, is amazed at her father's implacable resistance. How can her father's opposition to religious life be compatible with his political work as champion of Catholicism? Ironically, Moirans learns that he himself is the inspiration of his daughter's vocation. His walks with Clarisse to the Carmelite convent one day moved him to speak so reassuringly about religion that he quieted her fears of death. Clarisse now wants to live where she can rise every morning with the peace she then experienced. But Moirans proceeds to eclipse her spiritual sun with the clouds of his reasonings.

He accuses Clarisse of running away to a peaceful refuge, of avoiding temptation and evil, the inevitable lot of all men. But Clarisse denies seeking mere repose; her entrance is not a flight, but a confrontation; the struggle is most terrible at the summit where life's value is measured by agony and fervor; ecstatic immobilization in adoration is not her goal, but rather combat and victory. As for Moirans' position, Clarisse has some accusations of her own. Her father's faith is not authentic; he does not believe in a future life where her sacrifice will find fulfillment; his life has been one long lie, an imposture, a fraud that has utilized religion merely as a necessary restraint on human excesses. He has been a skeptic dabbling in religion as a pragmatic dilettante, professing a faith founded on no transcendent Being.

The shock of confrontation in this *crise de foi* brings father and daughter to a reciprocal clarification. Moirans is disgusted by what he sees in himself; he would seek deliverance through death, were he that courageous. He agrees with Clarisse that he must abandon his role of *defensor fidei* to which he does not really adhere. He will retire from politics, thus completing the severance with his life's central lie, as a first step toward moral integrity and salvation.

But Moirans' doubt has now contaminated his daughter. Suddenly Clarisse is in a storm of confusion. Was her vocation, after all, only a dream? Was it not really a temptation to escape? Recourse to an incompetent confessor only compounds her confusion. At this point, Moirans cyncially adds a diabolical condition to his retirement from political life, "provided Clarisse abandons her determination to enter the convent."[27]

A sudden emergency arises in which the Church needs Moirans. Monsignor Vielle petitions him to remain in public life, but Moirans counters that he is no longer a Catholic, has, in reality, never been one. The bishop's masterful rationalizations fail to hold Moirans at his post. Ironically, the bishop becomes for Moirans what Moirans has already become for Clarisse, a stumbling stone in the path of an authentic vocation. But where the bishop fails, Moirans succeeds. With the help of Clarisse, Moirans conquers the bishops' temptations. However, destroyed when his own faith collapses as "a palace of sand," the father now drags little Clarisse down with himself. Using his own sacrifice as a sort of blackmail, Moirans continues to urge Clarisse to give up her vocation. She gradually succumbs to the contagion of his incredulity. The priest had made some fatuous statements about convent life, making it appear frightful. In disgust, Clarisse decides her father is right and fulfills her end of the bizarre bargain. Moirans appears triumphant, but the price of his victory is that he has blinded with his own sightlessness the only being in the world he really loves.

Her paradise of prayers and peace gone, unhappy, alone and drifting, Clarisse drags out her existence "between heaven and earth. . . too low to live with God, too high to live among men."[28] When Pierre Servan asks her to marry him she replies: ". . . Because you will make me happy, I cannot accept. . . Some beings are born to be unhappy."[29] Although she really loves Pierre, Clarisse is suffering from the nostalgia for her lost paradise; now she will never be like other ordinary humans who marry and have children. But Pierre goes down fighting: "If you would not cling to your hope in the hereafter, you would not destroy the source of happiness, the origin of life itself. . . Your attitude is hideous. Had you seen, as I have hundreds of times, the life of the dying flickering like a frail flame on the verge of extinction, you would realize that this life is all there is that is precious. But no, hypnotized you walk toward mirages. True, you do not realize this. The dead do not repent. . . Allow me to unburden my whole soul as we will no longer see each other. I cannot even admire you, for, though the path you follow is certainly harsh, it brings you salvation; though its gate is narrow, it opens up on heaven."[30] "What do you know about heaven? What do you know about salvation?," replies Clarisse. "For you, these are but words or silly mirages. But the kingdom of heaven is within us. It is not a land of miracles promised for the day after death. It is a place of benediction where inexhaustible faith grows; eternal life is not a hope; it is not a future; it is today, the present."[31]

In the end Clarisse condemns her father for the spiritual murder he committed in bringing her to doubt her faith. "It was you who made me doubt and in doubting I became a different person. . . The spirit of pride was my master. Father, here is your crime. In wishing to explain my faith, you killed it. . . Never does faith die a natural death; in the realm of the spirit, there are only suicides and murders."[32] Life now becomes banal and intolerable for Clarisse; she is exiled and moves in a world of chimeras. One final blow falls. Her old, irksome, despotic mother, who has been away from home for a long time, is returning. Clarisse had some communion of thought with her father; her mother imposed the solitude of the tomb. But perhaps her mother could now help. "Mama, listen. . . I am here, Mama. . ." Clarisse is on her knees. "You are praying. To whom are you praying?,"[33] demands Moirans. Clarisse can answer nothing. Their loss of faith has closed off all communication between father and daughter.

Was the life of grace recaptured? We cannot say for certain. Grace, for Marcel, renders liberty possible. Speaking of the meaning of this liberty, Marcel says: "The fundamental difference between Sartre and myself is that I have never been able to consider liberty as an absolute, that, in my eyes, liberty can only exist on condition that it be joined and condemned with grace considered as such." Françoise and Gerard, Clarisse and Moirans certainly demonstrate this Marcellian affirmation. Intersubjectivity and communion are demanded for the heart of man by the ambiguity, by the invisible threshold that grace and liberty alone can transcend.

Period between the world wars

A Man of God (1921, a play in four acts)

Claude Lemoyne, a Huguenot pastor, is an ideal shepherd in the service of the holy gospel. A cultured man of the cloth, he feeds his parishioners on solid, well-reasoned sermons, eschewing superficial twaddle. His dedication is total; he mounts every breach, counsels, aids, consoles, relieves whoever is in need. And his wife Edmée is an excellent apostolic assistant. Into this relationship of family harmony an unexpected dissonance is sounded. A message arrives from Claude's brother, Dr. Francis Lemoyne, stating that Michel Sandier, the real father of the pastor's child, Osmonde, is dying and begs to see his daughter before the end.

Twenty years before, shortly after their marriage, Edmée had had as lover Michel Sandier; Osmonde was the fruit of their adulterous union. But Edmée had confessed her crime to Claude and begged his forgiveness. At the time of this shocking confession, Claude was in the throes of a prolonged temptation to abandon his ministry. From the depths of a soul blacked out by his wife's treason, a mysterious grace illumined Claude and he found the strength to forgive the betrayal. His surrender to forgiveness marvelously expanded his soul and inundated him with a renewed sense of the dignity of his mission. He related the experience to his mother: "Yes, I forgave her. And I shall never forget what that did for me, the inner peace it brought, the sense of a Power working with me and not instead of me, strengthening my will but not supplanting it. Since that day I've seen my way clear. Before I was groping in the dark. . . The test, Mother, the test. Before those terrible months the word sounded hollow to me. But after what I went through. . . .

Edmée's infidelity, by mutual accord, was erased and never beclouded their conjugal union. Osmonde was shielded from the sorry story. Yet the consciousness of this reality did disturb Edmée's relationship to Osmonde. Edmée is worried over Osmonde's frequent missions of mercy to the children of the tenant upstairs whose incurably sick wife has virtually rendered him a widower. Osmonde resents her mother's suffocating surveillance and appeals to her father for a life of normal freedom from suspicion. It is into this minor friction that Michel Sandier's petition comes as a catalyst for disintegration. Will Claude grant his plea to visit Osmonde? How can Claude justify a refusal? Would not a refusal to this legitimate request be an act of cowardice? Would it not prove that the past was not really dead? Where does forgiveness begin and end? As for Sandier, how brief his time for grace! Besides, refusal would undermine the foundation of Claude's apostolic mission!

But Edmée is terrified. How can Claude be so cold-blooded! Dare he invite her companion in adultery into their home? ''I'm sick of your tolerance; I'm sick of your broad-mindedness. It nauseates me....Yes, you forgave me, but it wasn't because you loved me...What was your forgiveness for?...What good is it to me?''[36]

So his charity toward Edmée these twenty years was all a professional gesture! He had only been playing the role of the good shepherd and reaping personal profits from that stellar performance. Claude's magnanimity, the cornerstone of his renewed life with Edmée, is now undermined. And Edmée's distrust infects her husband. The home of the Lemoynes totters on the sands of suspicion and falls before the winds of confusion and un-certainty. Claude loses his sense of spiritual direction, his sense of mission; he questions the genuinity of all he has done in the past, of whatever he is doing at present. An interior withering of soul plagues the entire family. Edmée is no longer sure of the sincerity of her remorse. Did she return to Claude for security reasons only? Did she ever love Claude, Michel or anyone else besides herself? Osmonde, estranged from her distrusting mother, is contemplating elopement with the married father upstairs.

Without awaiting an answer from the pastor, Michel Sandier appears at the Lemoyne home. He confronts Edmée and her husband. But Claude is temporarily called away, leaving the adulterous pair alone with each other. The ensuing dialogue is tense, coldly embittered, psychologically brilliant, one of the finest demonstrations of Marcel's skill as the dramatist who reveals the ''inside'' of souls in exile. Its temper is passionate; its pace swift, sure; not a useless word is uttered; the articulation of its various thoughts and emotions mounts to a crescendo of intersubjective agitation that is quite devastating. On the edge of the tomb, Michel wounds Edmée, despoiling their idyllic love of long ago. Edmée has only loved Edmée; pity, love, fidelity happened solely to her, never to *us*; jealousy is her canker; calculated cowardice her escape-hatch from moral insecurity. Edmée is terrified at being the guilty cause of Michel's dereliction. But Michel, who has ''gone to the dogs'' on her account, refuses ''the signed certificate of innocence''[37] she is desperately seeking. "If only you'd had more guts and less virtue, who knows...we might have made something of our lives together.''[38]

Michel has scarcely left when Claude returns to find a gravely shaken Edmée. Quickly they are again pitted against each other. Edmée's adultery is laid at Claude's door. Had he loved her more as a husband, less as an evangelist, she would never have been unfaithful. As for his forgiveness, he was using a marvelous opportunity for "saving the soul of a poor sinner." As the curtain falls on Act II, a livid Claude has sprung to his feet and is shouting at his envenomed wife: "Be silent, you are destroying me!''[39] The spectator is overwhelmed with tragic pity at the spiritual disintegration that is mutually inflicted by all the characters involved.

But the ultimate poignancy is achieved when Claude's last link to reality — Osmonde's trust and love — is snapped. When Claude eventually reveals to Osmonde the truth about her paternal origin, the girl is stunned. She reacts quickly and violently against her mother. "Oh, how I hate her!''[40] Toward Claude she feels the utmost compassion until she learns that, in a moment of shame, he lied to her about just having learned of Edmée's infidelity; he had known it all these many years. Now there is nothing left for any of them. "The three of us without any illusions left about one another.''[41] Osmonde, determined to break away from this maze of detestable compromises with false conventionalities, throws herself at the married man upstairs; Claude sighs for self-presence or suicide. "To be known as one is...or else to sleep.''[42] Edmée is frightened at the impending future of loneliness. In the end the poor pastor, touched by the kind act of some good parishioners, turns to prayer for the answer to his question: "Who am I? What am I? What am I worth?" Other sources had given him the lie; his family, his flock, he himself cannot solve this riddle. "To be known as one is..." is his agonized appeal to the Absolute Thou. And the drama closes on the hope that this man of God will rediscover his spiritual center, regain his metaphysical balance, reactivate his transcendent mission in the refound presence of the divine Thou to whom the grace-seeded tragedies of his life have driven him.

Le Dard (1936, a play in three acts)

As the clouds of World War II gathered over a Europe that was attempting to appease the Nazi beast by feeding it small, helpless neighbors, Marcel's dramatic work changed its focus. His "dramas of ambiguity" now echoed the heightened moral confusion that darkened the souls of men and nations. Everywhere the sickly spirit of surrender was corroding the spiritual stamina of Europe; the umbrella had supplanted the cross as the symbol of salvation. It was in this milieu of international illusion and treason that *Le Dard* was composed.

The play's conflict concentrates on the substance of human dignity; its clash occurs between professor Eustache Soreau and German singer Werner Schnee. Eustache Soreau is an embitterd, exasperated teacher of working-class roots who is bound to an affluent politician's daughter, Beatrice Durance Fresnel, by marriage, money and munificence. In his student days, he worked in the Socialist party with Gertrude Heuzard who was dismissed from her teaching post for seeding her students' minds with revolutionary propaganda. Eustache learned his lesson well and rose, not without great personal effort, from proletarian to patrician status. This accomplishment and accommodation earned him the caustic contempt of his former radical comrades. Unstable, suspicious, hypersensitive, Eustache is plagued by a bad conscience that justifies itself in violent, anti-Rightist rhetoric. His very success is the source of his bitter resentment, for it reveals that he is living the life of a lie, that he is a traitor to the social ideals of the revolution which still attracts his allegiance.

Earlier in his career, as a lecturer at the University of Marburg, Eustache and Werner Schnee had met and become fast friends. Werner, a singer of lieder of consummate artistry, has quit Nazi Germany, much to the displeasure of his wife, Gisela, in a venture of fraternal solidarity with his friend and accompanist, Rudolf Schontal, a Communist Jew who has been severely maltreated by the Nazis and lies dying in Switzerland. From the moment the Soreaus open their home to the refugee Schnees, the dissolution of the frienship begins. Eustache is a devotee of ideology; Werner despises abstractions. Much as he hates Nazism, Werner refuses to join any parties; he will not even associate with other German political refugees so as to avoid succumbing to the constricting emigré mentality. Above all, Werner aims at being a man; he rejects slogans and labels as vulgarian dilutions of the mystery that is man. On the other hand, Eustache's preoccupation with remaining loyal to his proletarian origins vitiates his whole personality. He accuses Werner of being an individualist, blames his wife for addiction to her privileged, bourgeois surroundings and scolds his mother for her fawning servitude toward her rich daughter-in-law. The partisan spirit is his moral disease and, as it metastasizes within him, it moves him to reduce all universality to ideology. Werner accuses Eustache of insufferable narrowness, of insolently judging others, not by their intrinsic, universal qualities, but by the categories into which he has imprisoned them. Eustache jealously resents his wife's concurrence in Werner's conclusions; the hostile struggle between them mounts. Finally, in a spirit of meanness, Eustache betrays Werner by revealing to Gisela a secret his old friend had committed to him under the strictest confidence. A government emissary from Germany had invited Werner to return to his nazified fatherland where he would receive top billing in an opera house, provided he espoused the Hitlerian cause. Werner categorically refuses this invitation to self-degradation. His superficial and light-headed wife, Gisela, explodes at his secrecy and refusal; she quits Werner and flees with a rich German baron from the intolerably harsh life of a refugee to the comfort of her homeland. Ironically, Eustache, who is haunted by a fear of treason against his proletarian masses, succeeds in committing the crime of treason against his friend.

But it seems as if no alienation occurs without some compensating communion and, thus, a bond of affection is born between Werner, who is endowed with the gift of moving hearts, and Beatrice who has lost her husband to the cause of ideology. Yet Werner refuses to exploit his gift for arousing sympathy, even when Beatrice, who has discovered Eustache's love affair with Socialist Gertrude, throws herself at him. Werner, uncertain that he can resist his love for Beatrice, decides to return to Germany, but not under the conditions offered by Hitler's henchmen. A scruple of conscience moves him to do something heroic for the political slaves in the Nazi concentration camps. Perhaps he can sing for them, become for them not so much a political ally as a companion in their suffering; he can give them the benefit of his presence, of his love. Has Werner been tainted by Eustache's guilty conscience? Perhaps. But he has no illusions as to his fate: arrest and deportation or execution. But before he goes, he must do his best to save Beatrice, to lift her to his own heights, to convince her that salvation springs from transcendence. Somehow he must make her see that his departure is not an act of suicide. Suicide! "Not in the least," Werner protests, "suicide is a crime...I am simply putting myself at the disposal...." "Of what?" asks Beatrice. "Of the cause? Of the revolution?" "I am not interested in the cause," Werner replies emphatically, "I am interested in men."[43] But Beatrice desires to hold him., Will not her husband Eustache abandon her and flee with Gertrude, that tart, that barbed dart who has speared him? Werner exhorts Beatrice to remain at the side of her husband for she alone can save him. "You cannot abandon him. You must always remember that you are the wife of a pauper...Poverty is not a deficiency of money, nor an absence of success. Eustache has had money; he has been a success. Yet he has remained poor and grown poorer still. Without a doubt, he will never be cured of his poverty. This is the greatest evil of our times; it is spreading like a plague. No physician has yet been found to take care of it. Nor has anyone as yet been able to diagnose it. Doubtless, the artist will be spared, even if he fasts and starves. And, to be sure, the true believer who gives himself to prayer...All other persons are in danger."

Beatrice protests that Werner is asking her to live with a leper. And Werner replies prophetically: "Leper colonies are going to multiply on earth, I fear. To very few people will grace be granted to live there knowing they are among lepers and yet not finding them repulsive. Much more than grace, they will need a viaticum to sustain them on their way."[45] Beatrice contends she lacks the bravery to face life without Werner. In the end, Werner exhorts her to find strength for the struggle where he himself is finding it for his coming ordeal in Germany — in communion with the beloved. "You will think of me as I think of Rudolf. Later I shall be in you a living presence, as Rudolf dwells on in me. You will remember then what I told you a few weeks ago. 'If there were only the living, Beatrice, I think life on this earth would be altogether impossible.'"[46]

Commenting philosophically on this drama from the Harvard University platform of the William James Lectures in 1961, Marcel said:

What *is* this poverty which is neither lack of money nor lack of success and which, we are told, is going to spread like leprosy? It might be said, I think, that it is the spirit of abstraction which finds in our own day — and we must not hesitate to say so — its most terrifying, though not its only incarnation in communism. But this spirit of abstraction cannot be separated from a certain lack of love, and by this I mean the inability to treat a human being as a human being, and for this human being the substituting of a certain idea, a certain abstract designation. The leper colonies which are going to multiply on earth (let me recall that this was written in 1936) are the popular democracies, to the extent that they are committed to the spirit of abstraction in its Marxist form.[47]

Le Dard leaves this fateful question yet unanswered: Which shall prevail — the rationalistic, egocentric, resentful spirit of equalitarianism (Eustache's ideology) or the realistic, heterocentric, neighborly spirit of fraternity (Werner's agapeology)? The nations, indeed, the citizens, will have to make a dreadful decision between the determinism of ideology and the liberty of agape. Marcel expects the salvation of man's dignity solely in that free life of transcendence which strengthens man's consciousness of his living bond with his fellow men.

Post-world war II period

L'Emissaire (1945-1948, a play in three acts)

Marcel was dejected at the excesses perpetrated by the Résistance in France's postwar purification program. During what he calls *des années noires,* the spirit of suspicion, fear and vengeance pitted Frenchmen against

Frenchmen. Each citizen felt called upon to prove he had not collaborated with the enemy; blackmail became the common weapon to bring down your adversary. The careful reader will notice that the existing state of confusion allows the characters involved to reveal themselves very gradually, like spies making contact with other unknown spies in enemy country. It is well for the reader or spectator, of this play especially, to recall Marcel's warning. "No more here than elsewhere did I start from abstract ideas to be dramatically illustrated afterwards."[48]

Clement Ferrier returns home after spending sixteen months in a prison camp in Polish Silesia. He remains ominously silent, displaying no sign of joy at reunion with his loved ones. People attribute his petrified silence to the intense sufferings he must have undergone, for he returned a wasted skeleton scarcely alive. But an uneasiness beclouds the minds of his neighbors. "How did he manage to return? Did he escape? Did he collaborate?" Clement refuses to see the press, to answer any questions, to make any statements. Yet to the congratulations of Antoine Sorgue, fiancé to his daughter, Sylvia, Clement explodes: "No, no, not joy; don't use that word, I beg you."[49] Poor Clement seems to be reliving a nightmare, destined to die with these frightening words on his lips, words that are constantly haunting his wife: "Mathilda, don't ever have a doubt about this...you are speaking to a dead man!"[50]

Some time later, a letter arrives at the Ferrier home from a doctor who was Clement's companion in captivity. Dr. Van Doren saved a Nazi leader's life in an epidemic which was raging in camp. The grateful leader offered Van Doren his freedom, but, in place of himself, the doctor persuaded the Nazi to free Clement whose condition was very grave and who had already attempted to poison himself. "I am sure," writes the doctor, "that he (Clement) is torturing himself on my account; no doubt he told you of this incident. He was unwilling to accept my proposal. But I felt I could hold out until the end, while he would doubtless have perished within a few weeks or even days."[51] So Clement was understandably ashamed. But how could he justifiably reject his family?

Mathilda belonged to a generation which still believed in conscience. Somewhat of a religious simpleton, she managed to confuse everything and confound everyone. To her the Résistance was rank sectarianism; she expected Clement's traumatic condition to be cured by a radiologist or an oculist as easily as one wipes away squalor and coal dust from a miner. Sylvia, Clement's youngest daughter, is a very ambivalent person. Shortly after the war, she had worked for the Résistance together with her friend Noemie Vitrel. But she had quit, after attending some secret meetings, to become engaged to Antoine Sorgue. Not long after this, Noemie was arrested and deported for working the mission originally given to Sylvia.

Antoine is a forthright, faithful, lucid Catholic, but hardly likable. Yet he is the one who lays bare the ambiguity of this drama. At first, Sylvia, who is strongly pro-Résistance, attempts to dissociate herself from him. But she eventually falls in love with him for the maturity and profound compassion with which Antoine understands the tragic condition of all the characters caught up in the maelstrom of the Résistance and the hateful collaboration. Antoine himself had been a prisoner of war, interned for a year in Saxony. Evacuated as sick, he later learned that he was freed through the intervention of a collaborator. Early in the occupation, he had worked for a publishing house that printed German propaganda. Anne-Marie, an older daughter of the Ferriers, and her husband Bertrand Sorel, had been very active members of the Résistance. Together with Roger, Bertrand's implacably atheistic brother, they suspect Antoine of being a collaborator and oppose Roland and his mother Madame de Carmoy for banking on a German victory. After the armistice, Roland is arrested as a collaborator. He hangs himself in his cell; his mother, on hearing of this tragedy, commits suicide. What was Roland's crime? A sincere young man, he had remained in the Holderin Philosophy Circle even after it had fallen under a "mixed patronage." It was Roland also who had intervened to help free Antoine. Moreover, he disapproved of the harsh methods of the French purification and was actually looking for a *rapprochement* with the Germans through the mediation of the intellectual élite on both sides. Roland may certainly have been naive, but he was not a traitor.

The double suicide shocks a chastened and sympathetic Sylvia back into the arms of Antoine, even though she feels that her original convictions against the collaborators are still valid. "Hundreds of thousands of men," she had told the collaborating Madame de Carmoy, "have known hell...hell, Madame! I suppose there is scarcely any mention of this word, which brings a smile to your face, in the elegant and reactionary parishes where you attend services. It would be improper, in bad taste...Nevertheless, hell exists...persons of your mentality, whose echo you've made yourself, are the caterers of hell. In one way or another, they have repeatedly fed hell to the human race. How can you fail to be ashamed of yourself? When I listen to you, it is as if I am inhaling the stench of the dirtiest of dungeons."[52]

Throughout the drama, both the men of the Résistance and the collaborators seem to be acting from a sincere consciousness of their responsibilities. The temptation to judge each side as categorically evil is great and both sides succumb to it with a vengeance. Yet ironically, great deeds and evil deeds are performed on both sides. Clement is liberated by a prisoner who survives him and unknowingly hastens him to an early grave. As for Roland, did he kill himself in a cowardly fashion? Or was

he too proud to submit to the grilling of the narrow partisans? Did his
mother dispatch herself to be with Roland, or was she dragged down into
his despair? Noemie returns from prison, a hate-breathing Communist,
convinced that Sylvia betrayed her. Sylvia herself is not so sure she did
not betray her friend and she has a guilty conscience over the lie of ill health
she advanced as the excuse for leaving the Résistance. Why did she refuse
to meet Noemie on the latter's return from prison? This flight seems to
prove the bad faith within which she has trapped herself. Roger, the atheist,
is disillusioned with the Résistance and embittered at the rejection of his
suit by Sylvia. He is tortured with a hunger for truth but can get no further
than the cry, ''yes, if only there were truth. . . . ''⁵³ Antoine is neither sure
of the purity of his motives nor of the genuinity of his patriotism. If only
the men of the Résistance and the collaborators could have understood .
each other, had more faith in each other. But the poignant tragedy is that
sometimes, despite the best will in the world, men cannot help causing
each other's misunderstandings and sorrows. The fundamental existential
situation is always ambiguous and sometimes hopelessly complicated. When
Sylvia asks Antoine if he has, at last, liberated himself from his mental
agony, Antoine answers: ''Yes and no, Sylvia, this is the only answer when
we ourselves are concerned: we believe and we do not believe, we love
and we do not love, we are and we are not. But if this is so, it is because
we are heading toward a goal which we see and do not see at the same
time.''⁵⁴

Perhaps Sylvia's response to her mother contains the truth that would
have saved them all: ''It may be that the important thing is not to be alive,
but only to be. . .reconciled.''⁵⁵ In the last analysis, Antoine's faith indicates
the road to transcendent salvation, to the time and place of unchanging
reconciliation: ''There is one thing I have discovered since my parents'
death: what we call being a survivor is in reality to live not so much *after*
as *under*; those we have never ceased to love with whatever is best in us
becoming something like a living, invisible arch which we sense and even
brush against, on the strength of which we are able to go on even as our
powers diminish, wrenched from ourselves, toward the moment when
everything will be caught up in love.''⁵⁶

Le Signe de la Croix (1938-1951, a play in three acts)

The time is 1938, the place Paris. Madame Lena Lilienthal is a refugee
Jew recently driven from Vienna and now living with her niece Pauline
Bernauer and Pauline's husband Simon, an accomplished musician whose
life is wrapt up in music. The Bernauers have four school-aged children,
three sons — David, Jean-Paul and Henri — and one daughter, Odette.
Simon Bernauer is eminently endowed with qualities that have distinguished

outstanding Jews throughout this people's long and glorious history. He is sensitively conscious of the universal brotherhood of man, has an incomparably compassionate disposition, suffers an acute nostalgia for the Absolute and ardently rejects all irrationally narrowing categories. Yet, such is the ambiguity of his personality, Simon is also a regular reader of *L'Action Francaise,* going along for the most part with Maurras' and Daudet's call to patriotism, but not with the vilification of the Jews. When David, his oldest, brilliant, high-spirited collegiate son, upbraids Simon for not gnashing his teeth while reading *L'Action's* attacks, Simon flies into a rage:

> So, I am condemned to think and feel like a Jew? Do you presume to wall me into a set way of thinking? Into a kind of mental ghetto? Don't you understand that the worst nonsense, the vilest imprisonment arises precisely from racism? Why, it is through such racism that you arm our very enemies. You justify in advance their most shocking and dangerous accustations. Oh! I have often thought that the Jews themselves have launched the idea of racism into the world.[57]

Simon refuses to club together with fellow Israelites in a segment of society that stands aside from the French citizenry. It is the practice of such unreasonable semitism that spawns an equally unreasonable anti-semitism. He complains that the Jews so stick together that one of their number no sooner arrives at a superior social and economic echelon than he turns and pulls the others up with himself. This is not evil in itself, but the tragedy of his people consists in their refusal to take root within the national fraternity that furthers their fortunes. In France they crave equality with all Frenchmen, yet simultaneously live as if they were members of a French Freemasonry. Simon seeks fraternity far more than equality; the former is an intersubjective presence of love, the latter is a hostile competition over things. Thus Simon excludes himself from any treasonable parasitic segment of society — the we-a-different-and-superior-people — for such a collectivity only divides the body politic.

Pauline, on the other hand, exudes the repulsive assurance that wealth bestows. She is fiercely clannish and hopes to hold her family together more by ethnic than ethical bonds. On learning that the brilliant Jewish contestants for high medical posts were all rejected on racial grounds, she exclaims: "If France rejects us, she is no longer our fatherland." But Simon is irritated by his wife's bigoted behavior. They argue bitterly. Pauline resents Simon's designation of his confreres as "a tribe." "We are a community," she cries, "and the more we are persecuted, the more we are bound to sense and affirm this community."[58] Simon vehemently

Women Priests and Other Fantasies

attempts to insert reason into their argument. "But you don't see, indeed, the vicious circle you are in. How tragic! How infernal! It is precisely because you are obstinate in keeping yourselves apart, in marching ceaselessly shoulder to shoulder that you advance your enemies and arm your persecutors."[59]

Jean-Paul, the second son, unable any longer to sustain a life committed to nothing, converts to Protestantism, with the tolerance of his father and against the bitter opposition of his mother. Meanwhile, in the collateral relationships, another tragedy is being enacted. Léon, Pauline's brother, is married to highly antisemitic Odette. Rejected in French medical circles, Léon is invited to practice in the United States. He would willingly accept, if only his beloved Odette would come back to him. But Odette has wandered into the arms of Xavier Reveillac and is seeking a divorce so as to marry him. Xavier is antisemitic not so much from hatred of the Jews but because an historical imperative calls for this posture at the present time. He predicts the war, the German victory and the inevitable extermination of the Jews. Once the fall and occupation of France is established, the arrest and deportation of the Jews begins. Simon, Pauline, Aunt Lena and the small children flee to the South of France. David and Jean-Paul remain in Paris. In a brazen show of racial pride and love of liberty, David attends the Bach concert at the home of the Colonnes, wearing the Jewish star for all to see. It was a rash disobedience against a specific order of the occupation forces. David is violently overpowered and disappears in the hands of the Nazi torturers, never to be heard from again. Jean-Paul escapes south to relate the tragedy to his family and friends.

Meanwhile, in the south a magnanimous priest, the Abbé Scheweigsam, offers to hide Aunt Lena from the Nazi dragnet which is slowly closing over the whole of France. Monsignor de Romière's refuge is opened only to Jews of French citizenship, thereby excluding Aunt Lena who is not yet a naturalized citizen. But the Abbé offers his home as a place of refuge for her, suggesting that she become a member of his family. Aunt Lena, with delicate finesse and warm sensibility, refuses, saying that she could not exploit for her own profit a religion to which she has never belonged. Instead, she consigns herself in faith to the transcendent Being and willingly accepts her approaching death by torture. "I belong more and more to another kingdom."[60]

As the German dragnet moves southward, Odette and Xavier offer to facilitate the escape of the Bernauers to America. Simon decides to remain with Aunt Lena, preferring to share the perils and dark destiny of his Jewish confreres than to escape to the comfort of America. Pauline, unwilling and unable to understand the profound commitment in Simon's soul, condemns him as a husband who is harsh and derelict in his duty toward his family.

She escapes with the children. As for Simon, his refusal to flee transforms him into a new man. The closer tragedy approaches his people, the more intensely he wills to participate in their sufferings. Persecution has created a new and stronger bond, a more than ordinary human bond, between Simon and all people, especially between him and the downtrodden. He now speaks of a "sacramental bond" which has sprung up between himself and his fellow Jews. And thus Simon remains in a spirit of self-oblation, convinced that to flee his suffering confreres would be an act of perfidious treason.

In an epilogue written in 1948, Marcel presents the survivors to us. A letter from a prisoner who has escaped the death camp shared with Simon is read by the Abbé to the Bernauer family. It relates that Aunt Lena was liquidated on arrival at the camp. Simon lingered on for a while, softened and sanctified by the suffering and example of Aunt Lena, in whose presence he moved. But his health failed rapidly and he died attended in his last moments by a Protestant minister. Odette is present at the reading; Léon and Pauline refuse her forgiveness. In an effort to bring them around, the Abbé reveals that Simon, before he died, forgave and prayed for Odette and Xavier who had saved his family. As for Xavier, he was later apprehended and executed by the Résistance. While in prison he had attempted suicide, but failed; he repented and returned to the faith of his childhood before his execution. Perhaps the prayers of Simon had saved him. Could not Pauline imitate her deceased husband's magnanimity? Bitter to the end, Pauline and Léon refuse to admit grace or miracles as possible, much less to accept them as facts.

And so the tragedy closes on an agonizing paradox. Simon and Aunt Lena cannot become Christians for fear of failing to identify themselves with their persecuted brethren. Yet they live and die in a faith and love that undoubtedly place them within the communion of the saints. The fire of persecution expanded the constricting mentality of the "we-a-special-and-superior-people" into the transcendent activity of compassionate communion. For the sign of the cross can always conquer superficial conformism and odious pharisaism whenever this symbol of suffering is embraced as a means of communion. Persecution can purify from clannishness; persecution orients man from the posture of the "we-who-stand-apart," to the "we-who-are-thine." The sign of the cross is meant to hold people and things together in him whom it shatters for the sake of the cosmos and the community. If this sign is freely accepted, it is a means of reconciliation. If it is rejected, it is the occasion for alienation and disintegration.

When we complete even a quick journey through Marcel's dramatic world, we come away imbued with the spirit of reverence toward the human individual that pervades every scene. The human person is seen as the

all-important center of experience — the center of this spinning earth, of
planetary revolutions, of an exploding universe, of an on-rushing history,
all of which are trifling when contrasted with the rise and fall of this demigod.
Persons, each unique and irreplaceable, are constantly being discovered
in an atmosphere of admiration, compassion, alienation. The plays are
orchestrations of intersubjectivity with harmony and disharmony resounding
from the clash of personalities. Even when the characters apparently
succumb to despair and suicide, the spectator is left with a ray of hope
that, perhaps beyond the invisible threshold, the inner conflict has been
healed and the protagonists lifted to a realm of transfiguring transcendence.
In any case, the individual tragedies always seem to promise hope for human
existence itself by inviting the spectator to go beyond particular failures
or successes to what is essentially and universally valid in human life —
"the sense and reality of communion which is to exist as little as possible
for oneself."[61] Drama is for Marcel the way of wisdom, the way to arouse
man to the spirit of gratitude for being alive and to invoke him to become
fully committed to the human calling to communion. The dramas are
certainly "psychological" in technique, dramas of thought, of the soul,
yet they are concerned not merely with the destiny of the individual characters, but with the destiny of human, spiritual survival which is necessarily
interlocked with the transcendent view of human existence. In the words
of Kenneth Gallagher, "Unless the spectator who beholds the action on
stage is moved to say, not 'so it is with them,' but 'so it is with me,' the
play remains relatively trivial."[62] But all Marcel's plays move men of
maturity to say, "so it is with us." For Marcel's drama rejects the decadent,
emasculated and tepid humanity that has lost faith in the individual person
and that opts for isolated, self-centered or collectivized existence — the
Sartrean society. His theater is rather addressed to men of flesh and blood
who, though immersed in a tragic milieu, are, nevertheless, dedicated to
a human way of life that knows how to fructify the marriage between the
visible and invisible, between the temporal and eternal into ascending
degrees of participation in being — into the communion of saints.

Notes

[1]R. Troisfontaines, S.J., *De l'existence a l'etre,* Vol. I (Paris: J. Vrin, 1953), p. 30.
[2]*Ibid.,* p. 30.
[3]M.-M. Davy, *Un philosophe itinérant: Gabriel Marcel* (Paris: Flammarion, 1959), p. 76.
[4]*Ibid.,* p. 74.
[5]G. Fessard, "Théatre et mystère," *Etudes,* April 5, 1938, p. 738
[6]Quoted by G. Fessard in *La Soif* (Paris: Desclée De Brouwer, 1938), p. 7.
[7]R. Troisfontaines, S.J., *op. cit.,* p. 35.
[8]J.P. Dubois-Dumée, "Solitude et communion dans le théatre de Gabriel Marcel," in
    Existentialisme chrétien, présentation de Gilson (Paris: Librairie Plon, 1947), p. 272.

[9]R. Troisfontaines, S.J., *op. cit.*, p. 35.

[10]J.P. Sartre, *No Exit and The Flies* (New York: Alfred A. Knopf, 1948), trans. Stuart Gilbert, p. 61.

[11]J.-P. Sartre, *L'etre et le néant* (Paris: Librairie Gallimard, 1943), p. 708.

[12]R. Troisfontaines, "What is Existentialism?", THOUGHT XXXII, No. 127 (Winter, 1957–1958), 527.

[13]G. Marcel, *La Grace* in *Le Seuil invisible* (Paris: Grasset, 1914), p. 31.

[14]*Ibid.*, p. 79

[15]*Ibid.*, pp. 79–80.

[16]*Ibid.*, p. 86

[17]*Ibid.*, p. 95.

[18]*Ibid.*, p. 107.

[19]*Ibid.*, p. 116.

[20]*Ibid.*, pp. 136–138.

[21]*Ibid.*, pp. 143–145.

[22]*Ibid.*, p. 159.

[23]*Ibid.*, pp. 200, 203.

[24]*Ibid.*, pp. 207, 208.

[25]*Ibid.*, p. 209.

[26]M.-M. Davy, *op. cit.*, p. 116.

[27]G. Marcel, *Le palais de sable* in *Le Seuil invisible* (Paris: Grasset, 1914), p. 346.

[28]*Ibid.*, pp. 385–386.

[29]*Ibid.*, p. 374.

[30]*Ibid.*, p. 378.

[31]*Ibid.*, p. 378.

[32]*Ibid.*, pp. 381–382.

[33]*Ibid.*, pp. 393, 398.

[34]*Ibid.*, M.-M. Davy, *op. cit.*, p. 123.

[35]G. Marcel, *Three Plays* (New York: Hill and Wang, 1958), trans. Rosalind Heywood and Marjorie Gabain, p. 47.

[36]*Ibid.*, p. 59.

[37]*Ibid.*, p. 74.

[38]*Ibid.*, p. 74.

[39]*Ibid.*, p. 79.

[40]*Ibid.*, p. 91.

[41]*Ibid.*, p. 108.

[42]*Ibid.*, p. 111.

[43]G. Marcel, *Le Dard* (Paris: Librairie Plon, 1936), p. 115.

[44]*Ibid.*, pp. 117–118.

[45]*Ibid.*, p. 118.

[46]*Ibid.*, pp. 87, 118.

[47]G. Marcel, *The Existential Background of Human Dignity* (Cambridge, Mass.: Harvard University Press, 1963), pp. 122–123.

[48]*Ibid.*, p. 117.

[49]G. Marcel, *L'Emissaire* in *Vers un autre royaume* (Paris: Librarie Plon, 1940), p. 32.

[50]*Ibid.*, p. 41.

[51]*Ibid.*, p. 88.

[52]*Ibid.*, pp. 71–72.

[53]*Ibid.*, p. 110.

[54]*Ibid.*, p. 108.

[55]*Ibid.*, p. 89.

[56]*Ibid.*, p. 109.
[57]G. Marcel, *Le Signe de la croix* in *Vers un autre royaume* (Paris: Librairie Plon, 1940), p. 161.
[58]*Ibid.*, pp. 170–171.
[59]*Ibid.*, p. 172.
[60]*Ibid.*, p. 199. It should be stressed that Marcel fully realized that diverse resonances would be awakened by his treatment of the delicate subject of semitism. He is willing to accept this fact and the enlightened criticism that will arise therefrom. But he opposes the interdiction of this subject from rational discussion, for no good can come from refusing to discuss the errors and illusions to which so many well-intentioned Israelites have succumbed since the end of the Second World War. Precisely on this point Marcel has written in the Postcript to the play:

"No one can question the fact that the problem of Israel has regained dramatic intensity. Today, as I am informed, conversions are growing among the Jews, but, on the other hand, a laicized and enraged Judaism is threatening to degenerate into a new form of nazism as indefensible as the former breed. Between these two extremes there are many Jews of genuine faith and good will. This play is written for their reflection" (*Ibid.*, p. 233).
[61]G. Marcel, *The Existential Background of Human Dignity* (Cambridge, Mass.: Harvard University Press, 1963), p. 125.
[62]Kenneth Gallagher, *The Philosophy of Gabriel Marcel* (New York: Fordham University Press, 1962), p. 114.

Reprinted from *Thought,* Summer 1965.

Pope John Paul II and Catholic Universities

In the December 1979 issue of the Irish monthly *The Furrow,* Fr. Charles E. Curran, professor of moral theology at the Catholic University of America, published an article entitled: "Academic Freedom: The Catholic University and Catholic Theology." In assessing the help that the recent Apostolic Constitution, *Sapientia Christiana,* issued by Pope Paul II on April 10, 1979, would give to a deeper appreciation and enlargement of the practice of academic freedom to teach in Catholic universities, Fr. Curran wrote:

> ...According to the most obvious interpretation of the new Apostolic Constitution, the Catholic college and university is not autonomous but is a continuation of the teaching function of the hierarchical Magisterium. Such a relationship explains why teachers need the *nihil obstat* from Rome and teachers in disciplines concerning faith and morals also need a canonical mission. In such a situation, there is no academic freedom because judgments about competency are not made by peers and promotion and tenure depends on judgments made by Church authority as such...

> If the Apostolic Constitution is literally applied, it will mean that such canonically erected Catholic institutions cannot be universities in the accepted sense of the term in the United States. Likewise, the theology done in such institutions will not have the necessary academic freedom to perform its function properly. As a result, canonically erected universities, Roman Catholic theology and the good of the whole Church will suffer.[1]

In effect Fr. Curran concludes that Pope John Paul II, by publishing *Sapientia Christiana,* has struck a fatal blow against the well-being of the Catholic Church. He has destroyed "canonically erected Catholic institutions" as "true universities in the accepted sense of the term in the United States." He has wiped out "the necessary academic freedom" theologians must have "to perform properly" in such institutions. Finally, he has jeopardized the good of such universities, of Roman Catholic theology and of the whole Church, foreshadowing sufferings for all three in the near future.

Underlying the harsh judgments made against the pope by Fr. Curran are three errors which vitiate his whole reasoning process on the compatibility of the Magisterium of the Church and the free university. First, there is his erroneous notion of academic freedom. Second, there is his treatment of the Catholic university as if it were merely another secular university.

Third, there is his contention that the faculties of Philosophy and Theology in a Catholic university enjoy a teaching authority wholly independent of the teaching authority of the Magisterium.

Speaking of the university in general, Fr. Curran has this to say: "The university as such must be a free and autonomous center of study with no external restraints limiting either its autonomy or its freedom."[2] Thus a university teacher can express his ideas without any interference whatever from political or ecclesiastical authority. Even administrative officials of the university may not censor the teaching of their faculty members. Inside the university the only restraining power on professors are committees of colleagues which can decide what methods of teaching are incompetent and who are to be dropped from faculties because of teaching contrary to professional ethics. Fr. Curran speaks repeatedly of "full" academic freedom, of "complete" academic freedom, never clarifying his meaning of these terms, but implying that academic freedom is limitless. Thus he invests academic freedom with the character of an absolute, with a sort of divine immunity from all control.

When he discusses the Catholic university, Fr. Curran adheres faithfully to the Land O'Lakes Statement issued in 1967 at the end of a congress which discussed "The Nature of the Contemporary Catholic University." That document states boldly, even defiantly, the doctrine of absolute academic freedom for the Catholic university:

> The Catholic university today must be a university in the full modern sense of the word, with a strong commitment to and concern for academic excellence. To perform its teaching and research functions effectively, the Catholic university must have a true autonomous and academic freedom in the face of authority of whatever kind, lay or clerical, external to the academic community itself. To say this is simply to assert that institutional autonomy and academic freedom are essential conditions of life and growth, and indeed, of survival for Catholic universities as for all universities.[3]

Fr. Curran then indicates that the revolution of Catholic universities against the Magisterium became even more focused and articulate in a statement put out by the North American Region of the International Federation of Catholic Universities (I.F.C.U.) in 1971. Needless to say, Fr. Curran enthusiastically endorses this statement: "The Catholic university is not simply a pastoral arm of the Church. It is an independent organization serving Christian purposes but not subject to ecclesiastical-juridical control, censorship or supervision."[4] Quite clearly, then, academic freedom means for Fr. Curran, the total absence of any limits being placed on the professional actions of academicians. Later we shall consider whether such freedom may not be in reality that complete illusion of true freedom which would destroy a university's liberty, rights and mission to pursue truth by plunging it into the chaos of endless academic and moral permissiveness, an abyss of total intellectual disorder.

Truth is at stake

Man alone in the whole visible creation is a *person*. That means each human being is unique, intelligent, free, irreplaceable and incommunicable. Each person holds his final destiny in his own power. What makes a person the image and likeness of God is the spirituality of his soul. This enables each person to enter the great dialogue with his Creator through the activities of his intellect and will. For man is able to accept God and creation as truth and to adhere to them in love. Hence all expressions of human freedom are gifts of God to man founded upon and deriving from man's rational nature, that is from his personhood. In the various private and social strata of man's conscious activities, freedom means the enjoyment of the ineffable spiritual power to choose, with preferential love, God, his eternal law, his providence for the whole of creation and especially for man. Freedom is the sublime spiritual power to choose authentic values, founded on reason and revelation, over idols, falsehood and wickedness. Now since it is an endowment of a creature, man's freedom is necessarily, metaphysically and morally limited. Unlimited human freedom is a contradictory illusion, a slogan hiding an impossible reality, the cruel hoax of a non-entity. Man can freely take positions; he can say yes or no to invitations to act in a certain way. But this very freedom is also the basis of all responsibility, a responsibility necessarily presupposed in him as a person capable of bearing metaphysical and moral values as well as disvalues.

Thus academic freedom is rooted in the intellectual activity of man whereby he alone, as a person is called to a dominion and stewardship of the universe through a conquest of truth. *Positively,* then, academic freedom is a generous guarantee to the unimpeded access to the evidence of the truth in any science. Academic freedom is thus bounded by the canons and axiomatic truths of each discipline of learning. Thus, *again positively,* academic freedom is both purposive and responsible. It is never an end in itself, but always a means to an end — to the true and the good. Hence it must never be absolutized, for it then degenerates into its antithesis — academic license. As limited, academic freedom has its own built-in rules. Its requirements are conditioned by predefined directions towards the truth of each particular science. Man's moral right to academic freedom arises from his indestructible natural activity which is necessary for the scientific achievement of truth. This right is founded on man's connatural inner dynamism of the human intellect's hunger for truth.

Negatively, academic freedom, at the very least, means the immunity from unreasonable restrictions, both from within and from outside the academic community, of the right to communicate the results of one's researches through lectures and publications, and the right to be immune from unreasonable restriction in the pursuit of the teaching profession.[5]

Now freedom of expression and teaching may require regulation under certain circumstances, especially when what is false is purposely taught as truth and what is immoral is presented as good. For true knowledge is intolerant of error, of falsehood, of quackery. No one in his right mind will entrust his body to a surgeon who is a quack doctor. Nor will anyone order his prescriptions from an incompetent pharmacist. Man must be intolerant of error, of incompetence, of quackery; his very life, well-being and, indeed the common good, depend on this healthy intolerance. Man's proper response to falsehood is to reject and denounce it; his proper response to truth is to seek and speak it. No professions will tolerate quacks. Why should the university? What we are emphasizing here is that academic freedom is inherently a restricted endowment. It must be a product of reason, of order. It has responsibilities as well as rights. It must meet these responsibilities and exercise these rights in a reasonable manner for its own preservation and vigorous advancement. For academic freedom itself needs protection. Hence it must normally regulate itself from within the university, even as it realizes that it is subordinate to the higher authorities whose communities it serves — the State and the Church of which it is itself a beneficiary. But if it will not regulate itself from within, it will have to be regulated from without for the sake of the common good.

Academic freedom, therefore, should not be entrusted to those who would work for its destruction by subverting the free State or Church societies within which a free university exists and flourishes. For such subverters would be the first to suppress academic freedom if they came to power. Thus no professor can claim the right to teach against the right of others to hear the truth. Civil or Church societies are not obliged to tolerate those who would not tolerate them if they had the power. Authorities are not obliged to tolerate those who would subvert the civil or ecclesiastical order under the cloak of freedom of study and teaching. In practice academic freedom must never be allowed to become a suicide pact. A free university, no more than a free nation or Church, can afford to tolerate a nest of ideologues whose total intellectual project is to subvert the truths and morals of the societies in which they function.[6] For example, in a free State a communist is unfit to teach; in a Catholic University a heretic is unfit to teach. The reason is because neither of them is a truly free person. The mental servitude to Party dictation in the former and to rebellion against the deposit of the faith in the latter has led them both to reject the metaphysical, moral and revelational values of Christian civilization. For, in the words of Christ, "The truth shall make you free." Whereas the communist works for the triumph of the Party over the Patria, the heretic works for the dethronement of Christian truth and the enthronement of falsehood. And both exploit the privileges of academic freedom because by training, purpose and dedication, they intend not to share but to twist and torture the truth. Both are useless and dangerous as teachers. As a matter of justice to the entire civil and ecclesiastical communities, who pay their salaries and bestow other privileges for a service they have prostituted, both should be removed from teaching and prevented from attaining other sensitive public positions in which the common good would be at stake for as long as they remain addicted to their wicked ideologies.

Curran's premises are false

One reason why Fr. Curran absolutizes academic freedom is that he isolates the university from all relational dependence on any "external" authority. Apparently, universities are to pursue truth in a solitary, Robinson Crusoe fashion.[7] Thus the Catholic Church is seen as an extern, an outsider when it comes to its own academic institutions. Fr. Curran arbitrarily, even invidiously, places the Catholic Church in the position of an adversary; he represents her as an alien power eager to suppress academic freedom. Indeed he accuses her of having "opposed modern liberties" in the 19th century. But history is an implacable witness to Fr. Curran's error in this matter. For the 19th century witnessed the publication of two famous encyclicals by Leo XIII, one explaining and extolling true *Liberty*, the other discoursing favorably *On the Christian Constitution of States*.

That the Church must be ostracized from her own academic institutions in order that they may enjoy academic freedom is a totally false premise. And this falsehood was rejected by the Vatican's Congregation for Catholic education in plenary session in October 1969:

> To fulfill its mission, a Catholic university must be seen as existing not only in the world, but also in the Catholic community and therefore it is related to those who preside over the Catholic community: the Catholic hierarchy. Obviously, the specific purpose of the Catholic university cannot be realized if those whose proper function it is to be the authentic guardians of the deposit of the faith are relegated to a marginal place in its life and activity.[8]

Another reason for Fr. Curran's egregious errors on the nature of academic freedom is that he equates the Catholic university with the secular university. He writes: "The Catholic university today must be a university in the full modern sense of the word...." But the "university in the full modern sense of the word'' differs profoundly from a true Catholic university in its general atmosphere and its philosophy of life. For State-controlled, and even private secularized, colleges have no particular convictions about God, philosophical truth or supernatural revelation. They function in a pseudo-scientific, pseudo-philosophical framework that is favorable to such erroneous systems of thought as scepticism, agnosticism, materialism, idealism, atheism, relativism, existentialism, collectivism, pragmatism and even militant anti-theism.[9] Now Fr. Curran expects Catholic academic institutions, if they are ever to become ''universities in the full modern sense,'' to conform to these ideological systems which are so dominant and so modern, in the full sense of the word, in the thoroughly secularized American universities. To accomplish this feat Catholic universities would necessarily have to break away from the Catholic Church and become free-thinking, free-wheeling academies without any allegiance to any truth whatsoever, rational or revelational.

Students' right to truth usurped

Just such a free-wheeling status did the delegates of Catholic universities from all over the world, led by a large militant North-American faction, fight for at the Second International Congress of Catholic universities held in the Vatican under the auspices of the Congregation of Catholic Education from November 20 to 30, 1972. After much heated and frank discussion, the delegates rejected the following amendment to the document being prepared on the role of the Catholic University in the modern world, an amendment which was proposed so as to harmonize the liberty of the Catholic University with the universal mission of the Catholic Church to spread the Gospel and bring all men to salvation in Jesus.

> The truth which the Catholic university has to research and transmit has a double source: science and revelation. Therefore, the Catholic university, in its statutes and regulations has to provide adequate means to guarantee in an autonomous and efficacious manner, fidelity in research and in teaching not only to science but also to Catholic doctrine, in conformity with its essential note of 'fidelity to the Christian message as it comes to us through the Church.'[10]

In effect, then the Catholic universities voted to reject any institutional, statutory, academic allegiance to the teachings of Jesus Christ as transmitted by his Church through the Magisterium. Unfortunately, in rejecting this amendment, the Catholic universities involved were rejecting what Cardinal Newman calls their ''necessary ancillary and ministrative role in the Church.'' Fr. Curran completely agrees with this revolutionary rejection of academic responsibility and fidelity to the Church by Catholic universities. But by behaving in this manner, such universities placed themselves on a par with, if not above, the supreme authority in the Catholic Church, usurping thereby a power and position they could never legitimately attain. At the same time they demonstrated a crude insensitivity for the grave responsibility of the hierarchy for the salvation of the souls committed to its care, many of whom are having their faith and morals undermined precisely on the campuses of modern Catholic universities where contradictions of the Church's teachings are academically featured and officially tolerated, if not openly fostered. Moreover, the fierceness with which this amendment was opposed evinced a coldly uncharitable indifference to the needs of their students who, in the words of Pope Pius XII, "have a strict right to instruction in harmony with the teaching of the Church, the pillar and ground of truth."

The light of faith transforms

As if foreseeing the rebellion of our day in the academic world against the Church, Cardinal Newman wrote over 100 years ago, apropos of the Catholic Church's presence in Catholic universities:

> Hence a direct and active jurisdiction of the Church over it and in it (the Catholic university) is necessary lest it should become the rival of the Church with the Community at large in those theological matters which to the Church are exclusively committed — acting as a representative of the intellect, as the Church is the representative of the religious principle. The Church has no call to watch over and protect science; but towards theology she has a distinct duty; it is one of the special trusts committed to her keeping. Where theology is, there she must be; and if a university cannot fulfill its name and office without the recognition of revealed truth, she must be there to see that it is a bona fide recognition, sincerely made and consistently acted upon.[11]

What, then, is the true nature and role of the Catholic university which Fr. Curran, and his fellow revolutionary clerical educators, would secularize and snatch from the bosom of the Church? The Catholic university is a community of minds associated together to teach and research the natural and social sciences, history, literature, philosophy, theology and so on. But what distinguishes the Catholic university is that it provides explicitly for a Faculty of Theology that teaches its own religious Creed as a science, that is, as a body of organized, researched dogmas and precepts, known as its religious philosophy of life. The Catholic university has a Theology Faculty which scientifically teaches and researches the articles of the Creed of the Catholic faith. "The Catholic college or university seeks to give the authentic message an institutional presence in the academic world. Several things follow from this. Christian commitment will characterize this academic community. While fully maintaining the autonomy concomitant with its being a college or university, the institution will manifest fidelity to the teaching of Jesus Christ as transmitted by his Church. The advancement of Christian thought will be the object of institutional commitment. The human sciences will be examined in the light of the Christian faith. The best of the Christian intellectual and spiritual tradition will be blended with the special dynamism of contemporary higher education in a way that enriches both."[12]

Moreover, the Catholic university will provide a chapel on campus, a place for worship and the administration of the sacraments and the religious service of spiritual counselors. In the Catholic university there is no compromise between the natural goals of academic excellence and the supernatural goals of the Catholic Church, namely the transformation of all natural truth in the new light of its relationship to the truth of revelation. Nor is there any compromise between the natural goals of moral excellence and the sublime goals of the Catholic Church, namely the elevation of natural moral goodness to the transcendent level of sanctity through man's acceptance of the grace of salvation in Christ. Once again Cardinal Newman is our teacher on the mind of the Catholic Church when she goes about founding her own universities. Expounding on why Pope Pius IX wanted a Catholic university in Ireland, Newman wrote:

> Surely what he (the Pope) does, he does for the sake of religion. And if he encourages and patronizes art and science, it is for the sake of religion. He rejoices in the wildest and most philosophical systems of intellectual education, from an intimate conviction that truth is his real ally, as it is his profession; and that knowledge and reason are sure ministers to faith... Nothing short of this can be his aim, if, as becomes the successor of the Apostles, he is able to say with St. Paul, 'I do not judge myself to know anything among you, except Jesus Christ and him crucified.'

> ...When the Church founds a university, she is not cherishing talent, genius or knowledge for their own sake, but for the sake of her children, with a view of their spiritual welfare and their religious influence and usefulness, with the project of training them to fulfill their respective posts in life better, and of making them more intelligent, capable, active members of society.[13]

Indeed the Catholic Church is the mother of the universities. At a time when Western Christianity was united by the bond of the Catholic faith, the Middle Ages produced its most unique achievement, the universities. What is the distinctly Catholic and medieval stroke of genius in the creation of universities, of which our own are the modern heirs, is the institutional embodiment of the educational ideal, the organization of the various faculties of arts and sciences, and the interdependent hierarchy of all the sciences under the light of the science of revelation, which brought them all to the full complement of learning and wisdom. Before the revolt of Luther, eighty-one (81) universities were dispersed throughout Christendom and the majority of these were founded by papal charters. The major universities numbered from five to twenty thousand students, lay and ecclesiastic. Under the guidance of natural and revealed theology of universal faith, sciences flourished in medieval universities and thousands of students crowded their lecture halls. But perhaps the most remarkable phenomena of the medieval universities which flourished under the unity of the faith were the divergent schools of philosophy — Augustinianism, Scotism, Thomism, Suarezianism plus the variations within each school.[4]

The intellect is activated

Thus, we see that Christian revelational doctrine, far from being repressive under a magisterial authority of the Church, supposedly opposed to academic freedom, instead unleashed a vigorous, intensely curious, open and penetrating intellectual activity. The religious unity of the Catholic faith did not then, nor has it since, nor need it at any time in the future put a quietus on the free intellectual pursuit of truth. Writing of that halcyon age, Cardinal Newman says:

> If ever there was a time when the intellect went wild and had a licentious revel, it was the date I speak of. Was there ever a more curious, more meddling, bolder, keener, more penetrating, more rationalistic exercise of the reason than at that time?...Did the Church take a high hand with philosophy then? No!...Yet it was a time when she had temporal power and could have exterminated the spirit of inquiry with fire and sword; but she determined to put it down by argument...She sent her controversalists into the philosophical arena. It was the Dominican and Franciscan doctors, the greatest of them being St. Thomas, who in those medieval universities fought the battle of revelation with weapons of heathenism. It was no matter whose the weapon was; truth was truth all the world over. With the jawbone of an ass, with the skeleton philosophy of pagan Greece did the Samson of the Schools put to flight his thousand Philistines.[15]

We are now in a position to assess Fr. Curran's accusation that Pope

378 Women Priests and Other Fantasies

John Paul II has jeopardized the well-being of Catholic universities, indeed
of the whole Church, by publishing *Sapientia Christiana*. What has the pope
really done? He has reminded Catholic universities of their fundamental
purpose for existence. They have been created by the Church and her
faithful, they are continually financed by the Church and her faithful so
that they will cooperate with the Church in the mission of evangelization
given to her by Christ. The Apostolic Constitution reminds Catholic
universities that their teachers are to carry on their work in full communion
with the authentic Magisterium. It promulgates new laws and regulations
in the hope of bringing back into the bosom of the Catholic Magisterium
universities which have wandered into the arms of the modern, secularized
magisterium. The Pope is striving to restore order and discipline in an
academic world within the Church where confusion and chaos have entered.
Catholic universities and faculties are now to submit their statutes to the
Sacred Congregation of Education for approval. Those teaching disciplines
concerning faith or morals must receive a canonical mission from the
chancellor of the university, "for they do not teach on their own authority
but by virtue of the mission they have received from the Church."[16]
Moreover, "all teachers, before they are given a permanent post or before
they are promoted to the highest category of teachers...must receive a
declaration of *nihil obstat* from the Holy See."[17] This is equivalent to
acquiring a tentured position of the highest faculty rank.

Where does responsibility lie?

The Holy Father, as successor of St. Peter, has been given by Christ
the solemn mandate to confirm his brethren in the faith. He must at times
use disciplinary measures to fulfill this obligation. Pope John Paul II, besides
publishing *Sapientia Christiana,* has also, through local bishops and official
organs of the Church, exercised his authority to discipline wayward Catholic
professors. French radical Dominican Fr. Jacques Pohier has been forbidden
to exercise his priestly functions for his contumacious heretical teachings
and publications. Swiss theologian Fr. Bernhard Hasler has been laicized
for his book which calumniates Pope Pius IX on, *How The Pope Became
Infallible.* Dutch scholar Dominican Fr. Edward Schillebeeckx has been called
to Rome for questioning on his ambiguous theological views. Brazilian
Franciscan Fr. Leonard Boff has had some of his writings, interpreting
Christ in a Marxist mode, condemned. And Swiss theologian Fr. Hans
Kung has been stripped of his mission to teach as a Catholic theologian
because of his heresies denying the divinity of Christ and the infallibility
of the Church, among many other errors.

The church is founded, must survive and advance on the rock of truth.
The truths contained in the deposit of the faith create and strengthen her

essential unity. Peter and his successors are endowed with divine authority and infallibility to teach that truth accurately and coherently. Pope John Paul II, by his writings and actions, has demonstrated that he will not tolerate a nest of theologians, enamoured by their own reckless originality of thought and sparkling plausibility, to turn the Catholic Church into a new Tower of Babel in which the cacophony of contradictory voices scatters the flock to the four ends of an earth sinking in spiritual darkness. Fr. Curran and his revolutionary confreres condemn the pope unjustly because he is courageously living up to the mandate given him by Christ. These dissidents foolishly introduce a non-existent opposition between freedom to teach and authority to maintain truth. The antinomy is not between freedom to teach and that authority, but between freedom to teach error — actually a perverted use of freedom — and the authority to maintain truth. The rebels are claiming a freedom to speak, teach and think on matters of faith and morals as they wish. Pope John Paul II rejects this spurious freedom and uses his authority wisely and firmly to discipline contumacious rebels.

The pope knows that "a house divided against itself cannot stand." True, all Christians are called to love and pray for their enemies, especially for formal heretics. But the pope knows too that the faithful cannot live in community with heretics. Not even love can bring this about by itself. For the absolutely essential basis for community is unity in the faith, in the same beliefs, a truth demonstrated in the Gospel. Many of Christ's followers "walked no more with him" because they could not accept his "hard saying" about the need of eating his flesh and drinking his blood in order to attain eternal life. When Christ testified to the logic of their leaving by asking his Apostles, "Will you also go away?" Peter replied for the group: "To whom shall we go, Lord? You have the words of eternal life."

Here is the correct answer for the Catholic university. It must go with Christ, with the Vicar of Christ, with Pope John Paul II, if it hopes to bear honorably the title of Catholic, to continue alive, and to enjoy vigorous academic freedom in the pursuit and certain attainment of truth. Unlike Fr. Curran, the Catholic university must not exhibit a simplistic naivete about the trustworthiness and integrity of scholars, simply because they are academic intellectuals, to guarantee truth and academic freedom. Perhaps there exists in society today no more biased group against the ancient Christian wisdom than the modern, secularized scholars who despise permanent religious doctrines and established, tried and true traditions. For such religiously uprooted intellectuals are obsessed with novelty, with change, with the lust for revolution and notoriety. Christ is not reported to have said: "He who hears you scholars, you theologians, you journalists, hears me." But, "He who hears you — Peter, the Apostles and their episcopal successors teaching in union with the Vicar of Christ — hears me." It is quite evident that Fr. Curran and his Catholic rebel confreres in the Catholic academic world are listening to strange voices and sounding off as uncertain trumpets.

Notes

[1] The whole article is reprinted in *Catholic Mind,* February 1980.
[2] Ibid.
[3] Ibid.
[4] Ibid.
[5] Rev. Joseph F. Costanzo, S.J., "Academic Freedom and the Intellectual," Cork University Press, Ireland, 1960.
[6] Rev. Joseph F. Costanzo, S.J., "The Academy and the City," Cork University Press, Ireland, 1961.
[7] Dietrich Von Hildebrand, "Academic Freedom and the Catholic University," *The Wanderer,* June 5, 1969.
[8] Quoted by Charles Rice, *Authority And Rebellion,* Doubleday & Co., N.Y., 1971, p. 178.
[9] Dietrich Von Hildebrand, op. cit.
[10] From the working documents of this Congress at which I was an invited observer. These documents are in my file.
[11] Cardinal Newman, *The Idea of a University,* pp. 222-223.
[12] U.S. National Conference of Bishops, Letter on Education, "To Teach as Jesus Did," in *L'Osservatore Romano,* Eng. ed. Nov. 15, 1972.
[13] Cardinal Newman, op. cit.
[14] Rev. Joseph F. Costanzo, S.J., *This Nation Under God,* Herder & Herder, N.Y., 1964, pp. 412, 413.
[15] Cardinal Newman, op. cit.
[16] *Sapientia Christiana,* St. Paul Editions, Boston, 1980, Art. 27.
[17] Ibid. Art. 27, No. 2.

Reprinted from *Homiletic & Pastoral Review,* January 1981.

The Virtue of Patriotism

"You will be hated by all on account of me." John 10:22

If you split the atom, the smallest unit of matter, tremendous physical disaster results from the explosive forces released. If you split the family, the smallest sacred cell of society, tremendous social disaster results from the explosive passions released. If you split the Church, the only unit of salvation, tremendous eternal disaster results from the satanic forces released. If you split the nation, the sacred unit of civil society, tremendous fraternal disaster results from the treacherous crimes released.

Now there is no law against splitting the atom. But God himself forbids the splitting of the family: "What God has joined together, let no man put asunder." And Christ, the Son of God, forbids the splitting of His Church: "He who is not with me is against me; and he who does not gather with me, scatters." Moreover—and this truth is too little known—God wills the existence and harmonious functioning of civil society. Leo XIII, in his Encyclical *Immortale Dei,* "On the Function of the State in the Modern World," wrote: "It is the Creator's will that civil sovereignty should regulate social life after the dictates of an order changeless in its universal principles, should facilitate the attainment in the temporal order by individuals of physical, intellectual and moral perfection, and should aid them to reach their supernatural end. Hence it is the noble prerogative and function of the state to control, aid and direct the private and individual activities of national life that they may converge harmoniously towards the common good."

Thus, it is for the harmonious development of man, as a private and social being, that society is designed by the Creator as a means.

The virtue of patriotism

Now the virtue which renders citizens loyal to the God-given institution of the state and courageous in working for its goal of the common good is the *virtue of patriotism.* This special virtue arises from the virtue known as *pietas* or piety. Piety pays homage and duty to God as the supreme source and sustainer of one's being; it pays homage and duty to one's parents as the source of one's individual being and nourishment; it also pays loving homage to a person's fatherland with all his fellow citizens as the source and sustainer of man's civic and social perfection. In public, political life, the virtue of piety becomes the virtue of patriotism. For patriotism is the love and devotion to one's country, to one's countrymen as members of the same social and political family. Patriotism, in the sense of man's love for his civic community, is also a duty flowing from an intelligent recognition and moral acceptance of the very form of man's creation. Having created Adam as a solitary individual, God immediately announced the fact of man's incompleteness in himself: "It is not good for man to be alone." Then in creating Eve, God confirmed the truth that the human family, the civic family must become the social source and necessary community milieu from which each person may attain both individual and social maturity.

Thus patriotism is a special form of love of one's fatherland, a preferential love arising from man's first supreme love for God the omnipotent author and finisher of his being and personhood. Patriotism, therefore, can be defined descriptively as the reverent, grateful acknowledgment of one's fatherland as it is expressed in history; it is a response of loyal love to one's fellow citizens and the land in which one's countrymen live and work together for a common good founded on justice and fraternal brotherhood. It is a special form of piety binding citizens to their historical and cultural sources. But patriotism must arise from and function on a profoundly moral basis. "It is never lawful, or even wise, to dissociate morality from the affairs of practical life." In the last analysis, then, patriotism, which is founded on zealous, reverential love of God and countrymen, functions on justice, a justice inflamed with a love that exalts a nation. Consequently, true patriotism rejects all forms of immorality, for it is sin and escalating crime that render a nation miserable.

The vice of treason

The vice that destroys the justice and order of any society is called treason. Treason is a special, unnatural hatred of God as the author of one's being; it is also hatred of one family which gives birth and nourishment to the person; it is hatred of one's fatherland which endows its subjects with citizenship in a social milieu that guarantees human dignity, liberty and peace. *Treason is the ultimate ingratitude.* Judas hated Jesus, his benevolent savior and sold him into the hands of his enemies. The betrayal of Judas created chaos in the community of the twelve. Benedict Arnold betrayed his countrymen and, for a price, fought against them in the ranks of their enemies. There is a satanic, despicable dimension in the character of every traitor.

All apostates, all heretics betray their religious families. They introduce disunity, disorder, disaster among the brethren. They create divided communities, houses that cannot stand, that hasten towards a fall and utter collapse. So too in the social community known as the state traitors work for the destruction of the fatherland by introducing *crooked councils* and *engaging* in *spy activities.* The mind, heart and feet of political rogues run towards wicked deeds. Shakespeare addressed treasonist persons thus: "O Villain, villain, smiling, damned villain. Thou little valiant, great in villainy!" Now we know that holy men and hypocrites often wear the same sacred vestments, that honest citizens and knaves quote the same divine decalogue. Yet Emerson tells us: "As there is a use in medicine for poison, so the world cannot move without rogues."

And so religious rogues are forced to face religious saints whom God raises up to thwart them. St. Athanasius, whose feast day we celebrate today, was a man who courageously unmasked the religious rogues known as the Arians. In his loyalty to Christ and his Church, Athanasius exposed the subtle, alluring doctrinal betrayal of Arius, a priest of Alexandria of Egypt. Arius denied the divinity of Christ and cleverly spread his false teachings throughout the Roman Empire. Indeed so successful was he at sowing his doctrinal tares that St. Jerome, commenting on the situation at the time of the Council of Nicaea in 325 A.D., the Council which condemned Arius, wrote: "The whole Christian world awoke to find itself Arian, with eighty per cent of the bishops having fallen victims to this religious disease."

Yet Athanasius, who was bishop of Alexandria for 45 years, persisted in opposing emperors and a world in love with heresy, by doggedly presenting the truth of Christ's divinity. For his loyalty, for his religious piety and patriotism, for his fidelity to truth, to God and his Church, Athanasius was exiled 5 times and suffered much at the hands of emperors, fellow-bishops and fellow Catholics. Yet such was his fortitude as an intrepid writer and champion of the true faith, that history has crowned him with the illustrious accolades of Doctor of the Church and Conqueror of the world: *Athanasius Victor contra mundum*, Athanasius Conqueror of the world of heretics.

In the history of nations there also arise types of the great religious defenders of faith and morality. In America many brave persons have sacrificed all in the service of unmasking rogues and traitors. In identifying, exposing and bringing to justice those who treacherously work for the enslavement of the fatherland, such patriots have not hestitated to sacrifice family peace, reputation, positions of honor, careers and even life. Such patriots have had to fight against an academic and media world of duped utopians in love with political heresies and fostering policies sure to destroy the dignity and rights not only of their fellow citizens but of all men in the entire world. Christ as the way, the truth and the life was hated and rejected by the world. The world will always hate and reject all who follow Christ and the truth. Athanasius recalled Christ's worlds as he suffered for truth and holiness: "You will be hated by all on account of me." Even so patriots who fight against the lies and crimes of the godless enemies of their fatherland will be hated and persectued. Today we honor the memory of a great American patriot, Senator Joseph McCarthy, who in his public office did not hesitate to fight for the protection of his fatherland against traitors who were scheming to reduce "the land of the free and the home of the brave" into a Gulag run by godless tyrants bent on dominating

millions of sycophants and slaves. Whatever the faults this patriot had—
and we are all sinners—it can be said of him, as it is said of St. Athanasius:
"Greater love than this no man has, to have spent his life for the brethren."
A true patriot, like a real saint, is most pleasing to God. For both are
tremendous lovers of truth and fighters for righteousness.

Reprinted from *Ecclesia* (St. Patrick's Cathedral, N.Y.C.)

The Governor's Crooked Wisdom

Michel Montaigne, illustrious French essayist, has written this pithy statement: "No one is exempt from talking nonsense: the misfortune is to do it solemnly." In an exclusive interview which Governor Mario Cuomo granted to *The Tablet,* a journalistic organ of the Brooklyn Diocese, the governor, while emphasizing his strong disagreement with Archbishop John J. O'Connor, the new ordinary of the Archdiocese of New York, is quoted as saying on the subject of Medicaid funds for abortion the following:

> Medicaid funds provide the poor with medical services available to others in our society. By what principle am I to deny such funds? People don't decide to have an abortion because it is funded like the rest of their medical services. Medical funds only prevent back alley abortions.

This statement contains a plethora of false principles. To begin with, the action of aborting a defenseless, innocent child in the womb of its mother is called euphemistically "a medical service to the poor." We have here the typical tactic of the double-minded humanitarian and half-believing Catholic politician who is eager to make concessions to a post-Christian, paganized world for the reward of public power. Shakespeare tells us that "the devil knew not what he did when he made man politic; he crossed himself by 't." And Henry Adams notes that "practical politics consists in ignoring facts." Both of these Machiavellian artifices are verified in the governor's crooked wisdom.

For in truth "a medical service" to anyone aims at fostering life, improving health of adults and infants, defeating disease. The pro-abortionists have succeeded in poisoning our language. In the words of Father William Smith, academic dean and professor of moral theology at St. Joseph's Seminary, Dunwoodie, New York, the abortionists and all their allies who attempt to undermine Christian morality, function with an evil but effective strategy. "Remember," they tell their cohorts, "that terminological engineering must precede social engineering, if the latter is to be accepted in practice by the legal, political and medical institutions of a society." Thus, the killing of innocent, defenseless children in the womb must be made to sound plausible, reasonable, humanitarian. How is this to be done? Well, redefine the killing of fetuses and the instruments used for their slaughter with such slogans as "medical services," "free choice," "termination of a pregnancy," "a woman's right over her body," "a medical procedure necessary to protect the physical or even mental health of the mother," "a procedure to prevent the patient from committing suicide," and, finally, in the governor's words, using "funds that only prevent back alley abortions." This is the tactic of manipulating language, of using "compassionate lies" to avoid calling murder murder. It is a form of psychological seduction that makes it easier to commit a crime against the divine natural law which is metaphysically present in every man's conscience. That conscience is the voice of the Supreme Legislator and Just Judge who rewards good and punishes evil.

The governor asks himself a good question: "By what principle am I to deny such funds (Medicaid funds) for abortion?" The principle should have been obvious to a man who received his law degree from St. John's Catholic University. "Thou shalt not kill!" the Lord thundered from the smoke and fire of Mt. Sinai. This command aimed at protecting all innocent human lives, especially the lives of defenseless children, born or as yet unborn. Moreover, it implies that no person may formally, that is knowingly and willing, cooperate in the killing of innocent, defenseless human life. But by knowingly providing funds for such criminal action, the governor becomes a formal cooperator in such action. And he is not free from moral condemnation, not even if the positive law provides for such funds. St. Thomas wrote a masterful thesis on law in his Summa Theologica. One of his fundamental principles for evaluating the morality of a law is expressed thus: *Mala lex, nulla lex.* An evil positive law is no law. It is a violation of the rights of man and of the divine natural law. There is not only no obligation to observe such a pseudo-law, but one is obligated to fight to abolish such a caricature of a just law. Thus the governor's double-standard posture on abortion is irrational, immoral, and anti-Christian.

The governor asks himself another pertinent question: "Where are the lines between individual religious commitment and public policy which avoid the charge of hypocrisy?" Again the answer should be obvious. The same moral code that governs private personal life is the moral code that governs public life and policy. The universal divine moral code is social as well as individual. For morals govern conduct between and among persons—between man and God, among men, communities and nations. The abortion issue is primarily an issue of personal and social conscience. The prohibition againt performing abortions thus binds the consciences of all men, whether they belong to any religious sect or not. Reason itself demands that every man must avoid the killing of innocent, defenseless human life. And if any man commits this crime or cooperates in its accomplishment, he should in justice be punished by law. Ethical philosophy teaches this same moral imperative. Hence the prohibition against the crime of abortion is also a philosophical issue. The abortion prohibition became a religious issue when revelation from God in the Old and New Testaments condemned this heinous crime. But what Governor Cuomo fails to realize is that the prohibition against abortion is also a political issue. It is unrealistic for him to say or imply that public law or policy may allow abortion while private and social consciences condemn it. Laws protecting the family and its action of begetting and raising children must be in harmony with the divine natural law. Such laws are necessary for the attainment of the common good of a nation, for the greatest resource of a nation is its new children. Therefore, the objectives of civil and political institutions must be eminently moral. They must work for personal justice, social justice, security, peace, and the legal protection of the natural rights of all citizens—rights which it is not in the power of the state to deny or abrogate, such as the right to life of every human being whether existing inside or outside of the womb. The distinction between positive law and the moral natural law is that of a part to a whole. The performance of every human act—and especially of every human act of political executives, legislators, and judges—is always under the jurisdiction of the universal divine moral law. The problem arises in the interpretation and application of the moral law to an action of public law or policy. Yet political authority may not shirk its responsibilities in assisting the moral life of its subjects. To do this it must see that positive law and public policy do not contradict the universal moral law governing men and society. For if they do, then an evil moral philosophy imposes evil moral conduct arbitrarily upon its citizens and no euphemistic rationalization can justify this tyranny.

I contend that Governor Cuomo—like so many other Catholic politicians who claim they are personally against abortion but publicly support it by their votes and policies—has fallen a victim to the psychological seduction of modern day sophists. They have ensnared him and millions of other pagan-thinking Catholics by their mendacious antics in semantics into accepting a false dichotomy between private and public morality. Moreover, these latter day liberal Modernists, being pagan in their profounder sentiments, have succeeded in spreading the "big lie" that the moral code which condemns abortion is concerned merely with a religious issue that is pertinent and restricted only to the faiths of Christian and orthodox Jewish sects. The truth is that the abortion issue is a philosophical and political issue as well; it concerns all men and societies because it pertains to their personal, family and common good.

As if he were not sure that his "medical services" slogan had adequately justified his pro-abortion policies, the governor then asserts: "Medical funds only prevent back alley abortions." This is a patently false statement. Medical funds, above all, foster abortion in the millions—15 million to date in the United States—in medical clinics. The governor's exaggerated "only" seems to indicate that he is not concerned about the truth in his statements. Moreover, the fact is that medical funds for abortion in medical clinics have not wiped out "back alley abortions." The back alley killers are still prospering. Even if for the sake of argument we were sure that medical funds did completely wipe out back alley abortions, that would be no argument for the use of medical funds to perform abortions in medical clinics. One intrinsically evil activity allowed by the law cannot be justified as a means of eradicating the same intrinsically evil activity which is being performed outside the law. Morally evil conduct may never be engaged in to fight other morally evil conduct. Here the end especially does not justify the means, for both means and end are intrinsically evil and never allowed under any circumstances.

In conclusion, May I suggest to Governor Cuomo that, as a Catholic, he ought to choose, even at the cost of votes, not to confine himself to a series of double-minded claimers and disclaimers on moral-political issues—like abortion and homosexuality—that concern the personal, family, and common good of all citizens. He might make a positive effort to correct his thinking on the intrinsically immoral nature of abortion and homosexuality, thus bringing himself to the unclouded realization that both are never allowed as human conduct under any circumstances. He might re-study his Catholic faith in depth so that his subjective disposition will approach and explain more positively to himself God's revealed law on these and kindred moral problems. His performance of his public duties would thereby be enriched by philosophical and revelational truth. He might point to the wonderful agreement of certain central Catholic truths with the American Declaration of Independence, and how the Church insists on the moral basis for education, patriotism, and the fulfillment of all civic duties. If the governor, as a Catholic, is challenged on matters of faith or morals, he should welcome the opportunity to make the truth of these matters better known, if not better understood. He might without any apology point to papal teachings on such moral problems that also are political problems. St. Thomas, praising the art of self-government as perhaps the noblest art man can engage in, tells us that one of the primary functions of a governor (prince or ruler) is to educate—through just laws, policies and ordinances—the citizens of his nation. If he does this, he will lead his citizens, as a civilized society, to realize and accept the unifying bond which the divine natural law creates among all men. Only then will there be a realist guarantee that the positive, man-made laws of a nation will be in harmony with that universal natural law impressed by God on the consciences of men. Only then will the governor be able to achieve, by his leadership under these laws, the common good.

Reprinted from *Fidelity*, June, 1984

Appendix

Declaration on the question of the admission of women to the ministerial priesthood

The role of women in modern society and the church

Among the characteristics that mark our present age, Pope John XXIII indicated, in his encyclical *Pacem in Terris* of April 11, 1963, ''the part that women are now taking in public life. . . . This is a development that is perhaps of swifter growth among Christian nations, but it is also happening extensively, if more slowly, among nations that are heirs to different traditions and imbued with a different culture.''[1] Along the same lines, the Second Vatican Council, enumerating in its Pastoral Constitution *Gaudium et Spes* the forms of discrimination touching upon the basic rights of the person which must be overcome and eliminated as being contrary to God's plan, gives first place to discrimination based upon sex.[2] The resulting equality will secure the building upon a world that is not levelled out and uniform but harmonious and unified, if men and women contribute to it their own resources and dynamism, as Pope Paul VI recently stated.[3]

In the life of the Church herself, as history shows us, women have played a decisive role and accomplished tasks of outstanding value. One has only to think of the foundresses of the great religious families, such as St. Clare and St. Teresa of Avila. The latter, moreover, and St. Catherine of Siena, have left writings so rich in spiritual doctrine that Pope Paul VI has included them among the Doctors of the Church. Nor could one forget the great number of women who have consecrated themselves to the Lord for the exercise of charity or for the missions, and the Christian wives who have had a profound influence on their families, particularly for the passing on of the faith to their children.

But our age gives rise to increased demands: ''Since in our time women have an ever more active share in the whole life of society, it is very important that they participate more widely also in the various sectors of the Church's apostolate.''[4] This charge of the Second Vatican Council has already set in motion the whole process of change now taking place: these various experiences of course need to come to maturity. But as Pope Paul VI also remarked,[5] a very large number of Christian communities are already benefiting from the apostolic commitment of women. Some of these women are called to take part in councils set up for pastoral reflection, at the diocesan or parish level; and the Apostolic See has brought women into some of its working bodies.

For some years now various Christian communities stemming from the sixteenth-century Reformation or of later origin have been admitting women to the pastoral office on a par with men. This initiative has led to petitions and writings by members of these communities and similar groups, directed towards making this admission a general thing; it has also led to contrary reactions. This therefore constitutes an ecumenical problem, and the Catholic Church must make her thinking known on it, all the more because in various sectors of opinion the question has been asked whether she too could not modify her discipline and admit women to priestly ordination. A number of Catholic theologians have even posed this question publicly, evoking studies not only in the sphere of exegesis, patrology and Church history but also in the field of the history of institutions and customs, of sociology and psychology. The various arguments capable of clarifying this important problem have been submitted to a critical examination. As we are dealing with the debate which classical theology scarcely touched upon, the current argumentation runs the risk of neglecting essential elements.

For these reasons, in execution of a mandate received from the Holy Father and echoing the declaration which he himself made in his letter of November 30, 1975,[6] the Sacred Congregation for the Doctrine of the Faith judges it necessary to recall that the Church, in fidelity to the example of the Lord, does not consider herself authorized to admit women to priestly ordination. The Sacred Congregation deems it opportune at the present juncture to explain this position of the Church. It is a position which will perhaps cause pain but whose positive value will become apparent in the long run, since it can be of help in deepening understanding of the respective roles of men and of women.

The church's constant tradition

The Catholic Church has never felt that priestly or episcopal ordination can be validly conferred on women. A few heretical sects in the first centuries, especially Gnostic ones, entrusted the exercise of the priestly ministry to women: this innovation was immediately noted and condemned by the Fathers, who considered it as unacceptable in the Church.[7] It is true that in the writings of the Fathers one will find the undeniable influence of prejudices unfavorable to women, but nevertheless, it should be noted that these prejudices had hardly any influence on their pastoral activity, and still less on their spiritual direction. But over and above considerations inspired by the spirit of the times, one finds expressed—especially in the canonical documents of the Antiochian and Egyptian traditions—this essential reason, namely, that by calling only men to the priestly Order and ministry in its true sense, the Church intends to remain faithful to the type of ordained ministry willed by the Lord Jesus Christ and carefully maintained by the apostles.[8]

The same conviction animates medieval theology,[9] even if the Scholastic doctors, in their desire to clarify by reason the data of faith, often present arguments on this point that modern thought would have difficulty in admitting or would even rightly reject. Since that period and up to our own time, it can be said that the question has not been raised again, for the practice has enjoyed peaceful and universal acceptance.

The Church's tradition in the matter has thus been so firm in the course of the centuries that the magisterium has not felt the need to intervene in order to formulate a principle which was not attacked, or to defend a law which was not challenged. But each time that this tradition had the occasion to manifest itself, it witnessed to the Church's desire to conform to the model left to her by the Lord.

The same tradition has been faithfully safeguarded by the Churches of the East. Their unanimity on this point is all the more remarkable since in many other questions their discipline admits of a great diversity. At the present time these same Churches refuse to associate themselves with requests directed towards securing the accession of women to priestly ordination.

The attitude of Christ

Jesus Christ did not call any women to become part of the Twelve. If He acted in this way, it was not in order to conform to the customs of His time, for His attitude towards women was quite different from that of His milieu, and He deliberately and courageously broke with it.

For example, to the great astonishment of His own disciples, Jesus converses publicly with the Samaritan woman (cf. Jn. 4:27); He takes no notice of the state of legal impurity of the woman who had suffered from hemorrhages (cf. Mt. 9:20-22); He allows a sinful woman to approach Him in the house of Simon the Pharisee (cf. Lk. 7:37ff.); and by pardoning the woman taken in adultery, He means to show that one must not be more severe towards the fault of a woman than towards that of a man (cf. Jn. 8:11). He does not hesitate to depart from the Mosaic Law in order to affirm the equality of the rights and duties of men and women with regard to the marriage bond (cf. Mk. 10:2-11; Mt. 19:3-9).

In His itinerant ministry Jesus was accompanied not only by the Twelve but also by a group of women: "Mary, surnamed the Magdalene, from whom seven demons had gone out, Joanna the wife of Herod's steward Chuza, Susanna, and several others who provided for them out of their own resources" (Lk. 8:2-3). Contrary to the Jewish mentality, which did not accord great value to the testimony of women, as Jewish law attests, it was nevertheless women who were the first to have the privilege of seeing the risen Lord, and it was they who were charged by Jesus to take the first paschal message to the Apostles themselves (cf. Mt. 28:7-10; Lk. 24:9-20; Jn. 20:11-18), in order to prepare the latter to become the official witnesses to the Resurrection.

It is true that these facts do not make the matter immediately obvious. This is no surpise, for the questions that the Word of God brings before us go beyond the obvious. In order to reach the ultimate meaning of the mission of Jesus and the ultimate meaning of Scripture, a purely historical exegesis of the texts cannot suffice. But it must be recognized that we have here a number of convergent indications that make all the more remarkable the fact that Jesus did not entrust the apostolic charge[10] to women. Even His Mother, who was so closely associated with the mystery of her Son, and whose incomparable role is emphasized by the Gospels of Luke and John, was not invested with the apostolic ministry. This fact was to lead the Fathers to present her as the example of Christ's will in this domain; as Pope Innocent III repeated later, at the beginning of the thirteenth century, "Although the Blessed Virgin Mary surpassed in dignity and in excellence all the Apostles, nevertheless it was not to her but to them that the Lord entrusted the keys of the Kingdom of Heaven."[11]

The practice of the apostles

The apostolic community remained faithful to the attitude of Jesus towards women. Although Mary occupied a privileged place in the little circle of those gathered in the Upper Room after the Lord's Ascension (cf. Acts 1:14), it was not she who was called to enter the College of the Twelve at the time of the election that resulted in the choice of Matthias: those who were put forward were two disciples whom the Gospels do not even mention.

On the day of Pentecost, the Holy Spirit filled them all, men and women (cf. Acts 2:1, 1:14), yet the proclamation of the fulfillment of the prophecies in Jesus was made only by "Peter and the Eleven" (Acts 2:14).

When they and Paul went beyond the confines of the Jewish world, the preaching of the Gospel and the Christian life in the Greco-Roman civilization impelled them to break with Mosaic practices, sometimes regretfully. They could therefore have envisaged conferring ordination on women, if they had not been convinced of their duty of fidelity to the Lord on this point. In the Hellenistic world, the cult of a number of pagan divinities was entrusted to priestesses. In fact, the Greeks did not share the ideas of the Jews: although their philosophers taught the inferiority of women, historians nevertheless emphasize the existence of a certain movement for the advancement of women during the Imperial period. In fact, we know from the book of the Acts and from the Letters of St. Paul that certain women worked with the Apostle for the Gospel (cf. Rom. 16:3-12; Phil. 4:3). St. Paul lists their names with gratitude in the final salutations of the Letters.

Some of them often exercised an important influence on conversions: Priscilla, Lydia and others; especially Priscilla, who took it on herself to complete the instruction of Apollos (cf. Acts 18:26); Phoebe, in the service of the Church of Cenchreae (cf. Rom. 16:1). All these facts manifest within the Apostolic Church a considerable evolution vis-à-vis the customs of Judaism. Nevertheless at no time was there a question of conferring ordination on these women.

In the Pauline Letters, exegetes of authority have noted a difference between two formulas used by the Apostle: he writes indiscriminately "my fellow workers" (Rom. 16:3; Phil. 4:2-3) when referring to men and women helping him in his apostolate in one way or another; but he reserves the title "God's fellow workers" (1 Cor. 3:9; cf. 1 Thes. 3:2) to Apollos, Timothy and himself, thus designated because they are directly set apart for the apostolic ministry and the preaching of the Word of God. In spite of the so important role played by women on the day of the resurrection, their collaboration was not extended by St. Paul to the official and public proclamation of the message, since this proclamation belongs exclusively to the apostolic mission.

Permanent value of the attitude of Jesus and the apostles

Could the Church today depart from this attitude of Jesus and the apostles, which has been considered as normative by the whole of tradition up to our own day? Various arguments have been put forward in favor of a positive reply to this question, and these must now be examined.

It has been claimed in particular that the attitude of Jesus and the apostles is explained by the influence of their milieu and their times. It is said that, if Jesus did not entrust to women and not even to His Mother a ministry assimilating them to the Twelve, this was because historical circumstances did not permit Him to do so. No one, however, has ever proved—and it is clearly impossible to prove—that this attitude is inspired only by social and cultural reasons. As we have seen, an examination of the Gospels shows on the contrary that Jesus broke with the prejudices of His time, by widely contravening the discriminations practiced with regard to women. One, therefore, cannot maintain that, by not calling women to enter the group of the apostles, Jesus was simply letting Himself be guided by reasons of expediency. For all the more reason, social and cultural conditioning did not hold back the apostles working in the Greek milieu, where the same forms of discrimination did not exist.

Another objection is based upon the transitory character that one claims to see today in some of the prescriptions of St. Paul concerning women, and upon the difficulties that some aspects of His teaching raise in this regard. But it must be noted that these ordinances, probably inspired by the customs of the period, concern scarcely more than disciplinary practices of minor importance, such as the obligation imposed upon women to wear a veil on the head (1 Cor. 11:2–16); such requirements no longer have a normative value. However, the Apostle's forbidding of women "to speak" in the assemblies (cf. 1 Cor. 14:34–35; 1 Tm. 2:12) is of a different nature, and exegetes define its meaning in this way: Paul in no way opposes the right, which he elsewhere recognizes as possessed by women, to prophesy in the assembly (cf. 1 Cor. 11:5); the prohibition solely concerns the official function of teaching in the Christian assembly. For St. Paul this prescription is bound up with the divine plan of creation (cf. 1 Cor. 11:7; Gn. 2:18–24): it would be difficult to see in it the expression of a cultural fact. Nor should it be forgotten that we owe to St. Paul one of the most vigorous texts in the New Testament on the fundamental equality of men and women, as children of God in Christ (cf. Gal. 3:28). Therefore there is no reason for accusing him of prejudices against women, when we note the trust that he shows towards them and the collaboration that he asks of them in his apostolate.

But over and above these objections taken from the history of apostolic times, those who support the legitimacy of change in the matter turn to the Church's practice in her sacramental discipline. It has been noted, in our day especially, to what extent the Church is conscious of possessing a certain power over the sacraments, even though they were instituted by Christ. She has used this power down the centuries in order to determine their signs and the conditions of their administration: recent decisions of Popes Pius XII and Paul VI are proof of this.[12] However, it must be emphasized that this power, which is a real one, has definite limits. As Pope Pius XII recalled: "The Church has no power over the substance of the sacraments, that is to say, over what Christ the Lord, as the sources of Revelation bear witness, determined should be maintained in the sacramental sign.[13] This was already the teaching of the Council of Trent, which declared: "In the Church there has always existed this power, that in the administration of the sacraments, provided that their substance remains unaltered, she can lay down or modify what she considers more fitting either for the benefit of those who receive them or for respect towards those same sacraments, according to varying circumstances, times or places."[14]

Moreover, it must not be forgotten that the sacramental signs are not conventional ones. Not only is it true that, in many respects, they are natural signs because they respond to the deep symbolism of actions and things, but they are more than this: they are principally meant to link the person of every period to the supreme Event of the history of salvation, in order to enable that person to understand, through all the Bible's wealth of pedagogy and symbolism, what grace they signify and produce. For example, the sacrament of the Eucharist is not only a fraternal meal, but at the same time the memorial which makes present and actual Christ's sacrifice and His offering by the Church. Again, the priestly ministry is not just a pastoral service; it ensures the continuity of the functions entrusted by Christ to the apostles and the continuity of the powers related to those functions. Adaptation to civilizations and times therefore cannot abolish, on essential points, the sacramental reference to constitutive events of Christianity and to Christ Himself.

In the final analysis it is the Church, through the voice of her magisterium, that, in these various domains decides what can change and what must remain immutable. When she judges that she cannot accept certain changes, it is because she knows that she is bound by Christ's manner of acting. Her attitude, despite appearances, is therefore not one of archaism but of fidelity: it can be truly understood only in this light. The Church makes pronouncements in virtue of the Lord's promise and the presence of the Holy Spirit, in order to proclaim better the mystery of Christ and to safeguard and manifest the whole of its rich content.

This practice of the Church therefore has a normative character: in the fact of conferring priestly ordination only on men, it is a question of an unbroken tradition throughout the history of the Church, universal in the East and in the West, and alert to repress abuses immediately. This norm, based on Christ's example, has been and is still observed because it is considered to conform to God's plan for His Church.

The ministerial priesthood in the light of the mystery of Christ

Having recalled the Church's norm and the basis thereof, it seems useful and opportune to illustrate this now by showing the profound fittingness that theological reflection discovers between the proper nature of the sacrament of Order, with its specific reference to the mystery of Christ, and the fact that only men have been called to receive priestly ordination. It is not a question here of bringing forward a demonstrative argument, but of clarifying this teaching by the analogy of faith.

The Church's constant teaching, repeated and clarified by the Second Vatican Council and again recalled by the 1971 Synod of Bishops and by the Sacred Congregation for the Doctrine of the Faith in its Declaration of June 24, 1973, declares that the bishop or the priest, in the exercise of his ministry, does not act in his own name, *in persona propria:* he represents Christ, who acts through him: "the priest truly acts in the place of Christ," as St. Cyprian already wrote in the third century.[15] It is this ability to represent Christ that St. Paul considered as characteristic of his apostolic function (cf. 2 Cor. 5:20; Gal. 4:14). The supreme expression of this representation is found in the altogether special form it assumes in the celebration of the Eucharist, which is the source and center of the Church's unity, the sacrificial meal in which the People of God are associated in the sacrifice of Christ: the priest, who alone has the power to perform it, then acts not only through the effective power conferred on him by Christ, but *in persona Christi,*[16] taking the role of Christ, to the point of being His very image, when he pronounces the words of consecration.[17]

The Christian priesthood is therefore of a sacramental nature: the priest is a sign, the supernatural effectiveness of which comes from the ordination received, but a sign that must be perceptible[18] and which the faithful must be able to recognize with ease. The whole sacramental economy is, in fact, based upon natural signs, on symbols imprinted upon the human psychology: "Sacramental signs," says St. Thomas, "represent what they signify by natural resemblance.[19] The same natural resemblance is required for persons as for things: when Christ's role in the Eucharist is to be expressed sacramentally, there would not be this "natural resemblance" which must exist between Christ and His minister if the role of Christ were not taken by a man: in such a case it would be difficult to see in the minister the image of Christ. For Christ Himself was and remains a man.

Christ is, of course, the firstborn of all humanity, of women as well as men: the unity which He re-established after sin is such that there are no more distinctions between Jew and Greek, slave and free, male and female, but all are one in Christ Jesus (cf. Gal. 3:28). Nevertheless, the Incarnation of the Word took place according to the male sex: this is indeed a question of fact, and this fact, while not implying an alleged natural superiority of man over woman, cannot be disassociated from the economy of salvation: it is, indeed, in harmony with the entirety of God's plan as God Himself has revealed it, and of which the mystery of the Covenant is the nucleus.

For the salvation offered by God to men and women, the union with Him to which they are called—in short, the Covenant—took on, from the Old Testament prophets onwards, the privileged form of a nuptial mystery: for God the Chosen People is seen as His ardently loved spouse. Both Jewish and Christian tradition has discovered the depth of this intimacy of love by reading and rereading the Song of Songs; the divine Bridegroom will remain faithful even when the Bride betrays His love, when Israel is unfaithful to God (cf. Hos. 1–3; Jer. 2). When the "fullness of time" (Gal. 4:4) comes, the Word, the Son of God, takes on flesh in order to establish and seal the new and eternal Covenant in His blood, which will be shed for many so that sins may be forgiven. His death will gather together again the scattered children of God; from His pierced side will be born the Church, as Eve was born from Adam's side. At that time there is fully and eternally accomplished the nuptial mystery proclaimed and hymned in the Old Testament: Christ is the Bridegroom; the Church is His bride, whom He loves because He has gained her by His blood and made her glorious, holy and without blemish, and henceforth He is inseparable from her. This nuptial theme, which is developed from the Letters of St. Paul onwards (cf. 2 Cor. 11:2; Eph. 5:22-23) to the writings of St. John (cf. especially Jn. 3:29; Rev. 19:7, 9), is present also in the Synoptic Gospels: the Bridegroom's friends must not fast as long as He is with them (cf. Mk. 2:19); the kingdom of heaven is like a king who gave a feast for his son's wedding (cf. Mt. 22:1-14). It is through this Scriptural language, all interwoven with symbols, and which expresses and affects man and woman in their profound identity, that there is revealed to us the mystery of God and Christ, a mystery which of itself is unfathomable.

That is why we can never ignore the fact that Christ is a man. And, therefore, unless one is to disregard the importance of this symbolism for the economy of Revelation, it must be admitted that, in actions which demand the character of ordination and in which Christ Himself, the author of the Covenant, the Bridegroom and Head of the Church, is represented, exercising His ministry of salvation—which is in the highest degree the case of the Eucharist—His role (this is the original sense of the word *persona*) must be taken by a man. This does not stem from any personal superiority of the latter in the order of values, but only from a difference of fact on the level of functions and service.

Could one say that, since Christ is now in the heavenly condition, from now on it is a matter of indifference whether He be represented by a man or by a woman, since "at the resurrection men and women do not marry" (Mt. 22:30)? But this text does not mean that the distinction between man and woman, insofar as it determines the identity proper to the person, is suppressed in the glorified state; what holds for us holds also for Christ. It is indeed evident that in human beings the difference of sex exercises an important influence, much deeper than, for example, ethnic differences: the latter do not affect the human person as intimately as the difference of sex, which is directly ordained both for the communion of persons and for the generation of human beings. In biblical Revelation this difference is the effect of God's will from the beginning: "male and female he created them" (Gn. 1:27).

However, it will perhaps be further objected that the priest, especially when he presides at the liturgical and sacramental functions, equally represents the Church: he acts in her name with "the intention of doing what she does." In this sense, the theologians of the Middle Ages said that the minister also acts *in persona Ecclesiae,* that is to say, in the name of the whole Church and in order to represent her. And, in fact, leaving aside the question of the participation of the faithful in a liturgical action, it is indeed in the name of the whole Church that the action is celebrated by the priest:

he prays in the name of all, and in the Mass he offers the sacrifice of the whole Church. In the new Passover, the Church, under visible signs, immolates Christ through the mystery of the priest.[20] And so, it is asserted, since the priest also represents the Church, would it not be possible to think that this representation could be carried out by a woman, according to the symbolism already explained? It is true that the priest represents the Church, which is the Body of Christ. But if he does so, it is precisely because he first represents Christ Himself, who is the Head and Shepherd of the Church. The Second Vatican Council[21] used this phrase to make more precise and to complete the expression *in persona Christi*. It is in this quality that the priest presides over the Christian assembly and celebrates the Eucharistic sacrifice "in which the whole Church offers and is herself wholly offered."[22]

If one does justice to these reflections, one will better understand how well-founded is the basis of the Church's practice; and one will conclude that the controversies raised in our days over the ordination of women are for all Christians a pressing invitation to mediate on the mystery of the Church, to study in greater detail the meaning of the episcopate and the priesthood, and to rediscover the real and preeminent place of the priest in the community of the baptized, of which he indeed forms part but from which he is distinguished because, in the actions that call for the character of ordination, for the community he is—with all the effectiveness proper to the sacraments—the image and symbol of Christ Himself who calls, forgives, and accomplishes the sacrifice of the Covenant.

The ministerial priesthood illustrated by the mystery of the church

It is opportune to recall that problems of sacramental theology, especially when they concern the ministerial priesthood, as is the case here, cannot be solved except in the light of Revelation. The human sciences, however valuable their contribution in their own domain, cannot suffice here, for they cannot grasp the realities of faith: the properly supernatural content of these realities is beyond their competence.

Thus one must note the extent to which the Church is a society different from other societies, original in her nature and in her structures. The pastoral charge in the Church is normally linked to the sacrament of Order: it is not a simple government, comparable to the modes of authority found in States. It is not granted by people's spontaneous choice: even when it involves designation through election, it is the laying on of hands and the prayer of the successors of the apostles which guarantee God's choice; and it is the Holy Spirit, given by ordination, who grants participation in the ruling power of the Supreme Pastor, Christ (cf. Acts 20:28). It is a charge of service and love: "If you love me, feed my sheep" (cf. Jn. 21:15-17).

For this reason one cannot see how it is possible to propose the admission of women to the priesthood in virtue of the equality of rights of the human person, an equality which holds good also for Christians. To this end use is sometimes made of the text quoted above, from the Letter to the Galatians (3:28), which says that in Christ there is no longer any distinction between men and women. But this passage does not concern ministries: it only affirms the universal calling to divine filiation, which is the same for all. Moreover, and above all, to consider the ministerial priesthood as a human right would be to misjudge its nature completely: baptism does not confer any personal title to public ministry in the Church. The priesthood is not conferred for the honor or advantage of the recipient, but for the service of God and the Church; it is the object of a specific and totally gratuitous vocation: "You did not choose me, no, I chose you; and I commissioned you. . . ." (Jn. 15:16; cf. Heb. 5:4).

It is sometimes said and written in books and periodicals that some women feel that they have a vocation to the priesthood. Such an attraction, however noble and understandable, still does not suffice for a genuine vocation. In fact, a vocation cannot be reduced to a mere personal attraction, which can remain purely subjective. Since the priesthood is a particular ministry of which the Church has received the charge and the control, authentication by the Church is indispensable here and is a constitutive part of the vocation: Christ chose "those he wanted" (Mk. 3:13). On the other hand, there is a universal vocation of all the baptized to the exercise of the royal priesthood by offering their lives to God and by giving witness for His praise.

Women who express a desire for the ministerial priesthood are doubtless motivated by the desire to serve Christ and the Church. And it is not surprising that, at a time when they are becoming more aware of the discrimination to which they have been subject, they should desire the ministerial priesthood itself. But it must not be forgotten that the priesthood does not form part of the rights of the individual, but stems from the economy of the mystery of Christ and the Church. The priestly office cannot become the goal of social advancement; no merely human progress of society or of the individual can of itself give access to it: it is of another order.

It therefore remains for us to meditate more deeply on the nature of the real equality of the baptized which is one of the great affirmations of Christianity: equality is in no way identity, for the Church is a differentiated body, in which each individual has his or her role. The roles are distinct, and must not be confused; they do not favor the superiority of some vis-à-vis the others, nor do they provide an excuse for jealousy; the only better gift, which can and must be desired, is love (cf. 1 Cor. 12–13). The greatest in the kingdom of heaven are not the ministers but the saints.

The Church desires that Christian women should become fully aware of the greatness of their mission: today their role is of capital importance, both for the renewal and humanization of society and for the rediscovery by believers of the true face of the Church.

His Holiness Pope Paul VI, during the audience granted to the undersigned Prefect of the Sacred Congregation on October 15, 1976, approved this Declaration, confirmed it and ordered its publication.

Given in Rome, at the Sacred Congregation for the Doctrine of the Faith, on October 15, 1976, the feast of St. Teresa of Avila.

Franjo Cardinal Seper, *Prefect*
+ Fr. Jerome Hamer, O.P., *Titular Archbishop of Lorium, Secretary*

Notes

[1]*Acta Apostolicae Sedis* 55 (1963), pp. 267-268.

[2]Cf. Second Vatican Council, Pastoral Constitution *Gaudium et Spes,* 29 (December 7, 1965): *AAS* 58 (1966), pp. 1048-1049.

[3]Cf. Pope Paul VI, Address to the members of the Study Commission on the Role of Women in Society and in the Church and to the members of the Committee for International Women's Year, April 18, 1975: *AAS* 67 (1975), p. 265,

[4]Second Vatican Council, Decree *Apostolicam Actuositatem,* 9 (November 18, 1965): *AAS* 58 (1966), p. 846.

[5]Cf. Pope Paul VI, Address to the members of the Study Commission on the Role of Women in Society and in the Church and to the members of the Committee for International Women's Year, April 18, 1975: *AAS* 67 (1975), p. 266.

[6]Cf. *AAS* 68 (1976), pp. 599-600; cf. *ibid.,* pp. 600-601.

[7]St. Irenaeus, *Adversus Haereses,* 1, 13, 2: *PG* 7, 580-581; ed. Harvey, I, 114-122; Tertullian, *De Praescrip. Haeretic.* 41, 5: *CCL* 1, p. 221; Firmilian of Caesarea, in St. Cyprian, *Epist.,* 75: *CSEL* 3, pp. 817-818; Origen, *Fragmentum in I Cor. 74,* in *Journal of Theological Studies* 10 (1909), pp. 41-42; St. Epiphanius, *Panarion* 49, 2-3; 78, 23; 79, 2-4; vol. 2, *GCS* 31, pp. 243-244; vol. 3, *GCS* 37, pp. 473, 477-479.

[8]*Didascalia Apostolorum,* ch. 15, ed. R.H. Connolly, pp. 133 and 142; *Constitutiones Apostolicae,* bk. 3, ch. 6, nos. 1-2; ch. 9, nos. 3-4: ed. F. H. Funk, pp. 191, 201; St. John Chrysostom, *De Sacredotio* 2, 2: *PG* 48, 633.

[9]St. Bonaventure, *In IV Sent.,* Dist. 25, art. 2, q. 1, ed. Quaracchi, vol. 4, p. 649; Richard of Middleton, *In IV Sent.,* Dist. 25, art. 4, n. 1, ed. Venice, 1499 f° 177ʳ; John Duns Scotus, *In IV Sent.,* Dist. 25: *Opus Oxoniense,* ed. Vives, vol. 19, p. 140; *Reportata Parisiensia,* vol. 24, pp. 369-371; Durandus of Saint Pourcain, *In IV Sent.,* Dist. 25, q. 2, ed. Venice. 1571, f° 364-v.

[10]Some have also wished to explain this fact by a symbolic intention of Jesus: the Twelve were to represent the ancestors of the twelve tribes of Israel (cf. Mt. 19:28; Lk. 22:30). But in these texts it is only a question of their participation in the eschatological judgment. The essential meaning of the choice of the Twelve should rather be sought in the totality of their mission (cf. Mk. 3:14): they are to represent Jesus to the people and carry on His work.

[11]Pope Innocent III, *Epist.* (December 11, 1210) to the bishops of Palencia and Burgos, included in *Corpus Iuris, Decret. Lib.* 5, tit. 38, *De Paenit.,* ch. 10 *Nova:* ed. A. Friedberg, vol. 2, col. 886-887; cf. *Glossa in Decretal, Lib. 1,* tit. 33, ch. 12 *Dilecta, v° Iurisdictioni.*

Cf. St. Thomas, *Summa Theologiae*, III (q. 27, a. 5 ad 3; Pseudo-Albert the Great, *Mariale*, quaest. 42, ed. Borgnet 37, 81.

[12]Pope Pius XII, Apostolic Constitution *Sacramentum Ordinis*, November 30, 1947: *AAS* 40 (1948), pp. 5-7; Pope Paul VI, Apostolic Constitution *Divinae Consortium Naturae*, August 15, 1971: *AAS* 63 (1971), pp. 657-664; Apostolic Constitution *Sacram Unctionem*, November 30, 1972: *AAS* 65 (1973), pp. 5-9.

[13]Pope Pius XII, Apostolic Constitution *Sacramentum Ordinis: loc. cit.,* p. 5.

[14]Session 21, chap. 2: Denzinger-Schönmetzer, *Enchiridion Symbolorum* 1728.

[15]St. Cyprian, *Epist.* 63, 14: *PL* 4, 397 B; ed. Hartel, vol. 3, p. 713.

[16]Second Vatican Council, Constitution *Sacrosanctum Concilium*, 33 (December 4, 1963): "... by the priest who presides over the assembly in the person of Christ...."; Dogmatic Constitution *Lumen Gentium*, 10 (November 21, 1964): "The ministerial priest, by the sacred power he enjoys, molds and rules the priestly people. Acting in the person of Christ, he brings about the Eucharistic Sacrifice, and offers it to God in the name of all the people..."; 28: "By the powers of the sacrament of Order, and in the image of Christ the eternal High Priest...they exercise this sacred function of Christ above all in the Eucharistic liturgy or synaxis. There, acting in the person of Christ..."; Decree *Presbyterorum Ordinis,* 2 (December 7, 1965): "...priests, by the anointing of the Holy Spirit, are marked with a special character and are so configured to Christ the Priest that they can act in the person of Christ the Head"; 13: "As ministers of sacred realities, especially in the Sacrifice of the Mass, priests represent the person of Christ in a special way"; cf. 1971 Synod of Bishops, *De Sacredotio ministeriali* I, 4; Sacred Congregation for the Doctrine of the Faith, *Declaratio circa catholicam doctrinam de Ecclesia*, 6 (June 24, 1973).

[17]St. Thomas, *Summa Theologiae* III, q. 83, art. 1, ad 3: "It is to be said that (just as the celebration of this sacrament is the representative image of Christ's cross; *ibid.* ad 2), for the same reason the priest also enacts the image of Christ, in whose person and by whose power he pronounces the words of consecration."

[18]"For since a sacrament is a sign, there is required in the things that are done in the sacraments not only the 'res' but the signification of the 'res,' " recalls St. Thomas precisely in order to reject the ordination of women: *In IV Sent.,* Dist. 25, q. 2, art. 1, quaestiuncula 1ª, corp.

[19]St. Thomas *In IV Sent., Dist.* 25, q. 2, quaestiuncula 1ª ad 4-um.

[20]Cf. Council of Trent, Session 22, chap. 1: *DS* 1741.

[21]Second Vatican Council, Dogmatic Constitution *Lumen Gentium*, 28: "Exercising within the limits of their authority the function of Christ as Shepherd and Head"; Decree *Presbyterorum Ordinis* 2: "that they can act in the person of Christ the Head"; 6: "the office of Christ the Head and the Shepherd." Cf. Pope Pius XII, Encyclical Letter *Mediator Dei:* "the minister of the altar represents the person of Christ as the Head, offering in the name of all His members": *AAS* 39 (1947), p. 556; 1971 Synod of Bishops, *De Sacerdotio Ministeriali,* I, 4: "(The priestly ministry)...makes Christ, the Head of the community, present...."

[22]Pope Paul VI, Encyclical Letter *Mysterium Fidei*, September 3, 1965: *AAS* 57 (1965), p. 761.

Name Index

Roberts, David E., 342n.
Robinson, Edward, 295n.
Roca, Canon M., 219, 220, 226n.
Rousseau, Jean-Jacques, 122, 173
Rushdouny, 197, 198, 203n.
Ruskin, 55

Saint Simon, 122
Samson, 133, 377
Samuel, 149, 152
Sangnier, Mark, 49
Santayana, George, 91, 92, 198, 232, 254
Sara, 6, 112
Sartre, Jean-Paul, 47, 57, 208, 228, 296,
  297, 299, 300, 301, 302, 303, 304, 305,
  306, 307, 330, 344, 345, 346, 354, 367n.
Satan, 8, 14, 55, 59, 86, 97, 98, 132, 134,
  140, 143, 144, 151, 153, 161, 165, 169,
  172, 174, 184, 185, 196, 198, 203, 212,
  215, 217, 219, 222, 224, 240, 259, 305
Saul, 149
Scheler, Max, 308
Schillebecckx, Edward, 64, 378
Schuschnigg, Chancellor, 309
Schwarz, Dr. Balduin, 295n., 327, 342n.
Scotus, John Duns, 67, 400n.
Seneca, i
Seper, Franz Cardinal, 400
Shakespeare, William, i, 55, 106, 161, 169,
  171n., 258n., 278, 382, 385
Sheed, Rev. Frank, 156
Shem, 5
Sim, Dr. Myre, 191
Simeon, 104, 132
Simon the Pharisee, 391
Simon the Sorcerer, 223
Simon the Zealot, St., 151
Smith, Professor, 176
Smith, Rev. William B., 385
Smits, O.F.M., Cap., Rev. Luchesius, 66,
  67, 68, 69, 70, 71, 72
Socrates, 10, 314
Solzhenitsyn, Aleksandr I., 144, 236, 241
Spalding, Bishop, 136
Spratt, Philip, 265
Stalin, Josef, 202, 240
Stein, Walter, 176
Strachan, Richard, 295n.
Strauss, David, 204
Suzanna, 16, 391

Taylor, Gordon Rattray, 189
Teresa, Mother, 184
Teresa of Avila, St., 389, 400
Tertullian, 44, 400n.
Thibon, Gustave, 328
Thomas, St. (Apostle), 60, 95, 151
Thorsen, Jens Joergen, 19
Thucydides, 28
Timofeyev, Fyodor, 202
Timothy, 158
Trilling, 22
Troisfontaines, S.J., Rev. R., 342n., 346,
  366n., 367n.
Tryphaena, 13
Tryphosa, 13
Tyrrell, Rev. George, 86, 89n.

Unamuno, Miguel de, 29, 33, 36n., 265,
  267n.

Verardo, 41
Vermeersch, S.J., Rev. A., 90, 97, 109
Virgil, 179, 185n.
von Bathasar, Rev. Hans, 33, 36n.
von Hildebrand, Adolf, 308
von Hildebrand, Alice Jourdain, 35n.,
  109, 172, 310, 312, 323, 326, 342n.
von Hildrebrand, Bruno, 309
von Hildebrand, Dietrich, i, 50, 58, 59,
  101, 109, 226n., 307n., 308, 309, 310,
  311, 312, 313, 326, 380n.

Wald, George, 193
Wall, Bernard, 342n., 343n.
Weisser, O.P., Rev. Donald M., 295n.
White, Associate Justice Byron R., 188
Whitehorn, Katharine, 120
Wilde, Oscar, 161, 171n., 234
Williams, Duncan, 21, 35n.
Wiltgen, S.V.D., Rev. Ralph M., 235

Yeats, 162, 170, 171n.

Zeus, 25
Zachary, 30, 104, 113, 155
Zachary (Prophet), 242
Zedong, Mao, 202, 232
Zwingli, 64, 68